W9-AAS-821

UNDERSTANDING
PUBLIC POLICY

UNDERSTANDING PUBLIC POLICY

sixth edition

THOMAS R. DYE
Florida State University

PRENTICE-HALL, INC., ENGLEWOOD CLIFFS, N.J. 07632

Library of Congress Cataloging-in-Publication Data

Dye, Thomas R.
  Understanding public policy.

  Includes bibliographies and index.
  1. United States--Social policy. 2. United States
--Social conditions--1960-   . 3. United States--
Politics and government--1974-   .)I. Title.
HN65.D9 1987   361.6'0973   86-15164
ISBN 0-13-936973-2

Editorial/production supervision and
  interior design: Marina Harrison
Cover design: Lundgren Graphics, Inc.
Manufacturing buyer: Barbara Kelly Kittle
Photo research: Barbara Scott
Photo editor: Lorinda Morris

© 1987, 1984, 1981, 1978, 1975, 1972, by Prentice-Hall, Inc.
A Division of Simon & Schuster
Englewood Cliffs, New Jersey 07632

*All rights reserved. No part of this book may be
reproduced, in any form or by any means,
without permission in writing from the publisher.*

Printed in the United States of America

10 9 8 7 6 5 4 3 2 1

ISBN 0-13-936973-2 01

Prentice-Hall International (UK) Limited, *London*
Prentice-Hall of Australia Pty. Limited, *Sydney*
Prentice-Hall Canada Inc., *Toronto*
Prentice-Hall Hispanoamericana, S.A., *Mexico*
Prentice-Hall of India Private Limited, *New Delhi*
Prentice-Hall of Japan, Inc., *Tokyo*
Prentice-Hall of Southeast Asia Pte. Ltd., *Singapore*
Editora Prentice-Hall do Brasil, Ltda., *Rio de Janeiro*

CONTENTS

5

POVERTY AND WELFARE

6

HEALTH

7

EDUCATION

the group struggle   169

8

DEFENSE POLICY

strategies for serious games   197

9

PRIORITIES AND PRICE TAGS

incrementalism at work   231

10

TAX POLICY

11

AMERICAN FEDERALISM

12

INPUTS, OUTPUTS, AND BLACK BOXES

PREFACE

Policy analysis is concerned with "who gets what" in politics and, more important, "why" and "what difference it makes." We are concerned not only with *what* policies governments pursue but also *why* governments pursue the policies they do, and *what* the consequences of these policies are.

Political science, like other scientific disciplines, has developed a number of concepts and models to help describe and explain political life. These models are not really competitive in the sense that any one could be judged "best." Each focuses on separate elements of politics and each helps us to understand different things about political life.

We begin with a brief description of eight analytic models in political science and the potential contribution of each of them to the study of public policy. They are:

an institutional model	a rational model
a process model	an incremental model
a group model	a game theory model
an elite model	a systems model

We then attempt to describe and explain public policy by the use of these various analytic models. Readers are not only informed about public policy in a variety of key domestic policy areas but, more important, they are encouraged to utilize these conceptual models in political science to explain the causes and consequences of public policies in these areas. The policy areas studied are:

civil rights	budgeting and spending
criminal justice	taxation
poverty and welfare	national defense
health	state and local spending and services
education	

Most public policies are a combination of rational planning, incrementalism, competition among groups, elite preferences, systematic forces, political processes, and institutional influences. Throughout this volume we employ these models, both singly and in combination, to describe and explain public policy. However, certain chapters rely more on one model than another.

Any of these policy areas might be studied by employing more than one model. Frequently our selection of a particular analytic model to study a specific policy area was based as much upon pedagogical considerations as anything else. We simply wanted to demonstrate how political scientists employ analytical models. Once readers are familiar with the nature and uses of analytic models in political science, they may find it interesting to explore the utility of models other than the ones selected by the author in the explanation of particular policy outcomes. For example, we use an elitist model to discuss civil rights policy, but the reader may wish to view civil rights policy from the perspective of group theory. We employ the language of game theory to discuss national defense policy, but the reader might enjoy reinterpreting defense policy in a systems model.

Each chapter concludes with a series of propositions, which are derived from one or more analytic models, and which attempt to summarize the policies discussed. The purposes of these summaries are to suggest the kinds of policy explanations that can be derived from analytic models and to tie the policy material back to one or another of our models.

In short, this volume is not only an introduction to the study of public policy, but also an introduction to the models political scientists use to describe and explain political life.

THOMAS R. DYE
Florida State University

UNDERSTANDING
PUBLIC POLICY

1

POLICY ANALYSIS

what governments do,
why they do it,
and what difference it makes

President Ronald Reagan delivers his State of the Union address to a joint session of the Congress of the United States. (Art Stein/Photo Researchers)

POLICY ANALYSIS IN POLITICAL SCIENCE

This book is about public policy. It is concerned with what governments do, why they do it, and what difference it makes. It is also about political science and the ability of this academic discipline to describe, analyze, and explain public policy.

Public policy is whatever governments choose to do or not to do.[1] Governments do many things. They regulate conflict within society; they organize society to carry on conflict with other societies; they distribute a great variety of symbolic rewards and material services to members of the society; and they extract money from society, most often in the form of taxes. Thus, public policies may regulate behavior, organize bureaucracies, distribute benefits, or extract taxes—or all these things at once.

Governments in the United States directly allocate about 35 percent of the Gross National Product, the sum of all of the goods and services produced in the nation each year. About two-thirds of the governmental sector of the GNP is accounted for by the federal government itself; the remaining one-third is attributable to eighty thousand state, city, county, township, school district, and special district governments combined. Overall government employment in the United States comprises 16 percent of the nation's workforce.

Public policies may deal with a wide variety of substantive areas—defense, energy, environment, foreign affairs, education, welfare, police, highways, taxation, housing, social security, health, economic opportunity, urban development, inflation and recession, and so on. They may range from the vital to the trivial—from the allocation of tens of billions of dollars for a mobile missile system to the designation of an official national bird.

Public policy is not a new concern of political science: the earliest writings of political philosophers reveal an interest in the policies pursued by governments, the forces shaping these policies, and the impact of these policies on society. Yet the major focus of attention of political science has never really been on policies themselves, but rather on the institutions and structures of government and on the political behaviors and processes associated with policy making.

"Traditional" political science focused its attention primarily on the institutional structure and philosophical justification of government. This involved the study of constitutional arrangements, such as federalism, separation of power, and judicial review; powers and duties of official bodies, such as Congress, president, and courts; intergovernmental relations; and the organization and operation of legislative, executive, and judicial agencies. Traditional studies described the *institutions* in which public policy was

---

[1]See insert, "Defining Public Policy: Playing Word Games."

DEFINING PUBLIC POLICY: PLAYING WORD GAMES

This book discourages elaborate academic discussions of the definition of public policy—we say simply that public policy is whatever governments choose to do or not to do. Books, essays, and discussions of a "proper" definition of public policy have proven futile, even exasperating, and they often divert attention from the study of public policy itself. Moreover, even the most elaborate definitions of public policy, upon close examination, seem to boil down to the same thing. For example, political scientist David Easton defines public policy as "the authoritative allocation of values for the whole society"—but it turns out that only the government can "authoritatively" act on the "whole" society, and everything the government chooses to do or not to do results in the "allocation of values."

Political scientist Harold Lasswell and philosopher Abraham Kaplan define policy as "a projected program of goals, values, and practices," and political scientist Carl Friedrick says, "It is essential for the policy concept that there be a goal, objective, or purpose." These definitions imply a difference between specific governmental actions and an overall program of action toward a given goal. But the problem raised in insisting that government actions must have goals in order to be labeled "policy" is that we can never be sure whether or not a particular action has a goal, or if it does, what that goal is. Some people may assume that if a government chooses to do something there must be a goal, objective, or purpose, but all we can really observe is what governments choose to do or not to do. Realistically, our notion of public policy must include *all actions* of government, and not what governments or officials say they are going to do. We may wish that governments act in a "purposeful goal-oriented" fashion, but we know that all too frequently they do not.

Still another approach to defining public policy is to break down this general notion into various component parts. Political scientist Charles O. Jones asks that we consider the distinction among various proposals (specified means for achieving goals); programs (authorized means for achieving goals); decisions (specific actions taken to implement programs); and effects (the measurable impacts of programs). But again we have the problem of assuming that decisions, programs, goals, and effects are linked. Certainly in many policy areas we will see that the decisions of government have little to do with announced "programs," and neither are connected with national "goals." It may be unfortunate that our government does not function neatly to link goals, programs, decisions, and effects, but as a matter of fact, it does not.

Political scientists Heinz Eulau and Kenneth Prewitt supply still another definition of public policy: "Policy is defined as a 'standing decision' characterized by behavioral consistency and repetitiveness on the part of both those who make it and those who abide by it." Now certainly it would be a wonderful thing if government activities were characterized by "consistency and repetitiveness"; but it is doubtful that we would ever find "public policy" in government if we insist on these criteria. Much of what government does is inconsistent and nonrepetitive.

So we shall stick with our simple definition: *public policy is whatever governments choose to do or not to do.* Note that we are focusing not only on government action, but also on government inaction, that is, what government chooses *not* to do. We contend that government *in*action can have just as great an impact on society as government action.

See David Easton, *The Political System* (New York: Knopf, 1953), p. 129; Harold D. Lasswell and Abraham Kaplan, *Power and Society* (New Haven: Yale University Press, 1970), p. 71; Carl J. Friedrich, *Man and His Government* (New York: McGraw-Hill, 1963), p. 70; Charles O. Jones, *An Introduction to the Study of Public Policy* (Boston: Duxbury, 1977), p. 4; Heinz Eulau and Kenneth Prewitt, *Labyrinths of Democracy* (Indianapolis: Bobbs-Merrill, 1973), p. 465; and Hugh Heclo, "Policy Analysis," *British Journal of Political Science,* 2 (January 1972), p. 85.

formulated. But unfortunately the linkages between important institutional arrangements and the content of public policy were largely unexplored.

Modern "behavioral" political science focused its attention primarily on the processes and behaviors associated with government. This involved the study of the sociological and psychological bases of individual and group behavior; the determinants of voting and other political activities; the functioning of interest groups and political parties; and the description of various processes and behaviors in the legislative, executive, and judicial arenas. Although this approach described the *processes* by which public policy was determined, it did not deal directly with the linkages between various processes and behaviors and the content of public policy.

Today many political scientists are shifting their focus to *public policy*—to the *description and explanation of the causes and consequences of government activity.* This may involve a description of the content of public policy; an analysis of the impact of social, economic, and political forces on the content of public policy; an inquiry into the effect of various institutional arrangements and political processes on public policy; and an evaluation of the consequences of public policies on society, in terms of both expected and unexpected consequences.

WHY STUDY PUBLIC POLICY?

Why should political scientists devote greater attention to the study of public policy?[2] First of all, public policy can be studied for purely *scientific reasons:* understanding the causes and consequences of policy decisions improves our knowledge of society. Public policy can be viewed as a dependent variable, and we can ask what socioeconomic forces and political system characteristics operate to shape the content of policy. Alternatively, public policy can be viewed as an independent variable, and we can ask what impact public policy has on society and its political system. By asking such questions we can improve our understanding of the linkages between socioeconomic forces, political processes, and public policy. An understanding of these linkages contributes to the breadth, significance, reliability, and theoretical development of social science.

Public policy can also be studied for *professional reasons:* understanding the causes and consequences of public policy permits us to apply social science knowledge to the solution of practical problems. Factual knowledge is a prerequisite to prescribing for the ills of society. If certain ends are desired, then the question of what policies would best implement these ends is a factual question requiring scientific study. In other words, policy

[2]See the "Policy Analysis Explosion" symposium in *Society*, Vol. 16 (September 1979).

studies can produce professional advice, in terms of "if . . . then . . ." statements, about how to achieve desired goals.

Finally, public policy can be studied for *political purposes:* to ensure that the nation adopts the "right" policies to achieve the "right" goals. It is frequently argued that political science should not be silent or impotent in the face of great social and political crises, and that political scientists have a moral obligation to advance specific public policies. An exclusive focus on institutions, processes, or behaviors is frequently looked upon as "dry," "irrelevant," and "amoral," because it does not direct attention to the really important policy questions facing American society. Policy studies can be undertaken not only for scientific and professional purposes but also to inform political discussion, advance the level of political awareness, and improve the quality of public policy. Of course, these are very subjective purposes—Americans do not always agree on what constitutes the "right" policies or the "right" goals—but we will assume that knowledge is preferable to ignorance, even in politics.

QUESTIONS IN POLICY ANALYSIS

What can we learn about public policy? First of all, we can *describe* public policy—we can learn what government is doing (and not doing) in welfare, defense, education, civil rights, health, energy, taxation, and so on. A factual basis of information about national policy is really an indispensable part of everyone's education. What does the Civil Rights Act of 1964 actually say about discrimination in employment? What did the Supreme Court rule in the *Bakke* case about affirmative action programs? What is the condition of the nation's social security program? What do the Medicaid and Medicare programs promise for the poor and the aged? What is the purpose of the MX missile, the B-1 bomber, or the Trident submarine? How much are we really spending on national defense and on social welfare? What is "Reaganomics"? How much money are we paying in taxes? How much money does the federal government spend each year? These are examples of descriptive questions.

Second, we can inquire about the *causes,* or determinants, of public policy. Why is public policy what it is? Why do governments do what they do? We might inquire about the effects of political institutions, processes and behaviors on public policies (Linkage B in Figure 1-1). Does it make any difference in tax and spending levels whether Democrats or Republicans control the presidency and Congress? What is the impact of interest group conflict on federal aid to education? What is the impact of lobbying by the special interests on efforts to reform the federal tax system? We can also inquire about the effects of social, economic, and cultural forces and

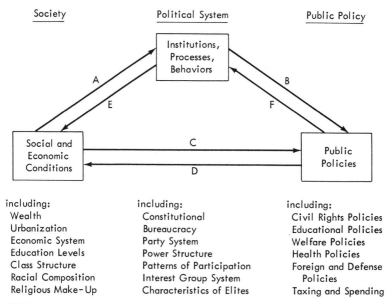

Society   Political System   Public Policy

including: including: including:
  Wealth   Constitutional   Civil Rights Policies
  Urbanization   Bureaucracy   Educational Policies
  Economic System   Party System   Welfare Policies
  Education Levels   Power Structure   Health Policies
  Class Structure   Patterns of Participation   Foreign and Defense
  Racial Composition   Interest Group System   Policies
  Religious Make-Up   Characteristics of Elites   Taxing and Spending

FIGURE 1-1 The policy system.

conditions in shaping public policy (Linkage C in Figure 1-1). What are the effects of changing public attitudes about race on civil rights policy? What are the effects of wars and recessions on government spending? What is the effect of an increasingly older population on the social security and Medicare programs?

Third, we can inquire about the *consequences,* or impacts, of public policy. What difference, if any, does public policy make in people's lives? We might inquire about the effects of public policy on political institutions and processes (Linkage F in Figure 1-1). What is the effect of tax cuts on Republican fortunes in Congress? What is the effect of increased defense spending on the president's influence in world affairs? We also want to examine the impact of public policies on social and economic conditions (Linkage D in Figure 1-1). Does capital punishment help to deter crime? Are welfare programs a disincentive to work? Is busing an effective means of ending racial inequalities in education?

All of these questions are interrelated. It may be helpful to think of a *policy system,* perhaps in the form shown in Figure 1-1. (We will say more about systems analysis in Chapter 2.) We can think of policy analysis as a series of questions abut the relationships, or linkages, between social and economic conditions, characteristics of political systems, and the content of public policy. This systems approach allows us to conceive of different types of questions in policy analysis:

Linkage A: What are the effects of environmental forces and conditions on political and governmental institutions, processes, and behaviors?

Linkage B: What are the effects of political and governmental institutions, processes, and behaviors on public policies?

Linkage C: What are the effects of environmental forces and conditions on public policies?

Linkage D: What are the effects (feedback) of public policies on environmental forces and conditions?

Linkage E: What are the effects (feedback) of political and governmental institutions, processes, and behaviors on environmental forces and conditions?

Linkage F: What are the effects (feedback) of public policies on political and governmental institutions, processes, and behaviors?

POLICY ANALYSIS AND POLICY ADVOCACY

It is important to distinguish *policy analysis* from *policy advocacy*. *Explaining* the causes and consequences of various policies is not equivalent to *prescribing* what policies governments ought to pursue. Learning *why* governments do what they do and what the consequences of their actions are is not the same as saying *what* governments ought to do, or bringing about changes in what they do. Policy advocacy requires the skills of rhetoric, persuasion, organization, and activism. Policy analysis encourages scholars and students to attack critical policy issues with the tools of systematic inquiry. There is an implied assumption in policy analysis that developing scientific knowledge about the forces shaping public policy and the consequences of public policy is itself a socially relevant activity, and that such analysis is a prerequisite to prescription, advocacy, and activism.

Specifically, *public analysis* involves:

1. *A primary concern with explanation rather than prescription.* Policy recommendations—if they are made at all—are subordinate to description and explanation. There is an implicit judgment that understanding is a prerequisite to prescription, and that understanding is best achieved through careful analysis rather than rhetoric or polemics.

2. *A rigorous search for the causes and consequences of public policies.* This search involves the use of scientific standards of inference. Sophisticated quantitative techniques may be helpful in establishing valid inferences about causes and consequences, but they are not really essential.

3. *An effort to develop and test general propositions about the causes and consequences of public policy and to accumulate reliable research findings of general relevance.* The object is to develop general theories about public policy that are reliable and that apply to different governmental agencies and different policy areas. Policy analysts clearly prefer to develop explanations that fit more than one

policy decision or case study—explanations that stand up over time in a variety of settings.

POLICY ANALYSIS IN ACTION: SOCIAL SCIENTISTS AND THE "BUSING" ISSUE

One of the more interesting examples of policy analysis over the years has been the social science research on equal educational opportunity and how to achieve it. "Busing" has been one of the most controversial topics in American politics, and social science has played an important role in policy making in this area. However, as we shall see, the more controversial the policy area, the more difficult it is to conduct policy research.

Early Research—the Coleman Report

The first influential report on educational opportunity in America was sociologist James S. Coleman's *Equality of Educational Opportunity*, frequently referred to as the "Coleman Report."[3] The Coleman Report dealt primarily with the *consequences* of educational policy—specifically, the impact of schools on the aspiration and achievement levels of pupils. Although Coleman's study was not without its critics,[4] it was nonetheless the most comprehensive analysis of the American public school system ever made. The Coleman Report included data on 600,000 children, 60,000 teachers, and 4,000 schools.

The results of Coleman's study undermined much of the conventional wisdom about the impact of public educational policies on student learning and achievement. Prior to the study, legislators, teachers, school administrators, school board members, and the general public assumed that factors such as the number of pupils in the classroom, the amount of money spent on each pupil, library and laboratory facilities, teachers' salaries, the quality of the curriculum, and other characteristics of the school affected the quality of education and educational opportunity. But systematic analysis revealed that these factors had *no* significant effect on student learning or achievement. "Differences in school facilities and curriculum . . . are so little

---

[3]James S. Coleman, *Equality of Educational Opportunity* (Washington, D.C.: Government Printing Office, 1966).

[4]For reviews of the Coleman Report, see Robert A. Dentler, "Equality of Educational Opportunity: A Special Review," *The Urban Review* (December 1966); Christopher Jenks, "Education: The Racial Gap," *The New Republic* (October 1, 1966); James K. Kent, "The Coleman Report: Opening Pandora's Box," *Phi Delta Kappan* (January 1968); James S. Coleman, "Educational Dilemmas: Equal Schools or Equal Students," *The Public Interest* (Summer 1966); James S. Coleman, "Toward Open Schools," *The Public Interest* (Fall 1967); and a special issue devoted to educational opportunity of *Harvard Educational Review*, vol. 38 (Winter 1968).

related to differences in achievement levels of students that, with few exceptions, their effects fail to appear even in a survey of this magnitude." Moreover, learning was found to be unaffected by the presence or absence of a "track system," ability grouping, guidance counseling, or other standard educational programs. Even the size of the class was found to be unrelated to learning, although educators had asserted the importance of this factor for decades. Finally, the Coleman study reported that the quality of teaching was not a very significant factor in student achievement compared to family and peer-group influences. In short, the things that "everybody knew" about education turned out not to be so!

The only factors that were found to affect a student's learning to any significant degree were (1) family background and (2) the family background of classmates. Family background affected the child's verbal abilities and attitudes toward education, and these factors correlated very closely with scholastic achievement. Of secondary but considerable significance were the verbal abilities and attitudes toward education of the child's classmates. Peer-group influence had its greatest impact on children from lower-class families. Teaching excellence mattered very little to children from upper- and middle-class backgrounds; they learned well despite mediocre or poor teaching. Children from lower-class families were slightly more affected by teacher quality.

Coleman also found that schools serving black pupils in this nation were *not* physically inferior to schools serving predominantly white student bodies. In the South, in fact, black schools were somewhat newer than white schools. Black teachers had about the same education and teaching experiences as white teachers, and their pay was equal. Black teachers, however, scored lower than white teachers on verbal tests, and their morale was reported to be lower than that of white teachers.

Reanalyzing Coleman's data for the U.S. Civil Rights Commission, Thomas F. Pettigrew and others found that black students attending predominantly black schools had lower achievement scores and lower levels of aspiration than black students *with comparable family backgrounds* who attended predominantly white schools.[5] When black students attending predominantly white schools were compared with black students attending predominantly black schools, the average difference in levels of achievement amounted to more than *two grade levels*. On the other hand, achievement levels of white students in classes nearly half-black in composition were *not* any lower than those of white students in all-white schools. Finally, special programs to raise achievement levels in predominantly black schools were found to have no lasting effect.

---

[5]U.S. Commission on Civil Rights, *Racial Isolation in the Public Schools*, 2 vols. (Washington, D.C.: Government Printing Office, 1967).

Policy Implications

The Coleman Report made no policy recommendations. But, like a great deal of policy research, policy recommendations can easily be inferred from its conclusions. First of all, if the Coleman Report is correct, it seems pointless to simply pour more money into the present system of public education—raising per pupil expenditures, increasing teachers' salaries, lowering the number of pupils per classroom, providing better libraries and laboratories, adding educational frills, or adopting any specific curricular innovations. These policies were found to have no significant impact on learning.

The findings of the Coleman Report are particularly important for Title I of the Elementary and Secondary Education Act (see Chapter 7). This piece of congressional legislation authorizes large amounts of federal assistance each year for "poverty impacted" schools. The purpose of this program is to remedy learning problems of disadvantaged children by increasing spending for special remedial programs. But the Coleman Report implies that compensatory programs have little educational value. They may have symbolic value for ghetto residents, or political value for officeholders who seek to establish an image of concern for the underprivileged, but they are of little educational value for children.

The U.S. Commission on Civil Rights used the Coleman Report to buttress its policy proposals to end racial imbalance in public schools in both the North and the South. Inasmuch as money, facilities, and compensatory programs have little effect on student learning, and inasmuch as the socioeconomic background of the student's *classmates* does affect his or her learning, it seemed reasonable to argue that the assignment of lower-class black students to predominantly middle-class white schools would be the only way to improve educational opportunities for ghetto children. Moreover, because the findings indicated that the achievement levels of middle-class white students were unaffected by blacks in the classroom (as long as blacks were less than a majority), the commission concluded that assigning ghetto blacks to predominantly white schools would not adversely affect the learning of white pupils. Hence, the commission called for an end to neighborhood schools and for the *busing* of black and white children to racially balanced schools.

The reaction of professional educators was largely one of silence. Perhaps they hoped the Coleman Report would disappear into history without significantly affecting the longstanding assumptions about the importance of money, facilities, classroom size, teacher training, and curricula. Perhaps they hoped that subsequent research would refute Coleman's findings. Daniel Moynihan writes:

> The whole rationale of American public education came very near to crashing down, and would have done so had there not been a seemingly general

agreement to act as if the report had not occurred. But it had, and public education will not now be the same. The relations between resource input and educational output, which all school systems, all legislatures, all executives have accepted as given, appear not to be given at all. At very least what has heretofore been taken for granted must henceforth be proved. Without in any way purporting to tell mothers, school teachers, school board superintendents what *will* change educational outcomes, social science has raised profoundly important questions as to what does not.[6]

The reactions of black leaders were mixed.[7] Some blacks were strongly offended by the report and its implications for public policy. The findings regarding compensatory education efforts were said to deal a "death blow to all black children" in the ghetto. They reasoned that integrated education is a physical impossibility in many big-city school systems with few white pupils, and it is a political impossibility in many other cities. Hence, to discredit compensatory education is to threaten the only hope for improvement in ghetto education. A more emotional reaction was the attack on the report as "racist" because it implied that ghetto black children could only learn by contact with middle-class white children. One commentator exclaimed: "I don't subscribe to the view that a black kid must sit next to a white kid to learn. The report is based on the myth of white supremacy."

The Coleman Report was frequently cited by proponents of busing— those urging deliberate government action to achieve racial balance in public schools. Courts and school officials in northern and southern cities cited the Coleman Report as evidence that racial imbalance denies equality of educational opportunity to black children, and as evidence that deliberate racial balancing in the schools, or busing, is required to achieve equal protection of laws guaranteed by the Fourteenth Amendment.

Research on Busing

However, in 1972, Harvard sociologist David Armor shocked the academic world with a careful review of the available evidence of the effect of busing on achievement levels of black students.[8] His conclusions: black students bused out of their neighborhoods to predominantly white schools do not improve their performance relative to white students, even after three or four years of integrated education. His interpretation of the impact of busing on the achievement levels of black students indicated that black students were not being helped "in any significant way" by busing, and he urged consideration of the question of whether psychological harm was

[6]Daniel P. Moynihan, *Maximum Feasible Misunderstanding* (New York: Free Press, 1969), p. 195.

[7]See Kent, "The Coleman Report: Opening Pandora's Box," 244–45.

[8]David J. Armor, "The Evidence on Busing," *The Public Interest*, no. 28 (Summer 1972), 90–126.

being done to black students by placing them in a situation where the achievement gap was so great. Note that Armor was not contradicting the Coleman Report. Coleman was observing black children who were attending predominantly white schools not as a result of deliberate government action, but rather within the previously existing pattern of "neighborhood schools." In contrast, Armor was observing black children who had been deliberately reassigned to integrated schools by government action.

The policy implications of Armor's work appear to support opponents of government-mandated racial balancing. Other social scientists have disputed Armor's review of the relevant research findings, including Thomas F. Pettigrew, who originally used the Coleman data in support of busing.[9] They contend that Armor's work undermines progress toward an integrated society and reinforces racism. But Armor replies that social science findings cannot be used only when they fit the political beliefs of social scientists, and ignored when their policy implications are painful.[10]

Busing and "White Flight"

Coleman himself reentered the fray in 1975 with the publication of a new report, *Trends in School Desegregation.*[11] This "Second Coleman Report" appeared to counter earlier implications about busing as a means to achieve equality of educational opportunity. In examining changes in segregation over time in twenty-two large cities and forty-six medium-sized cities, Coleman found that an increase in desegregation was associated with a loss of white pupils—"white flight." This white response to desegregation was greatest in large cities with large proportions of black school pupils, which were surrounded by predominantly white, independent, suburban school districts. Coleman predicted that the long-run effect of white-pupil

---

[9]Thomas F. Pettigrew et al., "Busing: A Review of 'The Evidence,'" *The Public Interest*, no. 31 (Spring 1973), 88–113.

[10]David J. Armor, "The Double Double Standard," *The Public Interest*, no. 31 (Spring 1973), 119–31. Still another reaction to the Coleman Report is found in the work of Harvard educator Christopher Jenks, *Inequality: A Reassessment of the Effect of Family and Schooling in America* (New York: Basic Books, 1972). Jenks reanalyzed Coleman's data and conducted additional research on the impact of schooling on economic success. He found that school quality has little effect on an individual's subsequent success in earning income. He concluded, therefore, that no amount of educational reform would ever bring about economic equality. Jenks assumed that *absolute equality* of income is the goal of society, not merely *equality of opportunity* to achieve economic success. Because the schools cannot ensure that everyone ends up with the same income, Jenks concludes that nothing short of a radical redistribution of income (steeply progressive taxes and laws preventing individuals from earning more than others) will bring about true equality in America. Attempts to improve the educational system, therefore, are a waste of time and effort. Thus, the Coleman findings have been used to buttress *radical* arguments about the ineffectiveness of *liberal* reforms.

[11]James S. Coleman et al., *Trends in School Desegregation 1968–1973* (Washington, D.C.: Urban Institute, 1975).

loss in these cities would offset government efforts to desegregate public schools and contribute to *greater* rather than less racial isolation. As Coleman explained:

> There are numerous examples of government policy in which the result of the interaction between policy and response is precisely the opposite of the result intended by those who initiated the policy. It is especially important in the case of school desegregation to examine this interaction, because many of the actions taken by individuals, and some of those taken by their local government bodies, have precisely the opposite effect to that intended by the federal government. The most obvious such individual action, of course, is a move of residences to flee school integration.[12]

Coleman had not lost his earlier belief in the achievement benefits of school integration. But he believed that large-scale busing had so many negative consequences, including white flight from the cities, that busing was self-defeating as a means of achieving equal educational opportunity.

Critics of the notion of "white flight" argue that there are many reasons besides desegregation which encourage white migration out of central cities.[13] Moreover, there are some big-city school districts which have *not* experienced "white flight" despite large-scale court-ordered desegregation plans involving busing.

Many *before* and *after* studies of black students bused to majority-white middle-class schools report significant gains by the black students in verbal and mathematical skills over several years. And almost all researchers report that desegregation has little, if any, effect on the achievement levels of white students.[14] There is very little racial interaction in desegregated schools except in supervised activities such as sports, band, and cheerleading.

Even more controversial social science research centers on the notion of a "tipping point"—a ratio of blacks and whites in schools, neighborhoods, or housing projects, beyond which whites begin to withdraw in large numbers, resulting in resegregation. The idea of a racial "tipping point" originated in early public housing studies: When blacks came to occupy more than one-third of a housing project, whites would leave so that soon the project became all-black. Evidence of a racial "tipping point" in public schools was presented by Florida researchers, who showed that white withdrawals from public schools ran at an annual rate of 2.3 percent when children were assigned to schools with less than 30 percent black enrollment

[12]Ibid, p. 2.

[13]See Edward J. Hayes, *Busing and Desegregation: The Real Truth* (Springfield: Charles C. Thomas, 1981).

[14]See Nicolaus Mills (ed.), *The Great School Bus Controversy* (New York: Teachers College Press, 1973); and Gary Orfield, *Must We Bus?* (Washington: Brookings Institution, 1978).

but leaped to 6.8 percent for schools over this ratio.[15] The policy implication of the "tipping point" hypotheses is that the desegregation can only be accomplished by carefully monitoring racial ratios and insuring that the black percentage does not exceed one-third.

The Boston Experience

The ultimate responsibility for insuring equal protection of laws under the Constitution of the United States lies with the federal courts. The U.S. Supreme Court had cited social science evidence in the historic *Brown v. Topeka* case in 1954 which showed that segregation in public schools had "a detrimental effect" upon black children.[16] Twenty years later, June 1974, U.S. Federal District Court Judge W. Arthur Garrity found that Boston school authorities built schools, assigned pupils, drew up attendance zones, and conscientiously endeavored to maintain racially segregated schools in that city. He ordered massive busing throughout the city. When the Boston School Committee refused to cooperate, he took over the governance of the school system himself. Serious violence accompanied attempts to bus students to and from high schools in working-class white neighborhoods. Violence, demonstrations, and racial hostilities continued for several years. Judge Garrity stuck to his plans: "No amount of public or parental opposition will excuse avoidance by school officials, of constitutionally imposed obligations."[17]

Prior to Judge Garrity's busing orders in 1973, Boston had 94,000 public school students, 57 percent of whom were white. When Judge Garrity finally removed himself from the case in 1985 and returned control of the schools to elected city officials, only 57,000 students remained in Boston's schools, and only 27 percent of them were white.[18] There was no creditable evidence that black students had improved their performance on standard test scores. Most white students in the Boston area attended either suburban schools or private schools (Judge Garrity lived in suburban Wellesley). Yet over time racial conflict in Boston subsided. The most vocal anti-busing politicians were eventually voted out of office. Boston's new school superintendent in 1985 was a black educator.

---

[15]Michael W. Giles, Everett F. Cataldo and Douglas S. Gatlin, "White Flight and Percent Black: The Tipping Point Re-examined," *Social Science Quarterly* vol. 56 (June 1975), 85–92; and "The Impact of Busing on White Flight," *Social Science Quarterly* vol. 55 (September 1974), 493–501.

[16]*Brown v. Board of Education of Topeka Kansas*, 347 U.S. 483 (1954).

[17]George M. Metcalf, *From Little Rock To Boston: The History of School Desegregation* (Westport Greenwood Press, 1983), p. 202.

[18]*The New York Times*, September 15, 1985.

Policy Analysis and Political Conflict

The point of this brief discussion is that policy analysis sometimes produces unexpected and even embarrassing findings, that public policies do not always work as intended, and that different political interests will interpret the findings of policy research differently—accepting, rejecting, or using these findings as they fit their own purposes.

POLICY ANALYSIS AND THE QUEST FOR "SOLUTIONS" TO AMERICA'S PROBLEMS

It is questionable that policy analysis can ever provide "solutions" to America's problems. War, ignorance, crime, poor health, poverty, racial cleavage, inequality, poor housing, pollution, congestion, and unhappy lives have afflicted people and societies for a long time. Of course, this is no excuse for failing to work toward a society free of these maladies. But our striving for a better society should be tempered with the realization that "solutions" to these problems may be very difficult to find. There are many reasons for tempering our enthusiasm for policy analysis, some of which are illustrated in the battle over busing and school desegregation.

First of all, it is easy to exaggerate the importance, both for good and for ill, of the policies of governments. It is not clear that government policies, however ingenious, could cure all or even most of society's ills. Governments are constrained by many powerful environmental forces—wealth, technology, population growth, patterns of family life, class structure, child-rearing practices, religious beliefs, and so on. These forces are not easily managed by governments, nor could they be controlled even if it seemed desirable to do so. In the final chapter of this volume we will examine policy impacts, but it is safe to say here that some of society's problems are very intractable. For example, it may be that the *only* way to ensure equality of opportunity is to remove children from disadvantaged family backgrounds at a very early age, perhaps before they are six months old. The weight of social science evidence suggests that the potential for achievement may be determined at a very young age. However, a policy of removing children from their family environment at such an early age runs contrary to our deepest feelings about family attachments. The forcible removal of children from their mothers is "unthinkable" as a governmental policy. So it may turn out that we never really provide equality of opportunity because cultural forces prevent us from pursuing an effective policy.

Second, policy analysis cannot offer "solutions" to problems when there isn't general agreement on what the problems are. The Coleman

Report assumed that raising achievement levels (measures of verbal and quantitative abilities) and raising aspiration levels (the desire to achieve by society's standards) were the "problems" to which our efforts should be directed. But others argue that racial segregation in the schools is constitutionally impermissible, whether or not integration improves the achievement levels of students. Judge Garrity, for example, refused to consider test scores in the Boston hearings; his goal was to end a dual school system.[19] In other words, there is no real agreement on what societal values should be implemented in educational policy. Policy analysis is not capable of resolving value conflicts. At best it can advise on how to achieve a certain set of end values; it cannot determine what those end values should be.

Third, policy analysis deals with very subjective topics and must rely upon interpretation of results. Professional researchers frequently interpret the results of their analyses differently. Social science research cannot be "value-free." Even the selection of the topic for research is affected by one's values about what is important in society and worthy of attention. As Louis Wirth explained,

> Since every assertion of a "fact" and the social world touches the interests of some individual or group, one cannot even call attention to the existence of certain "facts" without courting the objections of those whose very raison d'être in society rests upon a divergent interpretation of the "factual" situation.[20]

Another set of problems in systematic policy analysis centers around inherent limitations in the design of social science research. It is not really possible to conduct some forms of controlled experiments on human beings. For example, researchers cannot order middle-class white children to go to ghetto schools for several years just to see if it has an adverse impact on their achievement levels. Instead, social researchers must find situations in which educational deprivation has been produced "naturally" in order to make the necessary observations about the causes of such deprivation. Because we cannot control all the factors that go into a real-world situation, it is difficult to pinpoint precisely what it is that causes educational achievement or nonachievement. Moreover, even where some experimentation is permitted, human beings frequently modify their behavior simply because they know they are being observed in an experimental situation. For example, in educational research it frequently turns out that children perform well under *any* new teaching method or curricular innovation. It is difficult to know whether the improvements observed are a product of the new

---

[19]Metcalf, *From Little Rock to Boston: The History of School Desegregation*, p. 216.

[20]Louis Wirth, Preface to Karl Mannheim, *Ideology and Utopia: An Introduction to the Sociology of Knowledge* (New York: Harcourt Brace Jovanovich, 1936).

teaching method or curricular improvement or merely a product of the experimental situation. Finally, it should be noted that the people doing policy research are frequently program administrators who are interested in proving the positive results of their programs. It is important to separate research from policy implementation, but this is a difficult thing to do.

Perhaps the most serious reservation about policy analysis is the fact that social problems are so complex that social scientists are unable to make accurate predictions about the impact of proposed policies. *Social scientists simply do not know enough about individual and group behavior to be able to give reliable advice to policy makers.* Occasionally policy makers turn to social scientists for "solutions," but social scientists do not have any "solutions." Most of society's problems are shaped by so many variables that a simple explanation of them, or remedy for them, is rarely possible. A detailed understanding of such a complex system as human society is beyond our present capabilities. The fact that social scientists give so many contradictory recommendations is an indication of the absence of reliable scientific knowledge about social problems. Although some scholars argue that no advice is better than contradictory or inaccurate advice, policy makers still must make decisions, and it is probably better that they act in the light of whatever little knowledge social science can provide than that they act in the absence of any knowledge at all. Even if social scientists cannot predict the impact of future policies, they can at least attempt to measure the impact of current and past public policies and make this knowledge available to decision makers.

Policy Analysis As Art and Craft

Understanding public policy is both an art and a craft. It is an art because it requires insight, creativity, and imagination in identifying societal problems and describing them, in devising public policies which might alleviate them, and then, in finding out whether these policies end up making things better or worse. It is a craft because these tasks usually require some knowledge of economics, political science, public administration, sociology, law, and statistics. Policy analysis is really an applied subfield of all these traditional academic disciplines.

It is sometimes argued that a single "model of choice" can be applied to all kinds of problems—large and small, public and private.[21] (The "model of choice" is similar to the "rational model" described in Chapter 2 of this book.) But we doubt that there is any "model of choice" in policy analysis— that is, a single model or method which is preferable to all others and which consistently renders the best solutions to public problems.

[21]See Edith Stokey and Richard Zeckhauser, *A Primer for Policy Analysis* (New York: Norton, 1978), pp. 1, 23.

Instead we are in agreement with political scientist Aaron Wildavsky, who wrote:

> Policy analysis is one activity for which there can be no fixed program, for policy analysis is synonymous with creativity, which may be stimulated by theory and sharpened by practice, which can be learned but not taught.[22]

Wildavsky goes on to warn students that "solutions" to great public questions are not to be expected.

> In large part, it must be admitted, knowledge is negative. It tells us what we cannot do, where we cannot go, wherein we have been wrong, but not necessarily how to correct these errors. After all, if current efforts were judged wholly satisfactory, there would be little need for analysis and less for analysts.[23]

There is no one model of choice to be found in this book, but if anyone wants to begin a debate about different ways of understanding public policy, this book is a good place to begin.

BIBLIOGRAPHY

ANDERSON, JAMES E., DAVID W. BRADY, and CHARLES BULLOCK, *Public Policy and Politics in America*. Boston: Duxbury, 1978.

CHELF, CARL P., *Public Policymaking in America*, Santa Monica, Calif.: Goodyear, 1981.

COCHRAN, CLARKE E., et al., *American Public Policy: An Introduction*. New York: St. Martin's, 1982.

DYE, THOMAS R., *Policy Analysis: What Governments Do, Why They Do It, What Difference It Makes*. University, Ala.: University of Alabama Press, 1976.

LERNER, DANIEL, and HAROLD D. LASSWELL (eds.), *The Policy Sciences*. Stanford, Calif.: Stanford University Press, 1960.

STOKEY, EDITH and RICHARD ZECKHAUSER, *A Primer for Policy Analysis*. New York: Norton, 1978.

WILDAVSKY, AARON, *Speaking Truth to Power*. New York: John Wiley, 1979.

[22]Aaron Wildavsky, *Speaking Truth to Power* (New York: John Wiley, 1979), p. 3.
[23]Ibid., p. 401.

MODELS OF POLITICS
some help in thinking
about public policy

Secretary of Defense Caspar Weinberger rarely smiles at news conferences; he must defend the Defense Department against a critical media. (Dept. of Defense, photo by Ed Bosanko)

MODELS FOR POLICY ANALYSIS

A model is a simplified representation of some aspect of the real world. It may be an actual physical representation—a model airplane, for example, or the table-top buildings that urban planners use to show how things will look when proposed projects are completed. Or a model may be a diagram—a road map, for example, or a flow chart that political scientists use to show how a bill becomes a law.

The models we shall use in studying policy are *conceptual models*. These are word models which try to

1. simplify and clarify our thinking about politics and public policy;
2. identify important aspects of policy problems;
3. help us to communicate with each other by focusing on essential features of political life;
4. direct our efforts to better understand public policy by suggesting what is important and what is unimportant; and
5. suggest explanations for public policy and predict its consequences.

Over the years, political science, like other scientific disciplines, has developed a number of models to help us understand political life. Throughout this volume we will try to see whether these models have any utility in the study of public policy. Specifically we want to examine public policy from the perspective of the following models:

institutional model
process model
group model
elite model
rational model
incremental model
game theory model
systems model

Each of these terms identifies a major conceptual model which can be found in the literature of political science. None of these models was derived especially to study public policy, yet each offers a separate way of thinking about policy and even suggests some of the general causes and consequences of public policy.

These models are not competitive in the sense that any one of them could be judged "best." Each one provides a separate focus on political life, and each can help us to understand different things about public policy. Although some policies appear at first glance to lend themselves to explanation by one particular model, most policies are a combination of rational planning, incrementalism, interest group activity, elite preferences, systemic forces, game-playing, political processes, and institutional influences. In later chapters these models will be employed, singularly and in combination, to describe and explain specific policies. Following is a brief description of each model, with particular attention to the separate ways in which public policy can be viewed.

INSTITUTIONALISM: POLICY AS INSTITUTIONAL OUTPUT

Governmental institutions have long been a central focus of political science. Traditionally, political science has been defined as the study of governmental institutions. Political activities generally center around particular government institutions—Congress, the presidency, courts, states, municipalities, political parties, and so on. Public policy is authoritatively determined, implemented, and enforced by these institutions.

The relationship between public policy and governmental institutions is very close. Strictly speaking, a policy does not becomes a *public* policy until it is adopted, implemented, and enforced by some governmental institution. Governmental institutions give public policy three distinctive characteristics. First of all, government lends *legitimacy* to policies. Governmental policies are generally regarded as legal obligations which command the loyalty of citizens. People may regard the policies of other groups and associations in society—corporations, churches, professional organizations, civic associations, etc.—as important and even binding. But only government policies involve legal obligations. Second, government policies involve *universality*. Only government policies extend to all people in a society; the policies of other groups or organizations only reach a part of the society. Finally, government monopolizes *coercion* in society—only government can legitimately imprison violators of its policies. The sanctions that can be imposed by other groups or organizations in society are more limited. It is precisely this ability of government to command the loyalty of all its citizens, to enact policies governing the whole society, and to monopolize the legitimate use of force that encourages individuals and groups to work for enactment of their preferences into policy.

Traditionally, the institutional approach in political science did *not* devote much attention to the linkages between the structure of governmental institutions and the content of public policy. Instead, institutional studies usually described specific governmental institutions—their structures, organization, duties, and functions—without systematically inquiring about the impact of institutional characteristics on policy outputs. Constitutional and legal arrangements were described in detail, as were the myriad government offices and agencies at the federal, state, and local level. (See Figure 2-1 for an organizational description of the federal government.)

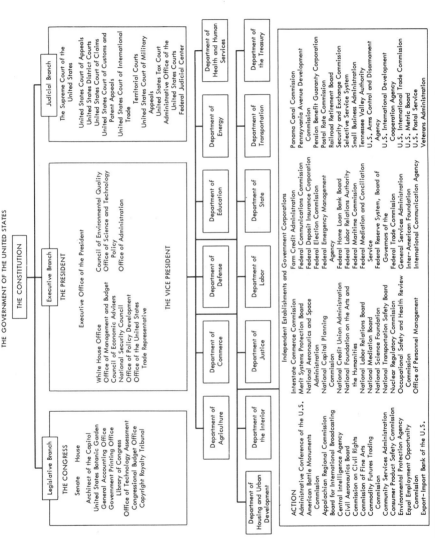

FIGURE 2-1 An institutional model: The organization of the United States government. (*U.S. Government Organization Manual.* Washington: Government Printing Office, 1983.)

However, the linkage between institutions and policy remained largely unexamined.

Despite the narrow focus of early institutional studies in political science, the institutional approach is not necessarily an unproductive one. Governmental institutions are really structured patterns of behavior of individuals and groups. By "structured" we mean that these patterns of behavior tend to persist over time. These stable patterns of individual and group behavior may affect the content of public policy. Institutions may be so structured as to facilitate certain policy outcomes and to obstruct other policy outcomes. They may give advantage to certain interests in society and withhold advantage from other interests. Certain individuals and groups may enjoy greater access to government power under one set of structural characteristics than under another set. In short, the structure of governmental institutions may have important policy consequences.

The institutional approach need not be narrow or descriptive. We can ask what relationships exist between institutional arrangements and the content of public policy, and we can investigate these relationships in a comparative, systematic fashion. For example, in the area of urban affairs we can ask: Are the policies of federal agencies (Congress, president, Department of Housing and Urban Development, etc.) more responsive to urban problems than are the policies of state or local governments? How does the division of responsibility among federal, state, and local governments affect the content of public policy? These questions can be dealt with systematically and involve a focus on institutional arrangements.

INSTITUTIONALISM: APPLYING THE MODEL

Governmental institutions and organizations are mentioned throughout this book. But in Chapter 11, "American Federalism: Institutional Arrangements and Public Policy," we shall examine some of the problems of American federalism—the distribution of money and power between federal, state, and local governments.

It is important to remember that the impact of institutional arrangements on public policy is an empirical question that deserves investigation. Too frequently, enthusiastic reformers have asserted that a particular change in institutional structure would bring about changes in public policy without investigating the true relationship between structure and policy. They have fallen into the trap of *assuming* that institutional changes will bring about policy changes. We must be cautious in our assessment of the impact of structure on policy. We may discover that *both* structure and policy are largely determined by social or economic forces, and that tinkering with institutional arrangements will have little independent impact on public policy if underlying forces remain constant.

PROCESS: POLICY AS POLITICAL ACTIVITY

Political processes and behaviors have been a central focus of political science for several decades. Modern "behavioral" political science since World War II has studied the activities of voters, interest groups, legislators, presidents, bureaucrats, judges, and other political actors. One of the main purposes has been to discover identifiable patterns of activities—or "processes." Recently some political scientists have tried to group various activities according to their relationship with public policy. The result is a set of *policy processes* which usually follow this general outline:

Identifying Problems	Demands are expressed for government action.
Formulating Policy Proposals	Agenda is set for public discussion.
	Development of program proposals to resolve problem.
Legitimating Policies	Selecting a proposal.
	Building political support for it.
	Enacting it as a law.
Implementing Policies	Organizing bureaucracies.
	Providing payments or services.
	Levying taxes.
Evaluating Policies	Studying programs.
	Reporting "outputs" of government programs.
	Evaluating "impacts" of programs on target and nontarget groups in society.
	Suggesting changes and adjustments.

In short, one can view the policy process as a series of political activities—problem identification, formulation, legitimation, implementation, and evaluation. A popular example of the process approach is shown in Table 2-1.

It has been argued that *political scientists* must limit their studies of public policy to these processes, and only these processes. According to political scientist Charles O. Jones:

> I maintain that the special purview of the political scientist is the political process and how it works. His or her interest in the substance of problems and policies, therefore, is in how it interacts with process, not necessarily in the substance itself. . . . this also suggests that my remedies for the social system tend to be of the process variety—more access for more interest, providing for criticism and opposition, publicizing decisions, and how they are made.[1]

[1]Charles O. Jones, *An Introduction to the Study of Public Policy*, 2nd ed. (Boston: Duxbury, 1978), p. 6.

TABLE 2-1   The Policy Process—A Framework for Analysis

FUNCTIONAL ACTIVITIES	CATEGORIZED IN GOVERNMENT	AND AS SYSTEMS	WITH OUTPUT
Perception Definition Aggregation Organization Representation	Problems to Government	Problem Identification	Problem to Demand
Formulation Legitimation Appropriation	Action in Government	Program Development	Proposal to Budgeted Program
Organization Interpretation Application	Government to Problem	Program Implementation	Varies (service, payments, facilities, controls, etc.)
Specification Measurement Analysis	Program to Government	Program Evaluation	Varies (jusification, recommendation, etc.)
Resolution/ Termination	Problem Resolution or Change	Program Termination	Solution or Change

Source: Charles O. Jones. *An Introduction to the Study of Public Policy*, 2nd ed. (Boston: Duxbury, 1978), p. 12. Copyright © 1977 by Wadsworth Publishing Co., Inc. Reprinted by permission of the publisher, Brooks/Cole Publishing Co., Monterey, California.

This argument allows the students of political science to study *how* decisions are made, and perhaps even how they *should* be made. But it does not permit students of political science to comment on the substance of public policy—who gets what and why. Books organized around the process theme have sections on identifying problems, formulating proposals, legitimating policies, and so on. It is not the *content* of public policy that is to be studied, but rather the *processes* by which public policy is developed, implemented, and changed.

Despite the narrow focus of the process model, it is still useful in helping us to understand the various activities involved in policy making. We want to keep in mind that *policy making* involves agenda setting (capturing the attention of policy makers); formulating proposals (devising and selecting policy options); legitimating policy (developing political support, winning congressional, presidential, or court approval); implementing policy (creating bureaucracies, spending money, enforcing laws); and evaluating policy (finding out whether policies work, whether they are popular).

Indeed, it may even be the case that the way policies are made affects the content of public policy and vice versa. At least this is a question that deserves attention. But again, just as we warned readers in our discussion of the institutional model: we do not want to fall into the trap of *assuming* that a change in the process of policy making will always bring about changes in the content of policy. It may turn out that social, economic, or technological constraints on policy makers are so great that it makes little or no difference in the content of policy whether the process of policy making is open or closed, competitive or noncompetitive, pluralist or elitist, or whatever. Political scientists are fond of discussing how a bill becomes a law, and even how various interests succeed in winning battles over policy questions. But changing either the formal or informal processes of decision making may or may not change the content of public policy.

We all may prefer to live in a political system where everyone has an equal voice in policy making, where many separate interests put forward solutions to public problems, where discussion, debate, and decision are open and accessible to all, where policy choices are made democratically, where implementation is reasonable, fair, and compassionate. But merely because we prefer such a political system does not necessarily mean that such a system would produce significantly different policies in national defense, energy, urban affairs, education, welfare, health, or criminal justice. The linkages between *process* and *content* must still be investigated.

PROCESSES: APPLYING THE MODEL

Political processes and behaviors are considered in each of the policy areas studied in this book. Additional commentary on the impact of political activity on public policy is found in Chapter 13, "The Policy-Making Process: Getting Inside the System."

GROUP THEORY: POLICY AS GROUP EQUILIBRIUM

Group theory begins with the proposition that interaction among groups is the central fact of politics.[2] Individuals with common interests band together formally or informally to press their demands upon government. According to political scientist David Truman, an interest group is "a shared-attitude group that makes certain claims upon other groups in the society"; such a group becomes political "if and when it makes a claim through or

---

[2]Group theory is explained at length in David B. Truman, *The Governmental Process* (New York: Knopf, 1951).

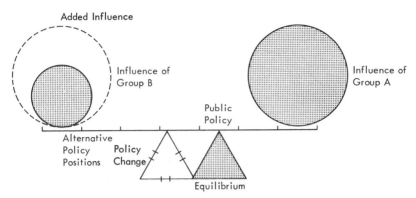

FIGURE 2-2   The group model.

upon any of the institutions of government."[3] Individuals are important in politics only when they act as part of, or on behalf of, group interests. The group becomes the essential bridge between the individual and the government. Politics is really the struggle among groups to influence public policy. The task of the political system is to *manage group conflict* by (1) establishing rules of the game in the group struggle, (2) arranging compromises and balancing interests, (3) enacting compromises in the form of public policy, and (4) enforcing these compromises.

According to group theorists, public policy at any given time is the equilibrium reached in the group struggle (see Figure 2-2). This equilibrium is determined by the relative influence of interest groups. Changes in the relative influence of any interest groups can be expected to result in changes in public policy; policy will move in the direction desired by the groups gaining in influence and away from the desires of groups losing influence. Political scientist Earl Latham described public policy from the group theory viewpoint as follows:

> What may be called public policy is actually the equilibrium reached in the group struggle at any given moment, and it represents a balance which the contending factions or groups constantly strive to tip in their favor.... The legislature referees the group struggle, ratifies the victories of the successful coalition, and records the terms of the surrenders, compromises, and conquests in the form of statutes.[4]

---

[3]Ibid., p. 37.

[4]Earl Latham, "The Group Basis of Politics," in Heinz Eulau, Samuel J. Eldersveld, and Morris Janowitz (eds.), *Political Behavior* (New York: Free Press, 1956), p. 239.

The influence of groups is determined by their numbers, wealth, organizational strength, leadership, access to decision makers, and internal cohesion.

Group theory purports to describe all meaningful political activity in terms of the group struggle. Policy makers are viewed as constantly responding to group pressures—bargaining, negotiating, and compromising among competing demands of influential groups. Politicians attempt to form a majority coalition of groups. In so doing, they have some latitude in determining what groups are to be included in the majority coalition. The larger the constituency of the politician, the greater the number of diverse interests, and the greater his latitude in selecting the groups to form a majority coalition. Thus, members of the House have less flexibility than senators, who have larger and generally more diverse constituencies; and the president has more flexibility than members of Congress and senators. Executive agencies are also understood in terms of their group constituencies.

Parties are viewed as coalitions of groups. The Democratic party coalition from the Roosevelt era until recently was composed of labor, central-city dwellers, ethnic groups, Catholics, the poor, liberal intellectuals, blacks, and Southerners. The difficulties of the Democratic party today can be traced largely to the weakening of this group coalition—the disaffection of the South and the group conflict between white labor and ethnic groups and blacks. The Republican coalition has consisted of rural and small-town residents, the middle class, whites, Protestants, white-collar workers, and suburbanites.

The whole interest group system—the political system itself—is held together in equilibrium by several forces. First of all, there is a large, nearly universal, *latent group* in American society which supports the constitutional system and prevailing "rules of the game." This group is not always visible but can be activated to administer overwhelming rebuke to any group that attacks the system and threatens to destroy the equilibrium.

Second, *overlapping group membership* helps to maintain the equilibrium by preventing any one group from moving too far from prevailing values. Individuals who belong to any one group also belong to other groups, and this fact moderates the demands of groups who must avoid offending their members who have other group affiliations.

Finally, the *checking and balancing resulting from group competition* also helps to maintain equilibrium in the system. No single group constitutes a majority in American society. The power of each group is checked by the power of competing groups. "Countervailing" centers of power function to check the influence of any single group and protect the individual from exploitation.

GROUP THEORY: APPLYING THE MODEL

Throughout this volume we will describe struggles over public policy. In Chapter 7, "Education: The Group Struggle," we will examine group conflict over public policy in our discussions of education and school issues. In Chapter 10, "Tax Policy: Battling the Special Interests," we will observe the power of interest groups in obtaining special treatments in the tax code and obstructing efforts to reform the nation's tax laws.

ELITE THEORY: POLICY AS ELITE PREFERENCE

Public policy may also be viewed as the preferences and values of a governing elite.[5] Although we often assert that public policy reflects the demands of "the people," this may express the myth rather than the reality of American democracy. Elite theory suggests that "the people" are apathetic and ill-informed about public policy, that elites actually shape mass opinion on policy questions more than masses shape elite opinion. Thus, public policy really turns out to be the preferences of elites. Public officials and administrators merely carry out the policies decided upon by the elite. Policies flow "downward" from elites to masses; they do not arise from mass demands (see Figure 2-3).

Elite theory can be summarized briefly as follows:

1. Society is divided into the few who have power and the many who do not. Only a small number of persons allocate values for society; the masses do not decide public policy.

2. The few who govern are not typical of the masses who are governed. Elites are drawn disproportionately from the upper socioeconomic strata of society.

3. The movement of nonelites to elite positions must be slow and continuous to maintain stability and avoid revolution. Only nonelites who have accepted the basic elite consensus can be admitted to governing circles.

4. Elites share consensus in behalf of the basic values of the social system and the preservation of the system. In America, the bases of elite consensus are the sanctity of private property, limited government, and individual liberty.

5. Public policy does not reflect demands of masses but rather the prevailing values of the elite. Changes in public policy will be incremental rather than revolutionary.

6. Active elites are subject to relatively little direct influence from apathetic masses. Elites influence masses more than masses influence elites.

[5]Elite theory is explained at length in Thomas R. Dye and Harmon Zeigler, *The Irony of Democracy*, 5th ed. (Monterey, Calif.: Brooks Cole, 1981).

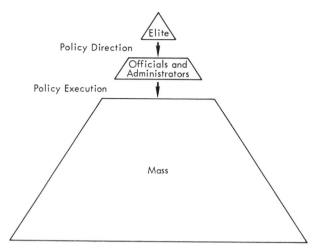

FIGURE 2-3 The elite model.

What are the implications of elite theory for policy analysis? First of all, elitism implies that public policy does not reflect demands of "the people" so much as it does the interests and values of elites. Therefore, change and innovations in public policy come about as a result of redefinitions by elites of their own values. Because of the general conservatism of elites—that is, their interest in preserving the system—change in public policy will be incremental rather than revolutionary. Public policies are frequently modified but seldom replaced. Changes in the nature of the political system occur when events threaten the system, and elites, acting on the basis of enlightened self-interest, institute reforms to preserve the system and their place in it. The values of elites may be very "public-regarding." A sense of *noblesse oblige* may permeate elite values, and the welfare of the masses may be an important element in elite decision making. Elitism does not mean that public policy will be against mass welfare, but only that the responsibility for mass welfare rests upon the shoulders of elites, not masses.

Second, elitism views the masses as largely passive, apathetic, and ill-informed; mass sentiments are more often manipulated by elites, rather than elite values being influenced by the sentiments of masses; and for the most part, communication between elites and masses flows downward. Therefore, popular elections and party competition do not enable the masses to govern. Policy questions are seldom decided by the people through elections or through the presentation of policy alternatives by political parties. For the most part these "democratic" institutions—elections and parties—are important only for their symbolic value. They help tie the masses to the political system by giving them a role to play on election day and a political party with which they can identify. Elitism contends that the masses have at best only an indirect influence over the decision-making behavior of elites.

Elitism also asserts that elites share in a consensus about fundamental norms underlying the social system, that elites agree on the basic "rules of the game," as well as the continuation of the social system itself. The stability of the system, and even its survival, depends upon elite consensus in behalf of the fundamental values of the system, and only policy alternatives that fall within the shared consensus will be given serious consideration. Of course, elitism does not mean that elite members never disagree or never compete with each other for preeminence. It is unlikely that there ever was a society in which there was no competition among elites. But elitism implies that competition centers around a very narrow range of issues and that elites agree on more matters than they disagree.

In America elite consensus includes constitutional government, democratic procedures, majority rule, freedom of speech and press, freedom to form opposition parties and run for public office, equality of opportunity in all segments of life, and sanctity of private property, the importance of individual initiative and reward, and the legitimacy of the free enterprise, capitalist economic system. Masses may give superficial support to democratic symbols, but they are not as consistent or reliable in their support for these values as elites.

ELITE THEORY: APPLYING THE MODEL

In Chapter 3, "Civil Rights: Elite and Mass Interaction," we will portray the civil rights movement as an effort by established national elites to extend equality of opportunity to blacks. Opposition to civil rights policies is centered among white masses in the states.

RATIONALISM: POLICY AS MAXIMUM SOCIAL GAIN

A rational policy is one that achieves maximum social gain. By "maximum social gain" we mean

> Governments should choose policies which result in gains to society which exceed costs by the greatest amount, and governments should refrain from policies if costs are not exceeded by gains.

Note that there are really two important guidelines included in this definition of maximum social gain. First of all, no policy should be adopted if its costs exceed its benefits. Second, among policy alternatives, decision makers should choose the policy that produces the greatest benefit over cost.[6]

In other words, a policy is rational when the difference between the values it achieves and the values it sacrifices is positive and greater than any other policy alternative. One should *not* view rationalism in a narrow dollars-and-cents framework, in which basic social values are sacrificed for dollar savings. Rationalism involves the calculation of *all* social, political, and economic values sacrificed or achieved by a public policy, not just those that can be measured in dollars.

To select a rational policy, policymakers must (1) know all the society's value preferences and their relative weights; (2) know all the policy alternatives available; (3) know all the consequences of each policy alternative; (4) calculate the ratio of benefits to costs for each policy alternative; and (5) select the most efficient policy alternative.[7] This rationality assumes that the value preferences of *society as a whole* can be known and weighted. It is not enough to know and weight the values of *some* groups and not others. There must be a complete understanding of *societal* values. Rational policy making also requires *information* about alternative policies, the *predictive capacity* to foresee accurately the consequences of alternate policies, and the *intelligence* to calculate correctly the ratio of costs to benefits. Finally, rational policy making requires a *decision-making system* that facilitates rationality in policy formation. A diagram of such a system is shown in Figure 2-4.

Many types of rational decision models are found in the literature of economics, political science, management, administrative science, and budgeting.[8] An example of a rational approach to resource allocation policy is portrayed in Figure 2-5.

The diagonal *Total Social Costs* shows costs increasing in direct proportion to the benefits provided. The curved line *Total Social Value* shows that the initial costs of a policy or program usually buy more benefits than later costs. As costs increase they usually do not buy as many benefits as the initial costs. (This reflects the familiar notion in economics of declining "marginal" value.) Eventually, increasing costs exceed benefits, where the straight line for *Total Social Costs* rises above the curved line for *Total Social Value*. Policy alternatives are represented by the perpendicular lines A, B, C, and D. A is not a rational policy alternative because costs exceed benefits. B provides the greatest amount of benefits but it is very costly; indeed,

[6]See Robert Henry Haveman, *The Economics of the Public Sector* (New York: John Wiley, 1970).

[7]See Yehezdel Dror, *Public Policy-Making Re-examined*, Part IV, "An Optional Model of Public Policy-Making" (San Francisco: Chandler, 1968).

[8]L. L. Wade and R. L. Curry, Jr., *A Logic of Public Policy: Aspects of Political Economy* (Belmont, Calif.: Wadsworth, 1970).

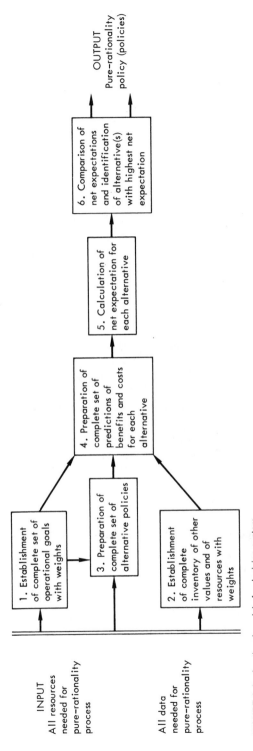

FIGURE 2-4 A rational model of a decision system.

INPUT
All resources
needed for
pure-rationality
process

All data
needed for
pure-rationality
process

1. Establishment
of complete set of
operational goals
with weights

2. Establishment
of complete
inventory of other
values and of
resources with
weights

3. Preparation of
complete set of
alternative policies

4. Preparation of
complete set of
predictions of
benefits and costs
for each
alternative

5. Calculation of
net expectation for
each alternative

6. Comparison of
net expectations
and identification
of alternative(s)
with highest net
expectation

OUTPUT
Pure-rationality
policy (policies)

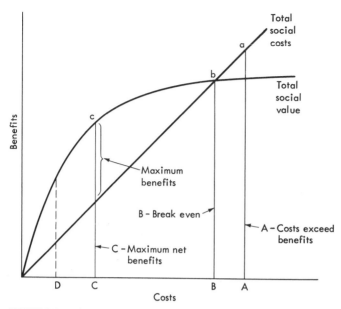

FIGURE 2-5 A model of maximum social gain.

costs and benefits are equal so we can consider *B* a "break-even" policy alternative. *C is the rational policy alternative because it provides the maximum net benefits (total benefits minus total costs).* In other words, *C* provides the maximum social gain.[9]

This model of maximum social gain can also be used to think about the optimal size of government. Governments, and government budgets, should increase until maximum net gain is achieved and then no more should be spent. The model of maximum social gain is applied to public policy making in benefit-cost analysis. The first applications were developed in the 1930s by the U.S. Corps of Engineers in programs for dams and river basin development. Today it is applied to virtually all government policies and programs. It is the principal analytic framework used to evaluate public spending decisions.

However, there are many barriers to rational decision making.[10] In fact, there are so many barriers to rational decision making that it rarely takes place at all in government. Yet the model remains important for analytic purposes because it helps to identify barriers to rationality. It assists

[9]An argument can also be made for policy *D* which yields a smaller maximum net benefit than *C*, but the ratio between its benefits and costs is lower. However, the maximum net benefit criterion is usually preferred over the largest benefit-cost ratio. See Edith Stokey and Richard Zeckhauser, *A Primer for Policy Analysis* (New York: Norton, 1978), p. 146.

[10]See Charles E. Lindblom, "The Science of Muddling Through," *Public Administration Review*, 19 (Spring 1959), 79–88; David Braybrooke and Charles E. Lindblom, *A Strategy of Decision* (New York: Free Press, 1963); Aaron Wildavsky, *The Politics of the Budgetary Process* (Boston: Little, Brown, 1964).

in posing the question: Why is policy making not a more rational process? At the outset we can hypothesize several important obstacles to rational policy making:

1. There are no *societal* benefits that are usually agreed upon, but only benefits to specific groups and individuals, many of which are conflicting.
2. The many conflicting benefits and costs cannot be compared or weighted; for example, it is impossible to compare or weigh the value of individual dignity against a tax increase.
3. Policy makers are not motivated to make decisions on the basis of societal goals, but instead try to maximize their own rewards—power, status, reelection, money, etc.
4. Policy makers are not motivated to *maximize* net social gain, but merely to *satisfy* demands for progress; they do not search until they find "the one best way" but halt their search when they find an alternative that "will work."
5. Large investments in existing programs and policies ("sunk costs") prevent policy makers from reconsidering alternatives foreclosed by previous decisions.
6. There are innumerable barriers to collecting all the information required to know all possible policy alternatives and the consequences of each alternative, including the cost of information gathering, the availability of the information, and the time involved in its collection.
7. Neither the predictive capacities of the social and behavioral sciences nor the predictive capacities of the physical and biological sciences are sufficiently advanced to enable policy makers to understand the full benefits or costs of each policy alternative.
8. Policy makers, even with the most advanced computerized analytical techniques, do not have sufficient intelligence to calculate accurately costs and benefits when a large number of diverse political, social, economic, and cultural values are at stake.
9. Uncertainty about the consequences of various policy alternatives compels policy makers to stick as closely as possible to previous policies to reduce the likelihood of disturbing, unanticipated consequences.
10. The segmentalized nature of policy making in large bureaucracies makes it difficult to coordinate decision making so that the input of all the various specialists is brought to bear at the point of decision.

RATIONALISM: APPLYING THE MODEL

In Chapter 4, "Criminal Justice: Rationality and Irrationality in Public Policy," we will show that rational policies to deter crime—policies ensuring certainty, swiftness, and severity of punishment—have seldom been implemented, and that the nation's high crime rate is partly a product of this irrationality. The problems of achieving rationality in public policy are also discussed in Chapter 5, "Poverty and Welfare: The Search for a Rational Strategy," and in Chapter 6, "Health: The Pathology Rationalism." We will describe the general design of alternative strategies in dealing with poverty, health, and welfare. We will observe how these strategies are implemented in public policy, and we will analyze some of the obstacles to the achievement of rationality in public policy.

INCREMENTALISM: POLICY AS VARIATIONS ON THE PAST

Incrementalism views public policy as a continuation of past government activities with only incremental modifications. Political scientist Charles E. Lindblom first presented the incremental model in the course of a critique of the traditional rational model of decision making.[11] According to Lindblom, decision makers do *not* annually review the whole range of existing and proposed policies, identify societal goals, research the benefits and costs of alternative policies in achieving these goals, rank-order preferences for each policy alternative in terms of the maximum net benefits, and then make a selection on the basis of all relevant information. On the contrary, constraints of time, information, and cost prevent policy makers from identifying the full range of policy alternatives and their consequences. Constraints of politics prevent the establishment of clear-cut societal goals and the accurate calculation of costs and benefits. The incremental model recognizes the impractical nature of "rational-comprehensive" policy making, and describes a more conservative process of decision making.

Incrementalism is conservative in that existing programs, policies, and expenditures are considered as a base, and attention is concentrated on new programs and policies and on increases, decreases, or modifications of current programs (see Figure 2-6). Policy makers generally accept the legitimacy of established programs and tacitly agree to continue previous policies.

They do this, first of all, because they do not have the time, information, or money to investigate all the alternatives to existing policy. The cost of collecting all this information is too great. Policy makers do not have sufficient predictive capacities, even in the age of computers, to know what all the consequences of each alternative will be. Nor are they able to calculate cost-benefit ratios for alternative policies when many diverse political, social, economic, and cultural values are at stake. Thus completely "rational" policy may turn out to be "inefficient" (despite the contradiction in terms) if the time and cost of developing a rational policy are excessive.

Second, policy makers accept the legitimacy of previous policies because of the uncertainty about the consequences of completely new or different policies. It is safer to stick with known programs when the consequences of new programs cannot be predicted. Under conditions of uncertainty, policy makers continue past policies or programs whether or not they have proven effective.

Third, there may be heavy investments in existing programs ("sunk costs" again) which preclude any really radical change. These investments may be in money, buildings, or other hard items, or they may be in psy-

---

[11]Lindblom, "The Science of Muddling Through," 79–88.

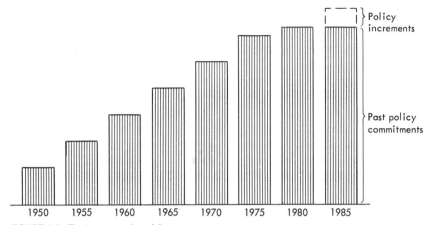

FIGURE 2-6 The incremental model.

chological dispositions, administrative practices, or organizational structure. It is accepted wisdom, for example, that organizations tend to persist over time regardless of their utility, that they develop routines that are difficult to alter, and that individuals develop a personal stake in the continuation of organizations and practices, which makes radical change very difficult. Hence, not all policy alternatives can be seriously considered, but only those which cause little physical, economic, organizational, and administrative dislocation.

Fourth, incrementalism is politically expedient. Agreement comes easier in policy making when the items in dispute are only increases or decreases in budgets, or modifications to existing programs. Conflict is heightened when decision making focuses on major policy shifts involving great gains or losses, or "all or nothing," "yes or no" policy decisions. Because the political tension involved in getting new programs or policies passed *every* year would be very great, past policy victories are continued into future years unless there is a substantial political realignment. Thus incrementalism is important in reducing conflict, maintaining stability, and preserving the political system itself.

The characteristics of policy makers themselves also recommend the incremental model. Rarely do human beings act to maximize all their values; more often they act to satisfy particular demands. People are pragmatic; they seldom search for the "one best way" but instead end their search when they find "a way that will work." This search usually begins with the familiar—that is, with policy alternatives close to current policies. Only if these alternatives appear to be unsatisfactory will the policy maker venture out toward more radical policy innovation. In most cases modification of existing programs will satisfy particular demands, and the major policy shifts required to maximize values are overlooked.

Finally, in the absence of any agreed-upon societal goals or values, it is easier for the government of a pluralist society to continue existing programs rather than to engage in overall policy planning toward specific societal goals.

INCREMENTALISM: APPLYING THE MODEL

We will give special attention to incrementalism in our discussion of government budgeting in Chapter 9. "Priorities and Price Tags: Incrementalism at Work."

GAME THEORY: POLICY AS RATIONAL CHOICE
IN COMPETITIVE SITUATIONS

Game theory is the study of rational decisions in situations in which two or more participants have choices to make and the outcome depends on the choices made by each of them. It is applied to policy making where there is no *independently* "best" choice that one can make—where the "best" outcomes depend upon what others do.

The idea of a "game" is that decision makers are involved in choices that are interdependent. "Players" must adjust their conduct to reflect not only their own desires and abilities but also their expectations about what others will do. Perhaps the connotation of a "game" is unfortunate, suggesting that game theory is not really appropriate for *serious* conflict situations. But just the opposite is true: game theory can be applied to decisions about war and peace, the use of nuclear weapons, international diplomacy, bargaining and coalition building in Congress or the United Nations, and a variety of other important political situations. A "player" may be an individual, a group, or a national government—indeed, any body with well-defined goals that is capable of rational action.

Game theory is an abstract and deductive model of policy making. It does not describe how people actually make decisions, but rather how they would go about making decisions in competitive situations if they were completely rational. Thus, game theory is a form of rationalism, but it is applied in *competitive* situations where the outcome depends on what two or more participants do.

The *rules of the game* describe the choices that are available to all the players. The choices are frequently portrayed in a "matrix"—a diagram which presents the alternative choices of each player and all the possible outcomes of the game. A two-by-two matrix is the simplest; there are only two players and each player has only two alternatives to choose from:

		PLAYER A	
		Alternative A_1	Alternative A_2
PLAYER B	Alternative B_1	outcome	outcome
	Alternative B_2	outcome	outcome

There are four possible outcomes to this simple game, each represented by a cell in a matrix. The actual outcome depends upon the choices of both Player *A* and Player *B*.

In game theory, *payoff* refers to the values that each player receives as a result of his or her choices and those of the opponent. Payoffs are frequently represented by numerical values placed on each outcome; these numerical values are placed inside each cell of the matrix and presumably correspond to the values each player places on each outcome. Because players value different outcomes differently, there are two numerical values inside each cell—one for each player.

Consider the game of "chicken." Two adolescents drive their cars toward each other at high speed, each with one set of wheels on the center line of the highway. If neither veers off-course they will crash. Whoever veers is "chicken." Both drivers prefer to avoid death but they also want to avoid the "dishonor" of being "chicken." The outcome depends on what both drivers do, and each driver must try to predict how the other will behave. This form of "brinkmanship" is common in international relations (see Figure 2-7).

Inspection of the payoff matrix suggests that it would be better for both drivers to veer in order to minimize the possibility of a great loss (−10). But the matrix is too simple. One or both players may place a different value on the outcomes than is suggested by the numbers. For example, one player may prefer death to dishonor in the game. Each player must try to calculate the values of the other and neither has complete

		DRIVER A	
		Stay on course	Veer
DRIVER B	Stay on Course	A: −10 B: −10	A: −5 B: +5
	Veer	A: +5 B: −5	A: −1 B: −1

FIGURE 2-7 A game-theoretic matrix for the game of "chicken." The game theorist him- or herself supplies the numerical values to the payoffs. If Driver *A* chooses to stay on course and Driver *B* chooses to stay on course also, the result might be scored as −10 for both players who wreck their cars. But if Driver *A* chooses to stay on course and Driver *B* veers, then Driver *A* might get +5 ("Courage") and Driver B −5 ("Dishonor"). If Driver *A* veers but Driver *B* stays on course, the results would be reversed. If both veer, each is dishonored slightly (−1) but not as much as when one or the other stayed on course.

information about the values of the opponent. Moreover, bluffing or the deliberate misrepresentation of one's values or resources to an opponent is always a possibility. For example, a possible strategy in the game of chicken is to allow your opponent to see you drink heavily before the game, stumble drunkenly toward your car, and mumble something about having lived long enough in this rotten world. The effect of this communication on your opponent may increase his estimate of your likelihood of staying on course, and hence provide incentive for him to veer and allow you to win.

A key concept in game theory is *strategy*. Strategy refers to rational decision making in which a set of moves is designed to achieve optimum payoff even after consideration of all of the opponent's possible moves. Game theorists employ the term "minimax" to refer to the rational strategy that either *minimizes the maximum loss or maximizes the minimum gain* for a player, regardless of what the opponent does. The minimax strategy is designed to protect a player against the opponent's best play. It might be viewed as a conservative strategy in that it is designed to reduce losses and insure minimum gains rather than to seek maximum gains at the risk of great losses. But most game theorists view minimax as the best rational strategy. (The rational player in the game of chicken will veer, because this choice minimizes his maximum loss.)

It should be clear from this discussion that game theory embraces both very complex and very simple ideas. The crucial question is whether any of these game theory ideas is really useful in studying public policy.

Game theory is more frequently proposed as an *analytic* tool by social scientists than as a practical guide to policy making by government officials. The conditions of game theory are seldom approximated in real life. Seldom do policy alternatives present themselves neatly in a matrix. More importantly, seldom can policy makers know the real payoff values for themselves or their opponents of various policy alternatives. Finally, as we have already indicated, there are many obstacles to rational policy making by governments.

Yet game theory provides an interesting way of thinking clearly about policy choices in conflict situations. Perhaps the real utility of game theory in policy analysis at the present time is in suggesting interesting questions and providing a vocabulary to deal with policy making in conflict situations.

GAME THEORY: APPLYING THE MODEL

Game theory is frequently applied in international conflict situations. We will explore the utility of game theory in our own efforts to describe and explain in Chapter 8 "Defense Policy: Strategies for Serious Games."

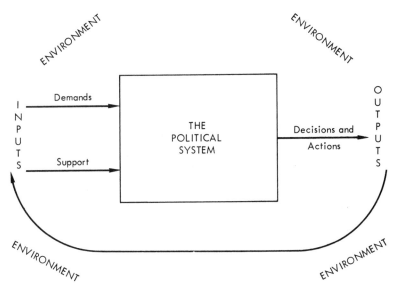

FIGURE 2-8 The systems model.

SYSTEMS THEORY: POLICY AS SYSTEM OUTPUT

Another way to conceive of public policy is to think of it as a response of a political system to forces brought to bear upon it from the environment.[12] Forces generated in the environment which affect the political system are viewed as *inputs*. The *environment* is any condition or circumstance defined as external to the boundaries of the political system. The political *system* is that group of interrelated structures and processes which functions authoritatively to allocate values for a society. *Outputs* of the political system are authoritative value allocations of the system, and these allocations constitute *public policy*.

This conceptualization of political activity and public policy can be diagramed as in Figure 2-8. This diagram is a simplified version of the idea of the political system described at great length by political scientist David Easton. The notion of a political system has been employed, either implicitly or explicitly, by many scholars who have sought to analyze the causes and consequences of public policy.

Systems theory portrays public policy as an output of the political *system*. The concept of *system* implies an identifiable set of institutions and activities in society that function to transform demands into authoritative

[12]This conceptualization is based upon David Easton, "An Approach to the Analysis of Political Systems," *World Politics*, 9 (1957), 383–400; and Easton, *A Framework for Political Analysis* (Englewood Cliffs, N.J.: Prentice-Hall, 1965).

decisions requiring the support of the whole society. The concept of *system* also implies that elements of the system are interrelated, that the system can respond to forces in its environment, and that it will do so in order to preserve itself. Inputs are received into the political system in the form of both demands and support. Demands occur when individuals or groups, in response to real or perceived environmental conditions, act to affect public policy. Support is rendered when individuals or groups accept the outcome of elections, obey the laws, pay their taxes, and generally conform to policy decisions. Any system absorbs a variety of demands, some of which conflict with each other. In order to transform these demands into output (public policies), it must arrange settlements and enforce these settlements upon the parties concerned. It is recognized that outputs (public policies) may have a modifying effect on the environment and the demands arising from it, and may also have an effect upon the character of the political system. The system preserves itself by (1) producing reasonably satisfying outputs, (2) relying upon deeply rooted attachments to the system itself, and (3) using, or threatening to use, force.

The value of the systems model to policy analysis lies in the questions that it poses:

1. What are the significant dimensions of the environment that generate demands upon the political system?
2. What are the significant characteristics of the political system that enable it to transform demands into public policy and to preserve itself over time?
3. How do environmental inputs affect the character of the political system?
4. How do characteristics of the political system affect the content of public policy?
5. How do environmental inputs affect the content of public policy?
6. How does public policy affect, through feedback, the environment and the character of the political system?

SYSTEMS THEORY: APPLYING THE MODEL

The systems model is particularly helpful in Chapter 12, "Inputs, Outputs, and Black Boxes," in examining public policies in the American states. By *comparing* states, we will assess the impact of various environmental conditions—particularly income—on levels of spending, benefits, and services in education, welfare, highways, police, corrections, and finance. We will see how federal policy sometimes tries to offset the impact of environmental variables on domestic policy in the states. We will examine the impact of political system characteristics—particularly party competition and voter participation—on levels of taxing, spending, benefits, and service, and attempt to compare the impact of these system characteristics on public policy with the impact of environmental conditions.

MODELS: HOW TO TELL IF THEY ARE HELPING OR NOT

A model is merely an abstraction or representation of political life. When we think of political "systems" or "elites" or "groups" or "rational decision making" or "incrementalism" or "games" we are abstracting from the real world in an attempt to simplify, clarify, and understand what is really important about politics. Before we begin our study of public policy, let us set forth some general criteria for evaluating the usefulness of concepts and models.

1. Certainly the utility of a model lies in its ability to *order and simplify* political life so that we can think about it more clearly and understand the relationships we find in the real world. Yet too much simplification can lead to inaccuracies in our thinking about reality. If a concept is too narrow or identifies only superficial phenomena, we may not be able to use it to explain public policy. On the other hand, if a concept is too broad, and suggests overly complex relationships, it may become so complicated and unmanageable that it is not really an aid to understanding. In other words, some theories of politics may be too complex to be helpful, while others may be too simplistic.

2. A model should also *identify* the really significant aspects of public policy. It should direct attention away from irrelevant variables or circumstances, and focus upon the "real" causes and "significant" consequences of public policy. Of course, what is "real," "relevant," or "significant" is to some extent a function of an individual's personal values. But we can all agree that the utility of a concept is related to its ability to identify what it is that is really important about politics.

3. Generally, a model should be *congruent with reality*—that is, it ought to have real empirical referents. We would expect to have difficulty with a concept that identifies a process that does not really occur, or symbolizes phenomena that do not exist in the real world. On the other hand, we must not be too quick to dismiss "unrealistic" concepts *if* they succeed in directing our attention to why they are unrealistic. For example, no one contends that government decision making is completely rational—public officials do not always act to maximize societal values and minimize societal costs. Yet the concept of "rational decision making" may be still useful, albeit "unrealistic," if it makes us realize how irrational government decision making really is and prompts us to inquire about why it is irrational.

4. A concept or model should also *communicate* something meaningful. If too many people disagree over the meaning of a concept, its utility in communication is diminished. For example, if no one really agrees on what constitutes an *elite*, then the concept of an *elite* does not mean the same thing to everyone. If one defines an *elite* as democratically elected public officials who are representative of the general public, then one is communicating a different idea in using the term than one who defines an *elite*

as an unrepresentative minority that makes decisions for society based on its own interests.

5. A model should help to *direct inquiry and research* into public policy. A concept should be operational—that is, it should refer directly to real-world phenomena that can be observed, measured, and verified. A concept, or a series of interrelated concepts (which we refer to as a *model*), should suggest relationships in the real world that can be tested and verified. If there is no way to prove or disprove the ideas suggested by a concept, then the concept is not really useful in developing a science of politics.

6. Finally, a model approach should *suggest an explanation* of public policy. It should suggest hypotheses about the causes and consequences of public policy—hypotheses that can be tested against real-world data. A concept that merely *describes* public policy is not as useful as a concept that *explains* public policy, or at least suggests some possible explanations.

BIBLIOGRAPHY

DUNN, WILLIAM N., *Public Policy Analysis: An Introduction.* Englewood Cliffs, N.J.: Prentice-Hall, 1981.

DYE, THOMAS R., and HARMON ZEIGLER, *The Irony of Democracy.* Monterey, Calif.: Brooks Cole, 1981.

EASTON, DAVID, *A Framework for Political Analysis.* Englewood Cliffs, N.J.: Prentice-Hall, 1965.

HAVEMAN, ROBERT HENRY, *The Economics of the Public Sector.* New York: John Wiley, 1970.

JONES, CHARLES O., *An Introduction to the Study of Public Policy,* 3rd ed., Monterey, CA: Brooks/Cole, 1984.

LINDBLOM, CHARLES E. *The Policy-Making Process.* Englewood Cliffs, N.J.: Prentice-Hall, 1968.

STOKEY EDITH, and RICHARD ZECKHAUSER, *A Primer for Policy Analysis.* New York: Norton, 1978.

TRUMAN, DAVID B., *The Governmental Process.* New York: Knopf, 1951.

WILDAVSKY, AARON, *The Politics of the Budgetary Process,* 4th edition. Boston: Little, Brown, 1984.

3
CIVIL RIGHTS
elite and mass interaction

The 1963 march on Washington: Stimulus to the Civil Rights Act. (AFL-CIO News)

The central domestic issue of American politics over the long history of the nation has been the place of blacks in American society. In describing this issue we have relied heavily on the elite model—because elite and mass attitudes toward civil rights differ a great deal, and public policy appears to reflect the attitudes of elites rather than masses. Civil rights policy is a response of a national elite to conditions affecting a minority of Americans, rather than a response of national leaders to majority sentiments. Policies of the national elite in civil rights have met with varying degrees of resistance from states and communities. We will contend that national policy has shaped mass opinion more than mass opinion has shaped national policy.

ELITE AND MASS ATTITUDES AND RACE

The attitudes of white masses toward blacks in American are ambivalent. Most whites believe that blacks are treated "the same as whites," but blacks do not agree. Most blacks believe that blacks are treated "not very well" or "badly." A majority of whites believed that blacks were treated the same as whites even *before* the Civil Rights Act of 1964! In short, there is little evidence that white masses have ever been overly concerned with the problems confronting blacks. This strongly suggests that the nation's civil rights laws were *not* a response of government to mass demands (see Table 3-1).

In general, white Americans are much more sympathetic toward blacks' rights today than they were in years past. A national sample of white Americans was asked the question, "Do you think white and black students should go to the same schools or separate schools?" over the years from 1942 to 1982. In 1942, not one American white in three approved of integrated schools (see Table 3-2). In 1956, two years after the historic *Brown v. Topeka* court decision, white attitudes had shifted markedly. Na-

TABLE 3-1 White Attitudes towards Treatment of Blacks
Question: In your opinion, how well do you think blacks are treated in this community—the same as whites are, not very well, or badly?

	SAME AS WHITES	NOT VERY WELL	BADLY	NO OPINION
1980 All	63	20	5	12
Whites	67	17	3	13
Blacks	35	41	16	8
1978 All	65	18	4	13
1968 All	67	19	2	12
1963 All	56	21	3	20

Source: *The Gallup Report*, February 1981.

TABLE 3-2 White Attitudes towards School Integration
Question: Do you think white students and Negro students should go to the same school or to separate schools?

	SAME SCHOOLS						
	1942	1956	1963	1966	1973	1980	1982
Total whites	30	49	62	67	82	88	91

Source: Paul B. Sheatsley, "White Attitudes Toward the Negro," *Daedalus*, 95, no. 1 (Winter 1966). Reprinted by permission of *Daedalus*, Journal of the American Academy of Arts and Sciences, Boston, Mass., Winter 1966, *The Negro American*-2. Updating from *Gallup Opinion Index* (October 1973), and *Public Opinion* (April/May, 1981), and (October/November, 1982). Prior to 1973 the term *Negro* was used in the question instead of *black*.

tionwide support for integration characterized about half of the white population. By 1963, two out of every three whites supported integrated schools. In recent years, there has been a continuation of the upward trend in the proportion of white Americans who favor school integration. Additional survey information suggests that whites are becoming increasingly accommodating toward equal rights for blacks over time in other areas as well. But it should be noted that white opinion generally *follows* public policy, rather than leading it.

There is a wide gap between the attitudes of masses and elites on the subject of black rights. The most hostile attitudes toward blacks are found among the less-privileged, less-educated whites. Lower socioeconomic status whites are much less willing to have contact with blacks than higher socioeconomic status whites, whether it is a matter of using the same public restrooms, or going to a movie or restaurant, or living next door. It is the affluent, well-educated white who is most concerned with discrimination and who is most willing to have contact with blacks.

The political implication of this finding is obvious: opposition to civil rights legislation and to black advancement in education, jobs, income, housing, and so on, is likely to be strongest among less educated and less affluent whites. Within the white community, support for civil rights will continue to come from the educated and affluent. In general, whites are willing to support laws eliminating direct discrimination. But what about compensatory efforts to overcome the effects of past discrimination and uplift the black community? Here the evidence is that most whites are not prepared to make any special effort to change the conditions of blacks. The overwhelming majority of white Americans and a majority of black Americans, *oppose* affirmative action programs (see Table 3-3). As we shall observe in this chapter, public policy in affirmative action, busing, and civil rights is not determined by public opinion but rather by the actions of Congress, the president, the bureaucracy, and especially the U.S. Supreme Court.

TABLE 3-3   Attitudes towards Affirmative Action
Question: Some people say that to make up for past discrimination, women and members of minority groups should be given preferential treatment in getting jobs and places in colleges. Others say that ability, as determined by test scores, should be the main consideration. Which point of view comes closest to how you feel in this matter?

	GIVE PREFERENCE	ABILITY MAIN CONSIDERATION	NO OPINION
Total	11%	83%	7%
Male	9	85	6
Female	11	82	7
White	7	87	6
Nonwhite	29	57	14

Source: *Public Opinion,* April/May, 1981.

THE DEVELOPMENT OF CIVIL RIGHTS POLICY

The initial goal in the struggle for equality in America was the elimination of discrimination and segregation practiced by governments, particularly in voting and public education. Later, discrimination in both public and private life—in transportation, theaters, parks, stores, restaurants, businesses, employment, and housing—came under legal attack.

The Fourteenth Amendment, passed by Congress after the Civil War and ratified in 1868, declares:

> All persons born or naturalized in the United States, and subject to the Jurisdiction thereof, are citizens of the United States and of the State wherein they reside. No State shall make or enforce any law which shall abridge the privileges or immunities of citizens of the United States; nor shall any State deprive any person of life, liberty, or property, without due process of law; nor deny to any person within its jurisdiction the equal protection of the laws.

The language of the Fourteenth Amendment and its historical context leave little doubt that its original purpose was to achieve the full measure of citizenship and equality for black Americans. During Reconstruction and the military occupation of the Southern states, some radical Republicans were prepared to carry out in Southern society the revolution this amendment implied. But by 1877, Reconstruction had been abandoned; the national government was not prepared to carry out the long, difficult, and disagreeable task of really reconstructing society in the eleven states of the former Confederacy. In the Compromise of 1877, the national government agreed to end military occupation of the South, gave up its efforts to rearrange Southern society, and lent tacit approval to white supremacy in that region. In return, the Southern states pledged their support of the Union, accepted national supremacy, and, of course, agreed to permit the

Republican candidate, Rutherford B. Hayes, to assume the presidency, even though his Democratic opponent, Samuel J. Tilden, had won more popular votes in the disputed election of 1876.

The Supreme Court agreed to the terms of the compromise. The result was a complete inversion of the meaning of the Fourteenth Amendment so that it became a bulwark of segregation. State laws segregating the races were upheld. The constitutional argument on behalf of segregation under the Fourteenth Amendment was that the phrase "equal protection of the laws" did not prevent state-enforced separation of the races. Schools and other public facilities that were "separate but equal" won constitutional approval. This separate-but-equal doctrine became the Supreme Court's interpretation of the Equal Protection Clause of the Fourteenth Amendment in *Plessy v. Ferguson*:

> The object of the [14th] Amendment was undoubtedly to enforce the absolute equality of the two races before the law, but in the nature of things it could not have been intended to abolish distinctions based upon color, or to enforce social, as distinguished from political, equality, or a commingling of the two races upon terms unsatisfactory to either. Laws permitting, and even requiring, their separation in places where they are liable to be brought into contact do not necessarily imply the inferiority of either race to the other, and have been generally, if not universally recognized as within the competency of the state legislatures in the exercise of their police power. The most common instance of this is connected with the establishment of separate schools for white and colored children, which has been held to be a valid exercise of the legislative power. . . . [1]

However, segregated facilities, including public schools, were seldom if ever equal, even with respect to physical conditions. In practice, the doctrine of segregation was "separate and *unequal*." The Supreme Court began to take notice of this after World War II. Although it declined to overrule the segregationist interpretation of the Fourteenth Amendment, it began to order the admission of individual blacks to white public universities where evidence indicated that separate black institutions were inferior or nonexistent.[2]

Leaders of the newly emerging civil rights movement in the 1940s and 1950s were not satisfied with court decisions that examined the circumstances in each case to determine if separate school facilities were really equal. Led by Roy Wilkins, executive director of the National Association for the Advancement of Colored People, and Thurgood Marshall, chief counsel for the NAACP, the civil rights movement pressed for a court decision that segregation itself meant inequality within the meaning of the Fourteenth Amendment, whether or not facilities were equal in all tangible

---

[1] *Plessy* v. *Ferguson,* 163 U.S. 537 (1896).
[2] *Sweatt* v. *Painter,* 339 U.S. 629 (1950).

respects. In short, they wanted a complete reversal of the "separate-but-equal" interpretation of the Fourteenth Amendment, and a ruling that laws *separating* the races were unconstitutional.

The civil rights groups chose to bring suit for desegregation in Topeka, Kansas, where segregated black and white schools were equal with respect to buildings, curricula, qualifications and salaries of teachers, and other tangible factors. The object was to prevent the Court from ordering the admission of blacks because *tangible* facilities were not equal, and to force the Court to review the doctrine of segregation itself.

The Court rendered its historic decision in *Brown* v. *Board of Education of Topeka, Kansas,* on May 17, 1954:

> Segregation of white and colored children in public schools has a detrimental effect upon the colored children. The impact is greater when it has the sanction of law, for the policy of separating the races is usually interpreted as denoting the inferiority of the Negro group. A form of inferiority affects the motivation of a child to learn. Segregation with the sanction of law, therefore, has a tendency to retard the educational and mental development of Negro children and to deprive them of some of the benefits they would receive in a racially integrated school system.
>
> Whatever may have been the extent of psychological knowledge of the time of *Plessy* v. *Ferguson,* this finding is amply supported by modern authority. Any language in *Plessy* v. *Ferguson* contrary to this source is rejected.[3]

The original *Brown* v. *Topeka* decision was symbolically very important. Although it would be many years before any significant number of black children would attend formerly segregated white schools, the decision by the nation's highest court undoubtedly stimulated black hopes and expectations. Black sociologist Kenneth Clark writes:

> This [civil rights] movement would probably not have existed at all were it not for the 1954 Supreme Court school desegregation decision which provided a tremendous boost to the morale of Negroes by its *clear* affirmation that color is irrelevant to the rights of American citizens. Until this time the Southern Negro generally had accommodated to the separation of the black from the white society.[4]

Note that this first great step toward racial justice in the twentieth century was taken by the *nonelective* branch of the federal government. Nine men, secure in their positions with lifetime appointments, responded to the legal arguments of highly educated black leaders, one of whom— Thurgood Marshall—would later become a Supreme Court justice himself.

---

[3]*Brown* v. *Board of Education of Topeka, Kansas,* 347 U.S. 483 (1954).
[4]Kenneth B. Clark, *Dark Ghetto* (New York: Harper & Row, 1965), pp. 77–78.

The decision was made by a judicial elite, not by "the people" or their elected representatives.

MASS RESISTANCE TO CIVIL RIGHTS POLICY

Although the Supreme Court had spoken forcefully in the *Brown* case in declaring segregation unconstitutional, from a *political* viewpoint the battle over segregation was just beginning. Segregation would remain a part of American life, regardless of its constitutionality, until effective elite power was brought to bear to end it. The Supreme Court, by virtue of the American system of federalism and separation of powers, has little formal power at its disposal. Congress, the president, state governors and legislatures, and the people have more power at their disposal than the federal judiciary. The Supreme Court must rely largely on the other branches of the federal government, on the states, and on private individuals and organizations to effectuate the law of the land.

Reverend Martin Luther King, Jr. won the Nobel Prize for his leadership in the American civil rights movement. (The Bergen Evening Record Corporation, Hackensack, N.J.)

Yet in 1954 the practice of segregation was widespread and deeply ingrained in American life. Seventeen states *required* the segregation of the races in public schools:

Alabama	Texas
Arkansas	Virginia
Florida	Delaware
Georgia	Kentucky
Louisiana	Maryland
Mississippi	Missouri
North Carolina	Oklahoma
South Carolina	West Virginia
Tennessee	

The Congress of the United States *required* the segregation of the races in the public schools of the District of Columbia. Four additional states—Arizona, Kansas, New Mexico, and Wyoming—*authorized* segregation upon the option of local school boards (see Figure 3-1.)

Thus, in deciding *Brown* v. *Topeka*, the Supreme Court struck down the laws of twenty-one states and the District of Columbia in a single opinion. Such a far-reaching decision was bound to meet with difficulties in implementation. In an opinion delivered the following year, the Supreme Court declined to order immediate nationwide desegregation, but instead turned over the responsibility for desegregation to state and local authorities under the supervision of federal district courts. The way was open for extensive litigation, obstruction, and delay by states that chose to resist desegregation.

The six border states with segregated school systems—Delaware, Kentucky, Maryland, Missouri, Oklahoma, West Virginia—together with the school districts in Kansas, Arizona, and New Mexico that had operated segregated schools, chose not to resist desegregation formally. The District of Columbia also desegregated its public schools the year following the Supreme Court's decision.

However, resistance to school integration was the policy choice of the eleven states of the Old Confederacy. Refusal of a school district to desegregate until it was faced with a federal court injunction was the most common form of delay. Segregationists also pressed for state laws that would create an endless chain of litigation in each of the nearly 3,000 school districts in the South in the hope that these integration efforts would drown in a sea of protracted court controversy. State laws that were obviously designed to evade constitutional responsibilities to end segregation were struck down in federal courts; but court suits and delays slowed progress toward integration. On the whole, those states that chose to resist desegregation were quite successful in doing so from 1954 to 1964. In late 1964,

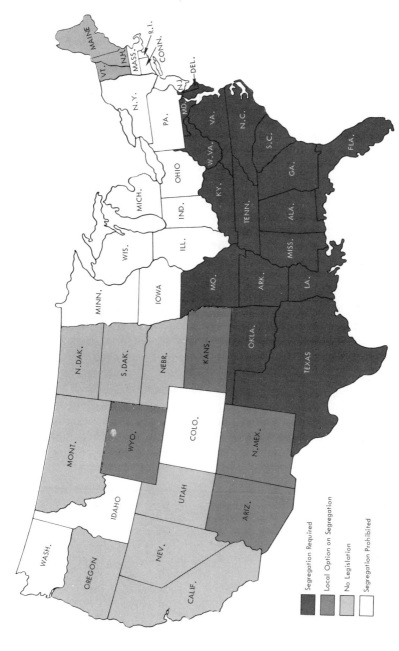

FIGURE 3-1 Segregation laws in the United States in 1954

Segregation Required

Local Option on Segregation

No Legislation

Segregation Prohibited

ten years after the *Brown* decision, only about 2 percent of the black school-children in the eleven Southern states were attending integrated schools!

Finally Congress entered the civil rights field in support of court efforts to achieve desegregation. The Civil Rights Act of 1964, Title VI, provided that every federal department and agency must take action to end segregation in all programs or activities receiving federal financial assistance. It was specified that this action was to include termination of financial assistance if states and communities receiving federal funds refused to comply with federal desegregation orders. Thus, in addition to *court orders* requiring desegregation, states and communities faced *administrative orders* or "guidelines" from federal executive agencies threatening loss of federal funds for noncompliance. Acting under the authority of Title VI, the U.S. Office of Education (now the Department of Education) required all school districts in the seventeen formerly segregated states to submit desegregation plans as a condition of federal assistance. "Guidelines" governing the acceptability of these plans were frequently unclear, often contradictory, and always changing, yet progress toward desegregation was speeded up.

The last legal excuse for delay in implementing school desegregation collapsed in 1969 when the Supreme Court rejected a request by Mississippi school officials for a delay in implementing school desegregation in that state. School officials contended that immediate desegregation in several southern Mississippi counties would encounter "administrative and legislative difficulties." The Supreme Court stated that no delay could be granted. The Court declared that every school district was obligated to end dual school systems "at once" and "now and hereafter" to operate only unitary schools.[5] The effect of the decision, fifteen years after the original *Brown* case, was to eliminate any further legal justification for the continuation of segregation in public schools.

DE FACTO SCHOOL SEGREGATION AND BUSING

In *Brown* v. *Board of Education of Topeka,* the Supreme Court quoted approvingly the view that segregation had "a tendency to retard the educational and mental development of Negro children and to deprive them of some of the benefits they would receive in a racially integrated school system." The U.S. Commission on Civil Rights reported that even when the segregation was *de facto*—that is, the product of segregated housing patterns and neighborhood schools rather than direct discrimination—the adverse effects on black students were still significant.[6] Black students at-

---

[5]*Alexander* v. *Holmes County Board of Education,* 396 U.S. 19 (1969).

[6]U.S. Commission on Civil Rights, *Racial Isolation in the Public School* (Washington, D.C.: Government Printing Office, 1966).

tending predominantly black schools had lower achievement scores and lower levels of aspiration than blacks with comparable socioeconomic backgrounds who attended predominantly white schools. When a group of black students attending school with a majority of advantaged whites was compared to a group of blacks attending school with a majority of disadvantaged blacks, the average difference in levels of achievement amounted to more than two grade levels. On the other hand, the commission found that the achievement levels of white students in classes roughly half-white in composition were not substantially different from those of white students in all-white schools. This finding comprises perhaps the best single argument for ending *de facto* segregation in both Northern and Southern school districts.

Ending racial isolation in the public schools frequently involves busing schoolchildren into and out of segregated neighborhoods. The objective is to achieve a racial "balance" in each public school, so that each has roughly the same percentage of blacks and whites as are found in the total population of the entire school district. Indeed, in some large cities where blacks comprise the overwhelming majority of public school students, desegregation may require city students to be bused to the suburbs and suburban students to be bused to the core city.

The argument *for* busing is that it is the most effective and efficient method of providing minority groups with equal opportunities in education. Black inner-city schools do not provide the same educational opportunities that are provided in predominantly white outer-city and suburban schools. As a black city councilman in Detroit put it:

> It's pragmatic. We don't have any desire to be close to white people just for the sake of being close to white people. We want the same thing everyone else wants so we can have the same opportunities for our kids to learn and grow.[7]

Blacks have a constitutional right to equal educational opportunities. Busing is an inconvenience, but it certainly is a minor inconvenience compared with the value of equal educational opportunity. Moreover, many supporters of busing argue that *de facto* segregation has indeed been abetted by government policies—for example, federal housing programs that build low-income public housing in central cities and promote middle-class home ownership in suburbs; transportation policies that make it easier for affluent white middle-class residents to leave the central city for homes in the suburbs while retaining their jobs in the cities—and therefore governments have a clear responsibility to take affirmative steps, including busing, to integrate public schools.

[7]*Time*, November 15, 1971, p. 64. Copyright 1971 Time Inc. All rights reserved. Reprinted by permission from *Time*.

TABLE 3-4   Mass Opinion on School Integration
QUESTION: Would you, yourself, have any objection to sending your children to a school where a few of the children are Negroes? Where half are Negroes? Where more than half are Negroes?

	PERCENTAGE OBJECTING	
	NORTHERN WHITE PARENTS	SOUTHERN WHITE PARENTS
Where a few are Negroes?		
1963	10%	61%
1970	6	16
1973	6	16
1980	5	5
Where half are Negroes?		
1963	33%	78%
1970	24	43
1973	23	36
1980	22	27
Where more than half are Negroes?		
1963	53%	86%
1970	51	69
1973	63	69
1980	51	66

Source: Data derived from *The Gallup Report* (February 1981), p. 30.

Not all opposition to busing is racist. Many middle-class parents feel that busing their children to inner-city schools will expose them to the social problems of the inner-city—crime, drugs, and violence. Middle-class whites who have moved to a suburb for the sake of its school system resent the fact that courts will order their children to be bused back to the poorer quality city schools. A Michigan mother argues: "I don't see any reason why they've got a right to come in here and tell me my kids can't use the school I bought and paid for.[8] Ending *de facto* segregation requires drastic changes in the prevailing concept of "neighborhood schools." Schools would no longer be a part of the neighborhood or the local community but rather part of a large citywide or areawide school system. Finally, the ending of *de facto* segregation would require school districts to classify students on the basis of race and use racial categories as a basis for school placement. Although this would supposedly be a benign form of racial classification, nevertheless it would represent a return to both government-sponsored racial classification and the differential application of laws to the separate races (in contrast to the notion that the law should be "colorblind").

The greatest opposition to busing comes when white middle-class children are ordered to attend predominantly black schools. Opposition is greatly reduced when black children are ordered to attend predominantly white middle-class schools (see Table 3-4). Most whites do not believe in

[8]Ibid., p. 57.

sending youngsters from a good school to a bad school in order to achieve
racial integration. Busing also destroys the concept of a neighborhood
school, where children are educated near their homes under the guidance
of their parents. Neighborhood schools are said to stimulate community
involvement in the educational process, bringing teachers, parents, and
students together more frequently. In addition, busing involves educational
time wasted in riding buses, educational funds spent on buses rather than
learning materials, and an unnecessary increase in the risk of accidents to
many children. Proponents of busing argue that it brings children of different cultures together and teaches them to live, work, and play with others
who are different from themselves. But racial balancing does not always
result in genuine integration; as one Pennsylvania high-school student re-
marked after a citywide busing program: "I thought the purpose of busing
was to integrate the schools, but in the long run, the white kids sit in one
part of the bus and the black kids in another part.[9]

BUSING: THE CONSTITUTIONAL QUESTION

The question of equality in public education, however, is a constitutional
question to be resolved by federal courts rather than public opinion. The
Fourteenth Amendment guarantees "equal protection of the laws." If the
Supreme Court requires busing and racial balancing in all public schools
in order to fulfill the constitutional mandate of the Fourteenth Amendment, then only another amendment to the Constitution specifically prohibiting busing and racial balancing could overturn that decision.

Where racial imbalance and *de facto* segregation are a product of past
or present discriminatory practices by states or school districts, the Supreme
Court has held that school officials have a duty to eliminate all vestiges of
segregation, and this responsibility may entail busing and deliberate racial
balancing to achieve integration in education. In the important case of
Swann v. *Charlotte-Mecklenburg Board of Education* (1971),[10] the Supreme
Court held that the racial composition of the school in a Southern district
that had previously been segregated by law could be used as evidence of
violation of constitutional rights, and busing to achieve racial balance could
be imposed as a means of ending all traces of dualism in the schools. The
Supreme Court was careful to say, however, that racial imbalance in school
is not itself grounds for ordering busing unless it is also shown that some
present or past government action has contributed to that imbalance. Thus,
the impact of the Swann decision falls largely on *Southern* schools.

The constitutional question in *Northern* cities is somewhat different
from that in Southern cities. In *Milliken* v. *Bradley* (1974), the Supreme

[9]Ibid., p. 63.
[10]*Swann* v. *Charlotte-Mecklenburg Board of Education,* 402 U.S. 1 (1971).

Court decided by a 5-to-4 vote that the Fourteenth Amendment does *not* require busing across city-suburban school district boundaries to achieve integration.[11] Where central-city schools are predominantly black, and sub-urban schools are predominantly white, *cross-district* busing is not required, unless it is shown that some official action brought about this segregation. The Supreme Court threw out a lower federal court order for massive busing of students between Detroit and fifty-two suburban school districts. Although Detroit city schools were 70 percent black, none of the Detroit area school districts segregated students within their own boundaries.

Chief Justice Burger, writing for the majority, said:

> The constitutional right of the Negro respondents residing in Detroit is to attend a unitary school system in that district. Unless petitioners drew the district lines in a discriminatory fashion, or arranged for the white students residing in the Detroit district to attend schools in Oakland or Macomb counties, they were under no constitutional duty to make provisions for Negro students to do so.

In a strong dissent, Justice Thurgood Marshall wrote:

> In the short run it may seem to be the easiest course to allow our great metropolitan areas to be divided up each into cities—one white, the other black—but it is a course, I predict, our people will ultimately regret.

This important decision means that largely black central cities, sur-rounded by largely white suburbs, will remain *de facto* segregated because there are not enough white students living within the city to achieve in-tegration.

Note that this decision applies only to city-suburban cross-district bus-ing. If a federal district court judge in any city, North or South, finds that any actions by governments or school officials have contributed to racial imbalances (for example, drawing school district attendance lines), the judge may still order busing within the city to overcome any racial imbalances produced by official action. In recent years, an increasing number of North-ern cities have come under federal district court orders to improve racial balances in their schools through busing.

EVALUATION: BUSING AND EDUCATION

Desegregation has *not* come to mean the elimination of racial imbalance in the public schools. Indeed, there is some evidence that government efforts to desegregate city schools in both the North and the South have resulted

---

[11]*Milliken v. Bradley,* 418 U.S. 717 (1974).

in *greater* racial imbalances. The reason, of course, is that many white parents confronted with busing and racial integration chose to move out of the city or to enroll their children in private schools. The result is the withdrawal of whites from city public schools and "resegregation" when black pupil percentages climb to 50, 75, or 95 percent of total public school enrollment. Thus, racial isolation in American schools remains quite high.

The most influential evidence of the failure of busing to achieve integration is sociologist James S. Coleman's *Trends in School Desegregation,* a 1975 study sometimes called the "Second Coleman Report," by the same scholar who provided the original evidence that racial imbalance lowers the scores of black schoolchildren (see Chapter 1). In this study, however, Coleman is concerned with whether court-ordered busing produces its intended effects, that is, improved racial balance—or whether it merely stimulates white flight and makes matters worse. In observing *all* U.S. cities, Coleman concludes that racial imbalance is decreasing, particularly in the South. However, among the largest metropolitan areas (1) there is a "sizable loss of whites" when government desegregation programs go into effect, and (2) white loss is greatest with larger black populations and surrounding white suburban rings.

Blacks now comprise the overwhelming majority of public school pupils in Detroit, Philadelphia, Boston, Atlanta, Chicago, Baltimore, Cleveland, Gary, Memphis, New Orleans, Newark, Richmond, St. Louis, and almost all the public school pupils in Washington, D.C.

THE CIVIL RIGHTS MOVEMENT

The first goal of the civil rights movement in America was to prevent discrimination and segregation by governments, particularly states, municipalities, and school districts. But even while important victories for the civil rights movement were being recorded in the prevention of discrimination by governments, particularly in the *Brown* case, the movement began to broaden its objectives to include the elimination of discrimination in *all* segments of American life, private as well as public. Governments should not only cease discriminatory practices of their own, they should also act to halt discrimination by private organizations and individuals.

The goal of eliminating discrimination in private life creates a positive obligation of government to act forcefully in public accommodations, employment, housing, and many other sectors of society. When the civil rights movement turned to combating private discrimination, it had to carry its fight into the legislative branch of government. The federal courts could help restrict discrimination by state and local governments and school authorities, but only Congress, state legislatures, and city councils could restrict discrimination practiced by private owners of restaurants, hotels and motels, private employers, and other individuals who were not government officials.

The leadership in the struggle to eliminate discrimination and segregation from private life was provided by a young black minister, Martin Luther King, Jr. King's father was the pastor of one of the South's largest and most influential congregations, the Ebenezer Baptist Church in Atlanta, Georgia. Martin Luther King, Jr., received his doctorate from Boston College and began his ministry in Montgomery, Alabama. In 1955 the black community of Montgomery began a year-long boycott with frequent demonstrations against the Montgomery city buses over segregated seating practices. The dramatic appeal and the eventual success of the boycott in Montgomery brought nationwide attention to its leader, and led to the creation in 1957 of the Southern Christian Leadership Conference.

Under King's leadership the civil rights movement developed and refined political techniques for minorities in American politics, including *nonviolent direct action.* Nonviolent direct action is a form of protest which involves breaking "unjust" laws in an open, "loving," nonviolent fashion. The general notion of civil disobedience is not new; it has played an important role in American history from the Boston Tea Party to the abolitionists who illegally hid runaway slaves, to the suffragettes who demonstrated for women's voting rights, to the labor organizers who formed the nation's major industrial unions, to the civil rights workers of the early 1960s who deliberately violated segregation laws. The purpose of nonviolent direct action is to call attention, or to "bear witness," to the existence of injustice. In the words of Martin Luther King, Jr., civil disobedience "seeks to dramatize the issue so that it can no longer be ignored."[12]

There should be no violence in true civil disobedience, and only "unjust" laws are broken. Moreover, the law is broken "openly, lovingly" with a willingness to accept the penalty. Punishment is actively sought rather than avoided, since punishment will help to emphasize the injustice of the law. The object is to stir the conscience of an elite, and win support for measures which will eliminate the injustices. By willingly accepting punishment for the violation of an unjust law, one demonstrates the strength of one's convictions. The dramatization of injustice makes news; the public's sympathy is won when injustices are spotlighted; and the willingness of demonstrators to accept punishment is visible evidence of their sincerity. Cruelty or violence directed against the demonstrators by police or others

---

[12]For an inspiring essay on nonviolent direct action and civil disobedience in a modern context, read Martin Luther King, Jr., "Letter from Birmingham City Jail," April 16, 1963, reprinted in Thomas R. Dye and Brett W. Hawkins, eds., *Politics in the Metropolis* (Columbus: Charles E. Merrill, 1967).

plays into the hands of the protesters by further emphasizing the injustices they are experiencing.[13]

In 1963 a group of Alabama clergymen petitioned Martin Luther King, Jr., to call off mass demonstrations in Birmingham. King, who had been arrested in the demonstrations, replied in his famous "Letter from Birmingham City Jail":

> In no sense do I advocate evading or defying the law as the rabid segregationist would do. This would lead to anarchy. One who breaks an unjust law must do it *openly*, *lovingly* (not hatefully as the white mothers did in New Orleans when they were seen on television screaming "nigger, nigger, nigger") and with a willingness to accept the penalty. I submit that an individual who breaks a law that conscience tells him is unjust, and willingly accepts the penalty by staying in jail to arouse the conscience of the community over its injustice, is in reality expressing the very highest respect for law.

It is important to note that King's tactics relied primarily on an appeal to the conscience of white elites. The purpose of demonstrations was to call attention to injustice and stimulate established elites to remedy the injustice by lawful means. The purpose of civil disobedience was to dramatize injustice; only *unjust* laws were to be broken "openly and lovingly," and punishment was accepted to demonstrate sincerity. King did *not* urge black masses to remedy injustice themselves by any means necessary; and he did *not* urge the overthrow of established elites.

In 1964, Martin Luther King, Jr., received the Nobel Peace Prize in recognition of his unique contributions to the development of nonviolent methods of social change.

Perhaps the most dramatic confrontation between the civil rights movement and the Southern segregationists occurred in Birmingham, Alabama, in the spring of 1963. In support of a request for desegregation of downtown eating places and the formation of a biracial committee to work out the integration of public schools, Martin Luther King, Jr., led several thousand Birmingham blacks in a series of orderly street marches. The demonstrators were met with strong police action, including fire hoses, police dogs, and electric cattle prods. Newspaper pictures of blacks being attacked by police and bitten by dogs were flashed all over the world. More than 25,000 demonstrators, including Dr. King, were jailed.

The year 1963 was probably the most important for nonviolent direct action. The Birmingham action set off demonstrations in many parts of

---

[13]For more detailed examinations of the purposes, functions, and rationale of civil disobedience, see Paul F. Power, "Civil Disobedience as Functional Opposition," *Journal of Politics,* 34 (February 1972), 37–55; and "On Civil Disobedience in Recent American Thought," *American Political Science Review,* 64 (March 1970), 35–47.

the country; the theme remained one of nonviolence, and it was usually whites rather than blacks who resorted to violence in these demonstrations. Responsible black elites remained in control of the movement and won widespread support from the white liberal community. The culmination of the nonviolent philosophy was a giant, yet orderly march on Washington, held on August 28, 1963. More than 200,000 blacks and whites participated in the march, which was endorsed by many labor leaders, religious groups, and political figures. The march ended at the Lincoln Memorial where Martin Luther King, Jr., delivered his most eloquent appeal, entitled "I Have a Dream."

> "I have a dream. It is a dream deeply rooted in the American dream. I have a dream that one day this nation will rise up and live up and live out the true meaning of its creed: 'We hold these truths to be self-evident, that all men are created equal.'"

In response President Kennedy sent a strong civil rights bill to Congress which was passed after his death—the famous Civil Rights Act of 1964.

The Civil Rights Acts

The Civil Rights Act of 1964 passed both houses of Congress by better than a two-thirds favorable vote; it won the overwhelming support of both Republican and Democratic members of Congress. It was signed into law on July 4, 1964. It ranks with the Emancipation Proclamation, the Fourteenth Amendment, and *Brown* v. *Topeka* as one of the most important steps toward full equality for blacks in America.

The Civil Rights Act of 1964 provides that:

1. It is unlawful to apply unequal standards in voter registration procedures, or to deny registration for irrelevant errors or omissions on records or applications.
2. It is unlawful to discriminate or segregate persons on the grounds of race, color, religion, or national origin in any public accommodation, including hotels, motels, restaurants, movies, theaters, sports arenas, entertainment houses, and other places that offer to serve the public. This prohibition extends to all establishments whose operations affect interstate commerce or whose discriminatory practices are supported by state action.
3. The attorney general shall undertake civil action on behalf of any person denied equal access to a public accommodation to obtain a federal district court order to secure compliance with the act. If the owner or manager of a public accommodation should continue to discriminate, he would be in contempt of court and subject to peremptory fines and imprisonment without trial by jury. [This mode of enforcement gave establishments a chance to mend their ways without punishment, and it also avoided the possibility that Southern juries would refuse to convict persons for violations of the act.]
4. The attorney general shall undertake civil actions on behalf of persons attempting orderly desegregation of public schools.

5. The Commission on Civil Rights, first established in the Civil Rights Act of 1957, shall be empowered to investigate deprivations of the right to vote, study, and collect information regarding the discrimination in America, and make reports to the president and Congress.
6. Each federal department and agency shall take action to end discrimination in all programs or activities receiving federal financial assistance in any form. This action shall include termination of financial assistance.
7. It shall be unlawful for any employer or labor union to discriminate against any individual in any fashion in employment, because of his race, color, religion, sex, or national origin, and that an Equal Employment Opportunity Commission shall be established to enforce this provision by investigation, conference, conciliation, persuasion, and if need be, civil action in federal court.

For many years "fair housing" had been considered the most sensitive area of civil rights legislation. Discrimination in the sale and rental of housing was the last major civil rights problem on which Congress took action. Discrimination in housing had not been mentioned in any previous legislation—not even in the comprehensive Civil Rights Act of 1964. Prohibiting discrimination in the sale or rental of housing affected the constituencies of Northern members of Congress more than any of the earlier Southern-oriented legislation.

The prospects for a fair housing law were not very good at the beginning of 1968. However, when Martin Luther King, Jr., was assassinated on April 4 the mood of Congress and the nation changed dramatically. Congress passed a fair housing law as tribute to the slain civil rights leader.

The Civil Rights Act of 1968 prohibited the following forms of discrimination:

Refusal to sell or rent a dwelling to any person because of his race, color, religion, or national origin.

Discrimination against a person in the terms, conditions, or privileges of the sale or rental of a dwelling.

Advertising the sale or rental of a dwelling indicating a preference or discrimination based on race, color, religion, or national origin.

Inducing persons to sell or rent a dwelling by referring to the entry into the neighborhood of persons of a particular race, religion, or national origin (the "blockbusting" technique of real estate selling).

But despite "fair housing" legislation, America is becoming *more* segregated over time, as black populations of large, central cities increase and white populations flee to surrounding suburbs. Black majorities will soon be found in more than a dozen of the nation's large cities: Washington, Atlanta, Newark, Detroit, Baltimore, St. Louis, New Orleans, Oakland, Cleveland, Gary. This suggests a developing pattern of predominantly black core cities, surrounded by nearly all-white suburbs. Even if direct discrimination is ended by "fair housing" laws, economic forces will continue to separate most black and white housing.

PUBLIC POLICY AND AFFIRMATIVE ACTION

Although the gains of the civil rights movement were immensely important, it must be recognized that they were *symbolic* rather than *actual* changes in the conditions under which most blacks live in America. Racial politics today center around the actual inequalities between blacks and whites in incomes, jobs, housing, health, education, and other conditions of life.

The problem of inequality is usually posed as differences in the "life chances" of blacks and whites. Figures can reveal only the bare outline of the black's "life chances" in American society (see Table 3-5). The average income of a black family is less than 60 percent of the average white family's income. Over 33 percent of all black families are below the recognized poverty line, while less than 12 percent of white families live in poverty. The black unemployment rate is almost twice as high as the white unemployment rate. Blacks are less likely to hold prestigious white-collar jobs in professional, managerial, clerical, or sales work. They do not hold many skilled craft jobs in industry, but are concentrated in operative, service, and laboring positions. The civil rights movement opened up new opportunities for black Americans. But equality of *opportunity* is not the same as *absolute* equality.

What public policies should be pursued to achieve equality in America? Is it sufficient that government eliminate discrimination, guarantee "equality of opportunity," and apply "colorblind" standards to both blacks and whites? Or should government take "affirmative action" to overcome the results of past unequal treatment of blacks—preferential or compensatory treatment that will favor black applicants for university admissions and scholarships, job hiring and promotion, and other opportunities for advancement in life?

The earlier emphasis of government policy, of course, was nondiscrimination, or *equal employment opportunity*. Equal employment opportunity ". . . was not a program to offer special privilege to any one group of persons because of their particular race, religion, sex, or national origin."[14] This appeared to conform to the original nondiscrimination approach of executive orders, beginning with President Harry Truman's decision to desegregate the armed forces in 1946, and carrying through Title VI and

---

[14]See David H. Rosenbloom, "The Civil Service Commission's Decision to Authorize the Use of Goals and Timetables in Federal Equal Employment Opportunity Programs," *Western Political Quarterly*, 26 (June 1973), 236–51.

TABLE 3-5   Change in Black-White Life Chances

MEDIAN INCOME OF FAMILIES							
	1950	1960	1970	1972	1975	1980	1984
White	$3,445	$5,835	$10,236	$11,549	$14,268	$20,502	$27,686
Black	$1,869	$3,230	$6,516	$7,106	$9,321	$12,380	$15,432

PERSONS BELOW POVERTY LEVEL

	MILLIONS		PERCENT OF TOTAL	
	BLACK	WHITE	BLACK	WHITE
1959	11.0	28.5	56	18
1965	10.7	22.5	47	13
1969	7.6	16.7	31	10
1975	7.5	17.8	31	9
1980	7.8	16.8	31	9
1984	9.5	22.9	34	12

OCCUPATION: BLACKS AND OTHER RACES AS PERCENT
OF ALL WORKERS IN SELECTED OCCUPATIONS

	1960	1970	1974	1978	1980
Professional	4	6	7	8	9
Medical	4	8	8	8	8
Teachers	7	10	9	9	10
Managers	2	3	4	5	5
Clerical	5	8	9	10	11
Sales	3	4	4	5	5
Craftsmen	5	7	7	7	8
Operatives	12	14	13	14	15
Nonfarm laborers	27	24	20	18	17
Private household	46	44	41	36	33
Other service	20	19	19	18	18

EDUCATION: PERCENTAGE OF PERSONS 25 TO 29 YEARS OLD

	WHO COMPLETED 4 YEARS OF HIGH SCHOOL OR MORE		WHO COMPLETED 4 YEARS OF COLLEGE OR MORE	
	BLACK	WHITE	BLACK	WHITE
1940	12	38	2	6
1950	22	53	3	8
1960	38	53	5	11
1970	56	75	7	16
1975	71	83	11	22
1980	77	86	12	23

Sources: Bureau of the Census, "The Social and Economic Status of the Black Population in the United States," *Current Population Reports*, Series No. 23; *Statistical Abstract of the United States, 1985.*

Title VII of the Civil Rights Act of 1964 to eliminate discrimination in federally aided projects and private employment.

Gradually, however, the goal of the civil rights movement shifted from the traditional aim of equality of opportunity through nondiscrimination alone, to affirmative action to establish "goals and timetables" to achieve absolute equality between blacks and whites. While usually avoiding the term *quota*, the notion of affirmative action tests the success of equal employment opportunity by observing whether blacks achieve admissions, jobs, and promotions in proportion to their numbers in the population.

Affirmative action programs are products of the federal bureaucracy. These programs were not enacted by Congress. Instead, these programs were developed by the federal executive agencies which were authorized by the Civil Rights Act of 1964 to develop "rules and regulations" for desegregating activities receiving federal funds (Title VI) and private employment (Title VII). President Lyndon B. Johnson gave impetus to affirmative action with Executive Order No. 11246 in 1965, covering employment and promotion in federal agencies and businesses contracting with the federal government. One of the first applications of affirmative action occurred in 1967 when the U.S. Office of Federal Contract Compliance issued the "Philadelphia Plan," which required contractors bidding on federal projects to submit affirmative action plans including specific percentage goals for the employment of minorities. At first the U.S. Civil Service Commission resisted the imposition of "goals" in federal employment.[15] But as pressure developed for greater minority representation, the Civil Service Commission relented and distinguished between "quotas" and "goals": "While quotas are not permissible, federal agencies may use numerical guidelines to assess progress toward equal employment opportunity and as one means of deterring the need for additional affirmative action regarding minority employment.[16] In 1972 the U.S. Office of Education issued guidelines which mandated "goals" for university admissions and faculty hiring of blacks and women. The Equal Employment Opportunity Commission, established by the Civil Rights Act of 1964 (Title VII) to eliminate discrimination in private employment, has carried the notion of affirmative action beyond federal contractors and recipients of federal aid into all sectors of private employment.

Federal officials generally measure "progress" in "affirmative action" in terms of the number of blacks admitted, employed, or promoted. The pressure to show "progress" and retain federal financial support can result in preferential treatment of blacks. It also puts pressure on traditional measures of qualifications—test scores and educational achievement. Blacks argue that these are not good predictors of performance on the job or in

---

[15]Letter from Civil Service Commission, July 24, 1970; cited ibid., p. 247.

[16]Letter from Civil Service Commission, February 3, 1971; cited ibid., p. 247.

school and that these measures are biased in favor of white culture. State and local governments, schools, colleges and universities, and private employers are under pressure to drop these standards.[17] But how far can any school, agency, or employer go in dropping traditional standards? It is not difficult to drop educational requirements for sanitation workers, but what about for physicians, surgeons, attorneys, pilots, and others whose skills directly affect health and safety?

The question becomes even more complex if we try to weigh the costs of some "reverse discrimination" against the value of achieving greater representation of blacks in all echelons of society. Perhaps it is better for society as a whole to make some sacrifices to bring black Americans into the mainstream of economic life—to give them a "stake in society," and hence to sew up the worn fabric of the social system. But who must make these sacrifices? It is not the established white upper classes, but the sons and daughters of white middle- and working-class families who are in direct competition with upwardly mobile blacks. Must the price of past discrimination against blacks now fall on these young whites? Another problem: can preferential treatment eventually create new injustices for blacks who have been recipients of such treatment? Will it create a façade of equality and representation, while actually patronizing black recipients? Does preferential treatment imply that blacks cannot "make it" without such treatment? Clearly there are sensitive moral and ethical questions surrounding this area of public policy, as well as the constitutional question of equal protection of the laws.

AFFIRMATIVE ACTION IN THE COURTS

The constitutional question posed by "affirmative action" programs is whether or not they discriminate against whites in violation of the Equal Protection Clause of the Fourteenth Amendment. A related question is whether or not affirmative action programs discriminate against whites in violation of the Civil Rights Act of 1964, which prohibits discrimination "on account of race," not just discrimination against blacks. Clearly, these are questions for the Supreme Court to resolve, but unfortunately the Court has failed to develop clear-cut answers.

In *Regents of the University of California* v. *Bakke* (1978), the Supreme Court struck down a special admissions program for minorities at a state medical school on the grounds that it excluded a white applicant because of his race and violated his rights under the Equal Protection Clause. Allan Bakke applied to the University of California Davis Medical School two

---

[17]See Frank J. Thompson, "Bureaucratic Responsiveness in the Cities: The Problem of Minority Hiring," *Urban Affairs Quarterly*, 10 (September 1974), 40–68.

consecutive years and was rejected; in both years black applicants with significantly lower grade point averages and medical aptitude test scores were accepted through a special admissions program which reserved sixteen minority places in a class of one hundred.[18] The University of California did not deny that its admissions decisions were based on race. Instead, it argued that its racial classification was "benign," that is, designed to assist minorities, not to hinder them. The special admissions program was designed (1) to "reduce the historical deficit of traditionally disfavored minorities in medical schools and the medical profession," (2) "to counter the effects of societal discrimination," (3) to "increase the number of physicians who will practice in communities currently underserved," and (4) to "obtain the educational benefits that flow from an ethnically diverse student body."

The Court held that these objectives were legitimate and that race and ethnic origin *may* be considered in reviewing applications to a state school without violating the Equal Protection Clause. However, the Court also held that a *separate* admissions program for minorities with a specified quota of openings which were unavailable to white applicants violated the Equal Protection Clause. "The guarantee of equal protection cannot mean one thing when applied to one individual and something else when applied to another. If both are not accorded the same protection, then it is not equal."

The Court ordered Bakke admitted to medical school and the elimination of the special admissions program. It recommended that California consider an admissions program developed at Harvard that considered disadvantaged racial or ethnic background as a "plus" in an overall evaluation of an applicant, but did not set numerical quotas or exclude any persons from competing for all positions.

Reaction to the decision was predictable: supporters of affirmative action, particularly government officials from affirmative action programs, emphasized the Supreme Court's willingness to allow minority status to be considered a positive factor; opponents emphasized the Supreme Court's unwillingness to allow quotas which excluded whites from competing for a certain number of positions. Since Bakke had "won" the case, most observers felt that the Supreme Court was not going to permit discriminatory quota systems.

However, in *United Steelworkers of America* v. *Weber* (1979), the Supreme Court approved a plan developed by a private employer and a union to

---

[18]Bakke's grade point average was 3.51; his MCAT scores were: verbal–96, quantitative–94, science–97, general information–2. The average for the special admissions students were: grade point average–2.62, MCAT verbal–34, quantitative–30, science–37, general information–18.

reserve 50 percent of higher paying, skilled jobs for minorities. Kaiser Aluminum Corporation and the United Steelworkers Union, under federal government pressure, had established a program to get more blacks into skilled technical jobs; only 2 percent of the skilled jobs were held by blacks in the plant where Weber worked, while 39 percent of the local workforce was black. When Weber was excluded from the training program, and blacks with less seniority and fewer qualifications were accepted, Weber filed suit in federal court claiming that he had been discriminated against because of his race in violation of Title VII of the Civil Rights Act of 1964. (Weber could not claim that his rights under the Fourteenth Amendment's Equal Protection Clause had been violated, because this clause applies only to the "state," that is, governmental discrimination, and not to private employers.) Title VII prevents *all* discrimination in employment on the basis of race; it does not specify only discrimination against blacks or minorities.

The Supreme Court held that Title VII of the Civil Rights Act of 1964 "left employers and unions in the private sector free to take such race-conscious steps to eliminate manifest racial imbalances in traditionally segregated job categories. We hold that Title VII does not prohibit such . . . affirmative action plans." Weber's reliance on the clear language of Title VII was "misplaced." According to the Court, it would be "ironic indeed" if the Civil Rights Act were used to prohibit voluntary private race-conscious efforts to overcome the past effects of discrimination.

The Weber ruling was applauded by the U.S. Equal Employment Opportunity Commission, as well as by various civil rights organizations, who hoped to use the decision to step up affirmative action plans in industry and government. The decision does not directly affect women, but it may be used as a precedent to strengthen affirmative action programs for them.

Yet the Supreme Court has continued to express concern about whites who are directly and adversely affected by government action solely because of their race. In *Firefighters Local Union* v. *Stotts* in 1984 the Court ruled that a city could not lay off white firefighters in favor of black firefighters with less seniority. The U.S. Justice Department under President Reagan used this decision to argue that any affirmative action plan which granted preference to one race over another was unconstitutional. But the Supreme Court has not yet adopted a completely "colorblind" standard.

How can the *Bakke* and *Weber* and *Stotts* decisions be reconciled into a coherent policy on affirmative action? They probably *cannot* be reconciled. It is true that the *Bakke* and *Stotts* cases struck down racial preferences established by *state* agencies while the *Weber* case upheld a quota system voluntarily established by a *private* employer under Title VII of the Civil Rights Act of 1964. But it is unlikely the Supreme Court will continue to differentiate between state agencies and private employers. Rather than search for consistency in the law, perhaps we should resign ourselves to some uncertainties about how far affirmative action programs can go without becoming "reverse discrimination." Perhaps each program will have to be judged separately, and no clear-cut national policy will emerge.

SEXUAL EQUALITY AND PUBLIC POLICY

The earliest active feminist organizations grew out of the pre–Civil War antislavery movement. The first generation of feminists included Lucretia Mott, Elizabeth Cady Stanton, Lucy Stone, and Susan B. Anthony. They learned to organize, hold public meetings, and conduct petition campaigns as abolitionists. After the Civil War, women were successful in changing many state laws which abridged the property rights of married women and otherwise treated them as "chattel" (property) of their husbands. Women were also prominent in the Anti-Saloon League, which succeeded in outlawing prostitution and gambling in every state (except Nevada) and providing a major source of support for the Eighteenth Amendment (Prohibition). In the early twentieth century the feminist movement concentrated on women's suffrage—the drive to guarantee women the right to vote. The early suffragettes employed mass demonstrations, parades, picketing, and occasional disruption and civil disobedience—tactics similar to those of the civil rights movement of the 1960s. The culmination of the early feminist movement was the passage in 1920 of the Nineteenth Amendment to the Constitution: "The right of citizens of the United States to vote shall not be denied or abridged by the United States or by any state on account of sex." The more moderate wing of the American suffrage movement became the League of Women Voters; in addition to women's right to vote, they sought protection of women in industry, child welfare laws, and honest election practices.

Renewed interest in feminist politics came after the civil rights movement of the 1960s. The feminist movement of recent years has worked in the states and in Congress on behalf of a wide range of reforms—the Equal Rights Amendment to the Constitution, equal employment opportunities for women, reform of divorce and child support laws, more convictions in sexual assault cases, and liberalization of laws regulating abortion. New organizations have sprung up to compete with the conventional activities of the League of Women Voters by presenting a more militant and activist stance toward women's liberation. The largest of these new organizations is the National Organization of Women (NOW) founded in 1966, which promises to change "the false image of women now prevalent in the mass media and in the texts, ceremonies, laws and practices of our major social institutions" which "perpetuate contempt for women by society and by women for themselves."[19]

Employment

The federal Civil Rights Act of 1964, Title VII, prevents sexual (as well as racial) discrimination in hiring, pay, and promotions. The Equal Employment Opportunity Commission (EEOC), which is the federal agency charged with eliminating discrimination in employment, has established guidelines barring stereotyped classifications of "men's jobs" and "women's jobs." State laws and employer practices which differentiate between men and women in hours, pay, retirement age, etc., have been struck down. Under active lobbying from feminist organizations, federal agencies, including the U.S. Office of Education and the Office of Federal Contract Compliance, have established affirmative action guidelines for government agencies, universities, and private businesses doing work for the government; these guidelines set goals and timetables for employers to alter their workforce to achieve higher female percentages at all levels.

Credit

The Federal Equal Credit Opportunity Act of 1974 prohibits sex discrimination in *credit* transactions. Most states now have similar laws. Both federal and state laws prevent banks, credit unions, savings and loan associations, retail stores, and credit card companies from denying credit because of sex or marital status. However, these businesses may still deny credit for a poor or nonexistent credit rating, and some women who have always maintained accounts in their husband's name may still face credit problems if they apply in their own name.

Education

In recent years, the states, particularly state colleges and universities, have been trying to comply with Title IX of the federal Education Amendment of 1972 dealing with sex discrimination in *education*. This federal law bars discrimination in admissions, housing, rules, financial aid, faculty and staff recruitment and pay, and—most troublesome of all—athletics. The latter problem has proven very difficult because men's football and basketball programs have traditionally brought in the money to finance all other sports, and men's football and basketball have received the largest share of school athletic budgets. To divide athletic budgets equally between

---

[19]Congressional Quarterly, *The Women's Movement* (Washington, D.C.: Congressional Quarterly Inc., 1973), p.14.

men's and women's sports might threaten the financial base of all school athletics. Currently, many schools are striving to upgrade women's sports and provide equal funding *per participant*. But it is not clear whether this satisfies the requirement of Title IX.

WOMEN AND JOBS

Sexual differences in the workplace have generated very important policy debates as more and more women have joined the nation's work force. In 1984, 62 percent of the adult female population worked outside of the home, compared to only 32 percent a generation earlier (1960).

Women's earnings are substantially less than men's earnings. In 1984 the median earnings for all men was $21,004 compared to $15,422 for women, indicating that women on the average earned only about 64 percent of what men did.[20] This earnings gap is not so much a product of direct discrimination, that is, women in the same job with the same skills, qualifications, experience, and work record being paid less than men. This form of direct discrimination has been illegal since the Civil Rights Act of 1964. Rather, the earnings gap is primarily a product of a division in the labor market between traditionally male and female jobs, with lower salaries paid in traditionally female occupations.

The initial efforts of the feminist movement were directed toward ensuring that women enjoyed equal access to traditionally male "white collar" occupations, for example, those of physician, lawyer, and engineer. Success in these efforts would automatically narrow the wage gap. And indeed, women have been very successful over the last several decades in increasing their representation in prestigious white collar occupations (see Table 3-6), although most of these occupational fields continue to be dominated by men.

Nonetheless, evidence of a "dual" labor market, with male-dominated "blue collar" jobs distinguishable from female-dominated "pink collar" jobs, continues to be a major obstacle to economic equality between men and women. A study sponsored by the National Academy of Sciences concluded that most of the differences in men's and women's earnings could be attributed to sex segregation in occupations.[21] These occupational differences were attributed to cultural stereotyping, social conditioning, and premarket training and education which narrow the choices available to women. While significant progress has been made in recent years in reducing occupational

[20]U.S. Bureau of the Census, "Money Income and Poverty Status of Families and Persons in the United States: 1984" (Washington, D.C.: U.S. Census Bureau, 1985).

[21]National Research Council, National Academy of Sciences, *Women's Work, Men's Work* (Washington: National Academy Press, 1985).

TABLE 3-6   Women at Work

"WHITE COLLAR"

Women are increasingly entering white collar occupation fields
traditionally dominated by men.

	1960	1983
Architects	3	13
Computer analysts	11	28
College and university teachers	28	36
Engineers	1	6
Lawyers and judges	4	16
Physicians	10	16

"PINK COLLAR"

Women continue to be concentrated in occupational fields traditionally dominated by women.

	1970	1980
Secretaries	98	99
Cashiers	84	54
Waitresses and waiters	91	88
Nurses	97	96
Office clerks	75	82

"BLUE COLLAR"

Women continue to be largely excluded from blue collar occupational fields traditionally
dominated by men.

	1970	1980
Truck drivers	1	2
Carpenters	1	2
Laborers	17	19
Auto mechanics	1	1
Factory production supervisor	10	15
Bartenders	21	44

Sources: U.S. Department of Labor, *Employment in Perspective: Working Women* (Washington: Government Printing Office, 1983); National Research Council, National Academy of Sciences, *Women's Work, Men's Work* (Washington: National Academy Press, 1985).

sex segregation, nonetheless many observers doubt that sexually differentiated occupations will be eliminated in the foreseeable future.

As a result of a growing recognition that the wage gap is more a result of occupational differentiation than direct discrimination, some feminist organizations have turned to a new approach—the demand that pay levels in various occupations be determined by "comparable worth" rather than by the labor market. "Comparable worth" means *more* than paying men and women equally for the same work; it means paying the same wages for jobs of comparable value to the employer. "Comparable worth" means that traditionally male and female jobs would be evaluated by government agencies or courts to determine their "worth" to the employer, perhaps by considering responsibilities, effort, knowledge, and skill requirements. Jobs adjudged to be "comparable" would be paid equal wages. Government agencies or the courts would replace the free labor market in the determination of wage rates.

Many feminist groups charge that the labor market is really a "dual market" in which women's work is valued less than men's work. But comparable worth raises problems of implementation: Who would decide what wages should be for various jobs? What standards would be used to decide? If government agencies set wage rates by law instead of the free market, would an illegal black market for labor arise? What penalties would be imposed on employers who paid wages different than those set by government? The U.S. Equal Employment Opportunity Commission has rejected the notion of comparable worth and declined to recommend wages for traditionally male and female jobs. And so far the federal courts have refused to declare that different wages in traditionally male and female occupations is evidence of sexual discrimination in violation of federal law. However, some state governments and private employers have undertaken to review their own pay scales to determine if traditionally female occupations are underpaid.

ERA

At the center of feminist activity in the 1970s was the Equal Rights Amendment to the Constitution. The amendment stated simply: "Equality of rights under the law shall not be denied or abridged by the United States or by any state on account of sex." The ERA passed the Congress easily in 1972 and was sent to the states for the necessary ratification of three-fourths (thirty-eight) of them. The amendment won quick ratification by half the states, but a developing "Stop ERA" movement slowed progress and eventually defeated the amendment itself. In 1979, the original seven-year time period for ratification—the period customarily set by Congress for ratification of constitutional amendments—expired. Proponents of the ERA persuaded Congress to extend the ratification period for three more years, to 1982. But despite heavy lobbying efforts in the states and public opinion polls showing national majorities favoring the ERA, the amendment failed to win ratification by the necessary thirty-eight states.[22]

[22]By 1982, thirty-four states had ratified the ERA. Three of them—Idaho, Nebraska, and Tennessee—subsequently voted to "rescind" their ratifications; but the U.S. Constitution does not mention "rescinding" votes. The states which had not ratified by 1982 were Nevada, Utah, Arizona, Oklahoma, Illinois, Indiana, Missouri, Arkansas, Louisiana, Mississippi, Alabama, Georgia, Florida, North Carolina, South Carolina, and Virginia.

Proponents of the ERA argued in the state legislatures that most of the progress women have made toward equality in marriage, property, employment, credit, education, and so on, depends upon state and federal *law*. The guarantee of equality of the sexes would be much more secure if this guarantee were made part of the U.S. Constitution. Moreover, the ERA would eliminate the need to pass separate laws in a wide variety of fields to ensure sexual equality. The ERA, as a permanent part of the U.S. Constitution, would provide a sweeping guarantee of equality, directly enforceable by court action. Finally, the ERA has taken on a great deal of symbolic meaning; even if federal and state laws prohibit sexual discrimination now, it is nonetheless important to many to see the ERA as part of the U.S. Constitution—"the supreme law of the land."

Opponents of the ERA charged that it would eliminate many legal protections for women, such as financial support by husbands, an interest in the husband's property, exemption from military service, and so forth. In addition to these specific objectives, opponents of "women's liberation" in general charged that the movement weakens the family institution and demoralizes women who wish to devote their lives to their families, husbands, and children.

ABORTION AND THE RIGHT TO LIFE

Potentially the most important and far-reaching decision in the recent history of the Supreme Court was its action in the legalization of abortion.[23] Historically, abortions for any purpose other than saving the life of the mother were criminal offenses under state law. About a dozen states acted in the late 1960s to permit abortions in cases of rape or incest, or to protect the physical health of the mother, and in some cases to protect mental health as well. Relatively few abortions were performed under these laws, however, because of the red tape involved—review of each case by several concurring physicians, approval of a hospital board, and so forth.

The movement for liberal abortion laws in America won a national victory when the Supreme Court ruled that the constitutional guarantee of personal liberty in the Fifth and Fourteenth Amendments included a woman's decision to bear or not to bear a child. In the *Roe* v. *Wade* and *Doe* v. *Bolton* decisions, the Supreme Court ruled the word *person* in the Constitution did *not* include the unborn child. Therefore the Fifth and Fourteenth Amendments to the Constitution, guaranteeing all persons "life, liberty, and property," did not protect the "life" of the fetus. The Court also ruled that a state's power to protect the health and safety of the mother could not justify any restriction on abortion in the first three months of

---

[23]*Roe* v. *Wade*, 410 U.S. 113 (1973); *Doe* v. *Bolton*, 410 U.S. 179 (1973).

pregnancy. Between the third and sixth months of pregnancy, the state could set standards for how and when abortions can be performed in order to protect the health of the mother; but the state cannot prohibit abortions in this period. Only in the final three months of pregnancy, the Supreme Court said, can a state ban all abortions to safeguard the life and health of the mother.

Abortion is a highly sensitive issue. It is not an issue that can easily be compromised. The arguments touch on fundamental moral and religious principles. Proponents of abortion, who often refer to themselves as "pro-choice," argue that a women should be permitted to control her own body and should not be forced by law to have unwanted children. They cite the heavy toll in lives lost in criminal abortions and the psychological and emotional pain of an unwanted pregnancy. Opponents of abortion, who often refer to themselves as "pro-life," generally base their belief on the sanctity of life, including the life of the unborn child, which they believe deserves the protection of law—the right to life. Many believe that the killing of an unborn child for any reason other than the preservation of the life of the mother is murder.

There are still many unresolved policy issues in abortion laws. Right-to-life groups have sprung up in many states to continue the fight against legalized abortion, as well as to push for a constitutional amendment to define the fetus as a person. Some states have passed legislation protecting doctors and nurses from loss of jobs or other penalties for refusing to carry out abortions because of their moral and religious convictions.[24] State laws are ambiguous about efforts to save aborted fetuses which emerge alive. Some state laws are still very restrictive in their definition of an "approved facility" for an abortion. Congress has spent many hours debating whether or not Medicaid funds for the poor should be used to pay for abortions. Currently, federal law allows the use of public funds for abortions only if the health of the mother is threatened. Some have argued that the "right" to an abortion should include public funds to pay for abortions for the poor. In summary, abortion legislation is still an important item on the agenda of Congress and state legislatures.

SUMMARY

Let us try to set forth some propositions that are consistent with elite theory and assist in describing the development of civil rights policy.

---

[24]However, in *Planned Parenthood of Central Missouri* v. *Danforth* (1976), the Supreme Court struck down state laws requiring a husband's consent for his wife's abortion, and also struck down state laws requiring parental consent for a minor's abortion.

1. Elites and masses in America differ in their attitudes toward blacks. Support for civil rights legislation has come from educated, affluent whites in leadership positions.

2. Mass opinion toward civil rights has generally *followed* public policy, and not led it. Mass opinion did not oppose legally segregated schools until after elites had declared national policy in *Brown* v. *Topeka*.

3. The greatest impetus to the advancement of civil rights policy in this century was the U.S. Supreme Court's decision in *Brown* v. *Topeka*. Thus, it was the Supreme Court, nonelected and enjoying life terms in office, which assumed the initiative in civil rights policy. Congress did not take significant action until ten years later.

4. Resistance to the implementation of *Brown* v. *Topeka* was centered in states and communities. Resistance to national policy was remarkably effective for over a decade; blacks were not admitted to white schools in the South in large numbers until all segments of the national elite—Congress and the executive branch, as well as the judicial branch—acted in support of desegregation.

5. The elimination of legal discrimination and the guarantee of equality of opportunity in the Civil Rights Act of 1964 were achieved largely through the dramatic appeals of middle-class black leaders to the consciences of white elites. Black leaders did not attempt to overthrow the established order, but to increase opportunities for blacks to achieve success within the American system.

6. Elite support for equality of opportunity does not satisfy the demands of black masses for absolute equality. Inequalities between blacks and whites in life chances—income, education, employment, health—persist, although the gap may be narrowing over the long run.

7. Affirmative action programs are pressed upon governments, universities, and private employers by federal agencies seeking to reduce inequalities. But white masses generally reject the notion of compensatory actions which they believe to disadvantage working-class and middle-class white males.

8. From its earliest beginnings, the feminist movement has frequently relied on the tactics of minorities—demonstrations, parades, and occasional civil disobedience—to convince governing elites to recognize women's rights. The Equal Rights Amendment won easy approval in Congress, but failed to win ratification by three-quarters of the states.

9. Abortion was prohibited by most of the states until the Supreme Court decided in *Roe* v. *Wade* and *Doe* v. *Bolton* in 1973 that women had a constitutional right under the Fifth and Fourteenth Amendments to terminate pregnancies. Thus, the Supreme Court established as a constitutional right what pro-abortion forces had failed to gain through political processes at the state level.

BIBLIOGRAPHY

BAXTER, SANDRA, and MARJORIE LANSING, *Women in Politics*. Ann Arbor: University of Michigan Press, 1980.

CARMICHAEL, STOKELY, and CHARLES V. HAMILTON, *Black Power*. New York: Random House, 1968.

CLARK, KENNETH B., *Dark Ghetto*. New York: Harper & Row, 1965.

FRANKLIN, JOHN HOPE. *From Slavery to Freedom*. 5th ed. New York: Knopf, 1978.

GLAZER, NATHAN, *Affirmative Discrimination*. New York: Basic Books, 1975.

KIRKPATRICK, JEANE, *The Politics of the Woman's Movement*. New York: D. McKay, 1975.

WALTON, HANES, JR., *Black Politics*. Philadelphia: Lippincott, 1972.

CRIMINAL JUSTICE
rationality and irrationality
in public policy

Non-violent civil disobedience demonstration in New York City. (Ken Karp)

Crime, violence, and social disorder are central problems confronting any society. So also is the problem of government repression. For thousands of years, philosophers and policy makers have wrestled with the question of balancing governmental power against individual freedom. How far can individual freedom be carried without undermining the stability of society and threatening the safety of others?

THE PROBLEM OF CRIME

It is not an easy task to learn exactly how much crime occurs in society. The *official* crime rates are based upon the Federal Bureau of Investigation's *Uniform Crime Reports,* but the FBI reports are based on figures supplied by state and local police agencies (see Table 4-1). The FBI has established a uniform classification of the number of serious crimes per 100,000 people that are reported to the police—murder and nonnegligent manslaughter, forcible rape, robbery, aggravated assault, burglary, larceny, and theft, including auto theft. But one should be cautious in interpreting official crime rates. They are really a function of several factors: (1) the willingness of people to report crime, (2) the adequacy of the reporting system tabulating crime, and (3) the amount of crime itself.

Between 1960 and 1975 the crime rate in America rose very rapidly. Every category of crime more than doubled, including the murder rate. Certainly some of this increase was a product of increased reporting—as more property is insured, people file more police reports in order to make insurance claims. And some of this increase can be attributed to the intro-

TABLE 4-1   Crime Rates in the United States: Offenses Known to the Police
(Rates per 100,000 Population)

	1960	1965	1970	1972	1975	1978	1980	1983
Murder	5	5	8	9	10	9	10	8
Forcible rape	9	12	18	22	26	31	36	34
Robbery	52	61	172	180	209	191	244	214
Aggravated assault	82	107	162	187	214	256	291	273
Burglary	465	605	1068	1126	1429	1424	1668	1334
Larceny and theft	1028	1521	2066	1980	2473	2744	3156	2866
Auto theft	179	251	454	423	461	455	495	429
Total crimes against persons	148	185	360	398	459	487	581	529
Total crimes against property	1672	2177	3588	3529	4363	4622	5319	4630

Source: Federal Bureau of Investigation, *Uniform Crime Reports,* in *Statistical Abstract of the United States 1981* (published annually by U.S. Bureau of the Census), p. 173.

duction of computers and sophisticated police data collection schemes. But *unquestionably crime itself was also on the rise.*

Recently, the crime rate has leveled off and even declined slightly from its highest years. We can only speculate about possible reasons for this modest success: (1) police are becoming more professional and effective; (2) business and industry are installing protective technology (steering locks on autos, for example), and they are hiring more private security guards; or more likely (3) the most "crime-prone" age group, persons fifteen to twenty-four years old, is no longer increasing as a percentage of the population.

How much crime is there in America today? We know that the FBI official crime rate understates the real amount of crime. Many crimes are not reported to the police and therefore cannot be counted in the official crime rate. In an effort to learn the real amount of crime in the nation, the U. S. Justice Department regularly surveys a national sample of people asking whether they have been a victim of a crime during the past year.[1] These surveys reveal that the "victimization rate" is many times greater than the official crime rate. The number of forcible rapes is three to five times greater than the number reported to police, burglaries three times greater, and robbery over twice the reported rate. Only auto theft and murder statistics are reasonably accurate, indicating that most people call the police when their car is stolen or someone is murdered.

Why do people fail to report crime to the police? The most common reason given by interviewees is the feeling that police cannot be effective in dealing with the crime. Other reasons included the feeling that the crime was "a private matter" or that the victim did not want to harm the offender. Fear of reprisal was mentioned much less frequently, usually in cases of assaults and family crimes.[2]

About 3 percent of Americans are victims of *violent* crime each year. While this percentage might seem small, this represents about six million victims of violent crime. Moreover, this figure applies only to victimizations that take place in a single year. The percentage of persons victimized sometime during their life is much higher. For example, Americans have a 1-in-10,000 chance of being murdered in any one year. But they have a 1-in-133 chance of *ever* becoming a murder victims.[3]

Blacks are victimized by crime more often than whites. For example, the lifetime risk of a black male becoming a murder victim is a startling 1-in-21, compared to a 1-in-131 risk for white males (see also Table 4-2).

[1]U. S. Department of Justice, *Criminal Victimization in the United States*, published annually. (Washington: Bureau of Justice Statistics).

[2]See Wesley G. Skogan, "The Validity of Official Crime Statistics: Empirical Investigation," *Social Science Quarterly*, 55 (June 1974), 25–38.

[3]U.S. Department of Justice, *The Risk of Violent Crime* (Washington: Bureau of Justice Statistics, 1985).

TABLE 4-2 Some Facts About Murder: Victims, Motives, Weapons

VICTIMS		MOTIVES		WEAPONS	
	Murder Rate (1981)		Percent (1983)		Percent (1983)
Total	10.3	Felony total	18.0	Guns, total	58
		Robbery	10.1	Handguns	44
White		Narcotics	2.0	Stabbing	22
Male	10.4	Sex Abuses	1.6	Blunt Object	6
Female	3.1	Other felony	3.9	Strangulation/beating	9
Black		Suspected felony	3.2	Arson	4
Male	64.8	Argument, total	43.7	Other	4
Female	12.7	Influence of alcohol,			
		drugs	4.1		
		Property or			
		money	2.8		
		Romantic	2.6		
		Other arguments	34.1		
		Other motives	14.2		
		Unknown, unnoticed	20.9		

Source: U.S. Bureau of the Census, *Crime in the United States,* in *Statistical Abstract of the United States 1985 (105th edition),* pp. 170–171.

Men are more likely to be murdered, robbed, or assaulted than women, although women are far more likely to be raped than men. The lifetime risk of murder for all males is 1-in-84, compared to 1-in-282 for all females.

It is fashionable today to dismiss or ignore crime statistics and to argue that "crime" is merely an activity which some legislative body has chosen to make illegal. But the FBI's Uniform Crime Reports does not count the so-called victimless crimes, including drug abuse, prostitution, and gambling. Murder, rape, robbery, aggravated assault, burglary, and theft are the *only* crimes reported by the FBI, and without question these crimes hurt people. Even if we assume that the "victimless" crimes do not hurt people (a very dubious assumption to anyone familiar with the life of a prostitute, a drug abuser, or a compulsive gambler), we must still be concerned with violent crime.

CRIME AND DETERRENCE

A rational strategy for dealing with crime would endeavor to make the costs of committing crimes far greater than any benefits potential criminals might derive from their acts. With advanced knowledge of these costs, rational individuals should be deterred from committing crimes. Deterrences would be enhanced by:

1. The *certainty* that a crime will be followed by costly punishment. Justice must be sure.
2. The *swiftness* of the punishment following the crime. Long delays between crime and punishment break the link in the mind of the criminal between the criminal act and its consequences. And a potential wrongdoer must believe that the costs of a crime will occur within a meaningful time frame, not in a distant, unknowable future. Justice must be swift.
3. The *severity* of the punishment. Punishment which is perceived as no more costly than the ordinary hazards of life on the streets which the potential criminal faces anyhow, will not deter. Punishment must clearly outweigh whatever benefits might be derived from a life of crime in the mind of potential criminals. Punishment must be severe.

These criteria for an effective deterrent policy are ranked in the order of their probable importance. That is, it is most important that punishment for crime be certain. The severity of punishment is probably less important than its swiftness or certainty.

The current system of criminal justice in America is not a serious deterrent to crime. Punishment for crime is neither certain, swift, nor severe. We will argue that the criminal justice system itself, by failing to deter crime, is principally responsible for the fact that *crime in the United States is more common than in any other advanced industrial nation of the world.*

Of course, there are many other conflicting theories of crime in America. For example, it is sometime argued that this nation's high crime rate is a product of its social heterogeneity—the multiethnic, multiracial character of the American population. Low levels of crime in European countries, Japan, and China are often attributed to their homogeneous populations and shared cultures. Blacks in the United States are both victims and perpetrators of crime far more frequently than whites. While blacks constitute only about 12 percent of the population, they account for 29 percent of all of persons arrested for serious crime (see Table 4-3). A larger segment of the black population is in the young crime-prone age (fifteen to twenty-four years), and these youths are more likely to live outside husband-wife families. It is argued that "the streets" of the nation's black inner cities produces a subculture which encourages crime.

It is also argued that crime is irrational, that is, the criminal does *not* weigh benefits against potential costs before committing the act. Many acts of violence are committed by persons acting in blind rage—murders and aggravated assaults among family members, for example. Many rapes are acts of violence, inspired by hatred of women, rather than efforts to obtain sexual pleasure. More murders occur in the heat of arguments than in the commission of other felonies (see Table 4-2). These are crimes of passion

TABLE 4-3   Arrests by Age, Sex, and Race

PERCENT OF TOTAL ARRESTS (1983)	
Male	83.4
Female	16.6
White	71.1
Black	28.9
Under 18	16.8
18–24	34.1
25–34	28.1
35–44	11.8
45–54	5.5
55 and over	3.6

Source: U.S. Bureau of the Census, *Crime in the United States* in *Statistical Abstract of the United States 1985 (105th edition)*, p. 173.

rather than calculated acts. Thus, it is argued, *no* rational policies can be devised to deter these irrational acts.

Crime is a young man's vocation. The most crime prone age is eighteen to twenty-four (see Table 4-3), and juveniles under eighteen also account for much of the nation's criminal activity. Much of the increase in crime from 1965 to 1980 may be a product of the fact that the proportion of young people in the population was increasing during those years. And the modest declines in crime rates recently may be a product of the fact that this same crime-prone age group is declining as a percentage of the nation's population.

The youthfulness of most criminal offenders detracts from the effectiveness of deterrent policies. It is sometimes argued that young people do not "think before they act" in crime. Older people are more prone to consider the costs and consequences of their acts than young people. Perhaps all we need to do is wait until the population grows older and crime rates will decline as a result of maturity.

Finally, we must recognize that the reduction of crime is not the overriding value of American society. Americans cherish individual liberty. Freedom from repression—from unlawful arrests, forced confessions, restrictions on movement, curfews, arbitrary police actions, unlimited searching of homes or seizures of property, punishment without trial, trials without juries, unfair procedures, brutal punishments, etc.—is more important to Americans than freedom from crime. Many authoritarian governments boast of low crime rates and criminal justice systems which ensure certain, swift, and severe punishment, but these governments fail to protect the personal liberties of their citizens. Indeed, given the choice of punishing all of the guilty, even if some innocents are also punished by mistake, or taking care that innocent persons not be punished, even if some guilty people escape, most Americans would choose the second alternative—protecting innocent persons.

Nonetheless, despite these problems, we shall argue that the frequency of crime in America is largely a product of the failure to adopt rational criminal justice policies.

Certainty

The best available estimates of the ratio between crime and punishment suggest that the likelihood of an individual being jailed for a serious crime is less than two in one hundred (see Figure 4-1). Police are successful in clearing only about one in five *reported* crimes by arresting the offender. The judicial system only convicts about one in four of the persons arrested and charged; others are not prosecuted, are handled as juveniles, are found not guilty, or are permitted to plead guilty to a lesser charge and released. Only about half of all convicted felons are given prison sentences.

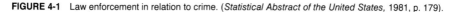

FIGURE 4-1 Law enforcement in relation to crime. (*Statistical Abstract of the United States,* 1981, p. 179).

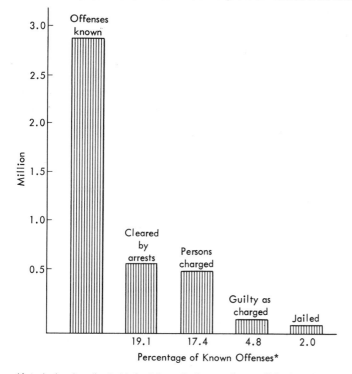

*Actual crime is estimated to be 3 times the known offenses. If the base is actual crime, these percentages would be one-third of those appearing in the figure. Thus, persons jailed as a percentage of actual crime is less than 1 percent.

Swiftness

The deterrent effect of a criminal justice system is lost when punishment is so long delayed that it has little relationship to the crime. The *bail system,* together with *trial delays,* allow criminal defendants to escape the consequences of their acts for long indefinite periods of time. Most criminal defendants are free on bail shortly after their arrest; only persons accused of the most serious crimes and adjudged to be likely to flee before trial are held in jail without bond. In preliminary hearings held shortly after arrest, judges release most defendants pending trial; even after a trial and a guilty verdict, many defendants are free on bail pending the outcome of lengthy appeals. The Constitution guarantees persons accused of crimes freedom from "excessive bail" (Eighth Amendment), and judges may not hold defendants in jail simply because they think the defendants might commit additional crimes while out on bail.

The court system works very slowly and delays favor the criminal defendant. Defendants request delays in court proceedings in order to remain free as long as possible. Moreover, they know that witnesses against them will lose interest, move away, grow tired of the hassle, and even forget key facts, if only the case can be postponed long enough. Some criminal cases are delayed for years.

Justice delayed destroys the deterrent effect, especially in the minds of youthful offenders who are "present oriented" rather than "future oriented." Inner-city youths, with no real prospects for the future anyhow, concentrate their attention on today, tomorrow and perhaps the next day, rather than years into the future. In their limited time frame of reference, they may consider the benefits of their criminal acts to be immediate, while the costs to be so far in the future that they have no real meaning to them. Or the costs may be estimated to be only the arrest itself and a night in jail before release on bail. For deterrence to work, the perceived costs of crime must be greater than the perceived benefits in *the minds of potential wrongdoers.*

Severity

More people are imprisoned today in America than at any previous time. Not only are there more inmates in the nation's prisons, but the *proportion* of the nation's population behind bars is the highest in recent history. (In 1970, 97 of every 100,000 persons was a federal or state prisoner, compared to 179 in 1983).[4] This increase in the prison population suggests that the court system is not really becoming any more lenient over time. On the contrary, in recent years there has been an increase in the

[4]*Statistical Abstract of the United States 1985,* p. 183.

likelihood of imprisonment as a punishment following conviction for a serious crime. Some state legislatures have recently enacted mandatory prison terms for repeat offenders, and determinate sentencing or sentencing guidelines (prescribed specific jail terms for specific criminal offenders). These reforms limit judicial discretion and make punishment policies more explicit.

Do prison sentences reduce crime? It is clear that removing habitual offenders from the streets reduces the crime they commit outside the prison walls for the duration of their sentences. Thus, long sentences can reduce crime rates by "incapacitating" habitual criminals for long periods. (Very few first offenders are sentenced to prison.) But there is no evidence that the prison experience itself deters people from committing more crime after they are released.

Punishment has no discernible effect on the subsequent criminal behavior of persons who have been convicted and imprisoned. An estimated 61 percent of persons admitted to prison are "recidivists," that is, persons who have previously served a sentence of incarceration as a juvenile, adult, or both. Of those 39 percent entering prisons without a prior record of incarceration, nearly 60 percent have prior convictions that resulted in probation. Thus, a total of 85 percent of all persons admitted to prison have prior convictions. An even more striking fact is that 28 percent of all persons entering prison would still have been in prison at the time of the new crime, conviction, and admission, if they had served out their maximum prior confinement sentence. These "avertible recidivists" were still on parole for a prior crime when they reentered prison. A total of 40 percent of all persons admitted to prison were on probation or parole at the time of their new conviction.[5] Clearly the criminal justice system did not "rehabilitate" those prison returnees. On the other hand, if they had been required to serve out their full sentences they would not have been free to commit the crimes that brought them back.

In summary, the severity of punishment does not deter crime, although it may protect the general public by incapacitating criminals.

POLICE AND LAW ENFORCEMENT

The principal responsibility for law enforcement in America rests with state and local governments. The Federal Bureau of Investigation in the Department of Justice was created in the 1920s and charged with the responsibility of enforcing only federal laws. Today, the role of the federal government in law enforcement is growing, but state and local governments

---

[5]U. S. Department of Justice, Bureau of Justice Statistics, *Examining Readmission.* February, 1985.

TABLE 4-4   Citizen Complaints Radioed to Police Vehicles

CALLS	NUMBER IN SAMPLE	PERCENTAGE
Information Gathering	69	22.1
Book and check	2	
Get a report	67	
Service	117	37.5
Accidents, illnesses, ambulance calls	42	
Animals	8	
Assist a person	1	
Drunk person	8	
Escort vehicle	3	
Fire, power line or tree down	26	
Property damage	6	
Maintenance of Order	94	30.1
Gang disturbance	50	
Family trouble	23	
Assault, fight	9	
Investigation	8	
Neighbor trouble	4	
Law Enforcement	32	10.3
Burglary in progress	9	
Check a car	5	
Open a door or window	8	
Prowler	6	
Make an arrest	4	
Totals	312	100.0

Source: James Q. Wilson, *Varieties of Police Behavior* (Cambridge: Harvard University Press, 1968), p. 18.

continue to carry the major burdens of police protection, judicial systems, and prison and parole programs. The federal government employs less than 50,000 persons in all law enforcement activities, compared with over one-half million state and local government law enforcement personnel. Federal prisons contain about 26,000 inmates, compared with over 400,000 in state prisons.

At least three important functions in society are performed by police: law enforcement, keeping the peace, and furnishing services. Actually, law enforcement may take up only a small portion of a police officer's daily activity, perhaps only 10 percent.[6] The service function is far more common—attending accidents, directing traffic, escorting crowds, assisting stranded motorists, handling drunks, and so on (see Table 4-4). The func-

[6]James Q. Wilson, *Varieties of Police Behavior* (Cambridge: Harvard University Press, 1968), p. 18; Arthur Niederhoffer, *Behind the Shield* (New York: Doubleday, 1967), p. 71.

tion of peace keeping is also very common—breaking up fights, quieting noisy parties, handling domestic or neighborhood quarrels, and the like. It is in this function that police exercise the greatest discretion in the application of the law. In most of these incidents, it is difficult to determine blame. Participants are reluctant to file charges and police must use personal discretion in handling each case.

Police are on the front line of society's efforts to resolve conflict. Indeed, instead of a legal or law enforcement role, the police are more likely to adopt a peace-keeping role. Police are generally lenient in their arrest practices; that is, they use their arrests powers less often than the law allows.[7] Rather than arresting people, the police prefer first to reestablish order. Of course, the decision to be more or less lenient in enforcing the law gives the police a great deal of discretion—the police exercise decision-making powers on the streets.

What factors influence police decision making? Probably the first factor to influence police behavior is the attitude of the other people involved in police encounters. If a person adopts an acquiescent role, displays deference and respect for the police, and conforms to police expectations, he or she is much less likely to be arrested than a person who shows disrespect or uses abusive language toward police.[8] This is not just an arbitrary response of police. They learn through training and experience the importance of establishing their authority on the streets.

The tasks assigned to police in an urban society would confound highly trained social scientists. Yet only recently have police officers been recruited from colleges and universities. Formal police training emphasizes self-control and caution in dealing with the public, but on-the-job experiences probably reinforce distrust of others. The element of danger in the police officer's job makes him or her naturally suspicious of others. Police officers see much of the "worst kind" of people, and they see even the "best kind" at their worst.

Police forces are semimilitary organizations engaged in rule enforcement. Police must be concerned with authority themselves, and they expect others to respect authority. It is often difficult for even the most well-meaning police officer to develop respect or sympathy for inner-city residents. One police officer described this problem as follows:

> The police have to associate with lower-class people, slobs, drunks, criminals, riffraff of the worst sort. Most of these . . . are Negroes. The police officers

---

[7]See Donald J. Black, "Social Organization of Arrest," in William B. Sanders and Howard C. Davidstel, eds., *The Criminal Justice Process* (New York: Holt, Rinehart & Winston, 1976).

[8]Stuart A. Sheingold, "Cultural Cleavage and Criminal Justice," *Journal of Politics,* 40, 865–97.

see these people through middle-class or lower-middle-class eyeballs. But even if he saw them through highly sophisticated eyeballs he can't go in the street and take this night after night. When some Negro criminal says to you a few times, "you white mother-fucker, take that badge off and I'll shove it up your ass," well, it's bound to affect you after a while. Pretty soon you decide they're all just niggers and they'll never be anything but niggers. It would take not just an average man to resist this feeling, it would take an extraordinary man to resist it, and there are very few ways by which the police department can attract extraordinary men to join them.[9]

The police officer's attitude toward ghetto residents is often affected by the high crime rates in ghetto areas. The police officer is suspicious of ghetto residents because crime rates tell him that his suspicions are often justified.

If police are overly suspicious of ghetto blacks, the attitudes of many ghetto blacks toward police are equally hostile. Black novelist James Baldwin writes of police in the ghetto:

Their very presence is an insult, and it would be, even if they spent their entire day feeding gumdrops to children. They represent the force of the white world, and that world's real intentions are simply, to keep the black man corralled up here, in his place. The badge, the gun and the holster and the swinging club make vivid what will happen should his rebellion become overt. . . .
He has never himself done anything for which to be hated—which of us has? And yet he is facing, daily and nightly, people who would gladly see him dead, and he knows it.[10]

Does increased police protection significantly reduce crime? The common assumption is that increased police manpower and increased police expenditures can significantly reduce crime in cities. But, unfortunately, it is very difficult to produce firm evidence to support this assumption. Studies of crime rates in relation to police manpower and expenditure have failed to find any strong evidence to support the more-police-activity-equals-less-crime theory.[11] So many other factors may affect crime rates in cities—size, density, youth, unemployment, race, poverty, etc.—that police activity appears insignificant. Or an increase in police activity may result in increased crime reporting, which tends to obscure any actual reduction in crime in official statistics.

[9]Wilson, *Varieties of Police Behavior*, p. 43.

[10]James Baldwin, *Nobody Knows My Name* (New York: Dell Pub. Co., Inc., 1962), pp. 61–62.

[11]E. Terrance Jones, "Evaluating Everyday Policies: Police Activity and Crime Incidence," *Urban Affairs Quarterly*, 8 (March 1973), 267–79.

CRIME AND GUNS

Many crimes involve the use of guns. Specifically, the FBI reports that in 1983 21 percent of all aggravated assaults, 37 percent of all robberies, and 58 percent of all murders were accomplished with guns.[12] Would registering guns, licensing gun owners, or banning handguns reduce crime?

Gun control legislation is a common policy initiative following murders or assassination attempts on prominent figures. The Federal Gun Control Act of 1968 was a response to the assassinations of Senator Robert F. Kennedy and Martin Luther King, Jr., in that year, and efforts to legislate additional restrictions occurred after attempts to assassinate Presidents Gerald Ford and Ronald Reagan. The rationale for licensing gun owners or banning guns altogether is that fewer crimes would be committed with guns if guns were less readily available. Murders, especially crimes of passion among family members or neighbors, would be reduced, if for no other reason than that it is physically more difficult to kill someone with only a knife, a club, or bare hands. Proponents of gun control note that the U.S. has less restrictive gun laws than other advanced nations and that it has the highest murder rate.

The Federal Gun Control Act of 1968 included the following:

1. A ban on interstate and mail-order sales of firearms and ammunition.
2. Prohibition of the sale of any firearms to a convicted felon, fugitive, or adjudicated mental defective.
3. A requirement that all firearms dealers must be licensed by the Federal Bureau of Alcohol, Tobacco, and Firearms of the Department of the Treasury.
4. A requirement that manufacturers record by serial number all firearms, and dealers record all sales. Dealers must require proof of identity and residence of buyers, and buyers must sign a statement certifying their eligibility to purchase.
5. Continued restrictions of private ownership of automatic weapons, military weapons, and other heavy ordinance. Prior Treasury Department approval of the purchaser and $200 tax is imposed on each of these weapons.

This important act was weakened in 1986 when Congress, under heavy pressure from the National Rifle Association, lifted the restriction on interstate sales of rifles and shotguns. (Only the ban on interstate sale of hand guns was retained.) The politically powerful National Rifle Association had argued for many years that the 1968 act was too broad and subjected innocent gun owners and sporting goods stores to harassment by federal agents. Congress also made it legal to transport an unloaded, "inaccessible" firearm anywhere in the United States, thus barring prose-

---

[12]*Statistical Abstract of the United States 1985*, p. 172.

cutions under state or local laws that prohibit carrying of a handgun in luggage or a vehicle.

State laws, and many local ordinances, also govern gun ownership. Handgun laws are common in the states. Most states require that a record of sale be submitted to state or local government agencies; some states require an application and a waiting period prior to purchase of a handgun; a few states require a license or a permit to purchase one; most states require a license to carry a "concealed" weapon; and four states (Illinois, Massachusetts, New Jersey, and New York) prohibit any handgun ownership except by persons licensed by law enforcement officials.

Gun ownership is widespread in the United States. Estimates vary, but there are probably 150 million firearms in the hands of the nation's 236 million people. Half of all American families admit in public opinion surveys to owning guns. A majority of gun owners say their guns are for hunting and sports; about one-third say the purpose of their gun ownership is self-defense. The proportion of gun owners who have ever used their gun in self-defense is infinitesimal. Indeed, the likelihood of being hurt with one's own weapon is far greater than the chance of inflicting harm upon an assailant. Interestingly, *both* those who favor a ban on handguns and those who oppose such a ban cite "crime" as the reason for their position. Those who want to ban guns say they contribute to crime and violence. Those who oppose a ban feel they need guns for protection against crime and violence. In opinion polls, majorities of Americans oppose any outright ban on the possession or sale of handguns, yet majorities also say they favor "strict" laws governing handguns.[13]

There is no systematic evidence that gun control laws can reduce violent crime. If we compare violent crime rates in jurisdictions with very restrictive gun laws (especially New York, Massachusetts, New Jersey, and Illinois) with violent crime rates in jurisdictions with very loose controls on gun ownership, we find no differences in rates of violent crime which cannot be attributed to social conditions. Gun laws, including purchase permits, waiting periods, carrying permits, and even complete prohibitions, seem to have no effect on violent crime, or even crimes committed with guns.[14] Indeed, gun laws do not even appear to have any effect on gun ownership. Even the Massachusetts ban on handguns, which calls for a mandatory prison sentence for unlicensed citizens found carrying a firearm, did not reduce gun-related crime.[15] The total number of persons imprisoned for gun crimes was essentially unchanged; however, more per-

---

[13]*The Gallup Report* (July 1981), pp. 26–31.

[14]Douglas R. Murray, "Handguns, Gun Control Laws and Firearm Violence," *Social Problems*, Vol. 23 (1975); James D. Wright and Peter H. Rossi, *Weapons, Crime, and Violence in America* (Washington, D.C.: U.S. Department of Justice, National Institute of Justice, 1981).

[15]David Rossman, *The Impact of the Mandatory Gun Law in Massachusetts* (Boston: Boston University School of Law, 1979).

sons without criminal records were arrested and charged with gun law violations. Of course, it might be argued that state and local laws are inadequate and only a rigorously enforced federal law could effectively ban handguns. But to date we must conclude that "there is little evidence to show that gun ownership among the population as a whole is, per se, an important cause of criminal violence."[16]

Public policies in the United States are seldom argued from a cross-national perspective; but gun control is an exception. A surprising amount of attention is devoted to comparisons between the United States and other nations. Gun control proponents cite the experience of Great Britain and Japan, where ownership of handguns is prohibited and violent crime is very rare (although the situation in Great Britain may be deteriorating). Opponents of gun control can cite the national experience in Israel, where military reservists (eighteen to fifty years of age) keep automatic weapons in their home and violent crime is virtually nonexistent. In short, cultural factors obscure any lessons that cross-national comparisons might teach about the value of gun control.[17]

The gun control debate also involves constitutional issues. The Second Amendment to the U.S. Constitution states: "A well regulated militia, being necessary to the security of a free state, the right of the people to keep and bear arms, shall not be infringed." Opponents of gun control view the right "to keep and bear arms" as an *individual* constitutional right, like the First Amendment freedom of speech or press. Proponents of gun control argue that the Second Amendment protects only the *collective* right of the people to form state militias, that is, the right of the states to maintain National Guard units. Either interpretation can be defended. Opponents of gun control argue that all rights set forth in the Bill of Rights are interpreted as individual rights. The history surrounding the adoption of the Second Amendment reveals the concern of colonists with the attempt by a despotic government to confiscate the arms of citizens and render them helpless to resist tyranny. James Madison writes in *The Federalist No. 46* that "the advantage of being armed which the Americans possess over the people of almost every other nation, . . . forms a barrier against the enterprise of [tyrannical] ambition." Early American political rhetoric is filled with praise for an armed citizenry able to protect their freedoms with force if necessary. And the "militia" was defined as every adult free male able to carry a weapon. Even the early English common law recognized the right of individuals "to have and use arms for self-protection and defense."[18] Proponents of gun control cite the U.S. Supreme Court decision in *United States*

---

[16]Wright and Rossi, *Weapons, Crime, and Violence in America*, p. 540.

[17]Barry Bruce-Biggs, "The Great American Gun War," *The Public Interest* (Fall 1976), 37–62.

[18]William Blackstone, *Commentaries of the Laws of England*, Vol. 1, p. 144.

v. *Miller* (1939).[19] In this case, the Court considered the constitutionality of the federal National Firearms Act of 1934, which, among other things, prohibited the transportation of sawed-off shotguns in interstate commerce. The defendant claimed that Congress could not infringe upon his right to keep and bear arms. But the Court responded that a sawed-off shotgun had no "relationship to the preservation or efficiency of a well-regulated militia." The clear implication of this decision is that the right to bear arms refers only to a state's right to maintain a militia.

Perhaps the argument over gun control really has nothing to do with reducing crime or with constitutional interpretations. Instead, two ethics are in conflict. There is the established upper-class liberal ethic of a civilized, educated, well-ordered society which can resolve conflict through laws, courts, and institutions. There is also the individualist ethic stressing one's own responsibility for the protection of family and property in a tough and sometimes dangerous world. These contrasting ethics in America are clearly in conflict over the gun control issue.

CRIME AND DRUGS

Public policy toward drug use in America is ambivalent. Alcohol and cigarettes are legal products, although the Office of the Surgeon General of the United States has undertaken educational campaigns to reduce their use, and Congress has banned the advertising of alcohol and tobacco on radio and television. (See Chapter 6 for a discussion of the effectiveness of these health measures.) Marijuana has been "decriminalized" in several states, making its use or possession a misdemeanor comparable to a traffic offense; a majority of states, however, have retained criminal sanctions against marijuana, and its manufacture and distribution are prohibited everywhere. The potential for drug abuse is found in many prescription medicines—amphetamines, barbiturates, and tranquilizers. The use and possession of cocaine is a criminal offense everywhere in the United States, yet this drug is increasingly popular, particularly among the upper and upper-middle classes. Heroin is a physically addictive drug, but its use in the United States is declining somewhat,[20] in part perhaps because of worldwide law enforcement activity.

It is difficult to estimate the various forms of drug use. According to the U.S. National Institute on Drug Abuse, there are 12 to 14 million "problem drinkers," or about 6 percent of the population. There are an

---

[19]*United States* v. *Miller*, 307 U.S. 174 (1939).

[20]Richard C. Schroeder, *The Politics of Drugs*, 2nd ed. (Washington, D.C.: Congressional Quarterly Inc., 1980), p. 80.

estimated 65 million cigarette smokers, or about 33 percent of the population (significantly less than the 45 percent of the population who smoked cigarettes in the 1940s and 1950s). There are an estimated 16 million regular users of marijuana, or about 7 percent of the population, although many more have smoked it at least once. Recent estimates of cocaine use have leaped upward to 10 million or about 5 percent of the population. There are an estimated one-half million users of heroin in the country.[21]

Public policy toward marijuana use illustrates many of the contradictions in elite and mass attitudes toward drug use. The medical evidence on the health effects of marijuana is mixed; conflicting reports have been issued about whether or not it is more dangerous than alcohol.[22] The U.S. prohibited the manufacture and use of alcohol for only thirteen years, during Prohibition, 1920 to 1933. Today the manufacture and sale of alcohol is legal in most U.S. jurisdictions, but marijuana is not. Marijuana arrests in the late 1960s and early 1970s approached one-half million per year. The estimates of the number of "problem drinkers" and regular marijuana users are very close. One explanation of the different public policies toward alcohol and marijuana centers on the different generations which use each drug. Marijuana became very popular in the United States in the 1960s, so its users tended to be young. As this generation of Americans grew older, the movement to "decriminalize" marijuana strengthened. "Decriminalizing" marijuana does not make its production or sale legal, but makes its possession (generally of an ounce or less) a civil offense, much like a traffic offense. Oregon was the first state to decriminalize marijuana possession and use in 1973.

Public policy toward heroin use has been far more consistent and restrictive over the years. Since the Harrison Narcotic Act of 1916, heroin use has been considered a major law enforcement problem. In contrast, in Great Britain since 1920 heroin use has been considered a medical problem and heroin is dispensed to addicted patients through physicians in the National Health Service. Heroin addiction in the United States is estimated to be greater than in Great Britain, as are the number of crimes committed by addicts. Over the years in the United States the extent of heroin addiction has varied with the success or failure of law enforcement. During the 1930s and 1940s with strong federal law enforcement efforts (almost one-third of all federal prisoners in 1928 were violators of the Harrison Act), heroin use declined. It rose again in the 1960s, but in the early 1970s the United States succeeded in pressing the Turkish government to ban opium poppy

[21]National Institute on Drug Abuse, *National Survey on Drug Abuse* (Washington, D. C., 1978).

[22]For a summary of this evidence and references to the relevant health literature, see Schroeder, *The Politics of Drugs*, ch. 4.

growing and law enforcement officials in the United States and France succeeded with their "French Connection" efforts to destroy a major drug smuggling syndicate, and use decline somewhat. In recent years cocaine has replaced heroin as the major drug smuggled into the United States. Most law enforcement officials doubt that heroin or cocaine traffic can ever be eliminated by law enforcement. As Schroeder reports, "It takes only 10 square miles of poppies to feed the entire American heroin market and they grow everywhere."[23]

The burgeoning market for cocaine currently challenges law enforcement efforts. Cocaine is not regarded as physically addictive, although the psychological urge to continue use of the drug is strong. It is made from coca leaves and imported into the Unites States. Its high cost, and celebrity use, have made it favored in upper-class circles, although there is yet to be any strong effort to "decriminalize" it. The health problems associated with its continuous use are fairly serious, as reported by the National Institute on Drug Abuse.[24] The power of the coca leaf has been known for hundreds of years; Coca-Cola originally contained cocaine, though the drug was removed from the popular drink in 1903.

Crime associated with drug trafficking is a serious national problem, whatever the health effects of various drugs. The world of drug trafficking is fraught with violence. Sellers rob and murder buyers and vice versa; neither can seek the protection of police or courts in their dealings with each other. Though some citizens might wish simply to allow dealers to wipe each other out, the frequency with which innocent bystanders are killed must be considered.

The U.S Drug Enforcement Administration (DEA) in the Department of Justice was created by Congress in 1973. It has the authority to enforce federal drug laws both in the United States and abroad. (Earlier responsibility had been shared by various agencies, including the Treasury Department's Bureau of Narcotics.) DEA officers may go abroad to collect international intelligence and to cooperate with foreign authorities; they do not participate in direct arrest actions in foreign nations. The U.S. Customs Service has the responsibility for stopping the entry of narcotics at U.S. borders. The U.S. Coast Guard cooperates in drug interception. The FBI monitors drug trafficking that contributes to other federal crimes. Surveillance of low-level buying and selling of drugs is usually left to state and local authorities. Federal "strike forces" composed of DEA, FBI, Customs inspectors, and U.S. attorneys are believed to be the most effective way to combat drug trafficking.

[23]Schroeder, *Politics of Drugs,* p. 148.
[24]Ibid., ch. 9.

CRIME AND THE COURTS

Former Chief Justice Warren E. Burger has argued persuasively that rising crime in America is partly due to inadequacies in our system of criminal justice. "The present system of criminal justice does not deter criminal conduct," he said in a special State of the Federal Judiciary Message. "Whatever deterrent effect may have existed in the past has now virtually vanished."[25] He urged major reforms in law enforcement courts, prisons, probation, and parole.

A major stumbling block to effective law enforcement is the current plight of America's judicial machinery.

Major congestion on court dockets that delays the hearing of cases months or even years. Moreover, actual trials now average twice as long as ten years ago.

Failure of courts to adopt modern management and administrative practice to speed and improve justice.

Increased litigation in the courts. Not only are more Americans aware of their rights, but more are using every avenue of appeal. Seldom do appeals concern the guilt or innocence of the defendant; they usually focus on procedural matters.

Excessive delays in trials. According to Burger, "Defendants, whether guilty or innocent, are human; they love freedom and hate punishment. With a lawyer provided to secure release without the need for a conventional bail bond, most defendants, except in capital cases, are released pending trial. We should not be surprised that a defendant on bail exerts a heavy pressure on his court-appointed lawyer to postpone the trial as long as possible so as to remain free. These postponements—and sometimes there are a dozen or more—consume the time of judges and court staffs as well as of lawyers. Cases are calendared and reset time after time while witnesses and jurors spend hours just waiting."

Excessive delays in appeals. "We should not be surprised at delay when more and more defendants demand their undoubtedly constitutional right to trial by jury because we have provided them with lawyers and other needs at public expense; nor should we be surprised that most convicted persons seek a new trial when the appeal costs them nothing and when failure to take the appeal will cost them freedom. Being human, a defendant plays out the line which society has cast him. Lawyers are competitive creatures and the adversary system encourages contention and often rewards delay; no lawyers want to be called upon to defend the client's charge of incompetence for having failed to exploit all the precedural techniques which we have deliberately made available."

Excessive variation in sentencing. Some judges let defendants off on probation for crimes that would draw five- or ten-year sentences by other judges. Although flexibility in sentencing is essential in dealing justly with individuals, perceived inconsistencies damage the image of the courts in the public mind

---

[25]Chief Justice Warren Burger, Address on the State of the Federal Judiciary to r American Bar Association, August 10, 1970.

Excessive "plea bargaining" between the prosecution and the defendant's attorney in which the defendant agrees to plead guilty to a lesser offense if the prosecutor will drop more serious charges.

Insufficient evidence and dismissal.   About half of all felony arrests result in dismissal of the charges against the defendant. This decision is usually made by the prosecutor (the *state's attorney, district attorney, county prosecutor,* as the office is variously designated in the states; or a prosecuting attorney in the U. S. Department of Justice in a federal criminal case). The prosecutor may determine that the offense is not serious, or that the offender is not a danger to society, or that the resources of his office would be better spent pursuing other cases. But the most common reason for the dismissal of the charges is insufficient evidence.

The exclusionary rule.   The exclusionary rule prevents illegally obtained evidence from being used in a criminal case. The rule is unique to the courts in the United States; it was adopted by the U.S. Supreme Court in *Mapp.* v. *Ohio* in 1961. Although illegally seized evidence may prove the guilt of the accused, it cannot be used in court and the accused may go free because the police committed a procedural error. The Fourth Amendment's prohibition against "unreasonable searches and seizures" has been interpreted to mean that police cannot conduct a search on private property without a court warrant. To obtain a warrant from a judge, police must show "probable cause" for their search and describe "the place to be searched and the persons or things to be seized." Errors on warrants are not infrequent; the addresses may be wrong or the names of the persons incorrect, or the articles misspecified. Any error results in exclusion of the evidence. There can be no blanket authorizations in a warrant to find evidence of *any* crime. In a public place, police cannot arrest persons without a warrant unless they have "probable cause" to believe that a crime has been committed. Immediately after making a warrantless arrest, police must take the accused before a magistrate to decide whether a probable cause existed to justify the arrest. Police do not have a general right to stop people on the streets or in their automobiles to make random checks or inspections.

Most trial proceedings today are not concerned with the guilt or innocence of the accused, but instead, center on possible procedural errors by police or prosecutors. If the defendant's attorney can show that an error was committed, the defendant goes free, regardless of his or her guilt or innocence. Supreme Court Justice Felix Frankfurter wrote many years ago: "The history of liberty has largely been the history of procedural safeguards." These safeguards protect us all from the abuse of police powers. But Chief Justice Warren Burger attacked the exclusionary rule for "the high price it extracts from society—the release of countless guilty criminals." Why should criminals go free because of police misconduct? Why not punish the police directly, perhaps with disciplinary measures imposed by courts which discover procedural errors, instead of letting guilty persons go free?

Right to counsel. In a series of cases, the Supreme Court under the leadership of Chief Justice Earl Warren greatly strengthened the Sixth Amendment's guarantee of the right to counsel.

> *Gideon* v. *Wainwright* (1963)—Ruling that equal protection under the Fourteenth Amendment requires that free legal counsel be appointed for all indigent defendants in all criminal cases.
>
> *Escobedo* v. *Illinois* (1964)—Ruling that a suspect is entitled to confer with counsel as soon as police investigation focuses on him or her, or once "the process shifts from investigatory to accusatory."
>
> *Miranda* v. *Arizona* (1966)—Requiring that police, before questioning a suspect, must inform him of all his constitutional rights, including the right to counsel, appointed free if necessary, and the right to remain silent. Although the suspect may knowingly waive these rights, the police cannot question anyone who at any point asks for a lawyer or indicates "in any manner" that he does not wish to be questioned. If the police commit an error in these procedures, the accused goes free, regardless of the evidence of guilt.

It is very difficult to ascertain to what extent these decisions have really hampered efforts to halt the rise in crime in America. Studies of police behavior following the *Mapp* v. *Ohio* decision show that at first police committed many procedural errors and guilty persons were freed; but after a year or so of adjustment to the new rules, successful prosecutions rose to the same level achieved before the decision.[26] The *Miranda* decision appears to have reduced the number of confessions. However, the Supreme Court under Chief Justice Burger has not reversed any of these important decisions. So whatever progress is made in law enforcement will have to be made within the current definition of the rights of defendants. It is important to note that Chief Justice Burger's recommendations for judicial reform center on the speedy administration of justice and not on changes in the rights of defendants.

Plea bargaining. Most convictions are obtained by guilty pleas. Indeed, about 90 percent of the criminal cases brought to trial are disposed of by guilty pleas before a judge, not trial by jury. The Constitution guarantees trial by jury (Sixth Amendment) and protects against self-incrimination (Fourth Amendment). All defendants have the right to a trial by jury to determine guilt or innocence. But guilty pleas outnumber trial by jury trials by ten to one.[27]

---

[26]Stephen Wasby, *The Impact of the United States Supreme Court* (Homewood: Dorsey Press, 1970).

[27]U. S. Department of Justice, Bureau of Justice Statistics, *The Prevalence of Guilty Pleas,* December, 1984.

"Plea bargaining," in which the prosecution either reduces the seriousness of the charges, or drops some but not all charges, or agrees to recommend lighter penalties, in exchange for a guilty plea by the defendant, is very common. Some critics of plea bargaining view it as another form of leniency in the criminal justice system which reduces its deterrent effects. Other critics view plea bargaining as a violation of the Constitution's protection against self-incrimination and guarantee of a fair jury trial. Prosecutors, they say, threaten defendants with serious charges and stiff penalties in order to force a guilty plea. Still other critics see plea bargaining as an "under-the-table" process which undermines respect for the criminal justice system.

While the decision to plead guilty or go to jury trial rests with the defendant, the decision is strongly influenced by the policies of the prosecutor's office. A defendant may plead guilty and accept the certainty of conviction with whatever reduced charges the prosecutor offers, and/or accept the prosecutor's pledge to recommend a lighter penalty. Or the defendant may go to trial confronting serious charges with stiffer penalties with the hope of being found innocent. However, the possibility of an innocent verdict in a jury trial is only one in six. This apparently strong record of conviction comes about because prosecutors have already dismissed charges in cases where the evidence is weak or illegally obtained. Thus, most defendants confronting strong cases against them decide to "cop a plea."

It is very fortunate for the nation's court system that most defendants plead guilty. The court system would quickly break down from overload if any substantial proportion of defendants insisted on jury trials.

EVALUATION: DETERRENCE AND CRIMINAL JUSTICE

Does the criminal justice system deter crime? This is a difficult question to answer. First we must distinguish between deterrence and incapacity. *Incapacity* can be imposed by long terms of imprisonment, particularly for habitual offenders; the policy of "keeping criminals off the streets" does indeed protect the public for a period of time, although it is done at a considerable cost ($15,000 to $25,000 per year per prisoner). The object of *deterrence* is to make the certainty, swiftness, and severity of punishment so great as to inhibit potential criminals from committing crimes.

For many years sociologists scorned the notion of deterrence, arguing that many crimes were committed without any consideration of consequences—particularly "crimes of passion." They argued that urbanization, density, poverty, age, race, and other demographic factors had more effect on crime rates than did the characteristics of the legal system. However, systematic studies have challenged this view. Sociologist Jack P. Gibbs studied criminal homicide rates and related them to the *certainty* and *severity* of imprisonment in the states.[28] The certainty of imprisonment for criminal homicides (the percentage of persons sent to prison divided by the number of homicides) ranged from 21 percent in South Carolina and South Dakota to 87 percent in Utah. The severity of imprisonment (the average number of months served for a criminal homicide) ranged from a low of 24 in Nevada to a high of 132 in North Dakota. Gibbs was able to analyze statistically these measures of certainty and severity in relation to homicide rates in the states. His conclusions:

1. States above the median-certainty and median-severity rates have lower homicide rates than states below both medians. Indeed, the homicide rate for low-certainty-rate and low-severity-rate states was three times greater than the average rate for high-certainty and high-severity states.
2. Certainty of imprisonment may be more important than severity of punishment in determining homicide rates, but there is conflicting evidence on which of these variables is more influential.
3. Both certainty and severity reduce homicide rates even after controlling for all other demographic variables.

Economists have generally confirmed these findings. Their general premise, of course, is that if you increase the cost of something (crime), less of it will be consumed (there will be fewer crimes). Their own studies confirm the deterrent effect of both the certainty and severity of punishment. Economist Gordon Tullock dismisses the notion that "crimes of passion" cannot be reduced by increasing the certainty and severity of punishment.

> The prisoners in Nazi concentration camps must frequently have been in a state of well-justified rage against some of their guards; yet this almost never led to their using violence against the guards, because punishment—which if they were lucky, would mean instant death, but was more likely to be death by torture—was so obvious and certain.[29]

Tullock argues that to increase the deterrent effect of punishment, potential criminals must be given information about it. Indeed, he suggests, governments might even lie—that is, pretend that punishment is more certain and severe than it really is—in order to reduce crime.

---

[28]See Maynard L. Erickson and Jack P. Gibbs, "The Deterrence Question," *Social Science Quarterly*, 54 (December 1973), 534–51; and Jack P. Gibbs, "Crime, Punishment, and Deterrence," *Social Science Quarterly*, 48 (March 1968), 515–30.

[29]See Gordon Tullock, "Does Punishment Deter Crime?" *The Public Interest* (Summer 1974), p. 108.

PRISONS AND CORRECTIONAL POLICIES

At least four separate theories of crime and punishment compete for preeminence in guiding correctional policies. First, there is the ancient Judeo-Christian idea of holding individuals responsible for their guilty acts and compelling them to pay a debt to society. Retribution is an expression of society's moral outrage and it lessens the impulse of victims and their families to seek revenge. Another philosophy argues that punishment should be sure, speedy, commensurate with the crime, and sufficiently conspicuous to deter others from committing crime. Still another philosophy in correctional policy is that of protecting the public from lawbreakers or habitual criminals by segregating these people behind prison walls. Finally, there is the theory that criminals are partly or entirely victims of social circumstances beyond their control and that society owes them comprehensive treatment in the form of rehabilitation.

Over two million Americans each year are prisoners in a jail, police station, juvenile home, or penitentiary. The vast majority are released within one year. There are, however, over 400,000 inmates in state and federal prisons in the United States. These prisoners are serving time for serious offenses: almost all had a record of crime before they committed the act that led to their current imprisonment.

If correctional systems could be made to work—that is, actually to rehabilitate persons as useful, law-abiding citizens—the benefits to the nation would be enormous. The Law Enforcement Assistance Administration estimates that 80 percent of all felonies are committed by repeaters—individuals who have had prior contact with the criminal justice system and were not corrected by it.[30] Penologists generally recommend more education and job training, more and better facilities, smaller prisons, halfway houses where offenders can adjust to civilian life before parole, more parole officers, and greater contact between prisoners and their families and friends. But as Daniel Glaser points out: "Unfortunately there is no convincing evidence that this investment reduces what criminologists call 'recidivism,' the offender's return to crime."[31] In short, there is no evidence that people can be "rehabilitated" no matter what is done! But prison policies now combine conflicting philosophies in a way that accomplishes *none* of society's goals. They do not effectively punish or deter individuals from crime. They do not succeed in rehabilitating the criminal. They do not even protect the public by keeping criminals off the streets; nineteen out of every twenty persons sent to prison will eventually return to society. Even the mainte-

---

[30]See *Crime and the Law* (Washington, D.C.: Congressional Quarterly, 1971), p. 11.

[31]See Daniel Glaser, *The Effectiveness of a Prison and Parole System* (Indianapolis: Bobbs-Merrill, 1964), p. 4.

nance of order *within* prisons and the protection of the lives of guards and inmates have become a serious national problem.

Over two-thirds of all prisoner releases come about by means of parole. Modern penology, with its concern for reform and rehabilitation, appears to favor parole releases rather than unconditional releases. The function of parole and postrelease supervision is (1) to procure information on the parolees' postprison conduct, and (2) to facilitate and graduate the transition between the prison and complete freedom. These functions are presumably oriented toward protecting the public and rehabilitating the offender. But states differ substantially in their use of parole: in some states, 90 percent of all releases come about because of parole, while in other states, parole is granted to less than 30 percent of all prisoners. Generally, urban industrial states with higher income and educational levels release a higher proportion of prisoners on parole than rural farm states with lower income and educational characteristics.

What is the effect of correctional expenditures, sentencing policies, and parole systems on *recidivism*—the percentage of released prisoners who return to prison for new crime? Unfortunately, the weight of evidence suggests *no* relationship between any specific means of handling prisoners and successful rehabilitation. For example, a ten-year study in Georgia comparing inmates released under parole (carefully selected, counseled, and supervised) with inmates released without parole showed no difference in the two groups in recidivism.[32] The parole system appears to be worthless. Similarly disappointing results were obtained in a California study comparing parolees given close supervision to those given little supervision; both groups committed the same number of new felonies. Finally, a comparative analysis of expenditures and manpower for corrections, parole, and probation in all fifty states revealed "the almost total absence of linkage between correction variables and recidivism." In summary, prisons do not rehabilitate. If rehabilitation is set as the goal, prisons are bound to be judged as failures.

CAPITAL PUNISHMENT: THE CONSTITUTIONAL ISSUES

Perhaps the most heated debate in criminal justice policy today concerns capital punishment. Opponents of the death penalty argue that it is "cruel and unusual punishment" in violation of the Eighth Amendment of the Constitution. They also argue that the death penalty is applied unequally. A large proportion of those executed have been poor, uneducated, and

[32]See Frank K. Gibson et al., "A Path Analytic Treatment of Corrections Output," *Social Science Quarterly*, 54 (September 1973), 281–91.

nonwhite. In contrast, there is a strong sense of justice among many Americans that demands retribution for heinous crimes—a life for a life. A mere jail sentence for a multiple murderer or rapist murderer seems unjust compared with the damage inflicted upon society and the victims. In most cases, a life sentence means less than ten years in prison under the current parole and probation policies of many states. Convicted murderers have been set free, and some have killed again. Moreover, prison guards and other inmates are exposed to convicted murderers who have "a license to kill," because they are already serving life sentences and have nothing to lose by killing again.

Prior to 1971, the death penalty was officially sanctioned by about half of the states. Federal law also retained the death penalty. However, no one had actually suffered the death penalty since 1967 because of numerous legal tangles and direct challenges to the constitutionality of capital punishment.

In *Furman* v. *Georgia* (1971) the Supreme Court ruled that capital punishment as then imposed violated the Eighth and Fourteenth Amendment prohibitions against cruel and unusual punishment and due process of law.[33] The reasoning in the case is very complex. Only two justices, Brennan and Marshall, declared that capital punishment itself is cruel and unusual. The other justices in the majority felt that death sentences had been applied unfairly: a few individuals were receiving the death penalty for crimes for which many others were receiving much lighter sentences. These justices left open the possibility that capital punishment would be constitutional, if it was specified for certain kinds of crime and applied uniformly.

After this decision, a majority of states rewrote their death penalty laws to try to ensure fairness and uniformity of application. Generally, these laws mandate the death penalty for murders committed during rape, robbery, hijacking, or kidnapping; murders of prison guards; murder with torture; and multiple murders. Two trials would be held—one to determine guilt or innocence and another to determine the penalty. At the second trial, evidence of "aggravating" and "mitigating" factors would be presented; if there were aggravating factors but no mitigating factors, the death penalty would be mandatory.

In a series of cases in 1976 (*Gregg* v. *Georgia, Profitt* v. *Florida, Jurek* v. *Texas*)[34] the Supreme Court finally held that "the punishment of death does *not* invariably violate the Constitution." The Court upheld the death penalty, employing the following rationale: the men who drafted the Bill of Rights accepted death as a common sanction for crime. It is true that the Eighth Amendment prohibition against cruel and unusual punishment

---

[33]*Furman* v. *Georgia*, 408 U.S. 238 (1971).
[34]428 U.S. 153 (1976).

must be interpreted in a dynamic fashion, reflecting changing moral values. But the decisions of more than half of the nation's state legislatures to reenact the death penalty since 1972 and the decision of juries to impose the death penalty on more than 450 persons under these new laws are evidence that "a large proportion of American society continues to regard it as an appropriate and necessary criminal sanction." Moreover, said the Court, the social purposes of retribution and deterrence justify the use of the death penalty. This ultimate sanction is "an expression of society's moral outrage at particularly offensive conduct." The Court reaffirmed that *Furman* v. *Georgia* only struck down the death penalty where it was inflicted in "an arbitary and capricious manner." The Court upheld the death penalty in states where the trial was a two-part proceeding, and during the second part the judge or jury was provided with relevant information and standards in deciding whether to impose the death penalty. The Court approved the consideration of "aggravating and mitigating circumstances." The Court also approved of automatic review of all death sentences by state Supreme Courts to ensure that the sentence was not imposed under the influence of passion or prejudice, that aggravating factors were supported by the evidence, and that the sentence was not disproportionate to the crime. However, the Court disapproved of state laws making the death penalty mandatory in first degree murder cases, holding that such laws were "unduly harsh and unworkably rigid."

CAPITAL PUNISHMENT: AN EVALUATION

Is the death penalty a deterrent to murder? Does capital punishment save lives because it prevents killings through the threat of execution? This is, indeed, a question of life or death, and it is a question which social science should be able to answer. Unfortunately, however, it is difficult to measure the deterrent effect of the death penalty because we cannot directly observe nonbehavior. We can never know for certain whether the fear of capital punishment was the reason why someone refrained from killing another person. All we can do is compare homicide rates in states which have used the death penalty over time with those states which have not; and in comparing states over time, we must remember than there are many other factors besides capital punishment which can raise or lower the homicide rate: age, race, gun ownership, and so on.

Perhaps the most controversial study in recent years is economist Isaac Ehrlich's analysis of the death penalty's use in forty-eight states between 1933 and 1969.[35] He studied execution rates and murder rates, controlling

---

[35]Isaac Ehrlich, "The Deterrent Effect of Capital Punishment: A Question of Life or Death," *American Economic Review*, 65 (June 1975), 397–414.

for many other variables, and concluded that the tradeoff between executions of convicted murderers and the reduction of killings was approximately one for eight. In other words, each execution was associated with saving the lives of eight potential victims.

However, other researchers, using similar methods, have *not* reported the same dramatic findings about the deterrent effects of capital punishment. Indeed, some social scientists specifically deny that the death penalty has any deterrent effect.[36] They attribute increases in the murder rate during the years and in the states which the death penalty was not used to a wide range of factors, including the increased ownership of handguns.[37]

Today, there are about fifteen hundred prisoners nationwide on "death row," that is, persons convicted and sentenced to death. But only about ten executions are actually carried out each year. The strategy of death row prisoners and their lawyers, of course, is to delay indefinitely the imposition of the death penalty with endless stays and appeals. So far the strategy has been successful for all but a few luckless murderers. As trial judges and juries continue to impose the death penalty, and appealable courts continue to grant stays of execution, the number of prisoners on death row grows. The few who have been executed have averaged ten years of delay between trial and execution.

The death penalty as it is employed today—inflicted on so few and so many years after the crime—has little deterrent effect. Nonetheless, it serves several purposes. It gives prosecutors some leverage in plea bargaining with murder defendants. They may choose to plead guilty in exchange for a life sentence, when confronted with the possibility that the prosecutor may win a conviction and the death penalty in a jury trial. Most importantly, however, the death penalty is symbolic of the value society places on the lives of innocent victims. The death penalty dramatically signifies that society does not excuse or condone the taking of innocent lives. It symbolizes the potential for society's retribution against hideous crime. Public opinion favors the death penalty by three to one. Only for a few years during the mid-1960s did public opinion appear to oppose the death penalty (see Figure 4-2). With increases in the crime rate from 1965–80, and accompanying increases in public fear and outrage over violent crime, heavy majorities swung back in favor of the death penalty.

---

[36]Hugo Adam Bedau, *The Death Penalty in America* (New York: Doubleday, 1967); Peter Passell, "The Deterrent Effect of the Death Penalty," *Standard Law Review*, 28 (November 1975), 61–80.

[37]Gary Kleck, "Capital Punishment, Gun Ownership, and Homicide," *American Journal of Sociology*, 84 (January 1979), 882–910.

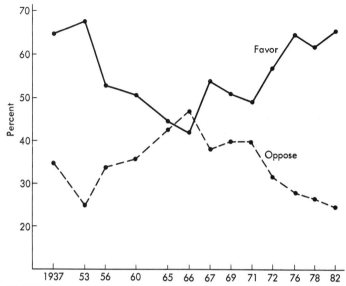

FIGURE 4-2 Question: "Are you in favor of the death penalty for persons convicted of murder?" Data from *The Gallup Report* (April 1981), p. 19.

SUMMARY

Crime is a central problem confronting society. We face a conflict between our desire to retain individual freedoms and our desire to ensure the safety of our people.

1. Crime rates rose steadily between 1960 and 1975; only recently have crime rates begun to level off. This leveling off is more likely a product of the relative decline of youth in the population than the crime deterrence policies of government. The "victimization rate" is several times greater than the reported crime rate. These statistics suggest that the current system of criminal justice is not a serious deterrent to crime.

2. A rational policy toward crime would endeavor to make the costs of crime far outweigh its benefits and in theory defer potential wrongdoers. Effective deterrence requires that punishment be certain, swift, and severe. However certainty and swiftness are probably of more importance to deterrence than severity.

3. But punishment for crime in the United States today is neither certain nor swift. The likelihood of going to jail for any particular crime is probably less than one in a hundred. "Speedy" trial and punishment are rare; criminal defendants usually succeed in obtaining long delays between arrest and trial and most are free on bail while awaiting trial.

4. Police provide many services to society in addition to law enforcement. Indeed, only a small proportion of their time is spent in fighting crime. It is

difficult to demonstate conclusively that increased police protection reduces the actual amount of crime.

5. Guns are used in a large number of violent crimes. Public policy on gun control varies throughout the nation. However, states with strict gun control laws do not have lower rates of violent crime, or even of gun-related crime, than states without such laws.

6. Public policies toward alcohol and drug use are ambivalent. Although the health dangers of cigarettes, alcohol, marijuana, cocaine, and heroin are widely known, the manufacture, sale, and use of each of these substances are treated differently in law enforcement.

7. According to Chief Justice Warren Burger, the court system fails to deter criminal conduct. Court congestion, increased litigation, excessive delays, endless appeals, variation in sentencing, and excessive plea bargaining all combine to detract from deterrence.

8. The exclusionary rule, which prohibits the use of illegally obtained evidence in court, has generated controversy since it was first announced by the Supreme Court in *Mapp* v. *Ohio* in 1961. It allows criminals to go free if police make an error.

9. About half of all serious charges are dismissed by prosecutors before trial. But most convictions are obtained by guilty pleas without jury trials. Plea bargaining is the most common means of resolving criminal cases. Without plea bargaining, the court system would break down from overload.

10. Prison and parole policies have failed to rehabilitate prisoners. Prisons can reduce crime only by incapacitating criminals for periods of time. Most prisoners are *recidivists*—persons who previously served a sentence of incarceration before being sentenced again. *Parolees*—persons released by officials for good behavior—are just as likely to commit new crimes as persons released after serving full sentences.

11. Social scientists disagree over whether the severity of the death penalty can be a deterrent to murder. But most agree that capital punishment as currently imposed—on very few persons and after very long delays—is not an effective deterrent.

BIBLIOGRAPHY

HELLMAN, DAVID, *The Economics of Crime*, New York: St. Martin's Press, 1980.

SCHROEDER, RICHARD C., *The Politics of Drugs*, 2nd ed. Washington, D.C.: Congressional Quarterly, 1980.

WILSON, JAMES Q., *Varieties of Police Behavior*. Cambridge, Mass.: Harvard University Press, 1968.

———, *Thinking About Crime*, New York: Basic Books, 1975.

———, *Crime and Public Policy*. New Brunswick: Transaction Books, 1983.

POVERTY AND WELFARE

the search for a rational strategy

Over 22 million Americans receive federal food stamps, yet reports of hunger persist. (Charles Gatewood)

POVERTY IN AMERICA

A rational approach to policy making requires a clear definition of the problem. But political conflict over the nature and extent of poverty in America is a major obstacle to a rational approach to social welfare policy.

Proponents of programs for the poor frequently make high estimates of the number of poor. They view the problem of poverty as a persistent one, even in an affluent society; they contend that many millions of people suffer from hunger, exposure, and remedial illness, and that some of them even starve to death. Their definition of the problem virtually mandates immediate and massive public welfare programs.

In contrast, others minimize the number of poor in America. They see poverty diminishing over time in a vigorous, expanding, free market economy. They believe the poor in America are considerably better off than the middle class of fifty years ago and even wealthy by the standards of most other societies in the world. They view government welfare programs as causes of poverty, destroying family life and robbing the poor of incentives to work, save, and assume responsibility for their own well-being. They deny that anyone needs to suffer from hunger, exposure, remedial illness, or starvation if they make use of the services and facilities available to them.

How Many Poor?

How much poverty really exists in America? According to the U. S. Social Security Administration there were about 34 million poor people in the United States in 1984. This is approximately 14 percent of the population. This official estimate of poverty includes all those Americans whose annual cash income falls below that which is required to maintain a decent standard of living. The definition of the "poverty line" by the Social Security Administration is derived by calculating "thrifty" food costs for families of various sizes and then multiplying these costs by three, on the assumption that poor families spend one-third of their income on food. The dollar amounts of these lines are flexible to take into account the effect of inflation; the amounts rise each year with the rate of inflation. In 1984 the poverty line for an urban family of four was approximately $10,609 per year (see Table 5-1). The median income for all families for the nation in that year was $26,433.[1]

This official definition of poverty has many critics. Some *liberal critics* believe poverty is underestimated because: (1) The official definition does

---

[1]All figures from U. S. Bureau of the Census, "Money Income and Poverty Status of Families and Persons in the United States 1984," Advance Report. Washington: Government Printing Office, September, 1985.

TABLE 5-1   Poverty in America

Poverty definition 1984	
Nonfarm family of four	$10,609
Number of poor	33.7 million
Poverty percentage of total population	14.4
Race (% poor)	
White	11.5
Black	33.8
Spanish	28.4
Age (% poor)	
Over 65	12.4
Family (% poor)	
Married couple	6.9
Male householder, no wife	13.1
Female householder, no husband	34.5

not take into account regional differences in the cost of living, climate, or accepted styles of living; (2) the "thrifty" food budget on which the poverty level is based is too low for good nutrition and health; (3) the official definition includes cash income from welfare and social security, and without this government assistance, the number of poor would be much higher, perhaps 25 percent of the total population; (4) the official definition does not count the many "near poor"; there are 40 million Americans or 18.1 percent of the population living below 125 percent of the poverty level; and (5) the official definition does not consider what people think they need to live. The Gallup Report said that in 1980 the public believed the "smallest amount of money" needed for a family of four was $250 per week or $13,000 per year, compared to the official poverty line of $8,414 in that same year.

Some *conservative critics* also challenge the official definition of poverty: (1) It does not consider the value of family assets. People (usually older people) who own their own mortgage-free homes, furniture, and automobiles may have current incomes below the poverty line yet not suffer hardship. (2) There are many families and individuals who are officially counted as poor but who do not think of themselves as "poor people"— students, for example, who deliberately postpone income to secure an education. (3) Many persons (poor and nonpoor) underreport their real income and this leads to overestimates of the number of poor. (4) More importantly, the official definition of poverty excludes "in kind" (noncash) benefits given to the poor by governments. These benefits include, for example, food stamps, free medical care, public housing, and school lunches. If these benefits were "costed out" (calculated as cash income), there may be only half as many poor people as shown in official statistics. The Social Security Administration itself estimates that if all government benefits to the poor were costed out, the proportion of the poor in America in 1984 would have been only about 9 percent. This figure might be thought of as the "net poverty" rate. Net poverty refers to people who remain poor even after counting their in-kind government benefits. The net poverty rate is shown together with the official poverty rate in Figure 5–1.

How persistent is poverty? Researchers from the Survey Research Center, University of Michigan, tracked 5000 American families for ten years and found that only *3 percent* were persistently poor, that is, they were poor throughout the entire period. This is a much smaller figure than the 11 to 14 percent reported as poor at any one time. This means that people slip into, and out of, the poverty category over time. People lose their jobs, retire, divorce or separate, become ill, and then later they find new jobs, remarry, get well, and their financial condition changes.

Figure 5-1   Three definitions of poverty.

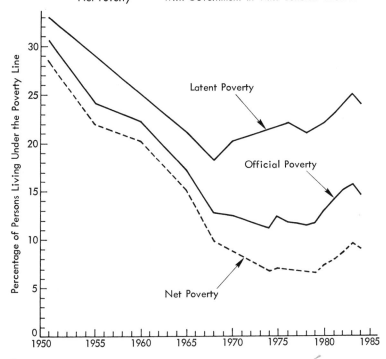

THREE DEFINITIONS OF POVERTY

Official Poverty = Cash Income
Latent Poverty = Without Government Benefits Counted
Net Poverty   = With Government In–Kind Benefits Counted

Sources: 1950 to 1980 from *Losing Ground: American Social Policy 1950–1980* by Charles Murray. Copyright © 1984 by Charles Murray. Reprinted by permission of Basic Books, Inc., Publishers. 1981–1984 by the author from U. S. Bureau of the Census, "Money, Income, and Poverty Status of Families and Persons in the United States," 1984 Advance Report. Washington: Government Printing Office, September, 1985.

How many people would be poor if we did *not* have government social security and welfare programs? What percentage of the population can be thought of as "latent poor," that is, persons who would be poor without the assistance they receive from federal programs? Charles Murray refers to the latent poverty figure as "the most damning statistic," because it counts the number of people in our society who are economically dependent and cannot stand on their own.[2] Latent poverty has been growing rapidly since the late 1960s when more and more people became dependent on government social security and welfare payment (see Figure 5-1). Latent poverty was estimated to be around 4 percent in 1984, well above the 14 percent in official poverty.

Who Are the Poor?

Poverty occurs in many kinds of families and all races and ethnic groups. However, some groups experience poverty in proportions greater than the national average.

Poverty is most common among female-headed families. The incidence of poverty among these families in 1984 was 34.5 percent, compared to only 6.9 percent for married couples (see Table 5–1). These women and their children comprise over two-thirds of all of the persons living in poverty in the United States. These figures describe "the feminization of poverty" in America. Clearly, poverty is closely related to family structure. Today the disintegration of the traditional husband-wife family is the single most influential factor contributing to poverty.

Blacks experience poverty in much greater proportions than whites. Over the years the poverty rate among blacks in the United States has been about three times higher than the poverty rate among whites (see Figure 5-2). Poverty among Hispanics is also significantly greater than among whites.

The relationship between race and family structure is a controversial topic. About 40 percent of all black families in the United States in 1984 were headed by females, compared to about 15 percent of all white families. Over 50 percent of all black female-headed families live in poverty.

These facts are not in dispute, but their implications have generated very controversial debate. U. S. Senator Daniel Patrick Moynihan (D.–N.Y.) ran into a firestorm of criticism when he first suggested in 1965 that the disintegration of black family life was a major cause of poverty. Although Moynihan argued that black families had been victimized by slavery and segregation, his views were interpreted by critics as racist.

The aged in America experience *less* poverty than the non-aged. The aged are not poor, despite the popularity of the phrase "the poor and the

---

[2]Charles Murray, *Losing Ground* (New York: Basic Books, 1984).

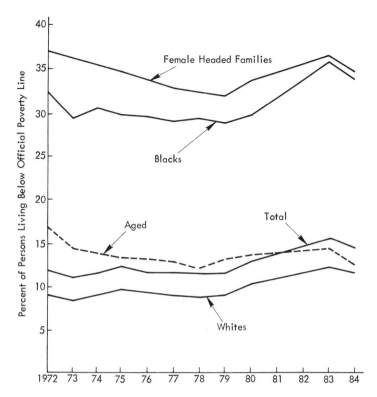

FIGURE 5-2 Who are the poor?

aged." The poverty rate for persons over 65 years of age is currently two full percentage points *below* the national average. Moreover, the aged are much wealthier than the non-aged. They are more likely than younger people to own homes with paid-up mortgages. A large portion of their medical expenses are paid by Medicare. With fewer expenses, the aged, even with relatively smaller cash incomes, experience poverty in a different fashion than a young mother with children. The lowering of the poverty rate among the aged is a relatively recent occurrence (see Figure 5-2). Continuing increases in social security benefits over the years are largely responsible for this singular "victory" in the war against poverty.

POVERTY AS INEQUALITY

Poverty can also be defined as "a state of mind"—some people think they have less income or material possessions than most Americans, and they believe they are entitled to more. Their sense of deprivation is not tied to any *absolute* level of income. Instead, their sense of deprivation is *relative* to what most Americans have, and what they, therefore, feel they are entitled to. Even fairly substantial incomes may result in a sense of "relative deprivation" in a very affluent society when commercial advertising and the mass media portray the "average American" as having a high level of consumption and material well-being.

Today the poor are not any more deprived, relative to the nonpoor, than in the past. However, they *feel* more deprived—they perceive the gap to be wider, and they no longer accept the gap as legitimate. Blacks are overrepresented among the poor; the civil rights movement made blacks acutely aware of their position in American society relative to whites. Thus, black advances contributed to a new awareness of the problem of poverty in terms of relative differences in income and conditions.

Defining poverty as "relative deprivation" really defines it as *inequality* in society. As Victor Fuchs explains:

> By the standards that have prevailed over most of history, and still prevail over large areas of the world, there are very few poor in the United States today. Nevertheless, there are millions of American families who, both in their own eyes and in those of others, are poor. As our nation prospers, our judgment as to what constitutes poverty will inevitably change. When we talk about poverty in America, we are talking about families and individuals who have much less income than most of us. When we talk about reducing or eliminating poverty, we are really talking about changing the distribution of income.[3]

Thus, eliminating poverty, if it is defined as relative deprivation, would mean achieving absolute equality of incomes and material possessions in America.

Let us try systematically to examine poverty as relative deprivation. Table 5-2 divides all American families into five groups—from the lowest one-fifth, in personal income, to the highest one-fifth—and shows the percentage of total family personal income received by each of these groups over the years. (If perfect income equality existed, each fifth of American families would receive 20 percent of all family personal income, and it would not even be possible to rank fifths from highest to lowest.) The poorest one-fifth received only 3.5 percent of all family personal income in 1929; in 1983, this group was still only receiving 4.7 percent of family personal income. The highest one-fifth of American families in personal income received 54.4 percent of all family personal income in 1929; in 1983, this percentage had declined to 42.7. This was the only income group to lose in relation to other income groups. The middle class improved their relative income position more than the poor. Another measure of income

[3]Victor R. Fuchs, "Redefining Poverty and Redistributing Income," *The Public Interest* (Summer 1967), 91.

**TABLE 5-2   The Distribution of Income in the United States
(Percent Distribution of Family Personal Income)**

Quintiles	1929	1936	1941	1950	1960	1970	1980	1983
Lowest	3.5%	4.1%	4.1%	4.5%	4.8%	5.4%	5.1%	4.7%
Second	9.0	9.2	9.5	12.0	12.2	12.2	11.6	11.1
Third	13.8	14.1	15.3	17.4	17.8	17.6	17.5	17.1
Fourth	19.3	20.9	22.3	23.4	24.0	23.9	24.1	24.4
Highest	54.4	51.7	48.8	42.7	41.2	40.9	41.6	42.7
Total	100.0	100.0	100.0	100.0	100.0	100.0	100.0	100.0
Top 5%	30.0	26.5	24.0	17.3	15.9	15.6	15.3	15.8

Source: *Statistical Abstract of the United States 1985*, p. 448.

equalization over time is the decline in the percentage of income received by the top 5 percent in America. The top 5 percent received 30 percent of all family income in 1929, but only 15.8 percent in 1983.

Although the income of the lowest fifth of the population appears small (4.7 percent) in comparison to the income of higher fifths, some of the hardships of this lowest fifth are reduced by in-kind government benefits, which are not counted as income. Indeed, one economist estimates that if these benefits are included, the "adjusted income distribution" of the lowest fifth would be raised to 12 percent.[4]

It is unlikely that income differences will ever disappear completely from a society that rewards skill, talent, risk taking, and ingenuity. If the problem of poverty is defined as relative deprivation—that is, *inequality*—then the problem is not really capable of solution. Regardless of how well-off the poor may be in absolute terms, there will always be a lowest one-fifth of the population receiving something less than 20 percent of all income. Income differences may decline over time, but *some* differences will remain, and even minor differences can be defined as a problem.

WHY ARE THE POOR POOR?

Inasmuch as policy makers cannot even agree on the definition of poverty, it comes as no surprise that they cannot agree on its causes. Yet rationality in public policy-making requires some agreement on the causes of social problems.

Low productivity.   Many economists explain poverty in terms of *human capital theory*. The poor are poor because their economic productivity is low. They do not have the human capital—the knowledge, skills, training, work

[4]Edgar K. Browning, "How Much More Equality Can We Afford?" *The Public Interest* (Spring 1976), 90–110.

habits, abilities—to sell to employers in a free market. Absence from the labor force is the largest single source of poverty. Over two-thirds of the poor are children, mothers of small children, aged or disabled people, who cannot reasonably be expected to find employment. No improvement in the general economy is likely to affect these people directly. Since the private economy has no role for these people, they are largely the responsibility of government. The poorly educated and unskilled are also at a disadvantage in a free labor market. The demand for their labor is low, employment is often temporary, and wage rates are low.

Economic stagnation.   Economists also recognize that some poverty results from inadequate aggregate demand. A serious recession and widespread unemployment raise the proportion of the population living below the poverty line. According to this view, the most effective antipoverty policy is to assure continued ecomonic growth and employment opportunity. Historically, the greatest reductions in poverty have occurred during prosperous times.

Discrimination.   Discrimination plays a role in poverty that is largely unaccounted for by economic theory. We have already observed that blacks are over three times more likely to experience poverty than whites. It is true that *some* of the income differences between blacks and whites are a product of educational differences between the races. However, blacks earn less than whites even at the same educational level. In 1980, black high school graduates earned an average of $12,109 per year, while white high school graduates earned $17,592. Black college graduates earned an average of $21,107, while white college graduates earned $25,071. If the "free" market operated without interference by discrimination, we would expect very little difference in income between blacks and whites with the same education.

The culture of poverty.   Yet another explanation of poverty centers on the notion of a "culture of poverty." According to this notion, poverty is a "way of life" which is learned by the poor. The culture of poverty involves not just a low income, but indifference, alienation, apathy, and irresponsibility. The culture of poverty fosters a lack of self-discipline to work hard, to plan and save for the future, and to get ahead. The culture of poverty also encourages family instability, immediate gratification, "present-orientedness," instead of "future-orientedness." All of these attitudes prevent the poor from taking advantage of the opportunities which are available to them. Even cash payments do not change the way of life of these hardcore poor very much. According to this theory, additional money will be spent quickly for nonessential or frivolous items.

Opponents of the culture of poverty idea argue that this notion diverts attention from the conditions of poverty that *foster* family instability, present-orientedness, and other ways of life of the poor. The question is really whether a lack of money creates a culture of poverty or vice versa. Reformers are likely to focus on the condition of poverty as the fundamental cause of the social pathologies that afflict the poor.

Disintegrating family structure.   Poverty is closely associated with family structure. As we have seen, poverty is greatest among female-headed households and least among husband-wife households. Family structure affects the income of both black and white families:

	1984 Median Income (dollars)
WHITE	
Married couple families	30,056
wife working	35,176
wife not working	24,246
Female-headed household	
no husband present	15,134
BLACK	
Married couple families	23,418
wife working	28,775
wife not working	14,502
Female-headed household	
no husband present	8,648

It may be fashionable in some circles to view husband-wife families as traditional or even antiquated and to redefine *family* as any household with more than one person. But no worse advice could be given to the poor.

Trends in family composition in the United States are not reassuring. Husband-wife families have declined from 87.5 percent of all families in 1960 to 82.5 percent in 1980, and these families are projected to decline to 75.9 percent of all households by 2000. Female-headed households with no husband present increased from 6.8 percent of all households in 1960 to 14.6 percent in 1980, and they are projected to rise to 20.0 percent of all households in 2000.[5] (The figures for the remaining male-headed households with no wife present are 2.7 percent for 1960, 2.9 percent for 1980, and 4.1 percent projected for 2000.)

Perhaps the most sensitive and controversial topic in social welfare policy is the difference in black and white family structure in America. Racial differences in family composition were observed many years ago;

---

[5]Census Bureau figures cited by U. S. senator Daniel Patrick Moynihan, "Family and Nation," Godkin Lectures, Harvard University, 1985.

these differences were attributed to the savage effects of slavery and discrimination on black families.[6] Yet as late as 1950 these differences were not very great; census figures for that year show 88 percent of white households headed by a husband and wife, compared to 78 percent of black households. By 1980, husband-wife families among white households had declined only slightly to 85.6 percent. But more significant changes occurred in black households: black husband-wife families declined from 78 percent to 59 percent of all black households. It is significant that almost all of this decline in black husband-wife families occurred in *poor* black households. Husband-wife family structure in black middle- and upper-class households has remained fairly stable at around 80 percent.[7]

Why have husband-wife families declined among poor blacks? Much of this decline has occurred in recent years, following the introduction of many new Great Society programs and huge increases in government welfare spending. Could it be that these government programs discouraged husband-wife family life among the poor, and by doing so actually contributed to an *increase* in poverty? We shall explore this possibility in the next section.

"Capitalist exploitation."   Finally, we might consider a Marxist explanation of poverty in a capitalist society. Typically Marxists argue that poverty is maintained by the ruling class in order to serve their self-interest. The poor are available to do society's "dirty work," to take jobs which are physically dirty or dangerous, temporary, dead-end, and underpaid. The poor buy old, used, and defective merchandise that others do not want. The poor are often punished and accused of wrong-doing as a means of upholding societal norms. For example, the poor are called lazy because society values hard-working, industrious people. Poverty allows those in the middle and upper classes to maintain their higher status in society. The poor allow others to improve their position in society by providng a market for legal (and illegal) business activities in the slums. The poor help fill the ranks of the "army of unemployed" who function to keep wage rates low by threatening to take the jobs of striking workers. If we accept this Marxist explanation, then the public policy in a capitalist society will be designed to maintain poverty. Welfare programs will not be designed to alleviate poverty or end poverty but rather to "regulate" the poor.[8] In other words

---

[6]Daniel Patrick Moynihan, *The Negro Family: The Case for National Action* (Washington: Government Printing Office, 1965).

[7]U. S. Bureau of the Census, *Characteristics of the Population Below the Poverty Level: 1980* (Washington: Government Printing Office, 1982). Cited by Charles Murray, *Losing Ground* (New York: Basic Books, 1985), pp. 129–132 and Appendix Table 25.

[8]Frances Fox Piven and Richard A. Cloward, *Regulating the Poor: The Functions of Public Welfare* (New York: Vintage Books, 1971).

welfare policy will be designed to avoid rioting, violence, or revolution, yet guarantee a continuation of poverty.

PUBLIC POLICY AS A CAUSE OF POVERTY

Does government itself create poverty by fashioning social welfare programs and policies which destroy incentives to work, encourage families to break up, and condemn the poor to social dependency? Does the current social welfare system sentence many millions of people to a life of poverty who would otherwise form families, take low-paying jobs, and perhaps with hard work and perseverance, gradually pull themselves and their children into the mainstream of American life?

Poverty in America steadily *declined* from 1950, when about 30 percent of the population was officially poor, to 1970, when about 11 percent of the population was poor. During this period of progress toward the elimination of poverty, government welfare programs were minimal. There were small AFDC programs for women with children who lived alone; eligibility was restricted and welfare authorities checked to see if an employable male lived in the house. There were also federal payments for aged, blind, and disabled poor. Welfare roles were modest; only about 1 to 2 percent of American families received AFDC payments.

With the addition of many new Great Society welfare programs, the downward trend in poverty was ended. Indeed, the numbers and proportion of the population living in poverty began to move upward in the 1970s and early 1980s (see Figure 5-1). This was a period in which AFDC payments were significantly increased and eligibility rules were relaxed. The Food Stamp program was initiated in 1965 and became a major new welfare benefit. Medicaid was initiated in the same year and by the late 1970s became the costliest of all welfare programs. Federal aid to the aged, blind, and disabled was merged into a new SSI program (Supplement Security Income) which quadrupled in numbers of recipients.

Did poverty increase in spite of, or because of, these new social welfare programs? Poverty increased in the 1970s despite a reasonably healthy economy. Discrimination did not become significantly *worse* during this period; on the contrary, the civil rights laws enacted in the 1960s were opening many new opportunities for blacks. Finally, poverty was reduced among the aged due to generous increases in social security benefits. The greatest increases in poverty occurred in families headed by *working age persons*. In short, it is difficult to find alternative explanations for the rise in poverty. We are obliged to consider the possibility that *policy* changes— new welfare programs, expanded benefits, and relaxed eligibility requirements—contributed to increased poverty.

According to Charles Murray, the persons hurt most by current welfare policies are the poor themselves. In his well-titled, yet controversial book *Losing Ground* he argues:

> The most compelling explanation for the marked shift in the fortunes of the poor is that they continued to respond, as they always had, to the world as they found it, but that we—meaning the not-poor and the un-disadvantaged— had changed the rules of their world. . . . The first effect of the new rules was to make it profitable for the poor to behave in the short term in ways that were destructive in the long term. Their second effect was to mask these long-term losses—to subsidize irretrievable mistakes.[9]

Murray contends that current social welfare policy provides many disincentives to family life. The break-up of the family, nearly everyone agrees, is closely associated with poverty. The effect of generous welfare benefits and relaxed eligibility requirements on employment has been argued for centuries. Surveys show that the poor prefer work over welfare, but welfare payments may produce subtle effects on the behavior of the poor. Persons unwilling to take minimum-wage jobs may never acquire the work habits required to move into better-paying jobs later in their lives. Welfare may even help to create a dependent and defeatist subculture, lowering personal self-esteem and contributing further to joblessness, illigitimacy, and broken families.

Murray's policy prescription is a drastic one. He recommends

> . . . scrapping the entire federal welfare and income-suport structure for working age persons, including AFDC (Aid to Families with Dependent Children), Medicaid, Food Stamps, Unemployment Insurance; workers compensation, subsidized housing, disability insurance, and the rest. It would leave the working-age person with no recourse whatever except the job market, family members, friends, and public or private locally funded services. . . . cut the knot, for there is no way to untie it.[10]

The result, he argues, would be less poverty, less illigitancy, more upward mobility, freedom and hope for the poor. "The lives of large numbers of poor people would radically changed for the better." The obstacle to this solution is not only the army of politicians and bureaucrats who want to keep their dependent clients, but more importantly the vast majority of generous and well-meaning middle-class Americans who support welfare programs because they do not understand how badly these programs injure the poor.

---

[9]Charles Murray, *Losing Ground* (New York: Basic Books, 1983), p. 9.
[10]Ibid., pp. 227–228.

Welfare recipients standing in line for the federal cheese giveaway program. (UPI/Bettmann Newsphotos.)

WELFARE DYNAMICS: HOW PERSISTENT IS POVERTY?

Is there a large "underclass" of the persistently poor who are dependent upon welfare payments for most of their lives? If welfare payments really *caused* dependency and poverty, then we would expect to see persons who get on welfare rolls to stay there for a long time. But most poverty is *not* long term, and most welfare dependency is relatively brief, lasting less than three years.

Tracing poor families over time presents a different picture of the nature of poverty and welfare from the "snapshot" view taken in any one year. For example, we know that over the last decade 11 to 15 percent of the nation's population has been officially classified as poor in any one year (see Figure 5-1). However, over a decade as many as 25 percent of the nation's population may have fallen under the poverty line at one time or another.[11] Only *some* poverty is persistent: about 6 percent of the population remains in poverty for over five years. This means that *most* of the people who experience poverty in their lives do so for only a short period of time.

The *persistently poor* are only a minority of the people who ever experience poverty. But the persistently poor place a disproportionate burden on welfare resources. About half of the people on welfare rolls at any one time are persistently poor, that is, likely to remain on welfare for eight or more years. An estimated 73 percent of all black children in the nation will receive welfare benefits sometime during a ten-year period. A smaller but significant 43 percent of all black children will remain on welfare rolls during most of a decade.

Welfare policy must be designed to deal with both persistent and temporary poverty. The Michigan study of 5,000 families showed that of all persons beginning their first spell on the AFDC rolls, 30 percent would go off welfare in 2 years, 40 percent would remain 3 to 7 years, and 30 percent would remain 8 or more years. Thus, for some welfare recipients, welfare payments are a relatively short term aid that helps people over life's difficult times. For others, welfare is a more permanent part of their lives.

What happens in people's lives that leads to welfare dependency? Divorce or separation is the single most common personal event associated with going onto welfare rolls (see Table 5-3). The second most common event is a child born to an unmarried woman. Getting off of welfare is most often associated with marriage. Finding a job and thereby increasing one's income is less frequent.

How frequent is "intergenerational poverty"? There is a great deal of interest in intergenerational aspects of welfare receipt—especially whether children growing up in households receiving welfare are themselves likely to receive it when they establish their own households. However, the University of Michigan studies report that a parent's reliance on welfare has no significant independent effect on welfare dependency of their children after their children reach adulthood.

What implications do these observations about welfare dynamics have for public policy? First of all, for most people who experience poverty, it is only a temporary happening in their lives. It is associated with divorce or separation, job loss, illness or disability, or some other misfortune. Conceivably, in the absence of government welfare programs, some people

[11]Greg J. Duncan, *Years of Poverty, Years of Plenty* (Ann Arbor: Institute of Social Research, 1984).

**TABLE 5-3   Personal Events Associated with Welfare Reliance
(Events Associated with the Beginnings and Endings
of AFDC Spells)**

BEGINNINGS		ENDINGS	
Divorce/Separation	45%	Marriage	35%
Childless, unmarried woman becomes a female head with children	30	Children leave parental home	11
Earnings of female head fell	12	Earnings of female head increased	21
Earnings of others in family fell	3	Earnings of others in family increased	5
Other income fell	1	Transfer Income Increased	14
Other (including unidentified)	9	Other (including unidentified)	14
All	100%	All	100%

Source: Greg J. Duncan and Saul D. Hoffman, "Welfare Dynamics and the Nature of Need." Paper presented at Policy Science Program Conference, Florida State University, Tallahassee, Florida March 5–6, 1986; using data from University of Michigan Panel Study of Income Dynamics.

might remain married who now separate or divorce, knowing that welfare would cushion the financial impact of their decision; and some people may leave an unsatisfactory job knowing that they can rely on welfare. But it is reasonable to assume that most of the *temporary* poverty in America is not a product of any structural characteristic of American society, including government welfare programs. For the temporary poor, welfare is short term assistance, and welfare programs are more akin to insurance—tiding people over the difficult events of life.

For the persistently poor, who constitute half of the nation's welfare rolls at any one time, welfare is not a temporary expedient but a way of life. Many of the persistently poor are single young women who came onto welfare rolls following the birth of their first child. If the welfare system itself is the cause of poverty, *then* its effects are most likely to be observed among these persistently poor. It is important to remember that most spells of welfare dependency are relatively short. This suggests that a brief experience with the welfare system does *not* necessarily create long-term dependency. However, a significant segment of welfare recipients are persistently poor and dependent. It is by no means certain that the welfare system itself causes this long term dependence. But a pattern of continuous welfare dependence may indeed be a product of attitudinal and behavioral characteristics toward family, work, and education which are caused in part by welfare policy itself.

RATIONALITY AND IRRATIONALITY IN THE WELFARE STATE

Nearly one-third of the population of the United States receives some form of government benefit—Social Security, Medicare or Medicaid, disability insurance, veterans' benefits, food stamps, or welfare payments. Since many of these programs overlap it is not really possible to know exactly the total number of people receiving government benefits. We know that in 1983 there were 24 million Social Security retirees, 4 million Social Security disability beneficiaries, 4 million veterans' beneficiaries, 7 million Social Security survivors' beneficiaries, 22 million persons receiving Medicaid, 22 million persons receiving food stamps, 12 million children receiving free school lunches, and over 15 million recipients of cash welfare payments.[12] The "welfare state" now encompasses a very large segment of our society.

A "welfare explosion" occurred in America in the decade between 1965 and 1975. For many years the liberal argument on behalf of social welfare followed clear lines: the United States was spending the largest portion of its budget for defense; programs for the poor, sick, and aged were underfinanced. In order to be more responsive to the needs of the people, it was argued in the 1960s that the nation should "change its priorities" and spend more for social programs than for defense. In 1965, defense expenditures accounted for 42 percent of the federal government's budget, while social welfare expenditures (Social Security, health, and public assistance) accounted for less than 25 percent. (See Figure 5-3). While the mass media focused on the Vietnam War and Watergate, a revolution in national policy priorities was occurring. By 1975, defense spending had dropped to 25 percent of the federal budget, while social welfare spending had grown to 43 percent of the budget. This change signaled a reversal of welfare and defense priorities.

Social welfare is now the largest function of the national government. The rise of the social welfare function occurred during both Democratic (Johnson) and Republican (Nixon and Ford) administrations and during the nation's longest war (Vietnam). Spending for social welfare and health have remained at high levels despite a significant increase in defense spending in the Reagan years.

It is not really possible in this chapter to describe all the problems of the poor in America or to describe all the difficulties in developing rational social welfare policies. But it is possible to describe the general design of

[12]U. S. Bureau of the Census, *Statistical Abstract of the United States 1985*. pp. 357, 36Q5.

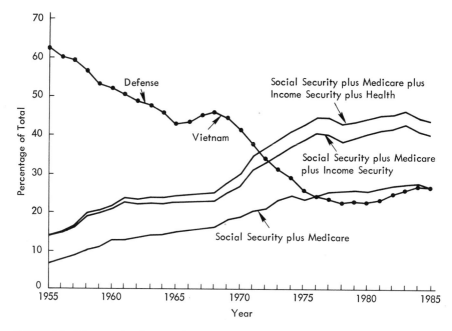

FIGURE 5-3 Defense and welfare spending as a percent of all federal spending.

alternative strategies to deal with poverty in America, to observe how these strategies have been implemented in public policy, and to outline some of the obstacles to a rational approach to the problems of the poor.

THE PUNITIVE STRATEGY: EARLY WELFARE POLICY

Public welfare has been a recognized responsibility of governments in English-speaking nations for almost 400 years. Prior to the 1930s, care of the poor in the United States resembled the early patterns of poor relief established as far back as the Poor Relief Act of 1601 by the English Parliament. Early Elizabethan welfare policy was a combination of punitive as well as alleviative strategies that discouraged all but the most desperately poor from seeking aid, and provided only minimal assistance to those persons clearly unable to care for themselves. The "able-bodied poor," those we call the unemployed, were sent to county workhouses; the "worthy poor"—widows, the aged, orphans, and the handicapped—were sent to poor-houses. Indigent persons who were mentally or physically ill were often kept in the same institutions. Destitute children were kept in county orphanages or sent to foster homes. Thus, public welfare was limited almost exclusively to institutional care; the distribution of food or clothing or other aid to homes of the poor was left to private charities. Whatever relief was provided by the public could never exceed the value of the income of the lowest-paid person in the community who was not on relief. Poor rolls were made public, and relief was forthcoming only if there were no living relatives who could be legally required to support a destitute member of their family.

Under Elizabethan law, the care of the poor was the responsibility of the local governments rather than the state and local governments. The parish in England, and the city or county in the United States, had to care for their poor out of their general tax funds. Because local governments wished to make certain that they were not caring for the poor of other communities, residence requirements were established for welfare care, and communities generally limited their support to those who had been born in the area or who had lived there for some time.

The rationale behind Elizabethan policy—a rationale that has not altogether disappeared from the welfare scene today—was that poverty was a product of moral or character deficiencies in the individual. Only a punitive strategy would dissuade people from indolence and keep poverty to a minimum.

During the period of rapid industrialization and heavy immigration in America (roughly 1870 to 1920) private charities, churches, and big-city political "machines" and "bosses" assisted the impoverished. The political machine operated as a large, although inefficient, brokerage organization. It traded off baskets of food, bushels of coal, minor patronage, and petty favors in exchange for the votes of the poor. To get funds to pay for this primitive welfare assistance, it traded off city contracts, protection, and privileges to business interests who paid off in cash. The machine was not very efficient as a welfare organization, because a great many middlemen came between the cash paid for a business franchise and the Christmas turkey sent to Widow O'Leary. But it worked. Recipients of such assistance were spared much of the red tape and delays experienced by recipients of public assistance today. More importantly, the aid was provided in a very personal fashion without making the recipient feel inferior or dependent. They were trading something valuable—their votes—for the assistance they received.

The Depression brought about significant changes in attitudes toward public welfare and in the policies and administration of welfare programs. Millions who had previously considered welfare recipients to be unworthy of public concern now joined the breadlines themselves. One out of four Americans was unemployed and one out of six was receiving some sort of welfare care. No longer were many people willing to believe that poverty was a product of the individual's moral or character faults. This widespread experience with poverty changed public attitudes toward welfare and led to a change away from Elizabethan policy.

THE PREVENTIVE STRATEGY: SOCIAL SECURITY

The administration of President Franklin D. Roosevelt brought conscious attempts by the federal government to develop rational programs to achieve societal goals. In the most important piece of legislation of the New Deal, the Social Security Act of 1935, the federal government undertook to establish the basic framework for welfare policies at the federal, state, and local levels, and, more importantly, to set forth a new strategy for dealing with poverty. The Depression convinced the national leadership and a great many citizens that indigency could result from forces over which the individual had no control—loss of his job, old age, death of the family breadwinner, or physical disability. The solution was to require individuals to purchase insurance against their own indigency resulting from any of these misfortunes.

The *social insurance* concept devised by the New Deal planners was designed to prevent poverty resulting from uncontrollable forces. Social insurance was based on the same notion as private insurance—the sharing of risks and the setting aside of money for a rainy day. Social insurance was not to be clarity or public assistance; it was to be preventive. It relied upon the individual's compulsory contribution to his own protection. In contrast, public assistance is only alleviative, and relies upon general tax revenues from all taxpayers. Indeed, when the Roosevelt administration presented the social insurance plan to Congress in the Social Security Act of 1935, it was contended that it would eventualy abolish the need for any public assistance program, because individuals would be compelled to protect themselves against poverty!

The distinction between a *social insurance* program and a *public assistance* program is an important one, and has on occasion been a major political issue. If the beneficiaries of a government program are required to make contributions to it before claiming any of its benefits, and if they are entitled to the benefits regardless of their personal wealth, then the program is said to be financed on the *social insurance* principle. On the other hand, if a program is financed out of general tax revenues, and if the recipients are required to show they are poor before claiming its benefits, then the program is said to be financed on the *public assistance* principle.

The key feature of the Social Security Act of 1935 is the Old Age Survivor's Disability and Health Insurance (OASDHI) program, generally known as Social Security. This is a compulsory social insurance program financed by regular deductions from earnings which gives individuals a legal right to benefits in the event of certain occurrences that cause a reduction of their income: old age, death of the head of household, illness in old age, or permanent disability[13] OASDHI is based on the same principle as private insurance—sharing the risk of the loss of income—except that it is a government program and it is compulsory for all workers. OASDHI now covers about nine out of every ten workers in the United States, including the self-employed. The only large group outside its coverage are federal employees who have their own retirement system. Both employees and employers must pay equal amounts toward the employees' OASDHI insurance. The money is paid into three federal "trust funds"— old age and survivor's disability, and Medicare.

Upon retirement, an insured worker is entitled to monthly benefit payments based upon age at retirement and the amount earned during working years. The average monthly amount for a retired worker, age sixty-five, with a spouse, was about $950 in 1985. For most recipients this income is tax-free. In 1972 Congress ordered automatic cost-of-living adjustments (COLAs) indexed to inflation. The formula for calculating CO-LAs increases benefits *faster* than actual cost-of-living increases for the elderly.

OASDHI also provides benefit payments to survivors of an insured worker, including a spouse if there are dependent children. But if there are no dependent children, benefits will not begin until the spouse reaches retirement age. OASDHI provides benefit payments to persons who suffer permanent and total disabilities that prevent them from working for more than one year. Finally, OASDHI provides prepaid health insurance for the aged under Medicare, which we will examine more closely later in the next chapter.

OASDHI is a completely federal program administered by the Social Security Administration in the Department of Health and Human Services. But it has an important indirect effect on state and local welfare programs: by compelling people to insure themselves against the possibility of their own poverty, Social Security has doubtlessly reduced the welfare problems that state and local governments would otherwise face. The growth of OASDHI in numbers of recipients (beneficiaries), average monthly payments, and percentage of the federal government's budget is shown in Table 5-4.

Social Security benefits are specifically exempted from federal income taxes. Persons over sixty-five also receive a double personal exemption on their federal income taxes.

A second important feature of the Social Security Act of 1935 was that it induced states to enact unemployment compensation programs through

---

[13]The original Social Security Act of 1935 did not include disability insurance; this was added by amendment in 1950. Health insurance for the aged—Medicare—was added by amendment in 1965; this is discussed in the next chapter.

TABLE 5-4   Social Security Benefits

	1940	1950	1960	1970	1980	1984
Numbers of Beneficiaries (in thousands)						
Old Age and Survivors	222	3,477	14,157	23,564	30,937	32,657
Disability	—	—	687	2,665	4,682	3,821
Average Monthly Benefit, Single Retired Worker	$18	$36	$63	$101	$305	$420

the imposition of the payroll tax on all employers. A federal unemployment tax is levied on the payroll of employers of four or more workers, but employers paying into state insurance programs that meet federal standards may use these state payments to offset most of their federal unemployment tax. In other words, the federal government threatens to undertake an unemployment compensation program and tax if the states do not do so themselves. This federal program succeeded in inducing all fifty states to establish unemployment compensation programs. However, the federal standards are flexible and the states have considerable freedom in shaping their own unemployment programs. In all cases, unemployed workers must report in person and show that they are willing and able to work in order to receive unemployment compensation benefits. In practice, this means that unemployed workers must register with the U. S. Employment Service (usually located in the same building as the state unemployment compensation office) as a condition of receiving their unemployment checks. States cannot deny workers benefits for refusing to work as strike-breakers or refusing to work for rates lower than prevailing rates. But basic decisions concerning the amount of benefits, eligibility, and the length of time that benefits can be drawn are largely left to the states.

EVALUATION: INTENDED AND UNINTENDED CONSEQUENCES OF SOCIAL SECURITY

The framers of the Social Security Act of 1935 created a "trust fund" with the expectation that a reserve would be built up from social insurance premiums from working persons. The reserve would earn interest, and the interest and principal would be used in later years to pay benefits. Benefits for an individual would be in proportion to his or her contributions. General tax revenues would not be used at all. It was intended that the system would resemble the financing of private insurance. But it turned out not to work that way at all.

The "trust fund."   The social insurance system is now financed on a pay-as-you-go, rather than a reserve, system. Political pressure to raise benefit levels while keeping payments low reduced the reserve to a very minor role in social security finance. Today, the income from all social insurance premiums (taxes) matches the outgo in Social Security benefits. Today, this generation of workers is paying for the benefits of the last generation, and it is hoped that this generation's benefits will be financed by the next generation of workers. Social Security "trust fund" revenues are now lumped together with general tax revenues in the federal budget.

The "dependency ratio."   Since current workers must pay for the benefits of current retirees and other beneficiaries, the "dependency ratio" becomes an important component of evaluating the future of Social Security. The "dependency ratio" for Social Security is the number of recipients as a percentage of the number of contributing workers. Americans are living longer and increasing the dependency ratio. A child born in 1935, when the Social Security system was created, could expect to live only to age sixty-one, four years *less* than the retirement age of sixty-five. The life expectancy of a child born in 1980 is seventy-four years, nine years *beyond* the retirement age. In the early years of Social Security, there were ten workers supporting each retiree—a dependency ratio of 10 to 1. But today, as the U. S. population grows older—due to lower birth rates and longer life span—there are only three workers for each retiree, and by 2010 the dependency ratio will rise to two workers for each retiree.

The "generational compact".   Taxing current workers to pay benefits to current retirees may be viewed as a compact between generations. Each generation of workers in effect agrees to pay benefits to an earlier generation of retirees, in the hope that the next generation will pay for their own retirement. But low birth rates (reducing the number of workers), longer life spans (increasing the number of retirees), and very generous benefits, are straining workers' ability to pay. The generational compact is likely to break before younger workers today reach retirement. Many of these workers, for good reason, have lost their confidence and trust in the system to support them in their old age.

Tax burdens.   Congress had gradually increased the Social Security payroll tax from 3 percent combined employee and employer contributions on the first $3000 of wages, to 14.3 percent combined contribution of the first $44,100 in 1986. The maximum employee contribution has grown from $30 to $3153 since the beginning of the program. The Social Security tax is now *the second largest source of federal revenue.* More important, it is also *the fastest growing source of federal revenue.* Social insurance and welfare payments are now *the largest expenditure of the federal government,* surpassing expenditures for national defense.

Regressive taxes. The Social Security tax is regressive. It takes a much larger share of the income of middle- and low-income workers than wealthy investors and others whose income is from sources other than wages. This was not a serious factor when the payments amounted to very little, but today the size of Social Security revenues—fully one-quarter of the federal government's income—has an important impact on the total revenue structure. The tax is only on *wages,* not total *income.* And wages above certain levels ($44,100 in 1986) are completely untaxed.

Generous benefits. The decline of the insurance concept began in the very first years of the program. The plan to build a large self-financing reserve fund was abandoned in 1939. Benefits are no longer really proportionate to contributions; they are figured more generously for those whose wages are low than for those wages are high. The only remaining aspect of an insurance program is that individuals must have paid into the system to receive its benefits, and beneficiaries are not required to prove they are needy. Most Americans view their benefits as a right.

Early retirement. Generous benefits also encourage early retirement, thereby reducing the number of tax-paying workers and increasing the number of Social Security beneficiaries. Currently workers may retire at age sixty-two with 80 percent of full benefits or at age sixty-five at full benefits. Fifty years ago, when this retirement age was established, people who reached this age had very few years to look forward to and perhaps had little to contribute to the economy. But today, the average person age sixty-five has nearly fifteen years of life remaining and can contribute more years of productive work.

COLAs. Currently social security COLAs are based upon the Consumer Price Index, which estimates the cost of all consumer items each year. These costs include home buying, mortgage interest, child rearing, and other costs which many retirees do not confront. Moreover, most *workers* do not have the same protection against inflation as retirees. Average wage rates do not always match the increases in cost of living. Over the years, the COLAs have improved the economic well-being of Social Security recipients relative to American workers.

Wealthy retirees.   Social Security benefits are paid to all eligible retirees, regardless of whatever other income they may receive. There is no means test for Social Security benefits. The result is that large numbers of affluent Americans receive government checks each month. Of course, they paid into Social Security during their working years and they can claim these checks as a legal "entitlement" under the insurance principle. But currently their benefits far exceed their previous payments.

The success of Social Security in reducing poverty.   Unquestionably Social Security has reduced poverty among the elderly to a point well below the national average (see Figure 5-2). Social Security is the government's only real success in the War on Poverty.

THE POLITICS OF SOCIAL SECURITY REFORM

Political obstacles to rational Social Security reform are awesome. The 36 million people receiving Social Security benefits are the largest block of recipients of *any* government program. They are especially sensitive to any talk of "reform" which suggests any reduction in their benefits. Mostly elderly, these persons vote more regularly than *any* other age category. They want to keep the Social Security program financially sound, but they do not want to give up any benefits, including annual cost-of-living increases.

Many rational changes have been proposed for the Social Security system in order to ensure its continued solvency, for example:

1. In the past, Social Security benefits were fully exempted from personal income taxes. If these benefits were taxed like other income, some money could be channeled back into the trust fund. Retirees whose only source of income was Social Security would not pay any taxes, but wealthy retirees with other income sources woud be required to do so.
2. Congress could reduce or eliminate the automatic cost-of-living increases for Social Security recipients. Benefits are tied to the general Consumer Price Index (CPI) overestimates the real effect of inflation on most retirees.
3. Congress could gradually increase the age at which individuals can retire and receive full Social Security benefits. If the retirement age were gradually moved from sixty-five to sixty-seven years of age, recipient payments would be delayed and the system could be financed on roughly the same basis as it is today. Vitality and life span have increased dramatically since the beginning of the system fifty years ago. A higher retirement age would better reflect the original intention of the system.
4. Congress could reduce the benefits of persons retiring early at age sixty-two to 30 or 50 percent of regular benefits instead of the 80 percent currently allowed.

5. Congress could encourage people to provide more for their own retirement needs and rely less upon Social Security. Indeed, in 1981, Congress moved boldly in this direction by allowing tax deductions for contributions to Individual Retirement Accounts (IRAs). Each income earner can deduct contributions up to $2,000 per year to his or her own IRA account; money in an IRA may be invested in stocks, bonds, bank certificates, and other securities. Interest and capital gains accumulated in an IRA account are not taxed. Money may be withdrawn from an IRA account without penalty after age 59. However, withdrawals are then taxed as ordinary income (in contrast to social benefits which are largely untaxed), but presumably retirees would be in a lower tax bracket than they were when their IRA money was accumulated.

Presidents often appoint special high-level study commissions to make policy recommendations in areas of great political sensitivity, especially when policy consensus is required. President Reagan appointed a National Commission on Social Security Reform in 1982, evenly divided between Republicans and Democrats, liberals and conservatives, and headed by a respected economist, Alan Greenspan. The commission was divided initially over which of the many reform proposals to adopt, but eventually it arrived at a compromise solution for the "short term" (to the year 2000). The commission skillfully involved both President Reagan and Democratic House Speaker Thomas T. "Tip" O'Neill in its compromise and thereby ensured success for its legislative proposals.

The resulting Social Security compromise plan included the following:

1. A one-time six-month delay in cost of living increases; and after 1988 the use of wage rates rather than prices as the basis of calculating cost of living increases.
2. A tax on Social Security benefits for beneficiaries earning over $25,000 ($32,000 for joint returns).
3. A speed-up of Social Security payroll tax increases to 15.3 percent by 1990 and thereafter.
4. Require all new federal employees to join the Social Security system (instead of the Federal Civil Service Retirement System), and prohibit withdrawals of state and local government employees from Social Security.

The commission itself did not recommend raising the retirement age, but it acknowledged that its recommendations would not necessarily solve the "long-term" (twenty-first century) problems confronting the system. The commission "agreed to disagree" on how to solve the future dependency ratio problems when the "baby boom" generation born in the 1950s and 1960s begins to retire. However, the Congress decided on a plan to gradually increase the retirement age from sixty-five to sixty-seven. This retirement age increase will not go into effect until after the year 2000; persons can still retire as early as age sixty-two, but only with reduced benefits. This increase in retirement age will probably solve the Social

Security system's long-term financial problems. One elated U.S. senator exclaimed, "The cynics are wrong. There are occasions when Congress will rally to the task and do what is politically hard."[14]

THE ALLEVIATIVE STRATEGY: PUBLIC ASSISTANCE

The Social Security and Unemployment Compensation programs were based upon the insurance strategy for preventing indigence, but the federal government also undertook in the Social Security Act of 1935 to help the states in providing public assistance payments to certain needy persons. This strategy was designed to alleviate the conditions of poverty; there was no effort to attack the causes of poverty. The notion was to provide a minimum level of subsistence to certain categories of needy adults—the aged, blind, and disabled—and to provide for the care of dependent children. This was to be done by providing small amounts of cash in monthly payments through state-administered weelfare programs. The federal grant-in-aid device was employed because welfare functions traditionally had been the responsibility of state and local governments. The entire federal effort in public assistance was supposed to be temporary in duration, declining in importance as social insurance took over the burden of assuring security.

Cash programs: SSI and AFDC.   Today the federal government directly aids three categories of welfare recipients—the aged, the blind, and the disabled—under the Supplemental Security Income program (SSI). The federal government also provides grants to the states to assist the fourth and largest category—families with dependent children. Within broad outlines of the federal policy, states retain considerable discretion in the Aid to Families with Dependent Children (AFDC) program in terms of the amounts of money appropriated, benefits to be paid to recipients, rules of eligibility, and rules of the programs. Each state may choose to grant assistance beyond the amounts supported by the national government. Each state establishes its own standards to determine need. As a result, there is a great deal of variation among the states in ease of access to welfare rolls and in the size of welfare benefits.

Federal standards for state AFDC programs, established as a prerequisite to receiving federal aid, allow considerable flexibility in state programs. Federal law requires the states to make financial contributions to their public assistance programs and to supervise these programs either

[14]Congressional Quarterly, *Weekly Report,* March 12, 1983, p. 487, quoting Senator William L. Armstrong (R.–Col.).

directly or through local agencies. Whatever standards a state adopts must be applicable throughout the state, and there must be no discrimination in these welfare programs. The federal government demands periodic reporting from the states, insists that states administer federally supported programs under a merit personnel system, and prevents the states from imposing unreasonable residence requirements on recipients. But in important questions of administration, standards of eligibility, residence, types of assistance, and amounts of payments, the states are free to determine their own welfare programs. Beginning in 1972, the federal government required "employable" welfare recipients to register for the Work Incentive (WIN) program; individuals prepared for work are referred to jobs while others are enrolled in training or job experience programs. But the definition of "employable" generally excludes the aged, the ill, and mothers of preschool children; indeed, only a tiny fraction of all welfare recipients have participated in the WIN program.

General assistance.   It is important to note that the federal government helps provide cash assistance to only four categories of needy persons— aged, blind, disabled (through SSI), and families with dependent children (through AFDC). Aid to persons who do *not* fall into any of these categories but who, for one reason or another, are "needy," is referred to as "general assistance." General assistance programs are entirely state-financed and state-administered. Without federal participation, these programs differ radically from state to state in terms of the persons aided, the criteria for eligibility, the amount and nature of benefits, and administration of financing. Many of these programs continue to resemble Elizabethan welfare policy. The average general assistance payment is lower than comparable payments in federally supported programs.

States also continue to maintain institutions to care for those individuals who are so destitute, alone, or ill that money payments cannot meet their needs. These institutions include state orphanages, homes for the aged, and homes for the mentally ill. They are, for the most part, state-financed as well as state-administered. However, persons living in these tax-supported institutions may be eligible for federal assistance—Social Security, SSI, and Medicare and Medicaid, for example.

In-kind programs.   Public assistance in the form of in-kind (noncash) benefits expanded very rapidly between 1965 and 1980. *Medicaid* is the costliest of these in-kind programs, providing federally assisted medical care for the poor. Over 22 million people or about 10 percent of the population of the United States receive Medicaid benefits. The Food Stamp program, administered by the Department of Agriculture, now costs more than either SSI or AFDC. Eligible persons may obtain free food stamps, generally from county welfare department. The stamps may then be used to purchase food at supermarkets. This program also enrolls about 22 million people or 10 percent of the population. Eligibility for both food stamps and Medicaid now extends to many low-income persons who are not poor enough to qualify for cash payments under SSI or AFDC.

Housing assistance is also a major in-kind benefit program for the poor. An estimated six million people live in two million low-income public housing units in the nation and many more benefit from various federal housing subsidies.

Public assistance recipients are generally eligible for participation in a variety of other social programs. These include school lunches and milk; job training; various educational and childcare programs and services; special food programs for women, infants, and children (WIC); home heating and weatherization assistance; free legal services; and more. Some of these programs are described elsewhere in this volume (Medicaid, Chapter 6; educational programs, Chapter 7).

The effect of these multiple social service programs on the alleviation of poverty is considerable. Indeed, it is difficult to determine just how poor the poor really are because it is difficult to cost out the dollar value of the many separate programs serving the poor.

EVALUATION: THE WELFARE MESS

While the social insurance programs (OASDHI, Medicare, and Unemployment Compensation) are politically popular and enjoy the support of large numbers of active beneficiaries, the public assistance programs are far less popular. They are disliked by many national, state, and local legislators who must vote the appropriations for them; they are resented by many taxpayers who must bear ever-increasing burdens; they are denounced by the officials and caseworkers who must administer them; and they are accepted with bitterness by those who were intended to benefit from them.

Social dependency. Certainly our public assistance programs have not succeeded in reducing dependency. Between 1965 and 1978 the number of welfare recipients more than tripled. It was the Aid to Families with Dependent Children (AFDC), and the Medicaid and Food Stamp programs, that became the largest and most expensive of all welfare programs, and the most controversial. In the 1980s enrollments leveled off in most major programs: SSI at about 4 million people, AFDC at about 11 million people, and Medicaid and Food Stamps at about 22 million each.

Photo by Fred W. McDarrah.

The working poor. Despite these levels of dependency upon welfare and the growing burden of welfare costs, many of the nation's poor do not receive public assistance. There were 34 million poor people in America in 1984, perhaps 10 million of whom receive no federal welfare benefits. Many of these poor are working poor, who are ineligible for welfare assistance because they hold jobs, even though these jobs pay very little.

Disparities among states. State administration of welfare has resulted in wide disparities among the states in eligibility requirements and benefits levels. For example, in 1982 average AFDC monthly payments ranged from a high of $422 per family in Wisconsin to a low of $89 per family in Mississippi.[15] In terms of welfare payments, it is far better to be poor in a wealthy high-tax state than in a poor low-tax one.

Administration. Operating policies and administration of welfare have produced a whole series of problems including disincentives to family life and work. Until recently, many states denied AFDC benefits if a man was living with his family, even though he had no work. This denial was based on the assumption that an employable man in the household meant that children were no longer dependent upon the state. Thus, if an unemployed husband lived with his family, he could watch them go hungry; if he abandoned them, public assistance would enable them to eat. Moreover, an unmarried mother could get on welfare rolls more easily than a married mother (who had to prove she was not receiving support from her husband). These rules have been relaxed in recent years, but it is still more difficult for whole families to get on public assistance than for fatherless families.

Cash versus in-kind assistance. The merits of cash versus goods and services as a form of public assistance have long been debated. It is frequently argued that cash payments are ineffective in alleviating poverty because recipients are often unable to manage household money. They fall prey to advertising which encourages them to spend money for nonessential items and to overlook the food and clothing needs of themselves and their children. Assistance in the form of goods (for example, food stamps which can only be used to purchase basic food items) and services (for example, health care, daycare for children, home management counseling) might represent a more effective approach. However, recipients themselves resent the goods and services approach, charging that it is paternalistic, that it curtails flexibility in family spending, and that it implies irresponsibility on the part of the recipient. Today most caseworkers argue for joint provision

---

[15]*Statistical Abstract of the United States 1985, p. 380.*

of cash and goods and services; they contend that cash is more effective when accompanied by services, and services are more effective when accompanied by cash.

Casework.   Welfare administration is made difficult by the heavy load assigned to caseworkers, many of whom are recent college graduates. They spend much of their time determining eligibility, computing payments, and filling out an avalanche of forms. With caseloads averaging up to 100 or 200 families, their contacts with recipients must be hurried, infrequent, and impersonal. Caseworkers are unable to develop any close bonds of friendship or rapport with persons in need of help. Recipients often come to view caseworkers with distrust or worse. The strain on caseworkers is very great; big-city welfare departments report high turnover among caseworkers.

Fraud.   Fraudulent welfare claims are a source of concern for federal and state administrators. The U.S. Office of Management and Budget cites surveys which indicate that 40 percent of all welfare claims under the AFDC program are inaccurate.[16] About 10 percent of AFDC recipients are not eligible for any payment, 23 percent are receiving greater payments than they should, and another 8 percent are underpaid. The Food Stamp program experiences about the same proportion of ineligibles and overpayments as the AFDC program. Most of these inaccuracies are technical errors rather than outright fraud. It is estimated that about 10 percent of Medicaid payments are also fraudulent. The recipients of fraudulent income under Medicaid are unethical doctors, clinics, and laboratories who charge Medicaid for services not actually provided to poor patients.

Work disincentives.   In most states, if a recipient of assistance takes a full-time job, assistance checks are reduced or stopped. If the recipient is then laid off, it may take some time to get back on the welfare roll. In other words, employment is uncertain, while assistance is not. More importantly, the jobs available to most recipients are very low-paying jobs which do not produce much more income than does assistance, particularly when transportation, childcare, and other costs of working are considered. All these facts discourage people from looking for work.

Social dependency and disincentives to work are magnified by the "pyramiding effect" of separate public assistance and social service programs. A family on the welfare rolls is generally entitled to participate in the Food Stamp program, to receive health care through Medicaid, to gain access to free or low-rent public housing, to receive free lunches in public

---

[16]*The Budget of the United States Government,* 1975 (Washington, D.C.: Government Printing Office, 1974), pp. 128–129.

schools, and to receive a variety of other social and educational benefits at little or no cost to themselves. These benefits and services available to the poor are not counted as income, yet the nonpoor must pay for similar services out of their own earnings. If a family head on welfare takes a job, he or she not only loses welfare assistance, but, more importantly perhaps, becomes ineligible for food stamps, Medicaid, public housing, and many other social services. Various studies have reported that an urban family would have to earn more than $20,000 per year to live as well as a family receiving just four basic social benefits—public assistance, food stamps, school lunches, and Medicaid.[17] Thus, only a fairly well-paying job would justify going off the welfare rolls.

THE CURATIVE STRATEGY: THE WAR ON POVERTY

"This Administration today, here and now, declares unconditional war on poverty in America." President Lyndon B. Johnson made this declaration in his 1964 State of the Union message and followed with a wide range of Great Society programs.[18] The "War on Poverty" promised a new *curative* strategy in dealing with the problems of the poor. In contrast to the alleviative strategy of public assistance, or the preventive strategy of social insurance, the curative strategy was supposed to break the cycle of poverty and provide escape routes by which the poor could become self-supporting and capable of earning adequate incomes. The emphasis was on "Rehabilitation, not Relief." Programs were aimed, whether accurately or inaccurately, at curing the cause of poverty rather than alleviating its symptoms.

Job training. Federal job training programs were a very important part of the curative strategy. These programs were designed to increase the skills and employment opportunities of the poor through both classroom and on-the-job training. A variety of programs begun in the Kennedy and Johnson administrations were brought together in 1973 under the Comprehensive Employment and Training Act (CETA).

CETA provided federal funds to both private and governmental employers who agreed to recruit and train low-skilled persons to fill regular job vacancies. The employers were reimbursed for the costs of training, remedial education, counseling, and supporting services. In addition, fed-

---

[17]Report prepared for the Joint Economic Subcommittee on Fiscal Policy released July 8, 1973, reported in Congressional Quarterly, *The Future of Social Programs* (Washington, D.C.: Congressional Quarterly, 1973), p. 87.

[18]Major social legislation of the Great Society included the Elementary and Secondary Education Act (1965), Medicare (1965), Medicaid (1965), and the Food Stamp Act (1964), all of which are discussed elsewhere in this book. The Great Society also included the Economic Opportunity Act (1964) and the many programs and services which evolved from it.

eral funds provided allowances for trainees to support them during the training period. In addition to CETA's job training program, a general "Public Service Employment" program was added in 1975 which simply provided federal money to local governments to create public service jobs. CETA was never a very popular program in Washington, and it was phased out by the Reagan administration. Public service jobs were viewed as dead-end, make-work, temporary jobs, which really did not assist the poor in becoming permanent productive members of the labor force. The public service jobs component of CETA was ended altogether in 1982. Federal allowances for trainees in job training programs were viewed as handouts which "enticed people to enter training programs for short-term income rather than long-term employability gains."

The Reagan Administration believed that general employment training block grants to the states would be more effective than CETA-administered grants for individual training programs throughout the country. The Job Partnership Training Act (JPTA) in 1982 authorized block grants for employment training in the states. Each state receives JPTA funds based on its number of poor and unemployed. Governors are required to establish private industry councils composed of business, labor, and community representatives in local areas. These councils are supposed to guide job training efforts and distribute federal funds.

The Job Corps was a specialized program for disadvantaged, unemployable youth. It provided education, vocational training, and work experience for its enrollees. The Job Corps was begun with the Economic Opportunity Act of 1964 under President Johnson and it continued for twenty years. The Reagan administration recommended its elimination arguing that it failed to meet the needs of those it was intended to serve. Training slots were estimated to cost $15,000 each, but 65 percent of all trainees dropped out without finishing training and only 35 percent of all participants were recorded as being placed in jobs.[19]

One major problem in dealing with unemployment is accurately assessing the meaning of the U. S. Labor Department's official "unemployment rate." The official unemployment rate is determined by a national survey conducted by the Bureau of Labor Statistics. The BLS asks a national sample of persons sixteen years of age and over, "Are you employed?" If the answer is no, BLS asks, "Are you looking for work?" If the answer is yes, then this person is counted as unemployed. Today's officially unemployed include teenagers, second and third wage earners in the same household, and individuals who sign up for jobs at the U. S. Employment Service because doing so is a requirement to receive certain welfare benefits. Years ago, the officially unemployed were almost exclusively heads of households with no other source of income. Hence, unemployment today is not the

[19]*Budget of the United States Government 1985*, pp. 5–98.

equivalent of unemployment a few decades ago. However, it should also be noted that the official rate does not include "discouraged workers"— those who say they are not currently looking for work because they have no hope of finding a job.

Community action. President Lyndon B. Johnson's Great Society also included the Economic Opportunity Act of 1964. Communities were urged to form "community action agencies," composed of representatives of government, private organizations, and, most importantly, the poor themselves. A federal Office of Economic Opportunity (OEO) gave financial support to antipoverty programs devised by the local community action agency. Projects might include (but were not limited to) literacy training, health services, homemaker services, legal aid for the poor, neighborhood service centers, manpower vocational training, and childhood development activities. The act also envisioned that a community action agency would help organize the poor so that they could become participating members of the community and avail themselves of the many public programs designed to serve the poor.

The most popular antipoverty project was Operation Head Start— usually a cooperative program between the community action agency and the local school district that permitted six to eight weeks of special summer preparation for preschoolers before their entry into kindergarten or first grade. There was never any clear evidence that Head Start actually helped remedy learning problems. Studies comparing poor children who attended Head Start with poor children who had not, showed that differences in achievement levels disappeared after several years. Nevertheless, Head Start remained popular among parents even if it had no lasting effect on children.

Another popular antipoverty project was the Legal Services program. Many community action agencies established free legal services to the poor to assist them in rent disputes, contracts, welfare rules, minor police action, housing regulations, and so on. Today the Legal Services Corporation is a nonprofit corporation financed by Congress from tax dollars. More than 5000 attorneys throughout the country are supported by the corporation.

Even before President Johnson left office in 1969, the War on Poverty had become another unpopular war. The Nixon administration "reorganized" OEO in 1973, turning over some programs like Head Start to other agencies. In 1975, the Ford administration and Congress abolished OEO altogether. The reasons for the failure of the War on Poverty are complex.

The Office of Economic Opportunity was always the scene of great confusion. New and untried programs were organized at breakneck speed. There was a high turnover in personnel. There was delay and confusion in releasing funds to local community action agencies. There was scandal and corruption, particularly at the local level. Community action agencies with young and inexperienced personnel frequently offended experienced governmental administrators as well as local political figures. Congressional action was uncertain, the project's life was extended for a year at a time, and appropriations were often delayed. But most damaging of all, even though programs were put in operation, there was little concrete evidence that these programs were successful in their objectives, that is, in eliminating the causes of poverty.

The demise of the economic opportunity programs cannot be attributed to political partisanship. Daniel P. Moynihan summarized the community action experiences as follows:

> Over and again the attempts by official and quasi-official agencies (such as the Ford Foundation) to organize poor communities led first to the radicalization of the middle-class persons who began the effort; next to a certain amount of stirring among the poor, but accompanied by heightened radical antagonism *on the part of the poor* if they happened to be black; next to retaliation from the larger white community; whereupon it would emerge that the community action agency, which had talked so much, been so much in the headlines, promised so much in the way of change in the fundamentals of things, was powerless. A creature of a Washington bureaucracy, subject to discontinuation without notice. Finally, much bitterness all around.[20]

WELFARE POLITICS: THE SOCIAL "SAFETY NET"

Welfare policy in a conservative administration can be expected to stress several themes: (1) Only the "truly needy" should receive benefits; these are the "deserving poor"—aged, blind, disabled, children, and others who cannot reasonably be expected to work. (2) Welfare benefits should not become disincentives to work or create welfare dependency. (3) Able-bodied adults should be required to work as a condition of aid. (4) Fraud should be eliminated. (5) The growth of welfare programs and welfare costs should be controlled. (6) Responsibility for administration and finance of welfare programs should be shifted to the state and local governments whenever possible. (7) Private charities should be encouraged to carry as much of the welfare burden as possible.

The Reagan administration, as part of its Program for Economic Recovery, attempted *to cut the rate of growth* in social insurance and public assistance programs. Despite widespread publicity given to welfare "cuts" by the Reagan administration, more dollars were spent for the major programs than during the Carter administration. Expenditures for Social Security, unemployment compensation, Medicare, Medicaid, SSI, AFDC, and

[20]Daniel P. Moynihan, *Maximum Feasible Misunderstanding: Community Action in the War on Poverty* (New York: The Free Press, 1969), pp. 1324–1325.

food stamps continued to rise each year but their *rate* of increase was less than in previous years.

The Reagan administration announced its intention of maintaining a social "safety net" for the truly needy. Initially the "safety net" programs would be free from significant alterations. These programs were:

Social Security (OASDHI)
Medicare
Unemployment Compensation
Supplemental Security Income (SSI)
Veterans Benefits

Note that the major thrust of these favored programs is care to the *aged*. Programs for the *poor* were not so favored, including:

Aid to Families with Dependent Children (AFDC)
Food Stamps
Medicaid
Public Housing
Job training
Legal Services

TABLE 5-5   Federal Social Welfare Program Expenditures

	BILLIONS $		
	1975	1980	1984
Social Insurance			
Social Security OASDI	63.7	118.1	178.2
Medicare	14.7	32.1	57.5
Federal Employee Retirement	13.3	26.6	38.1
Railroad Retirement	3.0	5.1	5.4
Unemployment Compensation	3.4	18.0	18.4
Public Assistance			
SSI	4.8	6.4	8.5
AFDC	7.5	6.9	8.9
Home Energy Assistance	—	1.7	2.0
Food Stamps	4.9	9.6	12.4
Child Nutrition	2.1	4.2	5.7
Medicaid	7.0	18.0	20.7
Housing Assistance	2.5	9.2	11.3
Total			
Dollars	126.9	255.1	367.1
Percent of Federal Expenditures	44.3%	44.2%	43.1%

Sources: *Statistical Abstract of the United States 1985*, pp. 356–357; *Budget of the United States Government 1986*.

The Reagan administration tried to reduce federal funding in this "lower tier" of social welfare programs but their effects were generally unsuccessful. Spending for AFDC, Food Stamps, Medicaid, and public housing continued to increase during the Reagan years (see Table 5-5), although the rate of growth was slower than in the previous decade. Job training was reorganized: CETA became the Job Partnership Training Act with block grants to the states, and overall federal spending for job training was reduced. Reagan fought hard for the elimination of the Legal Services Corporation, which is supposed to provide free legal services to the poor. But Legal Services successfully fought off all efforts to abolish it in the Congress.

In summary, the nation's social welfare system remained intact even during a conservative presidential administration. It is easy for liberal commentators to overlook this most important observation about social welfare policy in America: *major social welfare programs were virtually unchanged during the Reagan administration and spending for social welfare continued to rise.*

ALTERNATIVE STRATEGIES IN WELFARE POLICY

A different strategy in social welfare policy is set forth by advocates of the "negative income tax" or "guaranteed annual income." They argue that reforming current welfare programs is hopeless—welfare payments will always mean punitive rules, meddling social workers, and humiliation of the poor. They propose scrapping the welfare system altogether in favor of a general system of income payments entirely separate from any other kind of social service. The negative income tax would guarantee everyone a minimum income, and it would encourage recipients to work by allowing them to keep a proportion of their earnings without deducting them from the minimum guarantee. For example, a guarantee might be set at $6,000 for a family of four with an earnings reduction of 50 percent. Under such a system a family with no earnings would receive a payment of $6,000; a family with $6,000 in earnings would receive a payment of $3,000 for a total income of $9,000; and a family earning $12,000, the break-even point, would receive no government benefit. The proposal seems like a logical extension of the progressive income tax. Everyone would file a declaration of income as they do now; most would pay taxes as they do now, but those at the low end of the income scale would receive payments (negative taxes). Checks would be issued directly from the Treasury Department with little or no participation by federal or state welfare bureaucracies.

The advantages of the negative income tax strategy are: (1) it encourages work by phasing out benefits gradually as earnings increase; (2) administrative expenses and welfare bureaucracies are reduced by sending checks directly from the U. S. Treasury; (3) benefits would be the same nationwide; (4) the working poor would be aided.

However, the long-run impact of such a policy reform is difficult to predict. The first problem is cost: a negative income tax or guaranteed annual income plan would double the cost of welfare over the current system and might run three to four times greater. There is no reliable information on the number of working poor who would apply for assistance. Moreover, Congress would be under constant pressure to raise the minimum income for each year.

It is not certain whether this expansion of welfare assistance to many working families would increase or reduce economic dependency in America. It is conceivable that such an expansion in welfare assistance would destroy the "work ethic" and encourage dependence by making the acceptance of such assistance a common family practice, extending well up into the middle class. Certainly the percentage of the population receiving some form of public assistance would be greatly increased; it is conceivable that 20 percent of the population would eventually gain access to welfare rolls under a guaranteed annual income program. (Social science research on the effect of guaranteed income on the working behavior of the poor is discussed in Chapter 14.)

A guaranteed annual income does not necessarily tackle the problem of pyramiding welfare programs. Even if the prospect of keeping fifty cents on each dollar earned proved to be an incentive, benefits under multiple-income-test programs might be lost—notably, food stamps, Medicaid, and public housing—again leaving the working poor worse off than the non-working poor. Moreover, earnings would also be reduced by costs of working—transportation, clothing, etc.—and Social Security contributions. If working provides little improvement in the lives of the poor, we can hardly expect them to join the labor force.

There is widespread agreement that the nation's welfare system is in urgent need of reform. But there is little agreement on the direction of reform. The problems of welfare reform illustrate again the political obstacles to rational policy making.

SUMMARY

The difficulties of rational policy making are evidenced in policies and programs dealing with the poor.

1. Contrasting definitions of the problem of poverty constitute an obstacle to rational policy making. Official government sources define poverty in terms of minimum dollar amounts required for subsistence. Poverty, by this definition, is declining over time.

2. If poverty is defined in relative terms, then the problem of poverty is nearly insoluble. Income inequality is only slowly decreasing over time. However, unless all incomes in America are equalized among all persons, there will always be some individuals who fall below average income levels. Even if the differences in incomes are substantially narrowed, small differences may come to have great symbolic value and the problem of "poverty" will remain.

3. Contrasting explanations of poverty also make it difficult to formulate a rational policy. Is poverty a product of a lack of knowledge, skills, and training? Or recession and unemployment? Or a "culture of poverty"? Certainly the disintegration of the traditional husband-wife family is closely associated with poverty. How can government devise a rational policy to keep families together, or at least not encourage them to dissolve?

4. Government welfare policies themselves may be a significant cause of poverty. Poverty in America had steadily declined prior to the development of new Great Society programs, the relaxation of eligibility requirements for welfare assistance, and the rapid increase of welfare expenditures of the 1970s. To what extent do government programs themselves encourage social dependency and harm the long-term prospects of the poor?

5. Social welfare is now the largest function of the national government, even larger than national defense. Prior to 1965 it was argued that America should change its priorities and spend more on social welfare than national defense. Today America does just that, yet poverty remains, as well as dissatisfaction with welfare policies.

6. The strategy of early welfare policy was to discourage poverty by providing only minimal assistance, generally in institutions, to the most destitute in society. Heavy reliance was placed on local governments and upon private charity.

7. The social insurance concept was designed as a preventive strategy to insure persons against indigence arising from old age, death of a family breadwinner, or physical disability. But the Social Security "trust fund" idea remains in name only. Today each generation of workers is expected to pay the benefits for each generation of retirees. Yet after the year 2000 the "dependency ratio" will rise to a point when it will be very difficult for workers then to support the large number of Social Security recipients.

8. Rational reform of Social Security requires the political courage to raise taxes, tax benefits payments, limit cost of living allowance increases, or increase the retirement age. In 1983 the National Commission on Social Security Reform recommended a compromise reform package incorporating a combination of these reforms.

9. The federal government also pursues an alleviative strategy in assisting the poor with a variety of direct cash and in-kind benefit programs. The Supplemental Security Income program (SSI) provides direct federal

cash payments to the aged, the blind, and disabled. As a welfare program, SSI is paid from general tax revenues, and recipients must prove their need. The federal government also provides assistance to the states for the Aid to Families with Dependent Children (AFDC) welfare program. The largest in-kind welfare programs are the federal Food Stamp and Medicaid programs.

10. Social dependence under these programs grew rapidly during the 1970s despite a reasonably healthy economy. The Reagan administration has slowed the growth of these programs, but serious problems remain. Many of the nation's poor do not receive any aid, notably the working poor. Benefits are uneven among the states. Program policies include disincentives to both family life and work. Multiplication of programs makes estimates of the real income of the poor very difficult. A pyramiding of the many separate program benefits adds to the disincentives to work.

11. Despite a conservative administration in the White House, all major social insurance and welfare programs have not only survived intact but also grown in size and cost. Neither liberals nor conservatives, Democrats nor Republicans, have been able to achieve rational reform of social welfare policy.

BIBLIOGRAPHY

AARON, HENRY J., *Policies and the Professors: The Great Society in Perspective.* Washington: Brookings Institution, 1978.

ANDERSON, MARTIN, *Welfare: The Political Economy of Welfare Reform.* Stanford: Hoover Institution Press, 1978.

BANFIELD, EDWARD C., *The Unheavenly City.* Boston: Little, Brown, 1968.

DERTHICK, MARTHA, *Policy Making for Social Security.* Washington: Brookings Institution, 1979.

DUNCAN, GREG, J., *Years of Poverty, Years of Plenty.* Ann Arbor: Institute for Social Research, University of Michigan, 1984.

HARRINGTON, MICHAEL, *The Other America.* New York: Macmillan, 1962.

KAHN, ALFRED J., *Social Policy and Social Services.* New York: Random House, 1979.

LEVITAN, SAR A., *Programs in Aid of the Poor for the 1980's.* Baltimore: Johns Hopkins Press, 1980.

MORRIS, ROBERT, *Social Policy of the American Welfare State.* New York: Harper & Row, 1979.

MOYNIHAN, DANIEL PATRICK, *Maximum Feasible Misunderstanding: Community Action and the War on Poverty.* New York: Free Press, 1969.

————, *The Politics of a Guaranteed Income.* New York: Random House, 1973.

MURRAY, CHARLES, *Losing Ground.* New York: Basic Books, 1984.

PIVEN, FRANCES FOX AND RICHARD A. CLOWARD: *Regulating the Poor: The Functions of Public Welfare.* New York: Random House, 1971.

RODGERS, HARRELL R., *Poverty Amid Plenty: A Political and Economic Analysis.* Reading: Addison-Wesley, 1979.

SALAMON, LESTER M., *Welfare: The Elusive Consensus.* New York: Praeger, 1978.

HEALTH

the pathology of rational policy

Medicaid, providing medical care for the poor, is the most costly of all federal welfare programs. (Ken Karp)

HEALTH CARE OR MEDICAL CARE?

There is no better illustration of the dilemmas of rational policy making in America than in the field of health. Again, the first obstacle to rationalism is in defining the problem. Is our goal to be *good health*—that is, whether we live at all (infant mortality), how well we live (days lost to sickness), and how long we live (life spans and adult mortality)? Or is our goal to be *good medical care*—frequent and inexpensive visits to the doctor, well-equipped and accessible hospitals, and equal access to medical care by rich and poor alike?

Perhaps the first lesson in health policy is understanding that good medical care does *not* necessarily mean good health. Good health correlates best with factors over which doctors and hospitals have no control: heredity, lifestyle (smoking, eating, drinking, exercise, worry), and the physical environment (sewage disposal, water quality, conditions of work, etc.). Most of the bad things that happen to people's health are beyond the reach of doctors and hospitals.

Of course, doctors can set broken bones, stop infections with drugs, and remove swollen appendixes. And if you happen to be suffering from these or similar problems you want the careful attention of a skilled physician. But in the long run, infant mortality, sickness and disease, and life span are affected very little by the quality of medical care.[1] If you want a long healthy life, choose parents who have lived a long healthy life, and then do all the things your mother always told you to do: don't smoke, don't drink, get lots of exercise and rest, don't overeat, relax, and don't worry. You can spend millions on medical care, and you will not enjoy the same good health as you will by following these traditional guidelines.

Historically, most of the reductions in infant and adult death rates have resulted from public health and sanitation including immunization against smallpox, clean public water supply, sanitary sewage disposal, improved diets, and increased standards of living. Many of the leading causes of death today (see Table 6-1) including heart disease, stroke, cirrhosis of the liver, accidents, and suicides are closely linked to personal habits and lifestyles and beyond the reach of medicine. Thus, the greatest contribution to better health is likely to be found in altered personal habits and lifestyles, rather than in more medical care. Nonetheless, health policy in America is largely centered around the questionable notion that better medical care means better health.

The overall death rate in the United States (the number of deaths

---

[1]The literature on this point is extensive. See, for example, Victor R. Fuchs, *Who Shall Live? Health, Economics, and Social Choice* (New York: Basic Books, 1974); Nathan Glazer, "Paradoxes of Health Care," *The Public Interest* (Winter 1971), 62–77; Leon R. Kass, "Regarding the End of Medicine and the Pursuit of Health," *The Public Interest* (Summer 1975), 11–42.

TABLE 6-1 Leading Causes of Death[a]

	1960	1965	1970	1975	1980	1985
All Causes	954.7	943.2	945.3	888.5	883.4	875.9
Heart disease	369.0	367.4	362.0	336.2	334.3	325.2
Stroke (cerebrovascular)	108.0	103.7	101.9	91.1	80.5	64.8
Cancer	149.2	153.5	162.8	171.7	181.9	192.9
Accidents	52.3	55.7	56.4	48.4	48.4	38.9
Pneumonia	37.3	31.9	30.9	26.1	26.7	26.4
Diabetes	16.7	17.1	18.9	16.5	15.5	15.7
Cirrhosis	11.3	12.8	15.5	14.8	13.8	11.3
Infant diseases	37.4	28.6	21.3	12.5	10.1	10.8
Emphysema, asthma	[b]	14.4	15.2	12.0	10.0	9.0
Suicide	10.6	11.1	11.6	12.7	12.5	11.7
Homicide	4.7	5.5	8.3	10.0	9.4	8.2

[a]Deaths per 100,000 population per year.
[b]Not separately recorded.
Source: U.S. National Center for Health Statistics, *Vital Statistics of the United States,* published annually (Washington, D.C.: Government Printing Office); and *Monthly Vital Statistics Report,* October 1985.

per 100,000 people) continues to decline. Considerable progress is being made by the nation in reducing both infant and adult death rates for many of the major killers—heart disease, stroke, pneumonia, diabetes, and emphysema. However, the cancer death rate continues to rise despite increased medical spending, as does the number of deaths attributable to suicide and homicide. Moreover, death rates for the poor and blacks, although declining over time, remain much higher than the death rates for the nonpoor and nonblack.

HEALTH CARE FOR THE POOR

Society feels a special responsibility for providing health care to the poor. No one should be denied medical care for lack of money; no one should suffer or die for lack of financial resources to obtain adequate food; nor should anyone suffer desperation or pain for the lack of medical care that money can buy. We can find general agreement on these broad ethical principles. The tough questions arise when we try to find a way of implementing these principles.

It is not difficult to demonstrate that the poor and the black in America have higher mortality rates than the affluent and the white. For example, the infant mortality rate is used frequently as a general indicator of the adequacy of health care. Infant mortality rates have been consistently higher for blacks than for whites (see Figure 6-1). Infant mortality rates have

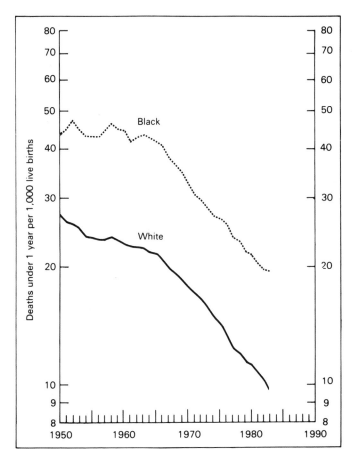

FIGURE 6-1   Infant Mortality Rates by Race. (Source: National Center for Health Statistics, "Advance Report of Final Mortality Statistics, 1982," *Monthly Vital Statistics Report,* Vol. 33, No. 9, Supplement, December 20, 1984, p. 6.)

declined for both races since 1950, but black infant deaths have continued to be significantly higher than white infant deaths. These and other figures clearly suggest that the poor do not enjoy the same good health as the affluent. But is this a product of inadequate medical care, or is it a product of nutrition, lifestyle, environment, and other nonmedical factors?

Contrary to popular stereotypes, the poor in America see doctors *more often* than the nonpoor. This situation has come about since 1965 with the beginning of the Medicaid program for the poor and Medicare for the aged. Indeed, the poor see their doctors about 20 percent more often than the nonpoor. Periodic examinations by physicians are considered good medical practice. We must therefore assume that the poor are receiving more, if not better, medical care than the nonpoor. Yet despite the increase in medical care for the poor, the health of the poor remains below the health of the nonpoor.

What has been accomplished for the poor? The health of the poor, relative to the nonpoor, does not improve with new government policies and programs. However, *access to medical care* for the poor has indeed improved with new government policies and programs. The poor see doctors more often than the affluent, but this is largely irrelevant to health.

MEDICAID: HEALTH CARE AS WELFARE

Medicaid is the federal government's largest single welfare program for the poor. The costs of Medicaid now exceed the costs of all traditional welfare programs—including AFDC, SSI, and the Food Stamp program. Medicaid was begun in 1965 and grew quickly into the nation's largest welfare program. Approximately 22 million people per year receive Medicaid payments.

Medicaid is a combined federal and state program. The states exercise fairly broad administrative powers and carry almost half of the financial burden. Medicaid is a welfare program designed for needy persons: no prior contributions are required, monies come from general tax revenues, and most recipients are already on welfare roles. Although states differ in their eligibility requirements for Medicaid, states must cover all AFDC families and most states also cover SSI recipients. In addition, a majority of states extend coverage to other "medically needy"—individuals who do not qualify for public assistance but whose incomes are low enough to qualify as needy. About half of the states extend Medicaid to families whose head is receiving unemployment compensation.

States also help set benefits under Medicaid. All states are required by the federal government to provide inpatient and outpatient hospital care, physicians' services, family planning, laboratory and X-ray, and nursing and home health care. States must also develop an early and periodic screening, diagnosis, and treatment program for all children under Medicaid. However, states themselves generally decide upon the rate of reimbursement to hospitals and physicians. Low rates can discourage hospitals and physicians from providing good care under Medicaid. To make up for low payments hospitals and doctors may schedule too many patients in too short a span of time or prescribe unnecessary tests and procedures designed to make treatment more expensive.

The costs of Medicaid have far exceeded original estimates. The rapid rise in welfare rolls in the late 1960s accounted for a large proportion of the increased costs of Medicaid. Another factor has been the high rate of inflation in medical care prices. Hospital costs and physicians' fees have raced ahead of even the high inflation rate affecting all segments of the economy. Ironically, part of the medical inflation has been produced by the Medicaid and Medicare programs themselves, which have created heavier demands for medical care. Finally, over one-third of all Medicaid payments go to nursing homes for the aged. The availability of Medicaid payments for nursing home care has spawned a large number of nursing homes and resulted in larger numbers of aged people being placed in nursing homes. Thus, Medicaid costs have run up due to (1) increase in welfare rolls, (2) inflation in medical costs, and (3) increased use of nursing homes.

MEDICARE: HEALTH CARE AS SOCIAL INSURANCE

Medicare, like Medicaid, was enacted in 1965 as an amendment to the nation's basic Social Security Act. Medicare provides prepaid hospital insurance for the aged, under Social Security and low-cost voluntary medical insurance for the aged, directly under federal administration. Medicare includes (1) HI—a compulsory basic health insurance plan covering hospital costs for the aged, which is financed out of payroll taxes which are collected under the Social Security system; and (2) SMI—a voluntary, supplemental medical insurance program that will pay doctors' bills and additional medical expenses, financed in part by contributions from the aged and in part by general tax revenues.

Only *aged* persons are covered by Medicare provisions. Eligibility is *not* dependent on income; *all* aged persons eligible for Social Security are also eligible for Medicare. Medicare is a part of the Social Security system—OASDHI: Old Age Survivor's Disability and Health Insurance—which compels employers and employees to pay into the program during their working years in order to enjoy the benefits, including health insurance, after retirement. Benefits include hospital insurance (HI) which covers a broad range of hospital services as well as nursing home care following hospital treatment. Benefits also include supplemental medical insurance (SMI) which covers physicians' services, outpatient hospital care, and other medical services. SMI is voluntary and open to all individuals over sixty-five, whether they are eligible for Social Security or not. No physical examination is required and preexisting conditions are covered. The costs of SMI are so low to the beneficiaries—approximately one hundred dollars per year— that participation by the elderly is almost universal. SMI insurance payments can be deducted automatically from Social Security payments.

Both the HI and SMI provisions of Medicare require patients to pay small **initial** charges or "deductibles." The purpose is to discourage unnecessary hospital or physician care. HI generally pays the full hospital charge, but many doctors charge higher rates than allowable under SMI. Indeed, it is estimated that only about half of the doctors in the nation accept SMI allowable payments as payment in full. Many doctors bill Medicare patients for charges *above* the allowable SMI payments. Medicare does *not* pay for prescription drugs, eyeglasses, hearing aids, or routine physical examinations.

EVALUATION: HEALTH CARE FOR THE POOR AND AGED

There is no doubt that Medicaid and Medicare have *improved access* to medicine by the poor and the aged. Both the poor and the aged now see physicians more often than the nonpoor and the nonaged. There are no clear indications, however, that Medicaid or Medicare has improved the health of the poor or the aged.

The nation's health, as measured by infant mortality rates, death rates due to specific causes, and average life spans, is improving over time. *But there is no indication that Medicaid or Medicare has been mainly or even partly responsible for these improvements.* Indeed, declines in the leading causes of death (shown in Table 6-1) were just as great *prior to* the enactment of Medicaid and Medicare (1950–1965) as they have been after the enactment of these programs. As Aaron Wildavsky observes:

> If the question is, "Does health increase with government expenditure on medicine?" the answer is likely to be "No." Just alter the question: "Has access to medicine been improved by government programs?" and the answer is most certainly with a little qualification, "Yes."[2]

No system of health care can provide as much as people will use. Each individual, believing his health and life are at stake, will want the most thorough diagnostic testing, the most constant care, the most advanced treatment. And doctors have no strong incentive to try to save on costs; they want the most advanced diagnostic and treatment facilities available for their patients. Under conditions of uncertainty in a medical situation—and there is always some uncertainty—physicians can always think of one more thing which might be done—one more consultation, one more test, one more therapeutic approach. The patient wants the best, and the doctor wants it too. Any tendency for doctors to limit testing and treatment is countered by the threat of malpractice suits; it is always easier to order one more test or procedure than to risk even the remote chance that the failure to do so will some day be cause for a court suit. So both patients and doctors push up the costs of health care, particularly when the public or private insurance pays.

Most health costs are not directly paid by either the patient or the

---

[2]Aaron Wildavsky, *Speaking Truth to Power* (Boston: Little, Brown, 1979), p. 286.

physician but by "third-party payers." Approximately 90 percent of the population is covered by some sort of health insurance—most by private insurance companies providing group insurance through employers—and the rest by Medicaid and Medicare.

One of the most pronounced effects of Medicaid and Medicare is their contribution to the spiraling inflation in health care costs. The costs of health care in the United States have risen much faster than prices in general. Medical costs have tripled over the last ten years. The nation's total medical bill is over 10 percent of the Gross National Product (see Figure 6-2).

Medicaid and Medicare have added significantly to the demand for medical services and thus contributed to this inflation. But these programs are certainly not the only causes of medical inflation. Another cause has been the rapid growth in *private* insurance plans. It is now estimated that two-thirds of the private costs of medicine are paid by private insurance companies, rather than directly by patients. Private insurance companies have been no more successful in holding down medical costs than government agencies.

Another cause of higher health costs has to do with advances in medical technology that require expensive equipment and highly trained personnel. Another cause of higher medical costs is an unnecessary expansion of hospital facilities. Tens of thousands of hospital rooms and beds are empty, yet the overhead costs of maintaining these facilities must be paid.

FIGURE 6-2 Total national health expenditures, selected years 1965 to 1990, in billions of dollars and percentage of gross national product. (Source: Congressional Quarterly, *Health Policy*. Washington, D.C.: Congressional Quarterly, Inc., 1980, p. 3.)

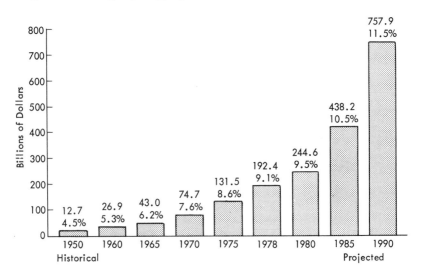

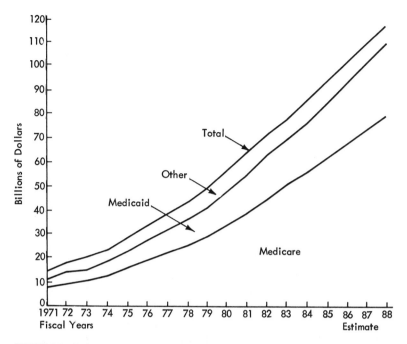

FIGURE 6-3   Federal outlays for health. (Source: *The Budget of the United States Government FY 1986.* Washington, D.C.: Government Printing Office, 1985.)

In short, modern high technology medical care is expensive (see Figure 6-3). There are few if any cost-control elements in the nation's current health care system. Patients and doctors want "the best." Private insurance, Medicaid, and Medicare remove most of the cost constraints from patients and doctors. Threats of malpractice encourage still more expenses, as doctors overtreat their patients to protect themselves from possible legal action.

COPING WITH MEDICAL COSTS

Medical care is a "scarce resource." There will never be enough of it available to satisfy the unlimited demands of every individual in society. If unlimited health care is a right and all costs are eliminated, then each patient and doctor can order the most elaborate diagnostic procedures (extensive lab work, CAT scanning, consultations with specialists), extraordinary treatments (renal dialysis, organ transplants), long hospital stays, extensive nursing care, frequent office visits, and so on. With potential unlimited demand, medical care must be rationed in *some* fashion.

Medicaid caps. Limits on payments to the states for Medicaid were initiated by the Reagan administration in the hope of slowing the rate of growth of Medicaid costs. Total federal and state Medicaid costs in 1985 exceeded $1,300 for each eligible beneficiary; this is more costly medical care than that received by the average consumer, who used less than $1,000 in medical care in that same year. Critics cite these figures as evidence that Medicaid is not cost-effective, that the "insulation" of patients, doctors, and hospitals from the cost consequences of their decisions unnecessarily inflates medical spending.

Medicare payments for diagnosis related groups. Controlling Medicare costs is a direct responsibility of the federal government. In 1983, the Reagan administration won congressional approval for a system of Medicare payment by "diagnosis-related groups" (DRGs). Prior to this reform, Medicare generally reimbursed hospitals for the total amount billed for each patient. This was a retrospective (after the fact) method of paying for hospital care. Now a prospective method of payment is being utilized in which the federal government specifies in advance what it will pay for the treatment of five hundred different illnesses or diagnosis-related groups. (Currently this DRG approach pertains only to hospital costs, not physician fees, and only to the Medicare and not the Medicaid program.) DRGs are interesting because hospitals which spend more to treat Medicare patients must absorb excess costs, but if the hospital spends less than the amount allotted to treat a patient, it is allowed to keep the difference. Hospitals may not charge Medicare patients more than DRG allotment. Obviously, the idea behind DRGs is to encourage hospitals to be more efficient in their treatment of Medicare patients. It appears that DRGs have had an effect, because in 1984 the average hospital stay was 7.5 days, down from 9.5 in 1983.[3] But critics charge that DRGs are harmful: "Patients are being discharged 'quicker and sicker,' sometimes more 'prematurely,' and are 'being sent out into a no-care zone, without access to the health care they so urgently need.' "[4]

DRGs under Medicare apply to hospital cost (HI) but not to physicians' fees (SMI). Efforts to contain costs under SMI have included freezes on the amount that participating physicians can charge to Medicaid patients. Participating physicians agree to accept Medicare reimbursement as payment in full for their services, while nonparticipating physicians may charge clients an addition to fees reimbursed by Medicare. There are some incentives for participating physicians such as prompter reimbursement by

[3]"Medicare Eyed For More Cuts," *Congressional Quarterly Weekly Report,* March 30, 1985, p. 577.
[4]"DRGs Leave Patients 'Sicker'," National Association of Social Workers, *NASW News,* April 1985, p. 10.

Medicare, and these physicians have been promised they will receive future fee increases from the government that will be denied to nonparticipating physicians.

Health services block grants.   In addition to Medicaid and Medicare, other health services are provided under block grants. These services include: community health centers which provide medical care to poor and near-poor persons in areas with few doctors or medical facilities; treatment for those with specific health problems such as hypertension; health programs for migrant workers; and rodent control programs. Less federal funding has been available for these health services since the block grants replaced numerous categorical grants.

HSAs and HMOs.   Approaches to cost containment that have already been tried include *health system agencies* (HSAs) and *health maintenance organizations* (HMOs). There are two hundred HSAs across the nation with authority to grant or withhold "certificates of need" for new medical facilities, building, and necessary costs. Withholding a "certificate of need" can lead to a withholding of Medicaid and Medicare payments to a hospital. But to date there is little evidence to suggest that HSAs have made any significant contribution to reducing medical inflation. HMOs are membership organizations which hire doctors and other health professionals at fixed salaries to serve dues-paying members. HMOs typically provide comprehensive health care for enrolled members. The members pay a regular fee and they are entitled to hospital care and physicians' services at no extra cost. Advocates of HMOs say that this is less costly than fee-for-service medical care because doctors have no incentive to overtreat patients. Moreover, HMOs emphasize preventive medicine and therefore minimize serious illnesses. However, there has been no rapid expansion in HMOs. Many of the complaints about HMOs correspond to complaints about service in other bureaucratic settings: patients see different doctors on different days; doctors in HMOs do not work as hard as private physicians; care is "depersonalized"; and so forth.

MENTAL HEALTH AND THE HOMELESS

For a pitiful few in America, sickness, hardship, and abandonment have risen dramatically in recent years *as a direct result of public policy.* These few are the nation's homeless "street people," suffering exposure, alcoholism, and chronic mental illness, while wandering the streets of the nation's larger cities. No one knows the total number of homeless; estimates vary from 200,000 to over 1 million. In most large cities, the street people are the most visible social welfare problem.

The current plight of the homeless is a direct result of "reforms" in public policy, notably the "deinstitutionalization" of care for the mentally ill, together with newly recognized rights to refuse treatment and the decriminalization of public intoxication.

Deinstitutionalization was a reform advanced by mental health care professionals and social welfare activists in the 1960s and 1970s to release chronic mental patients from state-run mental hospitals. It was widely recognized that aside from drugs, no psychiatric therapies have ever been found to have much success among the long-term mentally ill. Drug therapies can be administered on an outpatient basis; they usually do not require hospitalization. So it was argued that no one could be rightfully kept in a mental institution against their will; people who had committed no crimes and who posed no danger to others should be released. Federal and state monies for mental health were to be directed toward community mental health facilities which would treat the mentally ill on a voluntary outpatient basis. The nation's mental hospitals were emptied of all but the most dangerous mental patients. The population of mental hospitals declined from over 500,000 in 1960 to about 100,000 in 1984.[5]

Today most of the nation's chronic mentally ill persons and alcoholics are living in the community. Their constitutional right to liberty prevails over health care in the court system. Involuntary confinement has been abolished, unless a patient is adjudged in court to be "a danger to himself or others," which means a patient must commit a serious act of violence before the courts will intervene. For many homeless this means the freedom to "die with their rights on." The homeless are victimized by cold, exposure, hunger, the availability of alcohol and illegal drugs, and violent street crimes perpetrated against them, in addition to the ravages of their illness itself.

Community-based mental health care is largely irrelevant to the plight of the chronic mentally ill persons and alcoholics in the streets. Most are "uncooperative"; they are isolated from society; they have no family members or doctors or counselors to turn to for help. For them, community "care" is a Salvation Army meal and cot, or a police officer who makes a "mercy arrest," or a night in a city-run refuge for the homeless. "Care" is a ride to the city hospital psychiatric ward for a brief period of "observation" after which they must be released again to the streets. The nation's vast social welfare system provides them little help. They lose their social security, welfare, and disability checks because they have no permanent address. They cannot handle forms, appointments, or interviews; the welfare bureaucracy is intimidating. Welfare workers seldom provide the "aggressive care management" and mental health care that these people need.

---

[5]*Newsweek*, January 6, 1985, p. 16.

NATIONAL HEALTH INSURANCE: AN OLD DEBATE

When the original Social Security Act of 1935 was passed, efforts were made in Congress to include "a comprehensive national health insurance system with universal and mandatory coverage." But President Franklin D. Roosevelt backed off when he was convinced by representatives of the American Medical Association that the plan would not work without the support of the nation's physicians. President Harry Truman pushed hard for a national health insurance program tied to Social Security, but again opponents led by the American Medical Association were successful in defeating the proposal. President Lyndon Johnson opted for a somewhat narrower goal—health insurance for the poor and the aged (Medicaid and Medicare)—and he was successful in amending the Social Security Act to achieve these purposes in 1965. But the decades-old debate over national health care continues.

Current national health insurance proposals, notably the proposal which has long been recommended by Senator Edward M. Kennedy, call for compulsory national health insurance for *all* Americans. This insurance would be managed by a federal health insurance corporation. Financing would come mainly from payroll taxes paid by both employers and employees; but since the program is expected to cost a great deal, some financing would also come from general federal revenues.

National health insurance would *not* be "socialized medicine," that is, hospitals would not be federally owned and doctors would not be federal employees. Patients would still choose their own doctors and hospitals. However, a major portion of the medical *insurance* business would be government operated. Occasionally references are made in debate over national health insurance to the government-owned and -operated health care system in Great Britain. But a better analogy would be the national health insurance system in Canada "where the long waits and indifferent service that many complain about in England do not exist."[6]

Financially, the greatest obstacle to comprehensive health insurance for all Americans is the potentially ruinous inflation that might accompany such a program. Medicaid and Medicare turned out to be immensely more expensive than original estimates, and these programs have contributed significantly to medical inflation. Proponents of comprehensive health insurance have promised to tie such a program to strict cost containment efforts—limits on hospital charges and physicians' fees. But such efforts have not been particularly successful in the past in holding down medical inflation.

[6]Congressional Quarterly, Inc., *National Health Issues* (Washington, D.C.: Congressional Quarterly Inc., 1977), p. 19.

Politically, the greatest obstacle to comprehensive health insurance for all Americans is the success of Medicare and Medicaid. The existence of these programs for the aged and the poor removes much of the incentive for a comprehensive health insurance program. The programs subtract two important constituencies from a universal mandatory insurance program. Indeed, about 90 percent of all Americans are covered by some kind of medical insurance—private insurance, usually purchased through employers or unions, or Medicaid or Medicare. Half of all medical bills today are paid by "third parties," that is, by government or by private insurance companies.

Proponents of comprehensive health insurance argue that even though most people are covered by existing private and public insurance programs there are still major gaps in coverage. Many "working poor," whose incomes are too high to qualify for welfare or Medicaid, do not purchase insurance at all, or they purchase inadequate coverage. Or private insurance runs out after the first thirty or sixty days of hospital care, and eventually the seriously ill are impoverished by medical bills.

PREVENTIVE STRATEGIES: SUCCESSES AND FAILURES

Governments have long concerned themselves with the general health and safety of their citizens. Nonetheless, government efforts to reduce deaths due to accident or preventable illness have not always been successful.

Speed limits.   Occasionally government actions improve health or safety without setting out specifically to do so. When the United States adopted a national 55 MPH speed limit to save gasoline, the initial result was a reduction in annual highway accident deaths from over 55,000 per year to 46,000 per year—a saving of 9,000 lives each year. Rarely is any public health program so successful. It is ironic that this program was adopted in 1973 to save gas, rather than to save lives. It is also ironic that no giant Washington bureaucracy was established to implement this particular law, and relatively little federal money was spent to enforce it. Yet no other single action of the federal government has ever been so successful in saving so many lives. In recent years, average highway speeds have increased (even though the 55 MPH speed limit is unchanged), and highway deaths have begun to creep up toward the high levels of earlier years.

OSHA.   Just the opposite experience occurred with the creation of the Occupational Safety and Health Administration (OSHA) in 1970. OSHA was established as a large Washington bureaucracy with a substantial budget, amid a great deal of fanfare. Its responsibilities included the tasks of drawing up safety regulations for virtually every type of private employment and then enforcing these regulations with 2,500 inspectors issuing citations against businesses, large or small, found to be in violation of the regulations.

Approximately 14,000 persons die in work-related accidents each year. But there is no indication that OSHA ever affected this statistic. The number of work-related deaths declines slightly each year, but the declines were the same both before and after the creation of OSHA. It turned out that most of OSHA's regulation writers and inspectors had very little experience in the workplace. Their regulations were sometimes farcical: "All toilets must have U-shaped seats." Moreover, OSHA imposed requirements on businesses without regard to their costs, or more specifically, without weighing the benefits against the costs of these regulations. In recent years, OSHA has been instructed to concentrate its attentions on a few of the more dangerous industries (construction, heavy manufacturing, transportation, and petrochemicals) and to drop its more trivial safety rules. But it appears as if the bureaucratic command-control approach to safety and health is ineffective.

Smoking. In contrast to the government's failure with the bureaucratic approach in occupational health and safety, it is interesting to observe the government's success with the public education approach to smoking and health. The decrease in the percentage of adult smokers in recent years has been substantial. And yet, the federal government has not banned smoking or the manufacturing of cigarettes; no federal bureaucracy has been created specifically to implement antismoking laws; and relatively few tax dollars have been spent to curtail smoking. (On the contrary, the federal government spends millions each year to support the price of tobacco in its agricultural commodity credit program.)

According to the U.S. Public Health Service, the proportion of American adults who smoke decreased from 42.5 percent in 1965 to 33.5 percent in 1980.[7]

	1965	1980
Men	52.8%	36.8
Women	31.5	29.6
Total	42.5	33.5

What could account for this significant change in a health-related habit?

The American Cancer Society persuaded President John F. Kennedy to establish a special advisory commission to the surgeon general of the United States to undertake a comprehensive review of all the data relating

[7]*Statistical Abstract 1981*, p. 123.

to smoking and health. The famous "Surgeon General's Report" was published in 1964.[8] It concluded that cigarette smoking was a serious health hazard and that cigarette smoking was causally related to lung cancer. It also reported that cigarette smoking was associated with coronary disease, chronic bronchitis, and emphysema. The tobacco industry vainly tried to discredit the report, but cigarette sales dropped sharply. Although sales recovered after several years, increasing percentages of adults gave up smoking, or never started the habit.

The Federal Cigarette Labeling and Advertising Act of 1966 required all cigarette packages (and later all cigarette advertising) to be marked with the statement: "Caution: Cigarette Smoking May Be Dangerous to Your Health." In 1970, Congress approved legislation banning all cigarette commercials on radio and television. In 1971 the Interstate Commerce Commission restricted smoking to certain sections of buses and trains, and the Civil Aeronautics Board did the same on airlines in 1973.

Note that the federal government's actions in smoking have been largely *educational*. In this case, these efforts have met with significant success.

SUMMARY

A "rational" approach to health policy requires a clear definition of objectives, the development of alternative strategies for achieving these objectives, and a careful comparison and weighing of the costs and benefits of each alternative. But again in health, as well as welfare, there are seemingly insurmountable problems in developing a "rational policy":

1. The paramount objective in national health policy has never been clearly defined. Is it *good health,* as defined by lower death rates, less illness, and longer life? Or is it *better medical care,* as defined by easy access to inexpensive hospital and physician care?

2. If good health is the objective, then preventive efforts to change people's personal habits and lifestyles are more likely to improve health than anything else. For example, the 55 MPH speed limit reduced death rates more than any other recent governmental action. However, relatively little federal money is devoted to preventive measures.

3. Medical care does not contribute directly to good health. However, our ethical commitments require that we ensure adequate medical care for all, particularly the poor and the aged.

4. Medicaid is now the nation's costliest welfare program. The poor visit doctors more often and stay in hospitals longer than the nonpoor. But

[8]Report of the Advisory Committee to the Surgeon General of the Public Health Service, *Smoking and Health* (Washington, D.C.: Government Printing Office, 1964).

the health of the poor is still not as good as the health of the nonpoor. This suggests the public policy has succeeded in improving access to medical care but not necessarily improving the nation's health.

5. Medicare offers prepaid medical insurance for the aged under Social Security. Prior to the adoption of Medicare in 1965, the aged found it difficult to obtain medical insurance from private firms. Medicare removes the fear of impoverishment through hospital bills, even if it does not increase life span.

6. Both Medicaid for the poor and Medicare for the aged, together with private medical insurance, have contributed to inflation in medical care costs. The *success* of these programs (in terms of numbers of beneficiaries) has led to a new policy problem—medical care cost containment. In other words, solving one policy problem created another.

7. Alternative health care programs for the *entire* population have been proposed. Comprehensive health insurance would commit the federal government to pay a major share of all medical costs in the nation, an alternative that risks increased inflation, heavy taxing and spending, and greater controls over doctors and hospitals.

8. It is very difficult to predict the success or failure of preventive health programs. The U.S. Public Health Service's educational campaign against smoking has dramatically reduced the percentage of adult smokers. The Occupational Safety and Health Administration's control efforts have not significantly reduced accidents in the workplace.

BIBLIOGRAPHY

DAVIS, KAREN, and CATHY SCHOEN, *Health and the War on Poverty*. Washington, D.C.: Brookings Institution, 1978.

FUCHS, VICTOR R., *Who Shall Live? Health, Economics and Social Choice*. New York: Basic Books, 1974.

HOLAHAN, JOHN, *Financing Health Care for the Poor: The Medicaid Experience*. Boston: Heath, 1975.

KNOWLES, JOHN H., ed., *Doing Better and Feeling Worse: Health in the United States*. New York: Norton, 1977.

MARMOR, THEODORE R., *The Politics of Medicare*. New York: Aldine, 1973.

EDUCATION
the group struggle

Public education extends well beyond the "basics": reading, writing, and arithmetic. (Ken Karp)

Perhaps the most widely recommended "solution" to the problems that confront American society is more and better schooling. If there ever was a time when schools were only expected to combat ignorance and illiteracy, that time is far behind us. Today schools are expected to do many things: resolve racial conflict and build an integrated society; inspire patriotism and good citizenship; provide values, aspirations, and a sense of identity to disadvantaged children; offer various forms of recreation and mass entertainment (football games, bands, choruses, majorettes, and the like); reduce conflict in society by teaching children to get along well with others and to adjust to group living; reduce the highway accident toll by teaching students to be good drivers; fight disease and poor health through physical education, health training, and even medical treatment; eliminate unemployment and poverty by teaching job skills; end malnutrition and hunger through school lunch and milk programs; produce scientists and other technicians to continue America's progress in science and technology; fight drug abuse and educate children about sex; and act as custodians for teenagers who have no interest in education but whom we do not permit either to work or to roam the streets unsupervised. In other words, nearly all the nation's problems are reflected in demands placed on the nation's schools. And, of course, these demands are frequently conflicting.

It is important to note at the outset, however, that some of the pressures which have confronted American education are changing as total enrollments decline. Elementary and secondary school enrollments peaked around 1970; since then, declines in the birth rate (beginning in the 1960s) have gradually reduced the total number of children in school. Of course, enrollments are uneven across the nation: some school districts still face burgeoning enrollments, while others must close down classrooms and stop hiring new teachers. But overall, the problems confronting the nation's schools do not *now* include increasing enrollments. Even colleges and universities, which still managed small enrollment gains in the 1970s, have leveled off in enrollment in the 1980s (see Figure 7-1).

Educational policy affects a wide variety of interests, and stimulates a great deal of interest group activity. We will describe the major interests involved in federal educational policy. We will examine the constitutional provisions and court policies dealing with religion in the public schools. We will observe how both racial and religious group interests are mobilized in educational policy making, and we will see the importance of resolving group conflict in the development of educational policy. We shall also describe the structure of educational decision making and the resulting multiple points of group access in a fragmented federal-state-local educational system. We shall attempt to describe the broad categories of group interests—teachers, taxpayers, school board members, school administrators—involved in educational policy at the local level. Finally, we will ex-

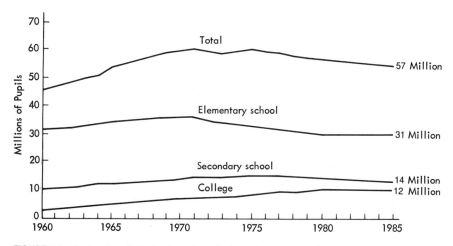

FIGURE 7-1   The leveling off of school enrollment in the United States. (Source: U.S. Bureau of the Census, *Statistical Abstract 1986.*)

amine the governing and financing of public higher education—the nation's investment in state colleges and universities.

THE FEDERAL GOVERNMENT'S ROLE IN EDUCATION

Traditionally, education in America has been a community responsibility. Only recently have state governments taken major responsibility for public education. The federal government remains largely an interested spectator in the area of educational policy. While it has taken the lead in guaranteeing racial equality in education, and separating religion from public schools, it has never assumed any significant share of the costs of education. State and local taxpayers have always borne over 90 percent of the costs of public elementary and secondary education; the federal share has never exceeded 10 percent (see Table 7-1). Similarly, federal expenditures for higher education have never exceeded 10 percent of the total costs.

Nonetheless the federal government's interest in education is a long-standing one. In the famous Northwest Ordinance of 1787, Congress offered land grants for public schools in the new territories and gave succeeding generations words to be forever etched on grammar school cornerstones: "Religion, morality, and knowledge, being necessary to good government and the happiness of mankind, schools and the means for education should ever be encouraged." The earliest democrats believed that the safest repository of the ultimate powers of society was the people themselves. If the people made mistakes, the remedy was not to remove

TABLE 7-1   Sources of Funds for Education in the United States

	Percentage of School Expenditures by Source		
	1960	1970	1984
Elementary and Secondary			
Federal	3.9	7.4	6.8
State	31.1	34.6	43.3
Local	53.3	47.7	38.4
Private	11.7	10.3	11.5
Higher Education			
Federal	7.5	9.7	7.5
State	23.9	25.5	30.2
Local	3.0	3.2	2.4
Other (inc. tuition)	22.4	25.5	26.1
Private	43.3	36.0	33.8

Source: *Statistical Abstract of the United States 1985*, p. 129

power from their hands but to help them in forming their judgment through education. If the common man was to be granted the right to vote, he must be educated to his task. This means that public education had to be universal, free, and compulsory. Compulsory education began in Massachusetts in 1852 and was eventually adopted by Mississippi in 1918.

In 1862 the Morrill Land Grant Act provided grants of federal land to each state for the establishment of colleges specializing in agricultural and mechanical arts. These became known as "land-grant colleges." In 1867 Congress established a U.S. Office of Education; in 1979, a separate, cabinet-level Department of Education was created. The Smith-Hughes Act of 1917 set up the first program of federal grants-in-aid to promote vocational education, enabling schools to provide training in agriculture, home economics, trades, and industries. In the National School Lunch and Milk programs, begun in 1946, federal grants and commodity donations were made for nonprofit lunches and milk served in public and private schools. In the Federal Impacted Areas Aid program, begun in 1950, federal aid was authorized for "federally impacted" areas of the nation. These are areas in which federal activities create a substantial increase in school enrollments or a reduction in taxable resources because of a federally owned property. Federal funds can be used for construction, operation, and maintenance of schools in these public school districts. This program is an outgrowth of the defense-impacted area aid legislation in World War II.

In response to the Soviet Union's success in launching the first satellite into space, Congress became concerned that the American educational system might not be keeping abreast of advances being made in other nations, particularly in science and technology. The Russian space shot created an intensive debate over education in America, and prompted Congress to reexamine the responsibilities of the national government in public education. "Sputnik" made everyone realize that education was closely related to national defense. In the National Defense Education Act of 1958, Congress provided financial aid to states and public school districts to improve instruction in science, mathematics, and foreign languages; to strengthen guidance counseling and testing; and to improve statistical services. It also established a system of loans to undergraduates, fellowships to graduate students, and funds to colleges—all in an effort to improve the training of teachers in America.

The Elementary and Secondary Education Act of 1965 established the single largest federal aid to education program. "Poverty-impacted" schools were the beneficiaries of ESEA, receiving instructional materials and educational research and training. ESEA provided for federal financial assistance to "local educational agencies serving areas with concentrations of children from low-income families" for programs "which contribute particularly to meeting the special needs of educationally deprived children." Grants were made on application to the Office of Education, awarded on the basis of the number of children enrolled from poverty-stricken families. Grants were also made to "public and private elementary and secondary schools" for the acquisition of school library resources, textbooks, and other instructional materials. Note that the act does include private church-related schools in some of its benefits, as long as the federal aid money is used for nonreligious purposes within such schools. However, the greatest amount of money distributed under ESEA has been to public schools in poverty-impacted areas.

It is difficult to demonstrate that these federal aid programs improved the quality of education in America. Indeed, during the years in which federal aid was increasing, student achievement scores were *declining* (see Table 7-3).

In an influential 1983 report "A Nation At Risk," the National Commission on Excellence in Education recommended a series of reforms in American education (see page 179) but reaffirmed that "state and local government officials, including school board members and governors, and legislators, have *the primary responsibility* for funding and governing the schools."

President Reagan clearly shared this preference for state and local responsibility for education. Earlier in his administration, he even proposed abolishing the U.S. Department of Education in order to emphasize that education should not become the federal government's responsibility. But educational interests were too well-organized in Congress to permit DOE to dissolve, and President Reagan came to recognize the role that the federal government could play in advising the states and stimulating and encouraging educational reform. Most of the cuts in federal school aid recommended by President Reagan were restored by Congress, but the president succeeded in *limiting the growth* of federal educational spending. The result has been a gradual decline in the 1980s of the federal percentage of total educational funding in the nation (see Table 7-1).

GROUP COMPROMISE: ESEA

The long struggle over federal aid to education is an excellent example of the power of interest groups in blocking legislation that has widespread public support, and the necessity of accommodating specific interest groups and finding workable compromises before a bill can be passed. Every year from 1945 to 1965—a period spanning two decades and the administrations of both Democratic and Republic presidents and both Democratic and Republican congressional majorities—federal aid-to-education bills were introduced and debated at great length. Yet no general aid-to-education bill passed the Congress in this period. These bills were lost *despite* overwhelming public support for federal aid to education revealed in all national opinion polls during this period, and *despite* announced presidential support for such aid. The failure of federal aid to education under these conditions can be attributed to the conflict between major *racial* and *religious* group interests in America over the character of such aid.[1]

Leading the fight for federal aid to education was the National Education Association. The NEA represents school administrators, state departments of education, university schools of education, as well as large numbers of dues-paying teachers. Whatever differences existed within these various categories of members, the NEA was united in its support of federal aid to education. The national office of the NEA, located in a modern, well-equipped office building in Washington, worked closely with the Office of Education (now the Department of Education) located only a few blocks away. The NEA also has affiliates in every one of the fifty states and most local school districts in the nation. Although the NEA was a strong advocate of federal aid, it actively opposed public funds for private church-related schools. Other groups supporting federal aid were the AFL-CIO (particularly its constituent union, the American Federation of Teachers, which frequently competes with the NEA for the loyalties of classroom teachers), Americans for Democratic Action, National Congress of Parents and Teachers, and many library and professional groups.

The first divisive issue was that of *race*. For many years the question of whether or not the federal government would assist racially segregated Southern schools posed a major obstacle to federal aid to education. Southern members of Congress stood to gain from any federal aid program designed to equalize educational expenditures among the states, because

---

[1] A detailed account of the long struggle leading to the passage of the Elementary and Secondary Education Act of 1965 is found in Eugene Eidenberg and Roy D. Morey, *An Act of Congress* (New York: Norton, 1969).

the Southern states are among the poorest in the nation. But this group strongly opposed the prospect of federal aid money being used as leverage to achieve integration. On the other hand, black and liberal groups opposed any federal aid to schools operated on a racially segregated basis. For many years federal aid-to-education bills were lost in racial controversy in Congress. The Civil Rights Act of 1964 greatly assisted the movement for federal aid to education, even though it made no direct mention of such aid. Title VI of the act specified that every federal department and agency must take action to end segregation by issuing rules, regulations, and orders (later known as "guidelines"), and by withholding federal aid from any programs that have failed to comply. The effect of the act was to clear the track of at least one obstacle to federal aid to education.

The second divisive issue in federal aid to education was *religion*, specifically whether or not federal aid should go to private, church-related schools. Catholic groups, particularly the National Catholic Welfare Conference, generally refused to support any federal aid bill that did not include aid to parochial schools. Yet many Protestant groups were equally convinced that federal aid to church-related schools would destroy the historic concept of separation of church and state. Many Protestant denominations, as well as the National Council of Churches, went on record against federal aid for parochial schools. The failure of President Kennedy's aid-to-education bill in 1961 is generally attributed to the religious conflict it engendered. In honoring a 1960 campaign pledge to Protestants, the nation's first Catholic president introduced a federal aid-to-education bill which *excluded* parochial schools.[2] To the school-aid bill's usual enemies— conservative Republicans wary of federal bureaucracy and Southern Democrats wary of integration efforts—President Kennedy added a substantial bloc of Catholic members of Congress, many of whom had supported aid to education in the past.

By 1965, twenty years of group struggle over federal aid to education convinced proponents of the policy that *compromise between major interest groups* was essential to its adoption. The key to success, then, was working out a compromise acceptable to the NEA and other educational groups, the National Catholic Welfare Conference and other representatives of the Catholic Church, and the National Council of Churches and other Protestant groups.

The Johnson administration skillfully emphasized "aid to children" rather than aid to schools, and particularly aid to children from low-income families. It was hoped that by placing the emphasis on the child, the church-state issue could be submerged. The president identified the program with his "War on Poverty" rather than with earlier aid-to-education efforts. The

---

[2]In a speech before the Greater Houston Ministerial Association in 1960 Kennedy stated: "I believe in an America where separation of Church and State is absolute . . . where no church or church school is granted any public funds or political preference."

greatest proportion of ESEA funds would be given under Title I to *public* school districts with children from low-income families. But as a concession to Catholic interests, the president's bill allowed parochial schools to receive funds along with public schools for libraries, textbooks, and instructional materials, and for supplementary educational centers and services. The NEA accepted the compromise despite its longstanding opposition to giving any public funds to church schools. Responsible spokesmen for Protestant churches also agreed to the compromise; they did not want to be charged with having hurt public education in America or blocking assistance to impoverished schoolchildren. Catholic groups were also unenthusiastic about the bill, because Catholic schools would not receive funding equal to public education. But in the end the Catholic groups agreed to the bill. Once support of the major interests was obtained, congressional approval of ESEA was practically certain. The ease and rapidity with which the bill passed Congress was a striking contrast to the bloody battles of earlier years. This turnabout in congressional behavior would have mystified anyone who was not aware of the interest group compromise.

GROUP STRUGGLE: TUITION TAX CREDITS

The group struggle over tuition tax credits for families with children in private schools illustrates what happens when groups fail to reach compromise.

Tuition tax credits would provide refundable federal income tax credit for half of the tuition (perhaps up to a maximum of $500) paid by a taxpayer to any private school. Initially these credits would extend to private elementary and high school tuitions and perhaps later to private college tuitions. The Reagan administration proposed these credits "as a matter of fairness" to allow families "to choose for their children those schools which best correspond to their own cultural and moral values."

Support for the proposal is strong among organized Catholic groups as well as other religious groups which maintain private schools. Catholic school enrollments have been slipping in recent years, but they have been offset by gains in other private schools. About 5.2 million pupils attend private schools in America or about 1 percent of the nation's pupil population (see Figure 7-2).

Proponents of tuition tax credits, including the Council for American Private Education, argue that these credits will reduce the family burden of paying private school tuition. Private schools, they argue, ensure pluralism in American education. They offer competition and standards of comparison for public schools. In addition, they save public education money by providing schooling for many pupils who would otherwise be assigned to public schools. Proponents also contend that minority students are well served, especially by Catholic schools whose enrollment is 17 per-

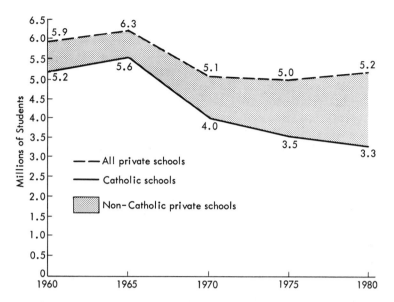

FIGURE 7-2   Private school enrollment. (Source: National Center for Educational Statistics.)

cent black and Hispanic. Black and Hispanic pupils are said to do better in Catholic schools than in public schools.[3] Private schools offer better discipline, higher academic standards, improved physical safety, less disruption in the classroom, and more emphasis on moral values than public schools.

Other reasons may also help to explain continued interest in private schools and the effort to enact tuition tax credits. Smaller families allow parents to provide the luxury of private education for their children. As the educational level of the entire population increases, there is a greater value placed on good schools. Many parents have enrolled their children in private schools to avoid busing. In big cities, white parents often choose private schools to avoid predominantly black public schools.

Strong opposition to tuition tax credits is led by the National Education Association and the American Federation of Teachers (AFL-CIO). They argue that tuition tax credits for private schools will undermine support for public education. The lost tax revenues from these credits could go to improving public schools. Lost revenue to public schools will accentuate all of the recognized problems of public education. The credits will encourage the growth of private schools; more middle-class children will be removed from public schools. An educational caste system may result, with the "haves" in private schools and the "have nots" in public schools. Private schools can be selective, while public schools must accept all children.

[3]Congressional Quarterly, Inc., *Education in America* (Washington, D.C.: Congressional Quarterly, Inc., 1981), p. 11.

Tax encouragements to private schools would contribute to an unequal educational system. Finally, it is argued that the tax credits would go mainly to middle-class families who need help the least. Private school families complain that they are paying taxes for schools their children do not use, but public school supporters argue that public education is available to all and that people who choose private education should be expected to pay for it themselves.

Perhaps the most divisive aspect of the controversy over tuition tax credits centers on religion. Since most private schools are church affiliated, government subsidies for private school tuitions raise the question of an "establishment" of religion in violation of the First Amendment of the U.S. Constitution. Not only must the policy of tuition tax credit win the approval of Congress, it must also win the support of the U.S. Supreme Court.

BACK TO BASICS

Citizen groups have confronted professional educators over the question of what should be taught in the public schools. Public sentiment is strongly in favor of teaching the "three R's" ("reading, 'riting, and 'rithmetic"), enforcing minimum standards with tests, and even testing teachers themselves for their mastery of the basics (see Table 7-2). Parents are less enthusiastic than professional educators about emotional growth, "getting along with others," the "new math," the "look-say" method of reading, and other "innovative" programs of education.

The SAT score controversy. For many years critics of modern public education cited declining scores on standardized tests, particularly the Scholastic Aptitude Test (SAT) required by many colleges and universities, as evidence of the failure of the schools to teach basic reading and mathematics skills. When the decline ended in 1982 (see Table 7-3), it was attributed to increasing emphasis on basic skills and standardized testing. But in all likelihood, changes in these test scores are really a function of how many students take the test. During the declining years, increasing numbers and

TABLE 7-2   Public Opinion on School Standards

Would you favor or oppose much more stress on teaching basic skills to children?	<u>Favor</u> 98%	<u>Oppose</u> 2%
All students should be required to pass a standardized basic skill test before they can graduate.	<u>Agree</u> 79%	<u>Disagree</u> 21%
Teachers should be required to pass a standardized test in the subject they will teach, before they can teach in the public schools.	<u>Agree</u> 90%	<u>Disagree</u> 10%

Source: *Public Opinion* (October/November 1981), p. 24.

TABLE 7-3   The SAT Score Controversy

ALL STUDENTS AVERAGE			AVERAGES BY GROUP		
YEAR	VERBAL	MATHEMATICAL		VERBAL	MATHEMATICAL
1963	478	502	Black	342	373
1965	473	498	Mexican-American	376	420
1970	460	488	Asian-Pacific	390	519
1975	437	473	Puerto Rican	366	400
1980	424	466	White	442	483
1981	424	466			
1982	426	467			
1983	425	468			
1984	426	471			

Source: College Entrance Examination Board, New York.

proportions of students were taking the test—students who never aspired to college in the past and whose test scores did not match those of the earlier smaller group of college-bound test takers.

A nation at risk.   The "back to basics" citizens' reform movement in education was given impetus by an influential 1983 report by the National Commission on Excellence in Education entitled "A Nation At Risk."[4]

> Our nation is at risk. Our once unchallenged prominence in commerce, industry, science, and technological innovation is being overtaken by competitors throughout the world. . . .
>
> If an unfriendly foreign power had attempted to impose on America the mediocre educational performance that exists today, we might well have viewed it as an act of war.

The commission cited as evidence of the nation's decline in educational achievement:

- international comparisons of student achievement among industrialized nations which often rank American students last and never first
- marked declines in student achievement over the preceding twenty years
- declining high school enrollments in courses in science, mathematics and foreign language, and increasing enrollments in cooking, marriage, driving, health, and recreational courses
- declining amounts of school homework
- rising school grades despite declining achievement scores
- the recruitment of new teachers from the bottom quarter of college graduates

---

[4]National Commission on Excellence in Education, *A Nation At Risk* (Washington, D.C.: Government Printing Office, 1983).

- the concentration of college credits of future teachers in educational courses, reducing the time spent in subject matter courses
- shortages of teachers in mathematics and science

The commission's recommendations set the agenda for educational policy debate in the states. Among the many recommendations were these:

- a minimum high school curriculum of four years of English, three years of mathematics, three years of social science, and one-half year of computer science
- four to six years of foreign language study beginning in the elementary grades
- standardized tests for achievement for all of these subjects
- more homework, a seven-hour school day, and a 200- to 220- day school year
- reliable grades and standardized tests for promotion and graduation
- "performance-based" salaries for teachers and rewards for "superior" teaching

MCT. Many state legislatures responded to the commission's report and the demand for greater achievement in basic skills by requiring minimum competence testing (MCT examinations) in the schools. These tests may be used as diagnostic tools to determine the need for remedial education, or minimum scores may be required for promotion or graduation. Currently, about half of the states require students to pass a minimum competency test in order to receive a high school diploma. These tests usually require performance at an eighth or ninth grade level.

Minimum competence tests force schools and teachers to place greater emphasis on the "basics." Professional educators have been less enthusiastic about testing than citizen groups and state legislators. Educators contend that MCT leads to narrow "test taking" education rather than broad preparation for life. MCT requires teachers to devote more time to coaching students on how to pass an exam rather than preparing them for productive lives after graduation.

But the most serious opposition to MCT has come from minority group leaders who charge that the tests are racially biased. Average black student scores are frequently lower than average white students scores, and larger percentages of black students are held back from promotion and graduation by testing than white students. Some black leaders charge that racial bias in the examination itself, as well as racial isolation in the school, contribute to black-white differences in exam scores. Denying a disproportionate number of black students a diploma because of the schools' failure to teach basics may be viewed as a form of discrimination. However, to date federal courts have declined to rule that MCT itself is discriminatory, as long as sufficient time and opportunity have been provided all students to prepare for the examination.

Testing teacher competency. Professional education groups have opposed teacher competency tests on the grounds that standardized tests cannot really measure competency in the classroom. The National Education Association has opposed all testing of teachers; the American Federation of Teachers is willing to accept competency testing only for new teachers. The Educational Testing Service (which prepares the SAT, GRE, LSAT, and other standardized national examinations) offers a National Teacher Examination (NTE) which measures general knowledge and basic comprehension and mathematical skills. Today, only a few states have adopted teacher competency tests, but the results have been disquieting. Large numbers of experienced teachers have failed the tests; black teachers have failed more often than white teachers.

Pay and recruitment. Another concern of the National Commission on Excellence in Education is the inability of the teaching profession to attract quality students. The commission noted that the average SAT scores of education majors were lower than the average scores of other students. Average starting salaries for teachers nationwide is less than 75 percent of the average starting salaries for other graduates. Years ago, when women were excluded from many other professions, teaching attracted many people of high ability even though salaries were low. But today, with expanded opportunities for women, the teaching profession cannot expect to attract quality graduates without offering competitive salary levels.

Merit pay. Few state legislators are willing or able to raise all teachers' salaries to the level of other professionals. The commission's recommendation for the adoption of "merit pay" provides a less costly option, yet one that promises to reward good teaching. Ideally, merit pay would help retain exceptional teachers and encourage quality teaching, without rewarding mediocrity through general (across-the-board) salary increases to all teachers. But the professional education groups fear that merit pay will become a substitute for adequate teachers' salaries. They also argue that there are no objective criteria for measuring "merit" in classroom teaching. Using student test scores would unfairly penalize teachers who taught disadvantaged students. And teacher scores on "pencil-and-paper" tests do not really measure classroom performance. And of course, the allocation of merit pay by principals and superintendents is attacked as potentially arbitrary. In short, merit pay plans often founder on an age-old question: What is good teaching?

Master teachers. Another proposal to recruit and retain the best among our nation's teachers centers on identification of master teachers, and a system of promotions, rewards, and responsibilities which encourages professional development. Exceptional classroom teachers might look forward to the designation "master teacher" with professional recognition and salary; they might undertake additional responsibilities in assisting other teachers. But, as with merit pay, problems of implementing a master teacher program abound: What objective criteria exist for identifying master teachers? Is the possession of a master's or Ph.D. degree evidence of effective teaching? Who should make the selection?

THE EDUCATIONAL GROUPS

Interest group activity in education includes many racial, religious, labor, and civil rights organizations, as well as educational groups. The professional educational groups are at the heart of most educational issues. The largest educational organization is the National Education Association (NEA) which claims a membership of two million teachers and school administrators. The NEA maintains a large Washington office for lobbying Congress and the executive branch and makes substantial campaign contributions to political candidates.

The American Federation of Teachers has a smaller membership, concentrated in big-city school districts, but as an affiliate of the AFL-CIO it can call upon assistance from organized labor. Because of the frequent involvement of racial and religious issues in education, such groups as the National Association for the Advancement of Colored People (NAACP), National Catholic Education Conference, the American Jewish Congress, Americans United for the Separation of Church and State, and the American Civil Liberties Union all become involved in educational policy. Support for federal aid to education is generally forthcoming from the NEA and AFT, organized labor (AFL-CIO), school-related organizations such as the National Congress of Parents and Teachers and the American Library Association, and liberal groups such as Americans for Democratic Action.

The educational groups not only lobby Congress but also the executive branch, particularly the Department of Education. Indeed, the Department of Education was created in 1979 largely because of President Carter's campaign pledge to the educational groups to create a separate education department. Formerly, most federal education programs were administered by the old U.S. Office of Education in the old Department of Health, Education, and Welfare (HEW); with the creation of the new Department of Education, HEW became HHS, the Department of Health and Human Services. Most educational groups believe that a separate cabinet-level Department of Education gives priority to educational needs.

School politics at the community level differ from one community to another, but it is possible to identify a number of political groups that appear on the scene in school politics almost everywhere. There is, first of all, that small band of voters who turn out for school elections. It is estimated that, on the average, only about one-third of the eligible voters bother to cast ballots in school elections. Voter turnout at school bond and tax elections also demonstrates no groundswell of public interest in school affairs. Perhaps even more interesting is the finding that the larger the voter turnout in a school referendum, the more likely the *defeat* of education proposals. In general, the best way to defeat a school bond referendum is to have a large turnout. Proponents of educational expenditures are better advised not to work for a large turnout, but for a better-informed and more educationally oriented electorate.

School board members constitute another important group of actors in local school politics. School board members are generally better educated than their constitutents. They are selected largely from among business owners, proprietors, and managers. There is some evidence that people who are interested in education and have some knowledge of what the schools are doing tend to support education more than do the less informed citizens. However, the occupational background of school board members suggests that they are sensitive to tax burdens placed upon business people and property owners.

Many professional educators are distrustful of the lay people who compose the school boards; they often feel that educational policy should be in the hands of professional educators. They may feel that important decisions about curriculum, facilities, personnel, and finances should be the special province of persons trained in education. They view the school board's role as one of defending the schools against public criticism and persuading the community to open its pocketbook. Professional educators often support the idea that "politics" should be kept out of education; to them, this means that lay persons should not interfere with decisions that professional educators wish to make for themselves. School boards and voters (those who supply money for public schools and therefore feel that it is their legitimate right to control them) believe that citizen control of education is a vital safeguard of democracy. But professional educators sometimes feel that school board members are uninformed about school problems and unwilling or unable to support the needs of education. As a case in point, school board members throughout the nation were much less likely to support federal aid to education than were professional educators. Many school board members felt that the federal government would strip them of their local power over the schools, while professional educators were less fearful of dictation from Washington.[5]

The professional educators can be divided into at least three distinct groups. Numerically, the largest group ($2\frac{1}{2}$ million) is the schoolteachers. But perhaps the most powerful group is the professional school administrators, particularly the superintendents of schools. A third group consists

[5]See Harmon Ziegler and M. Kent Jennings, *Governing American Schools* (Boston: Duxbury Press, 1974).

of the faculties of teachers colleges and departments of education at universities. This latter group often has contacts with state departments of education, diffuses educational innovations and ideologies to each generation of teachers, and influences requirements for teacher certification within the states.

Democratic theory assumes that schools are public institutions which should be governed by the local citizenry through their elected representatives. This was the original concept in American public education developed in the nineteenth century. But as school issues became more complex, the knowledge of citizen school boards seemed insufficient to cope with the many problems confronting the schools—teaching innovations, curricular changes, multimillion-dollar building programs, special educational programs, and so forth. In the twentieth century, the school superintendent and his or her administrative assistants came to exercise more and more control over day-to-day operations of the schools. Theoretically, the superintendent only implements the policies of the board, but in practice he or she has assumed much of the policy making in education. The superintendent is a full-time administrator, receiving direct advice from attorneys, architects, accountants, and educational consultants, and generally sets the agenda for school board meetings.

The resulting "professionalism" in education tangles directly with the "democratic" notion of control of school. There are few meetings of local school boards which do not involve at least some tug-of-war between board members and the superintendent. Professional educators often support the idea that "politics" should be kept out of education; this means that elected school board members should not interfere in educational decisions. But school board members and interested citizens generally believe that popular control of education is a vital component of democracy. Schools should be "responsive" to community needs and desires. Frequently, citizen criticism has focused on the schools' failure to teach basic skills—reading, writing, and arithmetic. These issues have in turn raised the underlying question— who should govern our schools, professional educators or interested citizens?

The struggle for power over the schools between interested citizens, school board members, and professional educators has now been joined by still another powerful force—the nation's growing teachers' unions. Most of the nation's two million teachers are organized into either the older, larger National Education Association (NEA), or the smaller but more militant American Federation of Teachers (AFT), an affiliate of the AFL-CIO. Until recently the NEA was considered a "professional" organization of both teachers and administrators. But today state and district chapters of the Classroom Teachers Association formed out of the NEA are demanding collective bargaining rights for their members and even threatening to strike to achieve them. Since its origin, the AFT has espoused the right to organize, bargain collectively, and strike in the fashion of other labor unions. The AFT is small in numbers but its membership is concentrated in the nation's largest cities where it exercises considerable power. Both AFT and NEA chapters have shut down schools to force concessions by superintendents, board members, and taxpayers—not only in salaries and benefits, but also in pupil-teacher relations, classroom conditions, school discipline, and other educational matters.

READING, WRITING, AND RELIGION

The First Amendment of the Constitution of the United States contains two important guarantees of religious freedom: (1) "Congress shall make no law respecting an establishment of religion . . ." and (2) "or prohibiting the free exercise thereof." The due process clause of the Fourteenth Amendment made these guarantees of religious liberty applicable to the states and their subdivisions as well as to Congress. Most of the debate over religion in the public schools centers around the "no establishment" clause of the First Amendment rather than the "free exercise" clause. However, it was respect for the "free exercise" clause that caused the Supreme Court in 1925 to declare unconsitutional an attempt on the part of a state to prohibit private and parochial schools and to force all children to attend public schools. In the words of the Supreme Court: "The fundamental theory of liberty upon which all governments in this Union repose excludes any general power of the state to standardize its children by forcing them to accept instruction from public teachers only. The child is not the mere creature of the state."[6] It is this decision that protects the entire structure of private religious schools in this nation.

A great deal of religious conflict in America has centered around the meaning of the "no establishment" clause, and the public schools have been the principal scene of this conflict. One interpretation of the clause holds that it does not prevent government from aiding religious schools or encouraging religious beliefs in the public schools, as long as it does not discriminate against any particular religion. Another interpretation of the "no establishment" clause is that it creates a "wall of separation" between church and state in America to prevent government from directly aiding religious schools or encouraging religious beliefs in any way.

Government Aid to Church-Related Schools

Those favoring government aid to church-related schools frequently refer to the language found in several cases decided by the Supreme Court, which appears to support the idea that government can *in a limited fashion*

---

[6]*Pierce* v. *The Society of Sisters,* 268 U.S. 510 (1925).

support the activities of church-related schools. In *Cochran v. Board of Education* (1930), the Court upheld a state law providing free textbooks for children attending both public and parochial schools on the grounds that this aid benefited the *children* rather than the Catholic Church and hence did not constitute an "establishment" of religion with the meaning of the First Amendment.[7]

In *Everson v. Board of Education* (1947), the Supreme Court upheld bus transportation for parochial school children at public expense on the grounds that the "wall of separation between church and states does not prohibit the state from adopting a general program which helps *all* children."[8] Interestingly in this case, even though the Supreme Court permitted the expenditure of public funds to assist children going to and from parochial schools, the Supreme Court voiced the opinion that the "no establishment" clause of the First Amendment should constitute a wall of separation between church and state. In the words of the Court:

> Neither a state nor the federal government can set up a church. Neither can pass laws which aid one religion, aid all religions, or prefer one religion over another. Neither can force nor influence a person to go to or to remain away from church against his will, or force him to profess a belief or disbelief in any religion. No person can be punished for entertaining or professing religious beliefs or disbeliefs, for church attendance or nonattendance. No tax in any amount, large or small, can be levied to support any religious activities or institutions, whatever they may be called, or whatever form they may adopt to teach or practice religion. Neither a state nor the federal government can, openly or secretly, participate in the affairs of any religious organizations or groups, and vice versa.[9]

So the *Everson* case can be cited by those interests which support the allocation of public funds for assistance to children in parochial schools, as well as those interests which oppose any public support, direct or indirect, of religion.

The question of how much government aid can go to church schools and for what purposes is still unresolved. Some states have passed bills giving financial support to nonpublic schools for such purposes as textbooks, bus transportation, and remedial courses. Proponents of public aid for church schools argue that these schools render a valuable public service by instructing millions of children who would have to be instructed by the state, at great expense, if the church schools were to close. There seemed to be many precedents for public support of religious institutions: Church

[7]*Cochran v. Board of Education*, 281 U.S. 370 (1930).
[8]*Everson v. Board of Education*, 330 U.S. 1 (1947).
[9]Ibid.

property has always been exempt from taxation; church contributions are deductible from federal income taxes; federal funds have been appropriated for the construction of religiously operated hospitals; chaplains are provided in the armed forces as well as in the Congress of the United States; veterans' programs permit veterans to use their educational subsidies to finance college educations in Catholic universities; federal grants and loans for college construction are available to Catholic as well as to public colleges, and so on.

Opponents of aid to church schools argue that free public schools are available to the parents of all children regardless of religious denomination. If religious parents are not content with the type of school that the state provides, they should expect to pay for the establishment and operation of special schools. The state is under no obligation to finance the religious preferences in education of religious groups. In fact, they contend that it is unfair to compel taxpayers to support religion directly or indirectly; furthermore, the diversion of any substantial amount of public education funds to church schools would weaken the public school system. The public schools bring together children of different religious backgrounds and by so doing supposedly encourage tolerance and understanding. In contrast, church-related schools segregate children of different backgrounds, and it is not in the public interest to encourage such segregation. And so the dispute continues.

One of the most important Supreme Court decisions in the history of church-state relations in America came in 1971 in the case of *Lemon* v. *Kurtzman*.[10] The Supreme Court held that it was unconstitutional for a state (Pennsylvania) to pay the costs of teachers' salaries or instructional materials in parochial schools. The Court acknowledged that it had previously approved the provision of state textbooks and bus transportation directly to parochial school children. But the Court held that state payments to parochial schools involved "excessive entanglement between government and religion" and violated both the "no establishment" and "free exercise" clauses of the First Amendment. State payments to religious schools, the Court said, would require excessive government controls and surveillance to ensure that funds were used only for secular instruction. Moreover, the Court expressed the fear that state aid to parochial schools would create "political divisions along religious lines . . . one of the principal evils against which the First Amendment was intended to protect." However, in *Roemer* v. *Maryland* (1976) the Supreme Court upheld general public grants of money to church-related *colleges:* "Religious institutions need not be quarantined from public benefits which are neutrally available to all."[11]

---

[10]*Lemon* v. *Kurtzman*, 403 U.S. 602 (1971).
[11]*Roemer* v. *Maryland*, 415 U.S. 382 (1976).

Prayer in Public Schools

Religious conflict in public schools also centers around the question of prayer and Bible-reading ceremonies conducted in public schools. A few years ago the practice of opening the school day with prayer and Bible reading ceremonies was widespread in American public schools. Usually the prayer was a Protestant rendition of the Lord's Prayer and Bible reading was from the King James version. In order to avoid the denominational aspects of these ceremonies, the New York State Board of Regents substituted a nondenominational prayer, which it required to be said aloud in each class in the presence of a teacher at the beginning of each school day.

> Almighty God, we acknowledge our dependence upon Thee, and we beg Thy blessings upon us, our parents, our teachers, and our country.

New York argued that this prayer ceremony did not violate the "no establishment" clause, because the prayer was denominationally neutral and because student participation in the prayer was voluntary. However, in *Engle* v. *Vitale* (1962), the Supreme Court stated that "the constitutional prohibition against laws respecting an establishment of a religion must at least mean in this country it is no part of the business of government to compose official prayers for any group of the American people to recite as part of a religious program carried on by government."[12] The Court pointed out that making prayer voluntary did not free it from the prohibitions of the "no establishment" clause; that clause prevented the establishment of a religious ceremony by a government agency, regardless of whether the ceremony was voluntary or not:

> Neither the fact that the prayer may be denominationally neutral, nor the fact that its observance on the part of the students is voluntary can serve to free it from the limitations of the establishment clause, as it might from the free exercise clause, of the First Amendment, both of which are operative against the states by virtue of the Fourteenth Amendment. . . . The establishment clause, unlike the free exercise clause, does not depend on any showing of direct governmental compulsion and is violated by the enactment of laws which establish an official religion whether those laws operate directly to coerce nonobserving individuals or not.

One year later in the case of *Abbington Township* v. *Schempp*, the Court considered the constitutionality of Bible-reading ceremonies in the public schools.[13] Here again, even though the children were not required to participate, the Court found that Bible reading as an opening exercise in the

---

[12]*Engle* v. *Vitale*, 370 U.S. 421 (1962).
[13]*Abbington Township* v. *Schempp*, 374 U.S. 203 (1963).

TABLE 7-4 Public Opinion on School Prayer

Do you mostly agree or disagree with this...The Supreme Court and Congress have gone too far in keeping religious and moral values like prayer out of our laws, our schools, and our lives.	Agree 73%	Disagree 27%
Generally speaking do you approve or disapprove of allowing prayer in public schools?	Approve 80%	Disapprove 20%
Do you favor or oppose a constitutional amendment ot allow daily prayers to be recited in school classrooms?	Favor 71%	Oppose 29%

Source: *Public Opinion* (June/July 1982), p. 40.

schools was a religious ceremony. The Court went to some trouble in its opinion to point out that it was not "throwing the Bible out of the schools," for it specifically stated that the study of the Bible or of religion, when presented as part of a secular program of education, did not violate the First Amendment, but religious *ceremonies* involving Bible reading or prayer, established by a state or school district, did so.

State efforts to encourage "voluntary prayer" in public schools have also been struck down by the Supreme Court as unconstitutional. When the state of Alabama authorized a period of silence for "meditation or voluntary prayer" in public schools, the Court ruled that this was an "establishment of religion." The Court said the law had no secular purpose, that it conveyed "a message of state endorsement and promotion of prayer," and that its real intent was to encourage prayer in public schools.[14] In a stinging dissenting opinion, Chief Justice Warren Burger noted that the Supreme Court itself opened its session with a prayer, that both houses of Congress opened every session with prayers led by official chaplains paid by the government. "To suggest that a moment of silence statute that includes the word *prayer* unconstitutionally endorses religion, manifests not neutrality but hostility toward religion."

The Supreme Court's interpretation of the "no establishment" clause ruling out prayer in the public schools is politically unpopular. Large majorities of Americans would prefer to see prayers in public schools and would support a constitutional amendment to reverse the Supreme Court's decision (see Table 7-4). Efforts in Congress to pass such an amendment and send it to the states for ratification have foundered so far. It is politically difficult for senators and representatives to directly oppose a prayer amendment but procedural rules have been used in Congress to prevent a clearcut vote on the issue.

[14]*Wallace* v. *Jaffree*, June 4, 1985.

PUBLIC POLICY AND HIGHER EDUCATION

State governments have been involved in public higher education since the colonial era. State governments in the Northeast frequently made contributions to support private colleges in their states, a practice that continues today. The first state university to be chartered by a state legislature was the University of Georgia in 1794. Before the Civil War, Northeastern states relied exclusively on private colleges, and the Southern states assumed the leadership in public higher education. The antebellum curricula at Southern state universities, however, resembled the rigid classical studies of the early private colleges—Greek and Latin, history, philosophy, and literature.

It was not until the Morrill Land Grant Act of 1862 that public higher education began to make major strides in the American states. Interestingly, the Eastern states were slow to respond to the opportunity afforded by the Morrill Act to develop public universities; Eastern states continued to rely primarily on their private colleges and universities. The Southern states were economically depressed in the post–Civil War period, and leadership in public higher education passed to the Midwestern states. The philosophy of the Morrill Act emphasized agricultural and mechanical studies rather than the classical curricula of Eastern colleges, and the movement for "A and M" education spread rapidly in the agricultural states. The early groups of Midwestern state universities were closely tied to agricultural education, including agricultural extension services. State universities also took the responsibility for the training of public school teachers in colleges of education. The state universities introduced a broad range of modern subjects in the university curricula—business administration, agriculture, home economics, education, engineering. It was not until the 1960s that the Eastern states began to develop public higher education, notably the huge, multicampus State University of New York.

Today public higher education enrolls three-quarters of the nation's college and university students. Perhaps more importantly, the nation's leading state universities can challenge the best private institutions in academic excellence. The University of California at Berkeley, the University of Michigan, and the University of Wisconsin are deservedly ranked with Harvard, Yale, Princeton, Stanford, and Chicago.

Federal aid to colleges and universities has come in a variety of forms. Historically, the Morrill Act of 1862 provided the groundwork for federal assistance to higher education. In 1890 Congress activated several federal grants to support the operations of the land-grant colleges, and this aid, although very modest, continues to the present. The GI bills following World War II and the Korean War (enacted in 1944 and 1952 respectively) were not, strictly speaking, aid-to-education bills, but rather a form of assistance to veterans to help them adjust to civilian life. Nevertheless, these bills had a great impact on higher education in terms of the millions of veterans who were able to enroll in college. Congress continues to provide educational benefits to veterans but at reduced levels from the wartime GI bills. The National Defense Education Act of 1958 also affected higher education by assisting students, particularly in science, mathematics, and modern foreign languages.

Federal support for scientific research has also had an important impact on higher education. In 1950 Congress established the National Science Foundation to promote scientific research and education. NSF has provided fellowships for graduate education in the sciences, supported the development of science teachers at all levels, supported many specific scientific research projects, and supported miscellaneous scientific enterprises. In 1965, Congress established a National Endowment for the Arts and Humanities, but funded these fields at only a tiny fraction of the amount given to NSF. In addition to NSF, many other federal agencies have granted research contracts to universities for specific projects. Thus, with federal support, research has become a very big item in university life.

Today higher education aid is concentrated in four types of programs:

Pell grants.   In 1972, Congress established a Basic Educational Opportunity Grant program, later named Pell Grants after the program's sponsor Senator Claybourne Pell (Democrat of Rhode Island). The program offers college students in good standing a maximum grant of $1,600 per year minus the amount the student's family would reasonably be expected to contribute to educational expenses. An estimate 1.8 million students per year receive Pell Grants.

Guaranteed student loans.   A Guaranteed Student Loan program seeks to encourage private banks to make low-interest loans to students. The federal government pays the interest charge while the student is in school and guarantees repayment in the event the student defaults on the payment after graduation. An estimated 2.8 million undergraduate students and 2.4 million graduate and professional school students have guaranteed student loans. The average loan is about $2,000. These loans must be paid back after graduation, but the program has a very high rate of default (12 percent) on loans.

Campus-based aid.   There are several aid programs administered by colleges and universities themselves with federal assistance, including a National Direct Student Loan program, supplemental educational opportunity grants, and the College Work-Study program. There are an estimated one million Work-Study students who earn $600 to $800 per year while going to school.

Institutional assistance. A variety of other programs provide direct aid to colleges and universities, usually for construction and maintenance of special facilities, but these general aid programs have been cut back in recent years.

Efforts by the Reagan administration to curtail spending in higher education were largely unsuccessful. Middle-class students and their parents, together with organizations representing public and private colleges and universities, were successful in their resisted efforts to eliminate some campus-based aid programs and to eliminate graduate students from the guaranteed student loan program.

GROUPS IN HIGHER EDUCATION

Among the influential groups in public higher education—aside from the governors and legislators who must vote the funds each year—are the boards of trustees (often called regents) that govern public colleges and universities. Their authority varies from state to state. But in nearly every state they are expected not only to set broad policy directions in higher education but also to insulate higher education from direct political involvement of governors and legislators. Prominent citizens who are appointed to these boards are expected to champion higher education with the public and the legislature.

Another key group in higher education is composed of university and college presidents and their top administrative assistants. Generally, university presidents are the chief spokesmen for higher education, and they must convince the public, the regents, the governor, and the legislature of the value of state colleges and universities. The president's crucial role is one of maintaining support for higher education in the state; he or she frequently delegates administrative responsibilities for the internal operation of the university to the vice-presidents and deans. Support for higher education among the public and its representatives can be affected by a broad spectrum of university activities, some of which are not directly related to the pursuit of knowledge. A winning football team can stimulate legislative enthusiasm and win appropriations for a new classroom building. University service-oriented research—developing new crops or feeds, assessing the state's mineral resources, advising state and local government agencies on administrative problems, analyzing the state economy, advising local school authorities, and so forth—may help to convince the public of the practical benefits of knowledge. University faculty may be interested in advanced research and the education of future Ph.D.s, but legislators and their constituents are more interested in the quality and effectiveness of undergraduate teaching.

The faculty of the nation's 2,800 colleges and universities—over $2\frac{1}{2}$ million strong—traditionally identified themselves as professionals with strong attachments to their institutions. The historic pattern of college and university governance included faculty participation in policy making—not only academic requirements but also budgeting, personnel, building programs, etc. But governance by faculty committee has proven cumbersome, unwieldy, and time-consuming in an era of large-scale enrollments, multimillion-dollar budgets, and increases in the size and complexity of academic administration. Increasingly, concepts of public "accountability," academic "management," cost control, and centralized budgeting and purchasing have transferred power in colleges and universities from faculty to professional academic administrators.

The traditional organization of a faculty has been the American Association of University Professors (AAUP); historically this group confined itself to publishing data on faculty salaries and officially "censuring" colleges or universities that violate longstanding notions of academic freedom or tenure. (Tenure is the tradition that a faculty member who has demonstrated his or her competence by service in a college or university position for three to seven years cannot thereafter be dismissed except for "cause"— serious infraction of established rules or dereliction of duty, to be proved in an open hearing.) In recent years, the American Federation of Teachers (AFT) succeeded in convincing some faculty that traditional patterns of individual bargaining over salaries, teaching load, and working conditions in colleges and universities should be replaced by collective bargaining in the manner of unionized labor. The AFT is growing in power and membership. The growth of the AFT has spurred the AAUP on many campuses to assume a more militant attitude on behalf of faculty interests. The AAUP remains the largest faculty organization in the nation, but most of the nation's faculty are not affiliated with either the AAUP or the AFT. Faculty collective bargaining is complicated by the fact that faculty continue to play some managerial role in academic governance—for example, in choosing deans and department heads and sitting on salary committees.

The nation's 10 million students are the most numerous yet least influential of the groups directly involved in higher education. Students can be compared to other "consumer" groups in society which are generally less well organized than the groups that provide goods and services. American student political activism has been sporadic and generally directed toward broad symbolic issues—the Vietnam War, the nuclear freeze movement, environmental issues. Most students view their condition in life as a short-term one; organizing for effective group action requires a commitment of time and energy which most students are unwilling to subtract from their studies and social life. Nonetheless, student complaints are often filtered through parents to state legislators or university officials.

SUMMARY

Let us summarize educational policy with particular reference to the group interests involved:

1. Historically, educational policy has been decentralized in America, with states and communities carrying the major responsibility for public elementary and secondary and higher education. However, federal aid to education is nearly as old as the nation itself. Historically, federal aid was distributed for specific programs and services—vocational education; school lunch and milk; federally impacted schools; science, mathematics, and foreign languages—rather than general support of education.

2. The Elementary and Secondary Education Act of 1965 was the first large-scale aid-to-education program. The long struggle over federal aid to education indicates the power of interest groups in blocking legislation that has widespread public support, and the necessity of accommodating specific interest groups in policy formation. The difficulty in securing passage of a significant federal aid-to-education bill can be attributed to conflict between major racial and religious group interests over the character of such aid rather than to opposition to the idea of federal aid. Success was finally achieved when major interest groups reached a compromise.

3. Today the issue of tuition tax credits illustrates the struggle of group interests in education—religious groups, private school interests, public school defenders. To date there has been no group compromise over the issue and it remains a heated one in Washington.

4. Ultimately, questions of religion and public education find their way to the U.S. Supreme Court. The Court must interpret the meaning of the "no establishment" clause of the First Amendment as it affects government aid to church-related schools and prayer in the public schools. The Supreme Court referees group struggle.

5. Important groups in local school politics include taxpayers who vote in school board elections; citizen school board members; professional school administrators; and schoolteachers. The American Federation of Teachers is a labor union representing many classroom teachers in large cities. The National Education Association, an older and larger professional group, represents school administrators and teachers; it has become more militant in recent years in protecting teacher interests.

6. The "back to basics" movement frequently involves conflict between citizen groups demanding greater emphasis on the "three R's" and achievement testing for students and teachers, and professional educators who have less confidence in test scores and a wider appreciation of the many goals of public education.

7. State aid to higher education began in America's colonial era and federal assistance began as early as the Morrill Land Grant Act in 1862. Today public education enrolls three-quarters of the nation's 11 million

college and university students. Widespread public support for student aid and effective lobbying for higher education has protected Pell grants, guaranteed student loans, and campus-based aid from elimination as federal programs, though these programs have experienced reduced funding levels.

8. Public higher education in the states involves many diverse groups—governors, legislators, regents, college and university presidents, and faculty.

BIBLIOGRAPHY

COLEMAN, JAMES S., *Equality of Educational Opportunity*. Washington, D.C.: Government Printing Office, 1966.

EIDENBERG, EUGENE, and ROY D. MOREY, *An Act of Congress*. New York: Norton, 1969.

THOMAS, NORMAN D., *Education in National Politics*. New York: D. McKay, 1975.

TIMPANE, MICHAEL, ed. *The Federal Interest in Financing Schools*. Cambridge, Mass.: Ballinger, 1978.

ZEIGLER, HARMON, and M. KENT JENNINGS, *Governing American Schools*. Boston: Duxbury Press, 1974.

DEFENSE POLICY
strategies for serious games

U.S. Lance missile can carry a small nuclear warhead for battlefield use in the defense of Western Europe. (U.S. Army photograph)

Many years ago the Nobel prize-winning philosopher and peace advocate Bertrand Russell observed that the game of "chicken" was played by youthful degenerates and world leaders. The statement is true. But whether we like it or not, our life, liberty, and security depend upon our national leaders being willing to play the game. For as Russell himself observes:

> Practical politicians may admit all this [the dangers and destructiveness of war], but they argue that there is no alternative. If one side is unwilling to risk global war, while the other side is willing to risk it, the side which is willing to run the risk will be victorious in all negotiations and will ultimately reduce the other side to complete impotence . . . We are, therefore, faced quite inevitably with the choice between brinkmanship and surrender.[1]

Game theory provides an interesting way of thinking about defense policy. Defense policies of major world powers are interdependent. Each major power must adjust its own defense policies to reflect not only its own national objectives but also its expectations of what other major powers may do. Outcomes depend on the combination of choices made in world capitals. Moreover, it is not unreasonable to assume that major powers strive for rationality in defense policy making. Nations choose defense strategies (policies) that are designed to achieve an optimum payoff even after considering all their opponents' possible strategies. Thus, national defense policy making conforms to basic game-theoretic notions. Our use of game-theoretic ideas is limited, however, to suggesting interesting questions, posing dilemmas, and providing a vocabulary for dealing with policy making in a competitive, interdependent world.

DETERRENCE STRATEGY AND NUCLEAR WAR

In order to maintain peace and protect the national interest of the United States, primary reliance is placed upon the strategy of *deterrence*. In a general sense, deterrence means that war and aggression are prevented by making the consequences of such acts clearly unacceptable to rational leaders of other nations. This is the irony of deterrence: massive destruction of civilization is prevented by maintaining weapons capable of inflicting the massive destruction they seek to prevent. The United States does not wish to use its nuclear deterrent *physically*, but rather *psychologically*, to inhibit potential enemies from engaging in war or aggression.

For over forty years, following the nuclear destruction of Hiroshima and Nagasaki in 1945, nations have added nuclear weapons to their arsenals. Yet they have not been used in war. Why? Because nations are

---

[1]Bertrand Russell, *Common Sense and Nuclear Warfare* (New York: Simon & Schuster, 1959), p. 30.

peace-loving, God-fearing, humane, trusting, caring, compassionate? Or because fear of retaliation has prevented nuclear war?

The strategy of deterrence assures that peace is maintained through mutual fear of retaliation. It is based on the rational self-interest of national leaders. It does not depend on their love of peace, or fear of God, or sense of humanity. We are not willing to risk the lives of hundreds of millions of people on anything other than rational self-interest. If America loses its deterrent—its ability to threaten retaliation—then peace would rest on the fragile hope that our potential enemies would be merciful, kind, and compassionate. No national leader can afford to take such a risk.

Assured Destruction Deterrence

Assured destruction deterrence is the notion that one can dissuade a potential enemy from aggression or war by maintaining the capability to destroy his society even after absorbing a well-executed surprise attack. Assured destruction deterrence considers the enemy's most menacing attack—a surprise, full-salvo, first-strike against our own offensive forces. It emphasizes our "second-strike capability"—the ability of our forces to survive such an attack by the enemy and then to inflict an unacceptable level of destruction on his homeland in retaliation. Generally, U.S. defense analysts believe that an enemy will consider one-third to one-half of his population killed and two-thirds to three-quarters of his industrial capacity destroyed to be "unacceptable," and hence this level of damage is believed to be sufficient to deter a nuclear attack.[2]

Note that the "second-strike capability" required for assured destruction deterrence is far more complex than the mere possession of nuclear weapons. It is not sufficient to merely count missiles or megatonnage or "overkill" capacity. The key question is the *survivability* of an effective deterrent strike force. Assured destruction deterrence considers what can be done *after* a successful surprise attack by the enemy. The surviving forces will be damaged and not fully coordinated because of the enemy's attacks on communications and command installations. These forces must operate in the confusion of a post-attack environment. The enemy's defenses will be altered. Yet the surviving forces must still retain a credible capability of penetrating the best-alerted defenses and inflicting unacceptably high casualties.

It is extremely important to realize that second-strike capability must be *communicated* to the enemy if it is to serve as a deterrent. It would be irrational to keep your second-strike capacity a secret. (Even if you did not

---

[2]Testimony of Robert S. McNamara, Committee on Armed Services, U.S. House of Representatives, 89th Congress, 1st session, February 1965. Reprinted in Mark E. Smith and Claude J. Johns, eds., *American Defense Policy*, 2nd ed. (Baltimore: Johns Hopkins University Press, 1968), p. 98.

have such a capability, you might bluff that you did.) Hence, U.S. policy makers regularly publicize the strength and size of U.S. strategic offensive forces. Deterrence is achieved only if the enemy knows that you have the capacity to deliver unacceptable damage even after absorbing a first strike.

Moreover, a second-strike deterrent must be *credible*. A potential enemy must never begin to suspect that in the event of attack you would lack the will to use your weapons. Even if you doubt the morality of a retaliatory strike which would kill millions of people, you must hide this doubt in order to preserve deterrence.

Finally, deterrence strategy assumes that potential enemies are *rational*. In this context, rationality means that an enemy would not deliberately choose a course of action that would produce mass death and destruction in his own country. Needless to say, an irrational leader (or a terrorist group) with nuclear weapons is an immense danger to the world.

In summary, assured destruction deterrence is a psychological concept. It requires (1) second-strike capability, (2) communication, (3) credibility, and (4) a rational opponent. The capability of this nation's forces to survive a surprise, full-salvo, nuclear attack must not be allowed to erode; potential aggressors must be informed of these capabilities; and the threat to use these capabilities in case of attack must be credible. If these requirements are met, then there should never be any need to use our nuclear weapons physically. Peace should be the outcome.

Mutual Assured Destruction—MAD

If *both* sides possess second-strike capability, each side can deter the other from launching a first strike. The mutual development of second-strike capability by both the United States and the USSR provides *stability* in strategic nuclear relations between the superpowers. *If* (1) both the United States and the USSR possess sufficient, protected retaliatory forces, so that either side could absorb any conceivable first strike by the other and still retain sufficient power to strike back and destroy the other; and *if* (2) each side communicates this retaliatory power to the other side; and *if* (3) both sides believe that the other side can survive a first strike; *then* the situation is one of mutual assured destruction or "MAD." MAD's balance of terror—each side restrained by knowledge of the second-strike capability of the other side—has maintained stability and protected the world from nuclear war for the past several decades. MAD produces stability because each side knows that any offensive action it might take could lead to *its own destruction* and thus be suicidal. MAD removes the need for trust and replaces it with the calculated self-interest in not being devastated. World peace under MAD does not rest on trust or love or brotherhood, but on rational calculation of what is in each side's self-interest.

MAD has the effect of holding the populations of each nation hostage against the possibility of a first-strike attack. The population of the USSR can be destroyed by a retaliatory strike by the United States, and the population of the United States can be destroyed by a retaliatory strike by the USSR. Hence, both nations are threatened with the annihilation of their own populations if they launch a first-strike attack.

Flexible Strategic Response—
Limited Nuclear Options

Assured destruction deterrence strategy threatens a potential attacker with a massive retaliatory strike—a strike which would be targeted on population and industrial centers. But is such a threat really creditable, particularly in response to an attack on only our offensive missile and bomber bases? If deterrence fails, and the Soviets launch an attack at military targets in the United States that causes relatively few civilian casualties, would it be rational to retaliate with a full-salvo city-busting attack? Such a retaliatory strike would certainly cause the Soviets to reply in a similar fashion, using whatever missiles they have left to kill millions of Americans. The Soviet threat of a second attack on our cities might "deter our deterrent." Knowing that we cannot really use our nuclear forces against Russian cities without incurring great loss of life ourselves, the Soviet leadership might be tempted to launch a limited-salvo attack against our offensive missile and bomber bases.

In recent years, U.S. defense policy makers have become increasingly concerned about the threat of a *limited* Soviet attack against our offensive nuclear forces. Some American officials believe that a massive U.S. response to such a limited attack would be irrational, and more importantly that the Soviet Union would not consider the threat of a massive U.S. retaliatory strike to be creditable. It is argued that to deter the Soviets from a limited attack on U.S. offensive nuclear forces, the United States must develop a more *flexible strategic response,* including "limited nuclear options."

A limited nuclear options strategy would allow the United States to respond to a limited Soviet attack with a limited attack of our own. A limited U.S. attack would be directed at "counterforce targets"—Soviet missile and bomber bases. Civilian casualties and damage to industry would be avoided. An effort would be made *not* to kill Soviet leaders, so that some resolution to conflict could be achieved before it escalates into an even more damaging nuclear war against cities. "What we need is a series of measured responses to aggression which bears some relation to the provocation, prospects of terminating hostilities before general nuclear war breaks out, and some possibility of restoring deterrence. . . . To be creditable, and hence effective over the range of possible contingencies, deterrence must rest on many

options and on a spectrum of capabilities to support these options.
. . . Flexibility of response is essential."[3]

Of course, there are many dangerous elements in a policy of limited nuclear options. First of all, by suggesting that the destruction caused by nuclear war might be controlled and limited primarily to military targets, the likelihood of nuclear war may be increased. As nuclear war becomes "thinkable," it becomes more acceptable; and the psychological barriers inhibiting political leaders from engaging in nuclear war would be weakened. Second, there is the fear that nuclear war can never be controlled. Once the nuclear threshold is crossed, there is no way to limit or manage the resulting destruction. Even limited nuclear attacks on military targets would kill millions of people in the United States and the Soviet Union. Escalation would be inevitable. Third, counterforce targeting threatens the second-strike capability of the enemy. It is the equivalent of the United States pursuing a disarming first-strike capability. If we achieve significant counterforce capability against the Soviets they will be encouraged to launch on warning to preserve *their* deterrent. This would create an even more delicate and dangerous world nuclear balance. Fourth, the pursuit of counterforce capability will lead to a very expensive and uncontrollable arms race between the superpowers. Counterforce weapons must have "hard target kill capability," and this means great accuracy, higher yields, and larger numbers of warheads.

Rational opponents of limited nuclear options continue to press for "stability"—the preservation of mutual assured destruction (MAD) capabilities. They perceive counterforce targeting and counterforce weapons as "destabilizing," that is, more likely to lead to war than to maintain the peace. They do not wish to minimize the costs of nuclear war, but rather to guarantee that the costs would be so great that no national leader would even consider a nuclear attack. They oppose damage limitation efforts (civil defense, ABMs, city evacuations) because these efforts imply that nuclear war is manageable; they would prefer instead to ensure that the potential damage to both sides in a nuclear conflict would be so great as to make nuclear war unthinkable.

STRATEGIC WEAPONS: THE EMBATTLED TRIAD

In striving to maintain assured destruction deterrence, the United States, over the past thirty years, has relied on a "TRIAD" of weapons systems: land-based missiles (ICBMs), submarine-launched missiles (SLBMs), and

---

[3]Secretary of Defense James R. Schlesinger, "Flexible Strategic Options," in John E. Endicott and Roy W. Stafford, eds., *American Defense Policy*, 4th ed. (Baltimore: Johns Hopkins University Press, 1977), p. 82.

manned bombers (B-52s). The strategic concept of the TRIAD includes the notion that any *one* of three sets of forces would give the United States assured destruction deterrence: if the ICBMs were destroyed in their silos by an enemy first strike, and all of the manned bomber force were destroyed, the United States could still retaliate with an SLBM attack which would itself inflict unacceptable damages on the enemy. Each "leg" of the TRIAD is supposed to be an independent, survivable, second-strike force. Each "leg" of the TRIAD poses separate and unique problems for an enemy in devising a way to destroy the U.S. second-strike deterrent.

ICBMs

Both the United States and the Soviet Union have developed long-range intercontinental ballistic missiles (ICBMs) that can travel between the United States and USSR in less than forty minutes. To improve their survivability, both sides have placed their ICBMs in "hardened" (concrete and steel) underground silos—designed and constructed so that they can be destroyed only by a direct hit. The United States built 1,000 Minuteman ICBMs in the early 1960s together with a few larger Titan missiles. These aging missiles continue to be this nation's complete ICBM force. The Minuteman is a solid-fuel missile which can be launched on short notice and can strike within one-quarter mile of any target in the Soviet Union. About half of the Minuteman force carries multiple independently targeted reentry vehicles (MIRVs) which are smaller nuclear warheads that separate from the missile itself and can be accurately directed to separate targets. These Minuteman III missiles carry three MIRVed warheads with 335 kiloton weapons. (While these weapons are small by today's standards, they are sixteen times more powerful than the 20-kiloton "Little Boy" A-bomb dropped on Hiroshima.) The destructiveness of various U.S. and Soviet missiles at various distances from the center of detonation is shown in Table 8-1.

Beyond replacing earlier Minuteman missiles with the MIRV-carrying Minuteman III, and improving the accuracy of the Minuteman guidance system, the United States did not deploy any new ICBMs for twenty-five years.

In contrast, the Soviet Union, during the past twenty-five years, continued the development of newer, larger, and more accurate MIRVed missiles. The result is a diversified Soviet Strategic Rocket Force which includes 1398 ICBMs of various types, as shown in Table 8-2. The SS-18 is currently the Soviets' major land-based ICBM. It dwarfs the Minuteman III. It carries *ten* MIRV warheads, each with a *one-megaton* weapon, and there is no reason to doubt its accuracy. The Soviets have 308 of these large ICBMs, which means that their SS-18 force can deliver 3080 one-megaton weapons.

The debate in Congress over the second Strategic Arms Limitation

TABLE 8-1   The Destructiveness of Nuclear Weapons

		WEAPON SIZE		
	40 KT U.S. POLARIS POSEIDON	170 KT U.S. MIRVed MINUTEMAN III, ONE WARHEAD	1 MT U.S. MINUTEMAN II UNMIRVed WARHEAD; USSR MIRVed SS18, ONE WARHEAD	5MT USSR SS17
Crater diameter[a]	.08	.13	.25	.70
Fireball radius	.20	.35	.70	1.40
150 PSI blast[b]				
(100% dead)	.20	.30	.60	1.00
5 PSI blast[c]				
(50% dead)	1.00	1.60	3.00	5.00
2 PSI blast[d]				
(5% dead)	1.60	2.70	5.00	8.00

[a]All figures expressed as miles or percentage thereof. Destruction of all facilities including hardened silos and underground command and control facilities.
[b]Fatal blast level for all unprotected populations, survival in reinforced concrete construction.
[c]Severe damage to unprotected populations, commercial buildings, and homes. However, standard fallout shelters can protect most of the population from blast pressures up to 7 PSI.
[d]Fatal injuries begin at 2 PSI. Population and buildings will survive outside this radius.
Source: Michael B. Donley, ed., *The SALT Handbook* (Washington, D.C.: The Heritage Foundation, 1979).

Treaty (SALT II) exposed Soviet superiority in numbers and size of their ICBM force. With their improved accuracy, the Soviets can now destroy the entire U.S. land-based missile force using only a small portion of their own ICBM force. This danger to the survivability of our ICBM force compelled President Carter and later President Reagan to announce plans for the development of a new ICBM system called the MX. Modernization of our land-based ICBMs, and the search for a *survivable* basing mode for

TABLE 8-2   Soviet ICBMs

TYPE	YEAR		WARHEAD	NUMBER
SS-11	1966		1-2 MT	520
SS-13	1968		1 MT	60
SS-17	1975		5 MT	150
SS-18	1975		10 × 1 MT (MIRV)	308
SS-19	1975		6 × 1 MT (MIRV)	360
SS-24	1986	Under development	10 × 1 MT (MIRV)	—
SS-25	1985	Nearing deployment (land mobile)	1 MT	—

Source: U.S. Department of Defense, *Soviet Military Power 1985* (Washington, D.C.: Government Printing Office, 1985).

them, now occupies defense planners, the president, and Congress. (See discussion below.)

Manned Bombers

The second "leg" of the TRIAD is the intercontinental bomber. Manned bombers can survive a first strike if they are in the air. A certain portion of a manned bomber force can be kept in the air during crisis periods. Given adequate warning (knowledge that the enemy has fired his ICBMs or SLBMs), a significant percentage of bombers can get off the ground before incoming missiles arrive. The range of intercontinental bombers (a 6000-mile two-way mission range, with added range from in-flight refueling) allows the United States to keep its bombers at home bases. Unlike missiles, manned bombers can be called back if the alert is an error; they can be redirected to other targets in flight; and they can be used in conventional nonnuclear war if needed. Manned aircarft can be equipped with short-range (25–75 mile) air-to-surface missiles (ASMs) or long-range air-launched Cruise missiles (ALCMs) to give the aircraft "stand off" capability, that is, the capability to launch nuclear attacks on targets without ever flying over the targeted area. The U.S. intercontinental manned bomber force is composed mainly of aged, slow, and large B-52s. This bomber was developed in 1952 as a high-penetration aircraft (a plane that would fly high over enemy air defenses), with a 6000-mile range and a capability of carrying large numbers of nuclear weapons as bombs and short-range air-to-surface missiles. But the B-52 is subsonic, that is, it flies at a maximum speed of 550 miles per hour. It is large, and therefore it presents a better target on radar for enemy air defense missiles and interceptor aircraft. It was produced between 1952 and 1962, and it is predicted to "wear out" in the 1980s. Indeed, many of the original force of 600 B-52s have been cannibalized to keep 241 aircraft "operational." The B-52 has undergone eight major improvements (to the B-52G and B-52H models) to try to offset Soviet air defenses. The latest improvement is the equipping of a small number of B-52s to carry long-range Cruise missiles. Soviet surface-to-air missiles (SAMs) now make high-altitude penetration very risky. Low-altitude penetration (as low as 100 to 200 feet) is preferred to make radar detection difficult and radar-guided SAMs less effective.

The Soviet Union has a supersonic, low-altitude penetration bomber, the TU22M, known in the United States as the "Backfire." The Soviets claim that this plane is not an intercontinental bomber and not a "strategic" weapon, because its range is less than 5000 miles. But, of course, with in-flight refueling the Backfire can penetrate any target in the United States. The Soviets are also developing a newer long-range Blackjack bomber. The development of the speedy Backfire and Blackjack offers clear evidence that the Soviets do *not* regard manned bombers as outmoded.

SLBMs

The third "leg" of the TRIAD is the submarine-launched ballistic missile (SLBM) force. At present, this is the most "survivable" force and therefore the best second-strike component of the TRIAD. Most defense analysts agree that Soviet antisubmarine warfare (ASW) capability is not now, nor will it be in the foreseeable future, capable of destroying a significant portion of our SLBM force.

For many years, the U.S. SLBM force was carried in 41 Polaris nuclear-powered submarines (SSBNs), each carrying 16 SLBMs which could be fired while submerged. This was a total force of 656 SLBMs, but at any given time only about two-thirds of the submarine force was at sea in a position to fire their missiles. The first Polaris submarines were completed in 1960 and they have accumulated many years of steady use. Today remodeled Poseidon SSBNs are armed with new Poseidon missiles, which have a 4000-mile range and can carry seven to ten MIRVed warheads. The United States is also building a force of new nuclear-powered Trident submarines. Each Trident carries twenty-four missiles with a 6000-mile range and ten MIRVed warheads. The first Trident entered service in 1981. The longer range of the Trident's missiles enable it to hide almost anywhere in the world's oceans and hit targets in the Soviet Union. Older Poseidon SSBNs are now being retired. Eventually the U.S. Navy expects to acquire eight to ten Tridents; such a force could carry a total of 240 SLBMS with 2400 separately targeted warheads. The Trident force should extend the American underwater deterrents beyond the year 2000.

The Soviets also have an SLBM force in nuclear-powered submarines. In 1985 the Soviets had 62 modern SSBNs carrying 928 nuclear-tipped missiles. But these "Hotel," "Yankee," and "Delta" class submarines cannot match the Trident in speed, range, sophistication, and numbers of missiles. However, recently the Soviets launched three new "Typhoon" SSBNs, the world's largest submarines, each with 20 long-range SLBMs.

STRATEGIC FORCE MODERNIZATION: MX, B-1, AND CRUISE

For twenty years, from the early 1960s to the early 1980s, the United States did not introduce any major changes in its strategic TRIAD. In effect, the United States engaged in a one-sided twenty-year "freeze" on strategic forces. The United States did not increase its number of ICBMs, or SLBMs, or B-52s (which declined in number) during this long period.

Qualitative improvements were made in U.S. strategic forces, including improved missile accuracy, MIRVing of warheads, and arming of B-52s with Cruise missiles. But no major new ICBM system was deployed, or new bomber added to our forces, or new strategic submarine built, until the first Trident was commissioned in 1981. But during this same twenty-year period the Soviet Union built the world's largest and heaviest ICBM force, the largest SLBM force, and its new supersonic, low-flying Backfire bomber.

The U.S. response to the massive Soviet buildup of strategic forces is a costly strategic modernization program which includes:

1. the Cruise missile, to be carried on older B-52 bombers to allow them to attack targets at a distance of 600 kilometers or more;
2. the B-1 bomber (to replace the B-52), a supersonic, low-flying aircraft which can penetrate Soviet air defenses;
3. the MX missile (to replace the Minuteman), a MIRVed missile with ten separately targeted warheads in a survivable basing mode;
4. the Trident submarine (to replace the Polaris) with 24 longer-range MIRVed SLBMs which allow the Trident to hide in millions of square miles of ocean.

The Cruise Missile

Cruise missiles are small, air-breathing, subsonic, low-flying guided missiles that can be fired from the ground (Ground Launched Cruise Missiles, GLCM), or from the air (Air Launched Cruise Missiles, ALCM), or from surface ships or submerged submarines (Sea Launched Cruise Missiles, SLCM). Cruise is very inexpensive to build compared to other weapons; tens of thousands could be built to overwhelm any possible air defense system and frustrate any possible attempt to destroy all of them on a first strike. Cruise missiles are very small (under 30 feet long); their size makes them mobile and difficult to locate; a single B-52 can carry twenty; and attack submarines can fire them under water from torpedo tubes. Although they are very slow-flying, their radar guidance system allows them to fly close to the ground; very few could be intercepted in a full-salvo attack; and they are very accurate. Currently the United States is extending the life of the B-52 by arming many of these with ALCMs. These ALCMs will allow the old slow-flying and vulnerable B-52s to avoid flying over enemy air defenses.

B-1 Bomber

An advanced manned bomber, the B-1 was developed and tested in the mid-1970s as a replacement for the aging B-52s. The B-1 is a small, intercontinental, supersonic (over 2000 miles per hour) bomber, designed for low-altitude penetration of modern air defenses. After successful test flying of this aircraft, the Carter administration cancelled production in 1977 arguing that the program was too costly and that Cruise missiles could extend the useful life of the B-52s. Criticism of this decision was widespread in Congress and the military. (To deflect some of this criticism the Carter administration announced that it was working on an even more advanced aircraft, designed to go undetected on enemy radar screens, the "Stealth," but this bomber has yet to be built.) The Reagan administration restored funding for the B-1. A production goal of 100 aircraft has been established, less than half of the original planned force.

MX

The MX missile is a land-based, intercontinental, solid-fueled missile which can carry ten MIRVed warheads. Research on the MX began in response to the improved accuracy of Soviet ICBMs, which placed our land-based Minuteman missiles in danger from a first strike. The central problem of the research was to find a *survivable* basing mode for land-based missiles. The original Carter plan would have mounted each of 200 MXs on large mobile carriers which could move around a "racetrack" to any one of twenty-six hardened sites spaced along tracks. The Soviets would not know which sites were empty and which sites contained operational MX missiles. The Reagan administration rejected the racetrack basing mode as too costly. It would use up many thousands of square miles of Western land, and there is always the possibility that the Soviets would devise a way to beat this giant "shell game" and learn where the real missiles are concealed. President Reagan went forward with a plan for 100 of the new missiles, but argument continued in Washington over how to deploy it in a survivable basing mode.

To help resolve the basing problem, President Reagan established an independent and bipartisan Commission on Strategic Alternatives, headed by former national security advisor General Brent Scowcroft. The commission recommended basing the MX in existing reinforced Minutemen silos. The Commission argued that the MX was required in order to threaten at least a portion of Soviet offensive missile forces. This counterforce threat would help deter the Soviets from a limited nuclear attack on the U.S.; with the MX, the U.S. could threaten a retaliatory strike at remaining Soviet missiles rather than at their cities. The commission also recommended the development of small, single-warhead, mobile missiles (quickly dubbed the "Midgetmen" by the press); these smaller missiles could be easily and quickly moved about the countryside, making them difficult targets for an attacker. The commission also recommended more efforts in arms control negotiations with the USSR to achieve agreement on equal numbers of *warheads*, so that neither nation could threaten to destroy all of the other's deterrent forces. President Reagan endorsed the commission's recommendations, but Congress so far has voted to fund only 50 MX missiles.

STAR WARS—THE STRATEGIC DEFENSE INITIATIVE

For over forty years, since the terrible nuclear blast of Hiroshima and Nagasaki, in 1945, the world has avoided nuclear war. Peace has been maintained by deterrence—by the threat of devastating nuclear attacks which would be launched in retaliation to an enemy first strike. While this balance of terror has kept the peace, many scholars, soldiers and citizens have tried to think of a better way of avoiding nuclear war. Instead of deterring war through fear of retaliation, perhaps we should seek a technological defense against nuclear missiles, one that will eventually render them "impotent and obsolete."

According to President Reagan,

> Our nuclear retaliating forces have deterred war for 40 years. The fact is, however, that we have no defense against nuclear ballistic missile attack . . . In the event that deterrence failed, a president's only recourse would be to surrender or to retaliate. Nuclear retaliation whether massive or limited, would result in the loss of millions of lives. . . .
>
> If we apply our great scientific and engineering talent to the problem of defending against ballistic missiles, there is a very real possibility that future presidents will be able to deter war by means other than threatening devastation to any aggressor—and by a means which threatens no one. . . .
>
> Emerging technologies offer the possibilities of non-nuclear options for destroying missiles and the nuclear warheads they carry in all phases of their flight. New technologies may be able to permit a layered defense by providing: sensors for identifying and tracking missiles and nuclear warheads; advanced ground and spaceborne intercepters and direct energy weapons to destroy both missiles and nuclear warheads; advanced ground and spaceborne intercepters and directed energy weapons to destroy both missiles and nuclear warheads; and the technology to permit the command control and communication necessary to operate a layered defense. . . .[4]

President Reagan's Strategic Defense Initiative (SDI) is a research program designed to explore means of destroying enemy nuclear missiles in space before they can reach their targets. Following the President's initial announcement of SDI in March 1983, the press quickly labeled the effort "Star Wars." At present, SDI is only a research program. The Soviets have two small ABM (antiballistic missile) systems permitted by SALT I, and the U.S. has successfully experimented in destroying a single object in space. But at present neither side can stop any significant portion of the other side's missiles once they have been fired. For many years to come, deterrence will continue to rest upon fear of retaliation.

As a broad research program, the SDI is not yet based on any single

---

[4]President Ronald Reagan, *The President's Strategic Defense Initiative*, White House, January 3, 1985.

type of ballistic missile defense. A *boost phase defense* might attempt to destroy enemy missiles shortly after they are launched. Sophisticated battle management satellites might keep watch over known Soviet missile fields. Antimissiles might be placed in orbit over Soviet missiles, ready to destroy these missiles during their initial boost phase. Or lasers or particle beams might be directed to mirrors orbiting over Soviet missile fields and bounced toward Soviet missiles in flight. If Soviet missiles escape these early boost phase defenses, perhaps *a layered defense* in space might be constructed in an effort to destroy missiles and warheads while they are traveling toward the United States. Defensive missiles or beams would have to locate, identify, track, and destroy perhaps thousands of separate missiles and warheads. Finally, those enemy warheads which survive a layer defense in space might be attacked in the *terminal phase* of their flight. Antiballistic missile defense might be set up specifically to defend expected targets, for example, the Capitol and command centers, or our own offensive missile sites. (Currently the Soviet Union has one ABM system defending Moscow and one defending their offensive ICBM fields; the U.S. has no operating ABM systems.)

Several different technologies are currently being explored for ballistic missile defenses. (1) *Conventional ABM* technologies featuring rocket-powered missile intercepters have been available for years; conceivably this "off-the-shelf" technology could be placed in space orbit over Soviet ICBM fields, as well as based on the ground to protect ICBM sites and command centers. (2) In the past, ABMs have contained conventional explosives and were guided by radar and heat sensors. Today research is providing an *electromagnetic rail gun* which would fling nonexplosive projectives ("smart rocks") along a magnetic beam in space. (3) *Chemical lasers* get their energy from combustion of fuels; this energy can be concentrated in beams which may destroy enemy missiles. Since chemical lasers can be distorted by the atmosphere, these weapons would also have to be placed in space. Perhaps "fighting mirrors" could be located in space over the Soviet Union, prepared to reflect laser beams generated by a chemical laser elsewhere in space. (4) However, more powerful *X-ray lasers* might be generated from the ground, somewhere in the United States, and projected by space-based mirrors toward Soviet missile sites. X-ray lasers are untroubled by atmospheric conditions. But X-ray lasers require an intense power source—perhaps an underground nuclear device. (This presents a political problem for President Reagan, who pledged a nonnuclear defense. The X-ray laser power source would be nuclear, although the destruction of enemy missiles would be accomplished by X-ray beams not by a nuclear blast.) The Soviets are so concerned with the X-ray laser program that they have offered a complete ban on all nuclear testing in the hope of halting U.S. development of this technology.

SDI requires the development of the most sophisticated and reliable computers ever developed. "Star Wars" weapons must be preprogrammed to fire at Soviet offensive missiles within seconds of their launch. Sophisticated battle management computations must be made—detecting, tracking, aiming, firing, assessing damage, coordinating firings, distinguishing decoys, and so on—for a giant space battle which would last less than 30 minutes. It is questionable whether reliable computer programs can be written for such large and complex tasks.

In addition to proving its feasibility, any ballistic missile defense technology must meet two important strategic tests in order to be effective. First, it must be cost-effective at the margin: it must be cheaper for the United States to add additional defenses than for the Soviet Union to add additional offensive missiles to overcome these defenses. A ballistic missile defense which is not cost-effective will simply encourage the Soviet Union to add additional offensive weapons. Secondly, it must be survivable itself and able to overcome Soviet countermeasures. This concern may give rise to a preference for ground-based lasers located in the United States over space-based lasers vulnerable to Soviet attack. Soviet ASAT (antisatellite) technology has already progressed for many years. Only recently has the United States begun ASAT research. Soviet ASAT capability is virtually indistinguishable from a capability to attack our proposed orbiting ballistic missile defenses.

Currently there is some confusion about the goals of SDI. Is the goal to create an impenetrable shield that will protect not only the population of the United States but the population of our European allies as well? Will this shield allow us to dismantle our retaliatory nuclear forces because deterrence will no longer be necessary? Or is the goal of SDI simply to enhance deterrence by protecting our second strike forces against a surprise disarming strike by the Soviets? If a completely impenetrable shield is not possible, will we not be required to keep some retaliatory forces as a deterrent? Will SDI reduce reliance on retaliation and allow some reduction in offensive weapons? If we eventually developed an effective defense against ballistic missiles, would we share this technology with the Soviets in order to calm their fears about a nuclear attack from a defended United States? It is important to remember that SDI is now only a research program; these questions will confront policy makers in the twenty-first century.

Opponents of President Reagan's Strategic Defense Initiative have made several important arguments:

1. U.S. efforts to defend itself against ICBMs may prompt the Soviets to build more and better ICBMs. SDI may simply stimulate an arms race. Even supporters of SDI acknowledge that missile defenses must be survivable, or else

the Soviets will simply attack the defense before launching their ICBMs. Supporters of SDI also acknowledge that defenses must be cheaper to build than ICBMs, or else the Soviets will simply build more ICBMs than we can build defenses.

2. The SDI might be interpreted by the Soviets as an effort by the U.S. to gain a "first strike" capability—the ability to launch a nuclear attack against the USSR and than defend ourselves against their weakened retaliatory response. This is the official line taken by the Soviets in objecting to "Star Wars." They claim we are seeking to "militarize space" in an effort to gain an advantage over them.

3. SDI might destabilize the balance of terror currently existing between the U.S. and the USSR. If the U.S. could defend itself against ICBMs and the Soviet Union could not, the U.S. would gain a strategic advantage.

4. SDI is technologically infeasible; efforts to build missile defenses will waste tens of billions of dollars. A complete protective "superdome" over the United States and its allies is impossible. Even a few nuclear weapons can cause millions of deaths.

5. SDI threatens to violate the SALT I Treaty prohibiting anti-ballistic missiles. Moreover, the SDI program may stand in the way of future agreements with the Soviet Union for promoting or reducing nuclear weapons. The Soviets have stated repeatedly that the U.S. must give up its SDI before any agreement on nuclear arms can be reached.

In contrast, supporters of the strategic defensive initiative argue that:

1. Technological advances offer the promise of maintaining peace by means of space defense, rather than the threat of nuclear retaliation. SDI is only a research program. Decisions about actually deploying a ballistic missile defense are many years in the future.

2. A ballistic missile defense is preferable to threats of retaliation for maintaining peace. What if deterrence fails someday? What if an irrational leader ignores our threat of retaliation and proceeds to attack the United States regardless of the consequences? A ballistic missile defense would provide the president and the nation with a means of defending ourselves in an actual attack.

3. A ballistic missile defense does not threaten millions of lives, in the fashion of our current deterrent strategy. Defensive weapons would be nonnuclear; they would be targeted on missile and warheads, not cities. A defensive strategy is morally preferable to threatening millions of lives.

4. A ballistic missile defense can offset the Soviet superiority in numbers and size of missiles. An effective missile defense may someday convince them that continuing increases in numbers of ICBMs are pointless. Indeed, the Soviets may be pressured to make reductions in their ICBMs in exchange for limiting the U.S. "Star Wars" program.

5. A ballistic missile defense, when employed in conjunction with our retaliatory forces, would improve deterrence. Any Soviet plans for a first strike against our retaliatory forces would be frustrated by the uncertainties created by our new defenses. Soviet generals could not guarantee that all of our retaliatory forces would be destroyed in a surprise attack.

ARMS LIMITATION GAMES

The United States and the Soviet Union have engaged in negotiations over strategic arms for many years. These negotiations began in 1970 under President Richard Nixon and his national security advisor Henry Kissinger and were originally labeled the Strategic Arms Limitation Talks (SALT). These talks produced the SALT I agreement in 1972 which was ratified by the U.S. Senate. Later, under President Jimmy Carter, they produced the SALT II agreement of 1979 which was *not* ratified by the U.S. Senate; however, both the United States and the USSR have avoided direct violations of the provisions of SALT II. President Carter formally withdrew the SALT II treaty from Senate consideration following the Soviet invasion of Afghanistan. President Reagan described SALT II as a "flawed" agreement, but he pledged that the U.S. would continue to honor the terms of this agreement as long as the Soviets did so. Reagan called for new talks aimed at arms "reduction" rather than "limitation," and renamed the talks Strategic Arms Reduction Talks or START. But in 1983 the Soviets walked out of these talks, protesting NATO's decision to deploy U.S. medium-range missiles in Europe to counter an earlier Soviet deployment of European missiles. However, the Soviet walkout failed to intimidate the Western European nations; a heavy-handed Soviet "peace" offensive failed; Reagan was reelected; and the "Star Wars" ballistic missile defense program was announced. In early 1985 the Soviets agreed to return to the bargaining table for new talks on nuclear and space arms at Geneva, Switzerland. In 1986 President Reagan announced that the U.S. would not be bound by SALT II treaty limits if the Soviets remained inflexible at the bargaining table.

SALT I

SALT I in 1972 was a milestone in that it marked the first effort by the superpowers to limit strategic weapons. SALT I consisted of a formal treaty halting further development of ABMs, and an executive agreement placing numerical limits on offensive missiles. The ABM treaty limited each side to one ABM site for defense of its national capital and one ABM site for defense of an offensive ICBM field. The total number of ABMs permitted was 200 for each side, 100 at each location. (The USSR already has both of its ABM sites constructed; the United States had one site at the Grand Forks, North Dakota, Minuteman field, which was deactivated in 1975.) Under the offensive arms agreement, each side was frozen at the total number of offensive missiles completed or under construction. The Soviet Union was permitted 1618 land-based missiles. The United States was permitted to maintain 1054 land-based missiles. Both sides were limited to the missile-carrying submarines operational or under construction at the time of the agreement; this also allowed the Soviets to gain an edge on the total number of SLBMs. Each nation agreed not to interfere in the electronic and satellite intelligence-gathering activities of the other nation.

Why would the United States and the USSR enter into such an agreement? First of all the USSR achieved what it had been struggling toward for decades: the United States officially recognized in a treaty Soviet superiority in the number and size of offensive weapons. The United States hoped to achieve a slowing of the Soviet momentum in the building of ICBMs and missile-carrying submarines. Bombers were not covered by the agreement, and at that time (prior to the deployment of the Soviet Backfire) the United States had superiority in numbers of long-range bombers. U.S. nuclear weapons in Europe, which were designed to defend NATO but *could* be used against the Soviets, were not included in the agreement, nor were the British and French SLBMs or bombers. Both sides agreed not to build large-scale ABM systems to defend their own cities. This meant that each agreed *not* to defend its own population. Each nation held the population of the other as hostage (a "stabilizing" condition) as long as neither developed a credible first-strike capability. Satellite reconnaissance made the SALT agreement self-enforcing; without satellite photography the question of verification would have doomed negotiations.

Experience with SALT

Soviet weapons development after SALT I continued at a rapid pace and soon began to threaten U.S. second-strike capability. SALT I did *not* limit MIRVs, nor the size or accuracy of missiles, nor the numbers of manned bombers. In all these areas, the Soviets made impressive gains. The Soviets deployed the world's largest missile, the SS-18, which carries *ten* one-megaton weapons. The Soviets built over 300 of these giant missiles—enough to carry over 3000 one-megaton warheads. The Soviets acquired the capability of destroying our ICBM forces using only their new SS-18s, while keeping the bulk of their ICBM and SLBM forces in reserve for threatened use against American cities if the United States attempted to retaliate. Finally, the Soviets deployed a new supersonic manned bomber, the Backfire, which is capable, with in-flight refueling, of penetrating U.S. air defenses and hitting any remaining targets.

SALT II

The SALT II agreement in 1979 was a complex one. Its major provisions included:

1. An overall limit on the number of strategic nuclear delivery vehicles (ICBMs, SLBMs, manned bombers) at 2250.

2. An overall limit on the total number of MIRVed ballistic missiles, ICBMs, and SLBMs and strategic bombers with long-range Cruise missiles.

3. A ban on the construction of *heavy* ICBMs. (This was a controversial item because the USSR already had 314 heavy ICBMs (the SS-18) while the United States had none. The treaty prevents the United States from building a heavy missile and recognizes the USSR monopoly in this weapon.)

4. A ban on the testing or deployment of new types of ICBMs, with the exception of one new type of light ICBM for each side. (This provision allowed the United States to build its new MX mobile missiles.)

5. A limit of ten MIRVed warheads on a single ICBM; a limit of fourteen MIRVed warheads on a single SLBM; and a limit of twenty Cruise missiles on a single bomber. (These limits represent current technology; they do not require changes in programs of either side.)

6. A ban on the rapid reload of ICBM launchers. (This affects the USSR program because only Soviet ICBMs can refire. Soviet reload missiles must be kept away from launch sites.)

7. An agreement by both sides not to interfere with national technical means (NTM) of verification of the provisions of the treaty. Neither side will interfere with photo-reconnaissance satellites or use deliberate concealment measures which impede verification. Electronic signals from test missiles, known as telemetry, cannot be encoded. (This is an extension of the SALT I provision prohibiting inteference in satellite and electronic intelligence.)

The Failure of SALT

Initially American leaders hoped that SALT would modify Soviet behavior and improve the political relationship between the United States and the USSR, a relationship commonly called *détente*. But Soviet expansionism was unchecked by the SALT agreements and SALT II was officially withdrawn from the U.S. Senate by President Carter in response to the Soviet invasion of Afghanistan. But objections were also raised to various strategic arrangements in SALT II:

1. The treaty recognized the Soviet monopoly in "heavy" missiles (SS-18s). The treaty did not require the dismantling of this large Soviet ICBM force, and did not permit the United States to build a comparable force. With its SS-18s, the Soviets continue to have a first-strike capability against our aging Minuteman ICBM force. This Soviet first-strike advantage against our land-based missiles will exist until the U.S. MX missile is fully deployed—and MX deployment may not be completed until 1990.

2. The treaty also recognized Soviet advantage in size, numbers, weight, deliverable warheads, and deliverable megatonnage in land-based ICBMs. SLBM forces were roughly equal, provided, of course, the the United States continued the Trident program.

3. The only "advantage" enjoyed by the United States was in "intercontinental" bombers—B-52s—which few people believe can be effective today. The treaty did *not* cover the Soviet Backfire bomber (except to limit its production to thirty per year), and this bomber *is* an effective modern weapon.

4. Finally, the long-term political effect of a SALT II treaty might have been to slow down American weapons development and deployment. Once a treaty is passed, U.S. defense programs may be set aside in the hopes that disarmament agreements will make them unnecessary. However, we can be reasonably certain that the *Soviets* will not deemphasize defense because of any arms agreement. We can expect that they will build right up to the limits of any agreement and continue work on weapons systems not covered by an agreement. In other words, arms agreements may be a ploy by the Soviets to bring about a relaxation of U.S. defense efforts while their own programs continue to move ahead rapidly.

START

Early in his administration President Reagan called for "substantial reductions in nuclear arms which would result in levels that are equal and verifiable."[5] The Reagan administration rejected the approach represented in earlier SALT negotiations that only future growth in nuclear arms be "limited." Instead, the goal in U.S. policy became "reductions" in nuclear arms. To symbolize this change, arms negotiations were relabeled START—Strategic Arms Reduction Talks.

The U.S. position in the START negotiations was based on the premise that the Soviet Union had acquired "a definite margin of superiority—enough so that there is risk."[6] If the U.S. and Soviet arsenals were frozen at current levels, not only would the United States be endangered, but also the prospects for negotiated reductions would disappear. With the United States frozen in a position of inferiority, there would be no incentive for the Soviets to negotiate reductions. Indeed, the Soviets would have no incentive to reduce their current arsenal unless convinced that the United States would rebuild its defenses to match the Soviet level. This meant that the success of the START negotiations depended on convincing the Soviets that the United States was really prepared to match Soviet forces if no agreement was reached. Thus under President Reagan, U.S. strategic force modernization efforts—the MX, Trident, B-1, and Cruise weapons—were defended as a means of forcing the Soviets to agree to arms reductions.

In all arms talks the Soviets have sought to count British and French nuclear missiles and aircraft against any limits placed on the U.S. side. They have also sought to count all U.S. nuclear forces located in Europe, including short- and medium-range battlefield nuclear weapons and all European-based U.S. aircraft, against any limits on U.S. "strategic" weapons. In short, the Soviets strive to be equal or superior to any *combination* of forces which could be arrayed against them anywhere in the world.

---

[5]Text of address of President Ronald Reagan on U.S. foreign policy, November 18, 1981.

[6]President Ronald Reagan, March 31, 1982, reported in *Congressional Quarterly Weekly Report*, April 3, 1982, p. 725.

According to the Soviets, their 1983 walkout of the START talks was a protest against NATO's decision to carry out the deployment of U.S. medium-range missiles in Europe. The original NATO decision regarding U.S. ground-launched Cruise and Pershing II missiles in Europe had been made in 1979 in response to the earlier deployment of Soviet mobile, multi-warhead, medium-range, SS-20 missiles targeted on the Western European nations. NATO had postponed the actual deployment of U.S. missiles in the hope that the Soviets would agree instead to withdraw their SS-20s.

The Geneva Talks

What brought the Soviets back to the negotiating table in 1985? The walkout failed to intimidate Western European governments; despite Soviet threats these governments went forward with the deployment of U.S. medium-range missiles. A Soviet "peace" offensive resulted in noisy demonstrations in European capitals, but failed to break up the NATO alliance. The reelection of Ronald Reagan promised a continuation of the U.S. defense modernization program. Finally, the president's announcement that the U.S. intended to begin a program of research on advanced ballistic missile defenses—the program labeled "Star Wars" by the press and the Soviets—seemed to motivate the Kremlin leaders to reopen talks. Although the Soviets publicly ridicule the prospect of an effective ballistic missile defense and claim to be able to defeat it with more and better ICBMs, the prospect of a race against the United States in advanced technology weapons appears to worry them.

The United States and the Soviet Union have agreed in the current Geneva talks to discuss three topics "in all of their interrelatedness":

1. Strategic nuclear arms, including ICBMs, SLBMs, and long-range aircraft.
2. Intermediate nuclear forces in Europe, including U.S. ground-launched Cruise and Pershing II missiles and Soviet SS-20s.
3. Space arms, including ground-based and spaced-based ballistic missile defenses.

In public statements, the Soviets have offered to agree to a 50 percent reduction in strategic arms by both sides, *if* the U.S. gives up research in ballistic missile defenses. But the Soviets' calculation of 50 percent would leave them with a heavy imbalance of strategic weapons over the U.S., and it would be impossible to verify whether the Soviets had given up their own ballistic missile defense research programs. The U.S. position calls for "sharply reduced and equal numbers of ICBMs and SLBMs and the aggregate number of warheads deployed on these systems." The U.S. has called for either the complete elimination of all intermediate nuclear missiles from Europe—the "zero" option—or alternatively a reduced and equal number of U.S. and Soviet missiles in Europe. The U.S. has implied that it might accept limits on the deployment of ballistic missile defenses but not on basic research into these systems.

THE NUCLEAR FREEZE MOVEMENT

When one side achieves a significant strategic advantage, it is in its interest to call for an arms "freeze" in order to guarantee its continued supremacy. In the early 1980s, the Soviet advantage in strategic weapons encouraged them to launch a worldwide political effort on behalf of a nuclear "freeze." The Soviet Union has nothing to lose and a great deal to gain from the international freeze movement: If the movement is successful, the Soviet strategic advantage would be recognized by treaty or agreement and Western nations would be legally prevented from restoring the balance of forces. Even if the movement fails to win a treaty freezing nuclear weapons, it brings pressure on democratic governments to make concessions in arms negotiations, and it may slow or halt development of specific weapons systems. Since the Soviets do not have to concern themselves greatly with democratic movements within their own nation, an international freeze movement poses no similar problems for the Soviet leadership.

Within Western nations the freeze movement finds support in different constituencies: (1) religious groups whose members believe that peace should not be maintained by deterrence (fear of retaliation) but rather by love, trust, or compassion; (2) persons who do not believe that the United States suffers from a strategic disadvantage but believe instead that both sides have "essential equivalence" and that a freeze would be mutually advantageous; (3) political groups who believe the Reagan administration has abandoned serious arms negotiations and who wish to pressure the administration to make new arms control initiatives. Early in the Reagan administration, the U.S. Congress responded to the nuclear freeze movement by considering resolutions calling upon the United States and the Soviet Union to negotiate "a mutual verifiable freeze on the testing, production, and further deployment of nuclear warheads, missiles and other delivery systems." In the Senate the resolution had the support of Massachusetts Democrat Edward M. Kennedy and Oregon Republican Robert Packwood.

Supporters of the freeze resolution argued that U.S. strategic forces were sufficient to deter a Soviet attack and therefore an "essential equivalence" existed between U.S. and Soviet forces. Soviet numerical advantages in ICBMs and SLBMs were not important; a Soviet first-strike was still an unacceptable risk. Continuation of the arms race was more dangerous than a freeze because one or both nations might achieve first-strike capability. No one could predict the ultimate outcome of the arms race; efforts by the United States to restore a strategic balance might only spur the Soviets to a new military effort of their own. The United States would be safer in the long run by accepting an imbalance of forces rather than risking the uncertainties and paying the enormous expenses of a continued arms race.

Opponents of the freeze resolution argued that: (1) a freeze would recognize and guarantee Soviet superiority in strategic nuclear forces. The Soviets might still be unlikely to launch a surprise first strike, but they would use their superiority to intimidate other nations. Western European nations would be pressured into neutralism, and Asian, African, Latin American, and Middle Eastern nations would perceive Soviet military superiority as proof that communism was the wave of the future. Over time, the Western will to resist Soviet expansionism would crumble. (2) A freeze would undermine U.S. efforts to reduce nuclear arms levels. Once a freeze was in place, the Soviets would have no incentive to reduce their nuclear arsenal. U.S. efforts to achieve "equal and substantially reduced levels of nuclear arms" would be undercut. (3) Only the United States would be affected by a nuclear freeze; the Soviets would continue adding to their nuclear advantage. A *de facto* U.S. "freeze" in the deployment of new strategic weapons between 1960 and 1980 was not emulated by the Soviet Union, which used this time period to gain strategic weapons superiority over the U.S. Continued erosion of U.S. deterrent forces would create real dangers of nuclear war by tempting the Soviets to either strike first or to directly threaten the United States. A democratic nation is unable to cheat on such an agreement, but there would be no real pressure on Soviet military leaders to curtail the large-scale strategic arms programs already underway in the nation.

The resumption of arms talks at Geneva quieted the nuclear freeze movement in the United States and Western Europe. But the notion of a nuclear freeze is politically appealing. It is a simple idea which appears to be fair and equal and which can be easily communicated to millions of people who fear nuclear weapons and have little knowledge of the complexities of nuclear deterrence or strategic arms. It promises relief from the burdens of defense spending for strategic weapons. The freeze movement may emerge again if the Geneva talks fail to make progress.

CONVENTIONAL WAR GAMES

Because of the high risks and costs of all-out nuclear war, and the *recognition* of these risks and costs by the United States and the USSR, limited conventional war is a more likely occurrence than a nuclear exchange. The notion of deterrence in nuclear war strategy involves the *psychological* use of very destructive weapons. But conventional war strategy is much more likely to involve the *physical* use of less destructive weapons—artillery, tanks, troops, and tactical aircraft.

America's active involvement in limited conventional wars in Korea and Vietnam has made most Americans realize that "war" is not a single, simple, or uniform action. Wars come in different varieties and sizes. Sometimes it is difficult for Americans to understand why this is so—why the United States does not seek "total victory" in every war and use any and every weapon in its arsenal to achieve that victory.

War is an instrument of national policy. Victory in war is not an end in itself; the purpose of war is to achieve some national objective—security, survival, credibility, protection of an ally, vital territory, resources. Nations are continually asserting their wills in conflict situations with other nations and using a variety of means of influence and coercion. At some point these conflicts become "war." War, then, is a matter of the degree and intensity of international conflict. It is not undisciplined mass violence.

War, if it is to be employed at all, must be employed in a rational fashion to serve national purposes. War is not simply a way of giving vent to hatred, malevolence, or sadism. Crushing the enemy is not the measure of success, but whether we have achieved our national purposes at a reasonable cost. For war to be a rational policy—that is, for its benefits to outweigh its costs—several conditions must be met. First of all, policy makers must clearly understand the objectives of the war and commit military forces in rough proportion to the value of these objectives. War is a very crude instrument of policy. Its violence and destruction can set off a chain of consequences that overshadow and defeat the original purposes of the war. Costs in lives and resources can easily spiral all out of proportion to the original objectives of the war. An increase in costs may itself cause a nation to expand its original objectives in order to rationalize higher costs. The enemy must then commit larger forces to prevent greater losses. Hence the necessity for close control and supervision of the level of violence. Diplomats must make continuing efforts to maintain political talks toward a negotiated settlement on the basis of national objectives.

If the object of the war becomes total victory over the enemy, there will be no limit on the enemy's use of force. Total victory for one nation implies total defeat for its opponent—a threat to national survival, justifying unlimited levels of violence. Political objectives are set aside for possible resolution after the war, and every effort is directed toward the complete destruction of the enemy's war-making power. As the dimensions of violence and destruction increase, the war arouses passionate fears and hatreds, which themselves come to replace rational objectives in the conflict. As the level of suffering and sacrifice increases, the goal becomes the blind unreasoning destruction of the enemy.

In a "stable" nuclear balance of terror—in which each side possesses assured destruction second-strike capability—conventional war becomes a more likely possibility. America's strategic nuclear forces have been designed to deter a direct attack on the continental United States. In *all* other conflicts the United States will probably rely on conventional weapons, or perhaps in case of a major attack on Western Europe, "tactical" nuclear weapons. *Exclusive* reliance on strategic nuclear weapons would place the United States in a terrible dilemma in confronting limited aggression—involving a choice between either surrender or nuclear war. In contrast, if the United States maintains a balance of forces—strategic nuclear, tactical nuclear, and conventional—it will be able to confront aggression anywhere in the world with weapons and forces appropriate to the situation.

Apart from their strictly military purposes, conventional forces also have an important psychological role to play. The deployment of U.S. troops in Berlin, West Germany, and Western Europe serves notice to the USSR that it cannot send Soviet divisions across the borders without engaging U.S. troops. Even though these U.S. troops are no match for the massive Soviet armies, nonetheless, the very fact that American troops would have to be killed in a Soviet attack in Western Europe *ensures* U.S. involvement in such a conflict. U.S. troops in Europe form a "plate-glass window": The Soviets know that to take Western Europe they would have to kill American troops, and this knowledge is a further deterrent to such an attack.[7] Deploying U.S. troops in Europe notifies friend and foe alike of the seriousness of our commitment to defend the area.

U.S. troops in Europe are equipped with tactical nuclear weapons. Obviously this fact has additional deterrent value. Not only do the Soviets know that U.S. troops would be immediately involved in any defense against aggression, but they also know that such a defense may involve the use of nuclear weapons, at least at the tactical level.

SOVIET SUPERIORITY IN CONVENTIONAL FORCES

The USSR has enjoyed a vast superiority in ground combat troops, tanks, and artillery since the end of World War II. The Soviets maintain 5.3 million persons under arms, compared to 2.1 million for the United States. The Soviets maintain 199 combat divisions, while the United States maintains sixteen Army divisions and three Marine divisions. The Soviets enjoy heavy advantages in numbers of tanks, combat aircraft, and artillery (See Table 8-3).

Part of the Soviet conventional superiority is dictated by the multiple missions assigned to the Soviet military: (1) to confront the NATO alliance

---

[7]Likewise, the deployment of U.S. forces in South Korea is a crucial psychological deterrent to another invasion by North Korea. North Korea has pledged itself to the "reunification" of Korea and has built large, paved, and lighted tunnels under the border in preparation for invasion. But the presence of U.S. troops—so far, at least—has deterred or postponed invasion plans.

TABLE 8-3   Balance of Forces: United States and USSR

STRATEGIC FORCES	U.S.	USSR
ICBM's		
Numbers	1,026	1,398
Warheads	2,126	5,840
SLBM's		
Submarines	37	62
Missiles	640	928
Warheads	5,344	1,781
Aircraft		
Long range	241	170
Medium range	56	130
TOTAL Launch Vehicles	1,963	2,496
GENERAL PURPOSE FORCES		
Armed Forces Personnel	2.1 million	5.3 million
Army		
Division	16 full	199[a]
	2 light	
Tanks	13,423	52,000
Artillery and Missiles	5,250	33,000
Helicopters	8,800	4,300
Marines		
Divisions	3	[b]
Aircraft	605	
Tanks	716	
Air Force		
Aircraft	4,000	4,480
Air Defense		
Aircraft	258	1,200
SAM	[c]	9,600
Navy		
Major Combat Surface Ships	213	293
Attack Submarines	95	201
Cruise Missile Submarines	4	66
Aircraft Carriers	14	6
Aircraft	1,350	875

[a]At full strength, Soviet combat divisions include about 8,000 men, compared to 14,000-16,000 men in U.S. combat divisions.
[b]U.S.S.R. has only small "Naval Infantry" units assigned to fleets.
[c]U.S. has no separate Air Defense Force. U.S. SAM included in Army Artillery.
Source: International Institute for Strategic Studies, *The Military Balance 1985–86* (London: Institute for Strategic Studies, 1984).

in Europe; (2) to keep the nations of Eastern Europe inside the Soviet bloc through armed intimidation; and (3) to defend against a growing Chinese threat in the Eastern Soviet Union. Indeed, defending its eastern boundaries against potential Chinese incursions now diverts over one quarter of the Soviet ground combat forces. The USSR must also divert about 20 percent of its ground combat forces to hold in check the populations of Poland, Hungary, East Germany, Rumania, Bulgaria, and Czechoslovakia. (In contrast, the United States can count on support, rather than opposition, from its NATO allies, including British, French, German, Belgian, Dutch, Italian, Greek, and Turkish forces.) An additional percentage of Soviet forces are engaged in a continuing war in Afghanistan. Thus, it can be argued that the USSR needs a larger ground combat capability than the United States.

American conventional arms—tactical aircraft, conventional bombs, tanks, antitank missiles, artillery, and battlefield missiles—are technologically equal or superior to Soviet conventional arms. But the USSR produces so many more conventional arms than the United States that the Soviets can send arms to their client nations in the Middle East, Asia, Latin America, and Africa without depleting their own armies.

The United States and USSR have different kinds of navies. The United States has large, aircraft carrier forces and a larger Marine Corps, which together can mount amphibious landing operations anywhere in the world with close air support. The Soviets have no such forces. They rely instead on missile cruisers and attack submarines, which give them the capacity to interrupt naval operations anywhere in the world. It would be difficult to estimate the outcome of a sea battle between U.S. forces relying on naval air attacks from carriers and Soviet forces relying on surface-to-surface missiles and submarine attacks. Perhaps the most worrisome aspect of Soviet naval power is its spectacular growth over the last decade. The Soviets built the largest combat surface fleet in the world in a very short period of time.

DEFENDING WESTERN EUROPE

The preservation of democracy in Western Europe has been the centerpiece of U.S. foreign and military policy for most of the twentieth century. The United States fought in two world wars and suffered one-quarter million battle deaths to preserve democracy in Europe. Today the combined economic output of the Western European nations exceeds the economic output of the Soviet Union. If the Soviets could add Western Europe to their empire, they would more than double their economic strength. Nowhere in the world does the United States have a greater stake in the preservation of national independence and democratic government than in Western Europe.

In response to aggressive Soviet moves in Europe after World War II, the United States, Canada, Belgium, Britain, Denmark, France, Iceland, Italy, Luxembourg, Netherlands, Norway, and Portugal joined in the North Atlantic Treaty Organization (NATO). Each nation pledged that "an armed attack against one . . . shall be considered an attack against them all." Greece and Turkey joined in 1952 and West Germany in 1955. More importantly, to give this pledge credibility, a joint NATO military command was established with a U.S. commanding officer (the first was General of the Army Dwight D. Eisenhower) to command the defenses of Western Europe. After the formation of NATO, the Soviets made no further advances in Western Europe. The Soviets themselves, in response to NATO, drew up a comparable treaty among their own Eastern European satellite nations—the "Warsaw Pact."

NATO is an international organization whose members are democracies. The fundamental difficulty in such an organization is finding agreement among the fifteen member nations on a common strategy. U.S. presidents have continually assured Western Europeans that a Soviet attack on them would be regarded as an attack on the United States itself. But ever since the Soviet Union acquired the ability to strike the U.S. homeland with nuclear weapons, skepticism in Western Europe about the U.S. commitment has grown. In 1966, France withdrew from the NATO military command (although not the NATO treaty) in order to develop its own independent nuclear war capability. The overwhelming Soviet advantage in conventional armies forced NATO to introduce tactical nuclear weapons in 1957. These nuclear weapons are designed for battlefield use; their purpose is to offset huge Soviet imbalances in tanks, artillery, and infantry. It is hoped that the threat of tactical nuclear weapons will help dissuade the Soviets from an attack on Western Europe. Tactical nuclear weapons are used *primarily* as psychological deterrents. However, tactical nuclear warfare is not unthinkable. It is a more likely possibility than strategic nuclear warfare.

The potential destructiveness of a war in Western Europe, particularly a war involving tactical nuclear weapons, creates serious political and strategic problems in Western European capitals. Resisting Soviet aggression may cause great destruction and loss of life in Europe. A limited war on European territory would not be "limited" for most Europeans; it would probably result in massive numbers of civilian casualties. Neutralist and leftist parties argue that it may be better to submit to Soviet demands, to avoid provoking the Soviets in any way, to disarm and disband NATO, in order to escape the damages of war. Thus far, the elected leadership of the Western European democracies have stood firm in their commitment to resist Soviet aggression. But there are strong Communist parties in most

European nations; the European "peace" movement is very strong; and the Soviets have brought strong pressure to bear to discourage defense efforts among European nations.

In recent years the Soviets have deployed over 300 nuclear-tipped intermediate range missiles (notably their mobile multiwarhead SS-20 missiles) aimed at the cities of Western Europe. The implied threat is that any attempt to resist Soviet aggression militarily by Western European nations will result in the massive destruction of European cities. These missiles place great pressure on the leaders of European nations to submit to Soviet demands.

In an effort to offset this Soviet pressure the United States and its Western allies have agreed to place 450 new, medium-range, ground-launched Cruise and Pershing II nuclear missiles in Europe. The range of these missiles would allow NATO forces to strike targets in Eastern Europe and even in the Soviet Union itself. These weapons are primarily a deterrent; they are designed to neutralize the Soviet SS-20 threat. Indeed, President Reagan has offered a "zero option" to the Soviets—the United States will cancel deployment of Cruise and Pershing II missiles in Europe if the Soviets withdraw their SS-20 missiles.

Since 1973, the NATO allies and the Soviet Union and Warsaw Pact nations have engaged in Mutual and Balanced Force Reduction (MBFR) talks in Vienna. These talks were originally aimed at reducing the number of conventional troops and weapons in Europe. No agreement has ever emerged from these talks. Indeed, there has never even been any agreement on how to count forces.

EVALUATION: THE PRICE OF PEACE

Soviet defense spending is significantly greater than U.S. defense spending. The Soviet Union is estimated to be spending 14 to 15 percent of its Gross National Product for defense, compared to about 5 percent for the United States. The massive Soviet buildup of strategic nuclear forces began after the Cuban missile crisis in 1962. For many years it was believed that the Soviets would be satisfied with a secure second-strike capability. But by the mid-1970s it was clear that the Soviet buildup was going far beyond this capability. At the same time, the Soviets vastly improved their intermediate-range and battlefield nuclear capabilities, posing a serious threat to the Western European democracies. Moreover, the Soviets continue to maintain conventional forces in Europe that are far too large to serve only in defense of Eastern European and Soviet territory. Finally, the USSR has created the world's largest fleet of combat surface ships.

During this enormous Soviet military buildup, U.S. defenses were neglected. In 1955 defense spending claimed 58.1 percent of all federal expenditures and equaled 10.5 percent of the Gross National Product. Ten years later, in 1965, defense spending had shrunk to 40.1 percent of federal spending and 7.2 percent of the GNP. In 1980 defense spending was down to only 23 percent of federal spending and 4.9 percent of the GNP. This was the lowest defense "effort" the United States had made since before World War II.

America's political leadership finally acknowledged the strategic and conventional imbalances during the Carter administration. The Carter administration announced plans to increase U.S. defense spending and won a pledge from NATO nations to increase their own defense spending by at least 3 percent above inflation rates. Figure 8-1 shows that defense spending as a percent of the GNP began to creep upward in 1980–81. The trend has continued under President Reagan through 1985. Defense spending is now about 6 percent of the GNP and 29 percent of the total federal budget. However, recent budget battles in Congress suggest that the U.S. effort to rebuild its defenses may be ending. It is doubtful that Congress will agree to significant defense increases in the next few years. Indeed, if annual defense increases fall below the inflation rate (currently about 4 percent per year) then U.S. defenses will gradually weaken again.

Defense outlays have no discernible effect on either social welfare spending or inflation. Total spending for welfare, social security, and health is more than double the defense budget. There is no evidence that increases

Figure 8-1   National defense outlays as a percent of GNP. (Source: *The Budget of the United States Government FY 1986. Washington, D.C.: Government Printing Office, 1985.*)

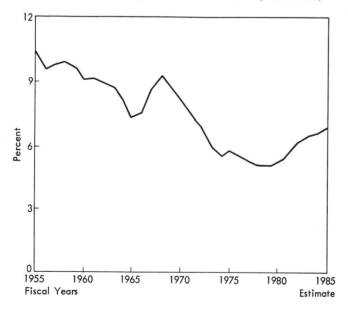

in the defense budget come at the expense of social spending. Nor is defense spending inflationary: From 1955 to 1965, when defense spending was heavy, there was very little inflation in the country; likewise inflation declined dramatically during the Reagan military buildup.

Personnel costs account for over one-half of the defense budget. An additional one-quarter of the budget is spent on operations. This leaves only one-quarter of the defense budget (only about 7 percent of the total federal budget) for the purchase of *all* new weapons—missiles, warheads, tanks, planes, ships, submarines, rifles.

The United States currently relies on an All Volunteer Force. The draft was ended following the Vietnam War. The All Volunteer Force is expensive, because pay and benefits must be made attractive. An economic recession increases enlistments when civilian jobs are hard to find; but it is difficult to maintain high standards among enlistees in a full-employment economy. The army usually has more difficulty in attracting quality recruits than the navy, air force, or marines.

SUMMARY

Decisions about defense policy in Washington, Moscow, Peking, and other world capitals are interdependent—the future of mankind depends on what is done at each of these major power centers and how each responds to the decisions of others. Game theory provides a vocabulary and a way of thinking rationally about decision making in competitive interdependent situations. Let us set forth several summary ideas about defense policy.

1. Assured destruction deterrence strategy is the basis of current national defense policy. It seeks to prevent nuclear war by making the consequences of a nuclear attack unacceptable to a rational enemy. The key to assured destruction deterrence is the *survivability* of one's forces—what can be done on a second strike after absorbing a successful surprise first strike by the enemy.

2. To maintain peace through assured destruction deterrence requires (1) second-strike capability, (2) communication of that capability to the enemy, (3) the enemy's belief in the credibility of the threat, and (4) a rational enemy.

3. If both sides maintain second-strike capability—that is, *mutual* assured destruction, or MAD—then a stable "balance of terror" is said to exist. Each side is restrained from launching an attack because it knows the second-strike capability of the other side. World peace does not rest on trust or love or brotherhood, but on a rational calculation of what is in each side's self-interest.

4. To implement its assured destruction deterrence, the United States has attempted to maintain a "TRIAD" of strategic forces—land-based mis-

siles, submarine-launched missiles, and manned bombers. However, declines in defense spending, opposition to the military generated during the Vietnam War, and underestimation of Soviet technological developments have threatened the survivability of land-based missiles and manned bombers. Defense planners are hopeful that the MX, the B-1, the Cruise missile, and the Trident submarine will modernize the TRIAD.

5. President Ronald Reagan began a large-scale research program into ballistic missile defenses. The Strategic Defense Initiative, or "Star Wars," is designed to reduce reliance on deterrence through retaliation and instead defend the U.S. by destroying enemy missiles in space. SDI will require the development of very sophisticated weapons and computer technologies.

6. Opponents of SDI argue that it will encourage the Soviets to build more offensive missiles, that the Soviets will interpret SDI as an attempt by the U.S. to gain a first-strike capability against them, that it will destabilize the balance of terror. Opponents also claim that SDI is unfeasible and a waste of money. Supporters of SDI argue that it promises to maintain peace through defense against missiles rather than the threat of nuclear retaliation against people.

7. In strategic arms talks, the United States seeks to achieve substantial reductions in nuclear arms to levels that are equal and verifiable. In SALT I (1972), both sides renounced ABM programs and placed overall numerical limits on strategic weapons. But the arms race continued, and so did Soviet momentum in new heavy missiles, SS-18s which now threaten to destroy the entire U.S. ICBM force on a first strike. The SALT II (1979) agreement placed a series of limits on strategic nuclear launch vehicles, and guaranteed national technical means of verification. However, it is also recognized Soviet monopoly in heavy ICBMs and placed no restrictions on Soviet Backfire bombers. SALT II failed to win Senate ratification, but both sides have avoided violating its provisions.

8. Current talks in Geneva cover three topics: Strategic arms, including ICBMs, SLBMs, and long-range bombers; intermediate-range nuclear missiles in Europe; and space-based missile defenses.

9. A nuclear "freeze" is the expected negotiating strategy of any nation that has achieved strategic superiority. Within Western nations the nuclear freeze movement finds support among religious groups whose members believe that deterrence is immoral and among leaders who do not believe that the United States suffers a strategic disadvantage.

10. Rational thinking in conventional war requires that the political purposes of the war should guide military operations. Unlimited, uncontrolled violence is not a rational strategy in a conventional war. For conventional war to be a rational policy, the benefits must outweigh the costs. Conventional forces also have a deterrent value; when potential aggressors know they must attack U.S. military forces to capture territory, the potential

risks may dissuade them. U.S. forces in Europe and South Korea have both a deterrent value and the physical capability of resisting aggression.

11. Soviet conventional forces far outnumber U.S. conventional forces. This poses a conventional military threat to Western Europe and allows the Soviets to supply arms to satellite nations in the Middle East, Asia, Africa, and Latin America.

12. The preservation of democracy in Western Europe has been a central goal of U.S. policy for most of the twentieth century. In the NATO alliance the United States and Western European nations pledge that an armed attack against one will be considered an armed attack against all. A joint NATO military command is designated to implement this pledge.

13. Intermediate range and tactical nuclear weapons in Europe pose a special threat to civilian populations. Even a "limited" war involving battlefield nuclear weapons would cause great destruction. The NATO nations have stood firm against Soviet threats to attack European cities with their SS-20 intermediate-range missiles. NATO has countered the Soviet threat with the introduction of U.S. ground-launched Cruise and Pershing II missiles in Europe.

14. The long decline in U.S. military spending as a percent of the GNP was reversed in 1980, as first the Carter administration and later the Reagan administration began to rebuild America's defenses. From 1980 to 1985 U.S. defense spending rose from 4.9 percent of the GNP to 6 percent, and from 23 percent of federal spending to 29 percent. But budget battles now threaten to end the U.S. defense buildup.

BIBLIOGRAPHY

DONLEY, MICHAEL B., *The SALT Handbook*. Washington, D.C.: Heritage Foundation, 1979.

KISSINGER, HENRY A., *Nuclear Weapons and Foreign Policy*. New York: Harper & Row, 1957.

REICHART, JOHN F., and STEVEN R. STORM, *American Defense Policy*, 5th ed. Baltimore: Johns Hopkins University Press, 1982.

SCHELLING, THOMAS C., *Arms and Influence*. New Haven, Conn.: Yale University Press, 1966.

9

PRIORITIES
AND PRICE TAGS
incrementalism at work

Political conflict over spending priorities shapes the budgetary process. (AP/Wide World photos)

Too often we think of budgeting as the dull province of clerks and statisticians. Nothing could be more mistaken. The budget is the single most important policy statement of any government. The expenditure side of the budget tells us "who gets what" in public funds, and the revenue side of the budget tells us "who pays the cost." There are few government activities or programs that do not require an expenditure of funds, and no public funds may be spent without budgetary authorization. Deciding what goes into a budget (the budgetary process) provides a mechanism for reviewing government programs, assessing their cost, relating them to financial resources, making choices among alternative expenditures, and determining the financial effort that a government will expend on these programs. Budgets determine what programs and policies are to be increased, decreased, lapsed, initiated, or renewed. The budget lies at the heart of public policy.[1]

DIMENSIONS OF GOVERNMENT SPENDING

Governments do many things that cannot be measured in dollars. Nevertheless, government expenditures are the best available measure of the overall dimensions of government activity. Budgets represent government policies with price tags attached.

The expenditures of *all* governments in the United States—the federal government, together with fifty state governments and eighty thousand local governments—grew from $1.7 billion in 1902 to over $1.3 trillion in 1985 (see Table 9-1). Some of the increase in government activity can be attributed to growth in the nation's population. And a great deal of the increase in dollar amounts spent by government is exaggerated by the diminishing value of the dollar—that is, by inflation. However, government activity has grown much faster than both the population and inflation.

A better yardstick of the growth of government activity is found in the relationship of government expenditures to the Gross National Product (GNP). The GNP is the dollar sum of all goods and services produced in the nation's economy. The growth of the GNP in the twentieth century reflects the expansion of the nation's economy: The GNP in dollar amounts grew from $21.6 billion to over $4 *trillion* today.

Government expenditures in relation to the Gross National Product had risen, somewhat bumpily, from 7.7 percent in 1902 to 35 percent in the late 1970s. If public programs financed by the government had grown

[1]See Aaron Wildavsky, *The Politics of the Budgetary Process*, 4th ed. (Boston: Little, Brown, 1984).

TABLE 9-1   Growth in Population, Wealth, and Government Activities
Over Eight Decades

	GNP		ALL GOVERNMENT SPENDING	
	POPULATION MILLIONS	BILLIONS	BILLIONS	PERCENT OF GNP
1902	79.2	21.6	1.7	7.7
1922	110.1	74.0	9.3	12.5
1932	124.9	58.5	12.4	21.3
1940	132.6	100.6	20.4	20.3
1944	138.9	211.4	109.9	52.0
1950	152.3	284.6	70.3	24.7
1960	180.7	502.6	151.3	30.1
1970	203.2	959.6	312.1	32.5
1980	226.0	2626.1	959.0	36.5
1985	238.0	3869.4	1348.5	34.8

Source: U.S. Bureau of the Census, *Historical Statistics on Governmental Finances and Employment* (Washington, D.C.: Government Printing Office, 1967); updating from U.S. Bureau of the Census, *Statistical Abstract of the United States*, and *The Budget of the United States Government, 1986.*

at the same rate as private economic activities, this percentage figure would have remained at the same level over the years. But government activity over the long run has grown even *faster* than private enterprise. By any yardstick, then, we find the growth of government activity in America has been substantial. Government activity now accounts for one-third of all economic activity in the nation.

Despite the growth of government activity over the years, the United States remains primarily a free enterprise economy. All modern economies use some combination of capitalist and socialist economic organization. In primarily capitalist countries like the United States, the government protects private property, provides some public goods, and regulates taxes and business, to modify the forces of supply and demand in the market. In socialist countries, government ownership and central control of the economy exist side-by-side with a small but often significant free market. Socialist governments forbid free markets in most goods (the Soviet Union refers to most market activities as "economic crimes"), although small "black markets" are allowed.

The table below presents a rough classification of governments in the world today according to their reliance on capitalist or socialist economic organization, plus the main features differentiating the two forms of economic organization.

FIGURE 9-1   All government expenditures as a percentage of the gross national product in the U.S.

TABLE 9-2

CAPITALIST									SOCIALIST
United States	Canada	Germany	France	England	Sweden Israel	Yugoslavia	China	Cuba	USSR
34	37	39	40	45	55	60	80	85	90

PROPORTION OF THE ECONOMY (GNP) PRODUCED BY THE GOVERNMENT

Productive resources owned by private individuals and firms	Productive resources owned by government
Workers employed by private individuals and firms or self-employed	Workers employed by government
Investment undertaken by private individuals and firms in search of profit	Investment ordered by government planners according to their own goals
Allocation of goods by market forces	Allocation of goods by goverment planners according to their own goals
Income determined by market forces that reward productivity and ownership	Income determined by government planners who may seek to reward productivity or achieve equality or any other goals they desire

Why Governments Grow

What accounts for the growth of government activity? There are many theories which offer explanations of government growth. We shall examine "incrementalism" in some detail, but first we should take note of some of the other leading theories of government growth. These theories are *not* mutually exclusive; indeed, probably all of the forces identified by these theories contribute to government growth.[2]

Wagner's law. Years ago, a European economist, Adolph Wagner, set forth a "law of increasing state activity" roughly to the effect that government activity increased faster than economic output in all developing societies.[3] He attributed his law to a variety of factors: Increasing regulatory services required to control a more specialized, complex economy; increasing involvement of government in economic enterprise; and increasing demands in a developed society for social services such as education, welfare, and public health. Thus the "law of increasing state activity" portrayed growth in government activity as an inevitable accompaniment of a developing society.

The displacement effect hypothesis. This theory assumes that government is responsive to public opinion and that public opinion usually limits government growth. However, during periods of social upheaval, especially war or economic dislocation, the public will accept higher than normal levels of taxation.[4] During these periods, then, government grows. After the stressful period is over, government size does not decline to its previous levels. Instead, new expenditures are substituted for those accepted during the crisis. There is some support for this theory in examining U.S. government expenditures in Figure 9-1; expenditures increase during crisis periods but never return to precrisis levels after the crises are over.

Fiscal illusion explanation. This explanation assumes that government officials can increase revenues, and then expenditures, by altering the revenue structure and tax-collecting devices so that voters do not realize how

---

[2]For a thorough survey of the literature on government growth, see P.D. Larkey, C. Stolp, and M. Winer, "Theorizing About the Growth of Government," *Journal of Public Policy* vol. 1 (February 1981), 157–220. See also D. Lowrey and W. Berry, "The Growth of Government in the United States," *American Journal of Political Science* vol. 27 (April 1980), 189–201.

[3]Adolph Wagner's major work is *Grundelgung der Politischen Oekonomie* (Leipzig, 1983). This work is discussed at length in Alan T. Peacock and Jack Wiseman, *The Growth of Public Expenditures in the United Kingdom* (Princeton, N.J.: Princeton University Press, 1961).

[4]Peacock and Wiseman, *The Growth of Public Expenditures in the United Kingdom.*

much money government is actually taking from them.[5] The federal income tax grew very rapidly *after* the introduction of "withholding" in 1943; wage earners never receive the money they earned and come to perceive it as "belonging" to the federal government. This illusion may also be accomplished through complex or indirect tax systems, for example social security payroll taxes, sales taxes, and value added taxes. These taxes make it difficult for taxpayers to directly associate the amount they pay in taxes to the cost of the services they receive.

Bureaucratic decision making.   Both bureaucrats and the legislators who decide upon their budgets are personally interested in expanding government budgets.[6] Bureaucrats are interested in increasing the amount of money they can spend and the number of employees under their supervision. Legislators want to increase the resources over which they have jurisdiction and enhance the government's capacity to deal with their own constituents.

Interest group interaction.   This explanation assumes that interest groups will want to increase the size of government programs that benefit their own members. Benefits are visible and concentrated. Costs, even though they may exceed the benefits, are diffused. All interests might prefer that no one gets these benefits at government expense, but each interest group is motivated to act on behalf of its own members.

The median voter.   The median voter explanation of public sector growth assumes that the level of government chosen by voters will be the level preferred by the median voter. However, it is highly unlikely that this level will be the most efficient level of government expenditures. The *median* voter will have less income than the *mean* income of all people, because income is unevenly distributed. Thus, the median voter would choose a level of government high enough to redistribute income from the richer to the poorer. The position of the median voter is also influenced by the fact that government employees, who in their own self-interest would support expanded government, are also voters.

Electoral competition.   This explanation assumes that politicians in competitive elections will be motivated to expand the size of government by offering specific groups of voters visible and exaggerated benefits while

[5]R.E. Wagner, "Revenue Structure, Fiscal Illusion and Budgetary Choice," *Public Choice* vol. 25 (Spring 1976), 45–61.

[6]W.A. Niskanen, *Bureaucracy and Representative Government* (Chicago: Aldine and Atherton, 1971).

hiding or minimizing the costs to other voters.[7] Moreover, competitive elections maximize incentives to pursue policies that will win the votes of the "have nots"—in particular, to increase social welfare services.

Leftist party control of government.   Another explanation of government growth centers on the control of government by liberal or left parties. Party activists in liberal and conservative parties hold strong and divergent views about the role of government in combating unemployment and controlling inflation. In most Western European democracies control of government by the liberal party is associated with significant increases in the public budget.[8]

Cumulative unintended consequences.   This explanation suggests that the size of the public sector is the result of previous efforts to solve other, often unrelated, problems. Since our comprehension capabilities are limited, we are unable to view the size of government in a holistic manner, taking all revenues and expenditures and their future consequences into account. Thus, manageable decisions are limited to relatively simple problems. However, even seemingly simple decisions have consequences for present and future expenditures. Over the years, the effects of all these decisions accumulate until the previously made commitments push the size of government beyond what anyone originally intended. Future generations are thus forced to live with the unintended consequences of previous decisions.

Incrementalism.   Incrementalism is both a theory of *why* government grows and *how* government grows. It suggests that budgetary decisions are made in an incremental fashion by policy makers who do not have the time, energy, or information to review every dollar of every budget request every year. Nor do policy makers wish to refight every political battle over every existing program each year. So they usually accept last year's *base* spending level as legitimate and focus attention on proposed increases for each program. The effect of this increment process overtime is to gradually increase total governmental spending. This is because existing programs are locked into the base and given very little scrutiny. Budget consideration is focused on *increases* over last year's budget. Indeed, in many programs "cost-of-living allowances" (COLAs) are automatically programmed into the base and not given much attention by decision makers.

[7]E.R. Tufte, *Political Control of the Economy* (Princeton, N.J.: Princeton University Press, 1978).

[8]Ibid.; and D. Hibbs, "Political Parties and Macroeconomic Policy," *American Political Science Review* vol. 72 (December 1977), 467–87.

INCREMENTALISM IN BUDGET MAKING

The incremental model of public policy making is particularly well suited to assist in understanding the budgeting process. Budgeting is *incremental* because decision makers generally consider last year's expenditures as a base. Active consideration of budget proposals is generally narrowed to new items or requested increases over last year's base. The attention of presidents, members of Congress, governors, legislators, mayors, and councils is focused on a narrow range of increases or decreases in a budget. A budget is almost never reviewed as a whole every year, in the sense of reconsidering the value of all existing programs. Departments are seldom required to defend or explain budget requests which do *not* exceed current appropriations; but requested increases in appropriations require extensive explanation. Reformers have proposed the "zero base" budget to force agencies to justify every penny requested—not just requested increases. In theory, zero base budgeting would eliminate unnecessary spending protected by incrementalism. But in practice, zero base budgeting may require so much wasted effort in justifying already accepted programs each year that executive agencies and legislative committees will grow tired of the effort and return to incrementalism.

Budgeting is very political. As Aaron Wildavsky was told by a federal executive, "It's not what's in your estimates, but how good a politician you are that matters."[9] Being a good politician involves (1) the cultivation of a good base of support for requests among the public at large and among people served by the agency, (2) the development of interest, enthusiasm, and support for a program among top political figures and legislative leaders, and (3) skill in following strategies that exploit opportunities to the maximum. Informing the public and the clientele of the full benefit of the services they receive from the agency may increase the intensity with which they will support the agency's request. If possible, the agency should inspire its clientele to contact members of congress, governors, mayors, legislators, and council members, and to help work for the agency's request. This is much more effective than the agency trying to promote its own requests.

Budgeting is also quite *fragmented*. In theory, the Office of Management and Budget (OMB), in the executive branch, and the Congressional Budget Office (CBO), in the legislative branch, are supposed to bring together budget requests and fit them into a coherent whole, while at the same time relating them to revenue estimates. But it is very difficult for the president, and almost impossible for the Congress, to view the total policy impact of a budget. Wildavsky explains that the fragmented character of the budgetary process helps to secure agreement on the budget as well

[9]Wildavsky, *The Politics of the Budgetary Process,* p. 19.

as reduce the burden of calculation. If each congressional subcommittee challenged the result of the others, conflict might be so great that no budget would ever be passed. It is much easier to agree on a small increase or decrease to a single program than it is to compare the worth of one program to that of all others. However, to counter the fragmentation in the federal budget, Congress not only established the Congressional Budget Office, but also House and Senate budget committees to examine the budget as a whole. We will describe their operation in the next section. But it is interesting to note that their purpose is to try to overcome the fragmentation in federal budget making.

Finally, budgeting is *nonprogrammatic*. Agency budgets typically list expenditures under the ambiguous phrases "personnel services," "contractual services," "travel," "supplies," "equipment." It is impossible to tell from such a listing exactly what programs the agency is spending its money on. Such a budget obscures policy decisions by hiding programs behind meaningless phrases. Reform-oriented administrators have called for budgeting by programs for many years; this would present budgetary requests in terms of end products or program packages, like aid to dependent children, vocational rehabilitation, administration of fair employment practices laws, and highway patrolling. Chief executives generally favor *program budgeting* because it will give them greater control over policy. But Wildavsky points out that there are some political functions served by *non*program budgeting. He notes that

> Agreement comes much more readily when the items can be treated in dollars instead of basic differences in policy. Calculating budgets in monetary increments facilitates bargaining and logrolling. It becomes possible to swap an increase here for a decrease there or for an increase elsewhere without always having to consider the ultimate desirability of the programs blatantly in competition.[10]

The most important influence over the size and content of this year's budget is last year's budget. One of the reasons for this is the continuing nature of most governmental programs and outlays. Over two-thirds of the federal budget is officially labeled "uncontrollable." The "uncontrollable" items are expenditures that are mandated by previous programs— for example, commitments to recipients of social security, Medicare, Medicaid, and public assistance; commitments to veterans; and interest that must be paid on the national debt.

Another reason for using last year's budget as a base is the cost that would be involved in generally reconsidering every government program and expenditure. There is not enough time and energy for the decision-

[10]Ibid., p. 136.

making process required to do this, so past programs are assumed to be worthy of continuation at previous levels of expenditures. It is considered a waste of time to view every budget as a blank slate and to ignore past experience. Moreover, the political instability that would ensue if every program were reevaluated every year would be too much for the system; every political battle that has ever been fought over a program would have to be fought all over again every year. Obviously, it is much more practical and political to accept past expenditures as a "base," and concentrate attention on new programs and increases and decreases in expenditures.[11]

"UNCONTROLLABLE" GOVERNMENT SPENDING

Government budgeting is incremental in part because of "uncontrollables" in the federal budget. "Uncontrollables" are items which are determined by past policies of Congress and represent commitments in future federal budgets. Almost *three-fourths* of all federal spending is "uncontrollable," that is, based on previous decisions of Congress and not easily changed in annual budget making (see Table 9-3). Sources of uncontrollable spending include:

TABLE 9-3   "Uncontrollables" in the Budget

ENTITLEMENTS	PERCENT OF BUDGET
Social Security	20.9
Federal Employees Retirement	3.8
Military Retirement	1.9
Unemployment Compensation	2.0
Medical Care (Medicaid, Medicare)	9.3
Welfare (SSI, AFDC)	2.4
Food Stamps	.4
Student Aid	.6
INTEREST	
Interest on the National Debt	13.0
FIXED CONTRACTS	
Defense	9.3
Nondefense	7.1
TOTAL	71.3

Source: *Budget of the United States Government, Fiscal Year 1986*, pp. 6–34.

[11]Richard F. Fenno, *The Power of the Purse: Appropriations Politics in Congress* (Boston: Little, Brown, 1966). See also Otto A. Davis, M.A.H. Dempster, and Aaron Wildavsky, "A Theory of the Budgetary Process," *American Political Science Review* 60 (September 1966), 529–47.

"Entitlement" programs. Federal programs which provide classes of people with a legally enforceable right to benefits are called "entitlement" programs. Entitlement programs account for two-thirds of all federal spending, including social security, public assistance, Medicare and Medicaid, and interest on the national debt. These entitlements are benefits that past Congresses have pledged the federal government to pay. Entitlements are not *really* uncontrollable: Congress can always amend the basic laws that established them; but this is politically difficult and might be regarded as a failure of trust.

Indexing of benefits. One reason that spending increases each year is that Congress has authorized automatic increases in benefits tied to increases in prices. Benefits are "indexed" to the Consumer Price Index under social security, SSI, food stamps, and veterans' pensions. This indexing would push up the cost of entitlement programs each year, even if the number of recipients stayed the same. Indexing, of course, runs counter to federal efforts to restrain inflation. Moreover the Consumer Price Index (which includes interest payments for new housing, the cost of new cars and appliances, etc.) generally overestimates the needs of recipients for cost-of-living increases.

Increasing costs of in-kind benefits. Rises in the cost of major in-kind (noncash) benefits, particularly medical costs of Medicaid and Medicare, also guarantee growth in federal spending. These in-kind benefit programs have risen faster in cost than cash benefit programs.

Interest on the national debt. Interest payments have grown rapidly as a percentage of all federal spending. The federal government has a long history of deficits. Only one year in the past twenty-five has the government balanced the budget. The result is a national debt in excess of $1 *trillion.* Each year the deficit increases, interest payments go up. Interest payments also rise with increases in interest rates.

Backdoor spending. Some federal spending does not appear on the budget. For example, spending by the Postal Service is not included in the federal budget. No clear rule explains why some agencies are in the budget and others are not. But "off budget" agencies have the same economic effects as other government agencies. Another form of backdoor spending is found in government-guaranteed loans. Initially government guarantees for loans—FHA housing, Guaranteed Student Loans, veterans' loans, etc.— do not require federal money. The government merely promises to repay the loan if the borrower fails to do so. Yet these loans create an obligation against the government.

THE FORMAL BUDGETARY PROCESS

It is difficult to imagine that prior to 1921 the president played no direct role in the budget process. The Secretary of the Treasury compiled the estimates of the individual agencies, and these were sent, without revision, to Congress for its consideration. The Budget and Accounting Act of 1921 provided for an executive budget giving the president responsibility for budget formulation, and thereby giving him an important means of controlling federal policy. The Office of Management and Budget (OMB), located in the Executive Office, has the key responsibility for budget preparation. In addition to this major task, the OMB has related responsibilities for improving the organization and management of the executive agencies, for coordinating the extensive statistical services of the federal government, and for analyzing and reviewing proposed legislation to determine its effect on administration and finance.

OMB—preparing the presidential budget.   Preparation of the federal budget starts more than a year before the beginning of the fiscal year for which it is intended. OMB, after preliminary consultation with the executive agencies and in accord with presidential policy, develops targets or ceilings within which the agencies are encouraged to build their requests. This work begins a full sixteen to eighteen months before the beginning of the fiscal year for which the budget is being prepared. In other words, work would begin in January 1987, on the budget for the fiscal year beginning October 1, 1988 and ending September 30, 1989. Budgets are named for the fiscal year in which they *end,* so this example describes the work on *The Budget of the United States Government Fiscal Year 1989* or more simply "FY89."

Budget materials and instructions go to the agencies with the request that the forms be completed and returned to OMB. This request is followed by about three months' arduous work by agency-employed budget officers, department heads, and the "grass roots" bureaucracy in Washington and out in the field. Budget officials at the bureau level check requests from the smaller units, compare them with previous year's estimates, hold conferences, and make adjustments. The process of checking, reviewing, modifying, and discussing is repeated on a larger scale at the department level.

The heads of agencies are expected to submit their completed requests to OMB by mid-September or early October. Occasionally a schedule of "over ceiling" items (requests above the suggested ceilings) will be included.

With the requests of the spending agencies at hand, OMB begins its own budget review. Hearings are given each agency. Top agency officials support their requests as convincingly as possible. On rare occasions dissatisfied agencies may ask the budget director to take their cases to the president.

In December, the president and the OMB director will devote time to the document which by now is approaching its final stages of assembly.

They and their staffs will "blue-pencil," revise, and make last-minute changes, as well as prepare the president's message which accompanies the budget to Congress. After the budget is in legislative hands, the president may recommend further alterations as needs dictate.

Although the completed document includes a revenue plan with general estimates for taxes and other income, it is primarily an expenditure budget. Revenue and tax policy staff work centers in the Treasury Department and not in the Office of Management and Budget. On January 15th the president presents *The Budget of the United States Government* for the fiscal year beginning October 1st to Congress (see Figure 9-2).

Congress—The power of the purse.   The Constitution gives Congress the basic authority to decide how the government should spend its money. Article I, Section 9, declares: "No money shall be drawn from the Treasury but in consequence of appropriations made by law." The Constitution also requires that the House of Representatives originate all tax legislation, and by tradition the House assumes the privilege of originating appropriations measures as well. Of course, the Senate must concur and appropriations bills travel the same path as other bills, including joint House-Senate conference committee in the event of a dispute between the houses. And appropriations bills are subject to veto by the president.

In an effort to consider the budget as a whole, Congress has established House and Senate budget committees and a Congressional Budget Office (CBO) to review the president's budget after its submission to Congress. These committees draft a first budget resolution (due May 15th) setting forth target goals to guide committee actions on specific appropriation and revenue measures. If appropriations measures exceed the targets in the budget resolution, it comes back to the floor in a reconciliation measure. A second budget resolution (due September 15th) sets binding budget figures for committees and subcommittees considering appropriations. In practice, however, these two budget resolutions have been folded into a single measure, because Congress does not want to reargue the same issues twice.

Gramm-Rudman deficit reduction.   Proposed spending and revenue laws, together with economic forecasts for the coming budget year, are then reviewed by the president's Office of Management and Budget (OMB) and the Congressional Budget Office (CBO). This review is to determine how large the projected *deficit* may be. (This is a new process introduced in 1985 by the Gramm-Rudman-Hollings Act discussed later in this chapter.) Their estimates of the deficit are sent to the independent General Accounting Office to resolve any differences and to declare whether or not the deficit exceeds limits set in the Gramm-Rudman-Hollings Act. If the deficit limits are exceeded, Congress and the president have thirty days to reduce spending or increase taxes in order to reduce the deficit. Otherwise, automatic

FIGURE 9-2

MAJOR STEPS IN THE BUDGET PROCESS

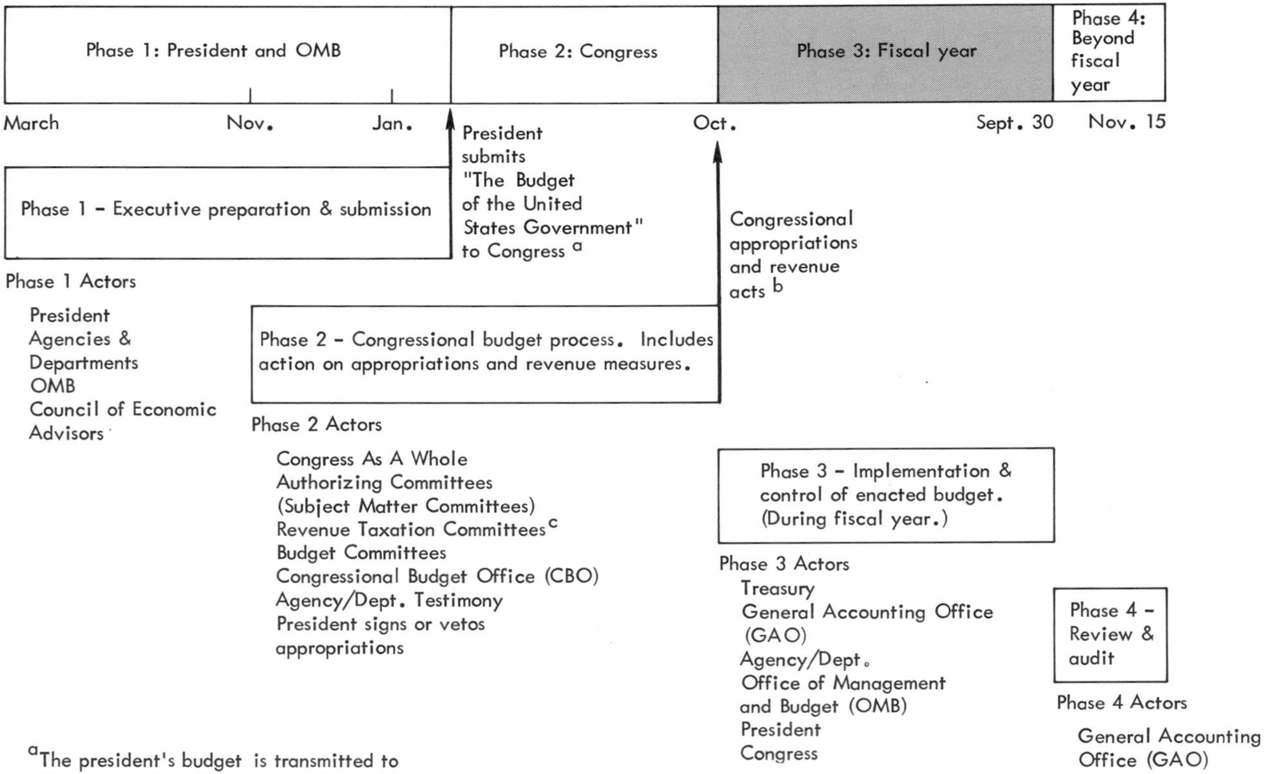

Phase 1: President and OMB	Phase 2: Congress	Phase 3: Fiscal year	Phase 4: Beyond fiscal year

March	Nov.	Jan.	Oct.	Sept. 30	Nov. 15

President submits "The Budget of the United States Government" to Congress [a]

Congressional appropriations and revenue acts [b]

Phase 1 – Executive preparation & submission

Phase 2 – Congressional budget process. Includes action on appropriations and revenue measures.

Phase 3 – Implementation & control of enacted budget. (During fiscal year.)

Phase 4 – Review & audit

Phase 1 Actors

President
Agencies & Departments
OMB
Council of Economic Advisors

Phase 2 Actors

Congress As A Whole
Authorizing Committees
(Subject Matter Committees)
Revenue Taxation Committees [c]
Budget Committees
Congressional Budget Office (CBO)
Agency/Dept. Testimony
President signs or vetos appropriations

Phase 3 Actors

Treasury
General Accounting Office (GAO)
Agency/Dept.
Office of Management and Budget (OMB)
President
Congress

Phase 4 Actors

General Accounting Office (GAO)

[a] The president's budget is transmitted to Congress within 15 days after Congress convenes.
[b] If appropriation action is not completed by Sept. 30, Congress enacts temporary appropriation (i.e., continuing resolution).
[c] House Ways and Means Committee, Senate Finance Committee

cuts will be made in defense and domestic spending levels, although social security and most welfare programs are exempted from these automatic cuts.

Appropriations acts. Congressional approval of each year's spending is usually divided into thirteen separate appropriations bills, each covering separate broad categories of spending. These appropriations bills are drawn up by the House and Senate appropriations committees and their specialized subcommittees. Indeed, House appropriations subcommittees function as overseers of the agencies included in their appropriations bill. The appropriations committees must stay within overall totals set forth in the budget resolutions adopted by Congress. All appropriations bills *should* be passed by both houses and signed by the president into law before October 1st, the date set for the start of the fiscal year. However, it is rare that Congress meets its own deadlines. The government usually finds itself beginning a new fiscal year without a budget. Legally the U.S. government is obliged to shut down if Congress does not pass an appropriations measure. However, Congress gets around this problem by adopting a "continuing resolution" authorizing government agencies to keep spending money for a specified period at the same level as the previous fiscal year.

An *appropriations* act provides money for spending and no funds can be spent without an appropriations act. An *authorization* is an act of Congress establishing a government program and defining the amount of money which it may spend. Authorizations may be for several years. However, the authorization does not actually provide the money which has been authorized; only an appropriations act can do that. Appropriations acts are almost always for a single fiscal year. Congress has its own rule that does not allow appropriations for programs which have not been authorized. However, appropriations frequently provide less money for programs than earlier authorizations.

Appropriations acts include both obligational *authority* and *outlays*. An obligation of authority permits a government agency to enter into contracts calling for payments into future years (new obligated authority). Outlays are to be spent in the fiscal year for which they are appropriated.

Appropriations subcommittees. Considerations of specific appropriations measures are functions of the appropriations committees in both houses. Committee work in the House of Representatives is usually more thorough than it is in the Senate; the committee in the Senate tends to be a "court of appeal" for agencies opposed to House action. Each committee, moreover, has about ten largely independent subcommittees to review the requests of a particular agency or a group of related functions. Specific appropriations bills are taken up by the subcommittees in hearings. Departmental officers answer questions on the conduct of their programs and defend their requests for the next fiscal year; lobbyists and other witnesses testify.

The appropriations subcommittees are of primary importance in congressional consideration of the budget. Because neither Congress nor the full committees have the time or understanding necessary to conduct adequate reviews, the subcommittee has become the locus of congressional budget analysis. Several factors contribute to its preeminent position. Each subcommittee specializes in a relatively small fraction of the total budget. It considers the same agencies and functions year after year. The long tenure characteristic of the membership of the prestigious appropriations committees guarantees decades of experience in dealing with particular programs. Although the work of the subcommittee is reviewed by the full committee, in practice it is routinely accepted with the expenditure of little time and debate.

Revenue acts. The House Committee on Ways and Means and the Senate Finance Committee are the major instruments of Congress for consideration of *taxing* measures. Through long history and jealous pride they have maintained formal independence of the appropriations committees, further fragmenting legislative consideration of the budget.

Presidential veto. In terms of aggregates, Congress does not regularly make great changes in the executive budget, rarely changing it more than 5 percent. The budget is approved by Congress in the form of appropriations bills, usually thirteen of them, each ordinarily providing for several departments and agencies. The number of revenue measures is smaller. As with other bills that pass Congress, the president has ten days to approve or veto appropriations legislation. He lacks the power to veto items in bills, and only rarely exercises his right to veto appropriations bills in their entirety.

Changing Priorities in Federal Spending Incrementalism may help to explain the process of budgetary decision making. But incrementalism appears unable to explain major changes in budgetary priorities over the years. Incrementalism views public policy as a continuation of past government activities, with only incremental modifications from year to year. "Revolutions" in spending patterns are not anticipated by incremental theory.

Nonetheless, the United States experienced a "revolution" in spending priorities during the 1970s. In a single decade America's "national priorities" in defense and social welfare were reversed. In 1965 national defense expenditures accounted for 40.1 percent of the federal budget, while health and welfare expenditures accounted for only 23.2 percent of the budget (see Table 9-4). While the mass media focused attention on the war in Vietnam and on Watergate, national budget priorities were reversed. By 1975, only a decade later, defense accounted for only 26.2 percent of the federal budget, while health and welfare expenditures had grown to 41.8

percent of the budget. This reversal of "national priorities" occurred during both Democratic (Johnson) and Republican (Nixon and Ford) administrations in Washington, *and* during the nation's longest war. In short, what we thought we "knew" about the effects of politics and war on social welfare spending turned out to be wrong.

Interestingly, not many people really noticed this reversal of national

TABLE 9-4   Federal Expenditures Over Two Decades

	BILLIONS OF DOLLARS						
	1960	1965	1970	1975	1980	1983	1985
National Defense	45.2	47.5	78.6	85.4	135.9	221.1	252.9
Welfare and Health	19.6	27.5	56.2	136.2	251.3	339.8	416.1
Veterans	5.4	5.7	8.7	16.6	21.2	24.4	26.4
Education and Training	1.0	2.1	8.6	15.9	30.8	21.6	29.3
Commerce and Housing	1.6	1.2	2.1	5.6	7.8	1.6	4.2
Transportation	4.1	5.8	7.0	10.4	21.1	19.6	25.8
Environment, Resources	1.6	2.5	3.1	7.3	13.8	9.9	13.4
Energy	.5	.7	1.0	2.2	6.3	4.2	5.7
Community Development	.2	1.1	2.4	3.7	10.1	7.3	7.7
Agriculture	2.6	3.9	5.2	1.7	4.8	4.5	25.6
Interest	8.3	10.4	18.3	30.9	64.5	112.5	129.4
Revenue Sharing	.2	.2	.5	7.2	8.6	6.7	6.4
International Affairs	3.0	5.2	4.3	6.9	10.7	12.0	16.2
Science and Space	.6	5.8	4.5	4.0	5.7	7.6	8.6
General Government	1.0	1.4	1.9	3.1	4.5	5.0	5.2
Justice	.4	.5	1.0	2.9	4.6	4.6	6.3
Total*	92.2	118.4	196.6	326.2	579.6	757.6	946.3

	PERCENTAGE DISTRIBUTION						
National Defense	49.0	40.1	40.0	28.2	23.4	29.2	26.7
Welfare and Health	20.7	23.2	28.6	41.8	43.3	44.9	44.0
Veterans	5.9	4.8	4.4	5.1	3.7	3.2	2.8
Education and Training	1.1	1.8	4.4	4.9	5.3	2.9	3.1
Commerce and Housing	1.7	1.0	1.1	1.7	1.3	.2	.4
Transportation	4.4	4.7	3.6	3.2	3.6	2.6	2.7
Environment, Resources	1.7	2.1	1.6	2.2	2.4	1.3	1.4
Energy	.5	.6	.5	.7	1.1	.5	.6
Community Development	.2	.9	1.2	1.1	1.7	.9	.8
Agriculture	2.8	3.3	2.6	.5	.8	.6	2.7
Interest	9.0	8.8	9.3	9.5	11.1	14.8	13.7
Revenue Sharing	.2	.2	.3	2.2	1.5	.9	.7
International Affairs	3.3	4.4	2.2	2.1	1.8	1.6	1.7
Science and Space	.7	4.9	2.3	1.2	1.0	1.0	.9
General Government	1.1	1.3	1.0	1.0	.8	.6	.5
Justice	.4	.4	.5	.9	.8	.6	.7

*Figures do not total correctly because of "offsetting receipts" from various programs.
Sources: *Statistical Abstract of the United States 1985. Budget of the United States Government 1987.*

priorities. Many people still believe the federal government spends more on defense than anything else. Old beliefs die hard.

Federal budget oulays over two decades for major programs are shown in Table 9-4, in both dollars and percentages of the total federal budget. Note how spending for *national defense* has grown very slowly in dollars and declined very rapidly as a percentage of total federal spending. In contrast, spending for health and welfare (including social security, public assistance, Medicare, and Medicaid) has grown very rapidly, both in dollars and in percentages of the federal budget.

The Reagan "revolution" in national priorities is reflected in budget figures for 1983 and thereafter. Spending for *national defense* has climbed back to 29 percent of total federal outlays. Spending for welfare and health (notably social security and Medicare) has continued to expand to about 42 percent of total federal outlays. Higher federal deficits have forced interest payments up to over 13 percent of the budget (see Figure 9-3). All other categories of spending have declined as a percentage of total federal outlays.

UNDERSTANDING REAGANOMICS

"The Failed Policies of the Past"

Since the Great Depression of the 1930s, America's established leadership believed that government could stabilize the economy through "countercyclic" fiscal and monetary policies. Government, it was believed, could manipulate aggregate *demand* levels for goods and services. In a recession, government could increase demand by increasing its own spending, lowering taxes, expanding debt, and increasing the money supply. When faced with inflation, government could reduce demand by reducing its own spending, increasing taxes, reducing debt, and contracting the money supply. The ideas of British economist John M. Keynes prevailed. In the short run at least, society's productive capacity—its ability to *supply* goods and services—was viewed as fixed. Keynes focused on government stimulation of *demand* as the key to maintaining prosperity.

But forty years of Keynesian economics had produced "stagflation" in the 1970s: inflation and high interest rates, and stagnant economic growth rates. While politicians had no difficulty *increasing* spending during recessions, it turned out to be impossible for them to reduce spending during inflation periods. The result was continuing government deficit spending during both recession and inflation, runaway "double-digit" (over 10 percent) annual inflation rates, and declining rates of economic growth. Keynesian economics was labeled by President Reagan as "the failed policies of the past."

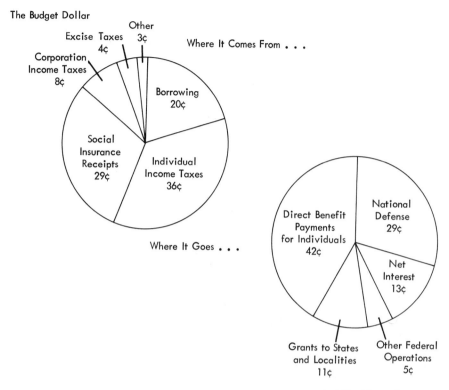

FIGURE 9-3 The budget dollar. (Source: The first page of *The Budget of the United States Government 1985.*)

What are the effects of inflation? If everyone correctly predicted the rate of inflation over future years, then all wages, prices, and interest rates could be adjusted (or "indexed") each year to protect everyone from suffering from inflation. But *uncertainty* over inflation produces many adverse consequences: (1) Inflation increases interest rates because lenders are fearful of repayment in less valuable dollars. (2) Inflation slows the rate of capital investment in new plants and facilities because of investors' fears that debt will be repaid in cheap money. (3) Inflation slows the rate of overall economic growth because of higher interest rates, less capital investment, and business uncertainty. (4) Inflation increases tax rates as taxpayers move into higher income brackets for tax purposes, even though their buying power remains the same.

Enter "Supply-Side" Economics

By 1980, the United States had experienced its worst decade-long inflation in history. Personal savings were disappearing rapidly. Uncertainty clouded investor decisions. Factories and machines were rapidly becoming outmoded. U.S. products (particularly steel, autos, and heavy machinery) could no longer compete with products from Europe and Japan in the world (and even the U.S.) market. Americans as a whole spent too much and saved too little. Federal tax and budget policies promoted immediate consumption instead of investment in the future.

Business and financial elites became concerned with declining economic growth rates, increasing rates of inflation, and increasing rates of taxation.

> *Declining growth:* Real per capita GNP (actual growth in the economy after controlling for inflation) averaged only 1.2 percent per year in the 1970s compared to 3.2 percent per year in the 1960s.
>
> *Inflation:* The Consumer Price Index (average prices paid by consumers) rose 112 percent in the 1970s compared to 31 percent in the 1960s.
>
> *Tax rates:* Federal taxes rose from 20 percent of total personal income in 1960 to 24 percent in 1980.

Supply-side economists argue that attention to long-term economic growth is more important than short-term manipulation of demand. Economic growth requires an expansion in the productive capacity of society. Economists argue that this requires an increase in one or more of the following: (1) natural resources, (2) labor, (3) capital, or (4) technology. Economic growth requires that we find and develop our natural resources, improve the productivity of our labor force, provide incentives for savings and capital investment, and improve our technology through continuing research and development.

Economic growth would increase the overall supply of goods and services, and thereby hold down prices. Inflation would be reduced or ended altogether. More importantly, everyone's standard of living would improve with the availability of more goods and services at stable prices. Economic growth would even increase government revenues over the long run.

Most supply-side economists believe that the free market is better equipped than government to bring about lower prices and more supplies of what people need and want. Government, they argue, is the problem, not the solution. Government taxing, spending, and monetary policies have promoted immediate consumption, instead of investment in the future. High taxes penalize hard work, creativity, investment, and savings. Government should provide tax incentives to encourage investment and savings; tax rates should be lowered in middle- and high-income brackets to encourage work and savings. Overall government spending should be held in check; if possible the governmental proportion of the GNP should be reduced over time. Government regulations should be minimized in order to increase productivity and growth. Overall, government should act to stimulate production and supply rather than demand and consumption.

A Program for Economic Recovery

The Reagan administration came into office with a comprehensive program for economic growth, officially labeled "A Program for Economic Recovery." This program was unofficially labeled "Reaganomics," and it was heavily influenced by supply-side economics.

Reaganomics includes the belief that past Keynesian policies had failed. High taxes, inflation, and stagnant economic growth had resulted from government attempts to increase demand. According to Reagan, the most important cause of the nation's economic problems—inflation, unemployment, low productivity, low investment—was the government itself. "The federal government through taxes, spending, regulating, and monetary policies, has sacrificed long-term growth and price stability for ephemeral, short-term goals."[12] Government efforts to reduce unemployment simply added to inflation.

The Program for Economic Recovery set forth a package of four sweeping policy directions:

1. Budget reform to cut the rate of growth in federal spending.
2. Tax reduction of 25 percent over three years on personal income and additional tax reductions to encourage business investment.
3. Relief from government regulations which cost industry large amounts of money for small increases in safety or environmental protection.
4. Slower growth of the money supply, to be achieved with the cooperation of the Federal Reserve Board.

These policies were designed to provide incentives for Americans to work, save, and invest. Theoretically, the economy would grow more rapidly because Americans could keep more of what they earned. Inflation would be brought under control by producing more goods. Americans would be encouraged to build new plants and provide new jobs.

Reducing Taxes to Stimulate Growth

Central to supply-side economics is the belief that high rates of taxation and oversized government reduce economic output and productivity. People will prefer leisure time over extra work if, for example, 50 percent of the additional money they make from the extra work is "snatched away" by income taxes. Individuals will not risk their money in new business investments if, for example, 70 percent of the income from the investment will be taken away by the income tax. High marginal tax rates also encourage

---

[12]Office of the President, *A Program for Economic Recovery*, February 18, 1981 (Washington, D.C.: Government Printing Office).

people to seek out "tax shelters"—special provisions in the tax laws which reduce personal income taxes. These shelters direct money to special investments (municipal bonds, commercial property, movies, horse farms) which are not really important for the nation's economic health. In addition, high tax rates encourage an "underground economy" in which people hide their real incomes and instead trade goods and services rather than conduct transactions which must be reported on income tax forms.

The Economic Recovery Tax Cut Act of 1981 was the first important step in implementing "Reaganomics." It reduced personal income taxes by 25 percent over a three-year period. Marginal tax rates were reduced from a range of 14 to 70 percent to a range of 11 to 50 percent. In addition, the act granted many new investment incentives for business, and "indexed" tax brackets against inflation in future years in order to prevent "bracket creep." (For a full discussion of the 1981 tax cuts and "bracket creep," see Chapter 10.)

The Effect of the Tax Cuts on the Budget

Tax cuts are politically very popular. Many Democrats joined President Reagan and the Republicans in Congress to support the 1981 tax cuts. The Reagan administration argued that the tax cuts would stimulate the economy so that much of the lost revenue would be recovered from taxes on increased personal and corporate income even at lower rates. But this "Laffer curve" effect (see Chapter 10) never happened. Lower tax rates brought less federal revenue. As a result, budget deficits soared.

The idea behind the tax cuts was that they would stimulate investment, create employment, and expand output. The improved economy would quickly make up lost revenues and the budget would come into balance. But even Reagan's budget director, David Stockman, had his doubts: He did not believe that a tax cut would expand the economy enough to cover the revenue loss. He was concerned when the Congress cut deeply into expected tax revenues but failed to make equivalent cuts in proposed spending. Later he confided in a reporter, "We didn't think it all the way through. We didn't add up all the numbers."[13] When Reagan saw such quotes in print, Stockman was "taken to the woodshed" and obliged to publicly apologize for his comments.

Evaluating "Reaganomics"

It is very difficult to accurately evaluate Reagan's economic policies, or any government policies for that matter. The problem is that the economy is constantly changing, independently of government policies. For

[13]Quoted by William Greider, "The Education of David Stockman," *Atlantic Monthly* (December 1981), 27–54.

example, as more women enter the labor force, the economy must create many new jobs just to absorb the larger percentage of the population who are seeking work. The unemployment rate may increase even though many more people are working, simply because jobs cannot be created as fast as new workers enter the job market.

Another problem is that the economy often requires one or two years to respond to government policies. The first two years of the Reagan administration, 1981–1983, saw the deepest recession in the United States since the 1930s. Did this recession occur because of Reagan policies, or did it occur as a product of high inflation and high interest rates in the preceding Carter administration? Finally, government policies can have different effects, some good and some bad. Political opponents of the administration in power will emphasize the bad effects, while the administration itself emphasizes the good.

On the positive side we can note that the annual *inflation rate* declined from 14.5 percent to 4.5 percent, a truly impressive performance. Unemployment remained stubbornly high, even though the economy absorbed about 6 million new workers during the five-year period. The *participation rate* in the labor force (the percentage of the population who are working) has increased slightly. Real growth in the GNP (growth measured in constant dollars) has rebounded from the sluggishness of the late 1970s to about 4 percent per year, a very healthy growth rate if it can be sustained.

The Reagan administration succeeded in cutting *the rate of growth* of government spending, even though government spending continued to increase during the Reagan years. Both domestic and defense spending under Reagan continued to rise, although defense spending increased faster than domestic spending. The result was that defense took a larger share of the federal budget (29 percent) in 1985 than in 1980 (24 percent).

The Reagan tax cuts in 1981 did *not* result in greatly increased revenues as predicted by some supply-side economists. Instead, the tax cuts slowed the rate of growth of government revenue. Domestic spending was not slowed sufficiently to offset these lost revenues, and defense spending was increased. Reagan had promised a balanced budget, but it was impossible to cut taxes, increase defense spending, and maintain social security and other popular domestic spending programs, without increasing the federal deficit. Indeed, in recent years the federal government has run *the largest peacetime deficits in history.*

These deficits threaten the future of the economy. As the federal government borrows high amounts of capital to fund its debts, less capital is available to the private market for economic growth. Interest rates are kept high by the government's own demand for loans.

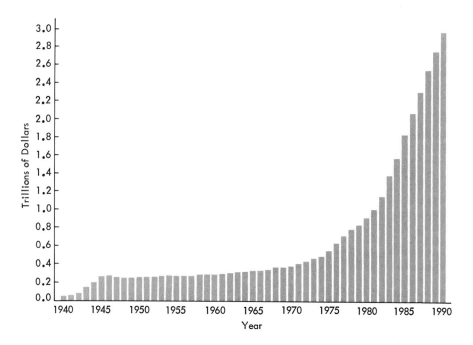

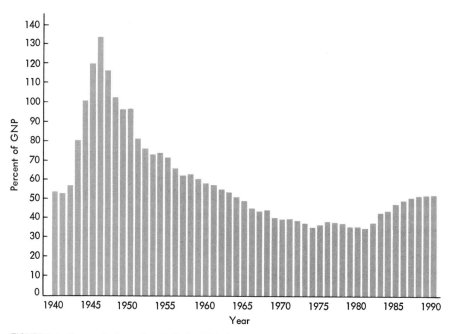

FIGURE 9-4   Top graph shows the total federal debt between 1940 and 1990; bottom graph shows federal debt as percentage of GNP during the same period.

The Burden of Government Debt

Traditional Keynesian economics encouraged government deficit spending during recessions. In theory, Keynesian economics called for surpluses during expansionary periods, but in practice Congresses hardly ever wished to tax more than they spent. The U.S. government has incurred a deficit in every one of the past twenty-five years. The total federal debt exceeds 2 *trillion* dollars, or nearly $10,000 for every man, woman and child in the nation (see Figure 9-5).

Liberal economists traditionally minimized the burdens of government debt; recently they have been joined by some Reagan administration officials. The U.S. government debt is owed mostly to banks and financial institutions and private citizens who buy U.S. Treasury bonds. As old debt comes due, the U.S. Treasury Department sells new bonds to pay off the old, that is, it continues to "roll over" or "float" the debt. The debt today is smaller as a percentage of the gross national product than at other periods in U.S. history (see Figure 9-5). Indeed, in order to pay the costs of fighting World War II, the U.S. government ran up a debt of 110 percent of GNP; the current debt is the highest in history in dollar terms but only 40 percent of the GNP. This suggest that the debt is still manageable, because of the size and strength of the U.S. economy.

The ability to float such a high debt depends on public confidence in the United States government—confidence that it will continue to pay interest on its debt, that it will pay off the principal of bond issues when they come due, and that the value of the bonds will not decline over time because of inflation.

Interest payments on the national debt are now 14 percent of total federal expenditures and the third largest expenditure of the federal government, after social security and national defense. These payments come from current taxes and they divert money away from all other government programs. Even if the federal government manages to balance its current budgets, these payments will remain obligations of the children and grandchildren of the current generation of policy makers and taxpayers. In short, today's high spending and low taxing is shifting the burden of debt from the current generation to future generations.

The size of the U.S. government debt and the resulting need for the Treasury Department to sell billions of dollars of bonds each month keeps interest rates high. The Treasury Department must compete with private borrowers for available savings money—home buyers seeking mortgages, car buyers seeking loans, corporations seeking loans for capital expansion, and so forth. So even though inflation declined in the 1980s (which should have reduced interest rates), real interest rates remain at historic high levels. (The "real" interest rate is the difference between the inflation rate and current interest rates; if inflation is 4 percent per year, and the average interest rate on Treasury bonds 10 percent, then the "real" interest rate is 7 percent.) High interest rates slow the growth of the GNP.

High interest rates paid on U.S. dollars raise the value of these dollars on international markets. A "strong" dollar hurts U.S. export businesses because foreigners must pay for U.S. goods with high-priced dollars. But imports are cheaper because U.S. dollars can buy more foreign goods. The result is a trade imbalance, with the U.S. buying more abroad than it sells abroad. Another result is a rapid decline of American industries which cannot compete well against foreign imports—especially steel, clothing, and textiles.

No one expects the United States to ever default on its debt—that is, to refuse to pay interest or principal when it comes due, although other debt-ridden nations have done so in the past and many threaten to do so today. But there is always the possibility that a future administration in Washington might "monetarize" the debt, that is, simply print currency and use it to pay off bondholders. Of course, this currency would flood the nation and soon become worthless. Hyperinflation would leave U.S. bondholders with worthless money. These financial disasters—default or hyperinflation—are unlikely, but the existence of a high federal deficit means that such disasters are not unthinkable.

Dealing with Deficits

The simple and responsible solution to the federal deficit is to have the president and Congress prepare and pass only balanced budgets. But that solution has eluded policy makers for over a quarter-century. Neither presidents nor Congresses, Democrats nor Republicans, have been willing to reduce expenditures or raise taxes to balance budgets. American politics has reached a level of irresponsibility where calls for a balanced budget are considered "naive" and "unrealistic." So Washington searches for politically "painless" remedies.

The balanced budget amendment. Constitutions govern government. Presumably, if "the people" wish to discipline their government they can do so by amending the Constitution to restrict the actions of officials. Indeed, according to the National Taxpayers Union, some thirty-one states have petitioned Congress to call a constitutional convention to balance the budget. Under Article V of the Constitution, a convention must be called if two-thirds of the states (thirty-four) request one. However, no procedure exists to force Congress to do so, or to determine when or how such a convention would be held, how delegates would be elected, or what the authority of the convention would be. Realistically, the call for a constitutional convention to balance the budget is only a means of pressuring Congress to pass a constitutional amendment itself to require balanced budgets.

President Ronald Reagan led an unsuccessful effort in 1982 to get Congress to pass a balanced budget amendment and send it to the states for ratification. Yet, even in the year that the Republican president proposed this amendment, he also submitted a budget with the largest peacetime deficit in history! Congressional Democrats viewed the amendment as a partisan attempt by Reagan to shift attention away from his own red ink. The amendment failed to win the necessary two-thirds vote in the Democrat-controlled House of Representatives in 1982.

Gramm-Rudman-Hollings.   Congress devised its own deficit reduction plan in 1985 which calls for "mandatory" reductions in annual federal deficits each year until a balanced budget is reached in 1991. The plan was originally proposed by Senators Phil Gramm (R.–Tex.), Warren B. Rudman (R.–N.H.), and Ernest F. Hollings (D.–N.C.). Of course, no Congress can really "mandate" that future Congresses do anything they do not wish to do. But Gramm-Rudman establishes automatic budget cuts which will take effect if Congress and the president cannot agree on deficit reductions.

The Gramm-Rudman-Hollings deficit reduction plan is supposed to work as follows:

- Gradually lowered ceilings are placed in the annual federal deficit from 1986 to 1991, when a balanced budget is required.
- The president's OMB and Congress's CBO jointly predict the size of the projected deficit each year. (The independent General Accounting Office resolves any differences in estimates.)
- If Congress and the president fail, through the ordinary budget process, to achieve these targeted deficit amounts, the president would be required to order spending cuts in all nonexempt programs.
- However, Congress exempted about half of all federal spending programs from the mandatory provisions of the plan. The privileged programs include:
  —Social Security, including generous cost of living allowances
  —Welfare: SSI and AFDC
  —Food Stamps
  —Medicaid
  —Veterans benefits
  —Interest on the national debt.
- Half of the cuts will automatically come from military spending and the other half from domestic programs which were not exempted.

Why would Congress be willing to give up part of its constitutional powers over spending in favor of "automatic" cuts by budgetary bureaucracies? Obviously Congress does not have the political courage to make the decisions that it is elected to make—that is, to decide to raise taxes or cut spending or both. They want an "invisible hand" to make the tough taxing and spending decisions. Perhaps the threat of "meat ax" automatic cuts in defense and domestic spending will be enough to force Congress to confront the hard budget choices itself. Or perhaps the threat to defense programs from automatic cuts will be enough to force the president to ask for tax increases. Gramm-Rudman does not rule out tax increases as a means of reaching the targeted deficit ceilings. In short, perhaps Gramm-Rudman will encourage responsible budget policies on both the president and Congress.

SUMMARY

Government budgeting lies at the heart of public policy making. Budgets tell us "who gets what" from government, and "who pays the cost." The theory of incrementalism helps us to understand the budget process and budget outcomes.

1. Government activity has grown in relation both to the size of the population and the economy. Government activity now accounts for about one-third of all economic activity in the United States. Nonetheless, the governmental percentage of the GNP in the United States is lower than that of most other nations.

2. Government expenditures as a proportion of all economic activity in the nation spurt upward in response to wars and depressions. When these crises subside, government expenditures associated with them decline somewhat, but stabilize at levels higher than before the crises. War forces citizens to tolerate major increases in government activity. During war, government domestic spending declines; but after a war, domestic spending displaces defense spending and achieves a higher plateau than before the war.

3. The budgetary *process* itself is incremental, political, fragmented, and nonprogrammatic. Policy makers generally consider last year's expenditure as a base and focus their attention on a narrow range of increases and decreases in expenditures. Evaluating the desirability of *every* public program *every* year might create politically insoluble conflict as well as exhaust the energies of budget makers.

4. The range of decisions available to policy makers in the development of an annual budget is really quite small. "Uncontrollable" items account for over two-thirds of the federal budget.

5. Among public expenditures, income security (social security, welfare, and social services) now takes highest priority. Defense spending, which was once the largest share of all federal spending, is now much less than spending for social programs. This shift in national priorities occurred between 1965 and 1975, during both a Democratic and a Republican administration and during the nation's longest war. This reversal of federal budget priorities raises questions about whether budgeting is truly "incremental."

6. Reaganomics views traditional countercyclical taxing and spending as "the failed policies of the past" which produced inflation, high interest rates and a stagnant economy. Higher government taxing and spending levels promoted immediate consumption instead of investment in the future, and penalized hard work, creativity, and savings. President Reagan's Program for Economic Recovery included cutting the rate of growth of government spending; reducing personal income tax rates by 25 percent over three years, and indexing future taxes; reducing government regulations; and slowing the growth of the money supply.

7. The economic record of the Reagan years includes lower inflation, a slower rate of growth of government spending, and lower taxes. Although the economy has absorbed many millions of new workers, unemployment remains high by historical standards. But the federal government has incurred the highest annual deficits in history.

8. Huge federal deficits direct federal tax dollars away from defense and domestic needs and into interest payments. These deficits and interest payments will burden future generations. Americans today are spending at the expense of their children. Deficits also help keep interest rates high and contribute to trade imbalances.

9. In over twenty-five years neither presidents nor Congresses, Republican or Democratic, have acted responsibly regarding deficits. Washington has been politically unable and unwilling to reduce spending (or to raise taxes) in order to balance the federal budget.

10. A constitutional amendment requiring a balanced budget is lost in political controversy and might not succeed in its objective even if it were to pass. An effort by Congress to discipline itself—the Gramm-Rudman-Hollings Act—promises gradually reduced deficits through automatic cuts in defense and nonprivileged domestic programs until a balanced budget is reached in 1991. But Congress can ignore, repeal, or amend its own law.

BIBLIOGRAPHY

CONGRESSIONAL QUARTERLY, *Budgeting for America*. Washington, D.C.: Congressional Quarterly, Inc., 1982.

FENNO, RICHARD, *The Power of the Purse*. Boston: Little, Brown, 1966.

SCHICK, ALLEN, *Congress and Money*. Washington, D.C.: The Brookings Institution, 1980.

WILDAVSKY, AARON, *The Politics of the Budgetary Process*, 4th ed. Boston: Little, Brown, 1984.

TAX POLICY
battling the special interests

Roscoe Egger, Internal Revenue Commissioner, tries to explain the "simplified" 1040A federal income tax form. (UPI/Bettmann Newsphotos)

The interplay of interest groups in policy making is praised as "pluralism" by many political scientists. Robert A. Dahl, for example, proclaimed the "central guiding thread of American constitutional development" to be "the evolution of a political system in which all the active and legitimate groups in the population can make themselves heard at some critical stage in the process of decision."[1] Public policy is portrayed by interest group theory as the equilibrium in the struggle between interest groups (see Chapter 2). While this equilibrium is not the same as majority preference, it is considered by pluralists to be the best possible approximation of the public interest in a highly organized society.

But what if only a small proportion of the American people are organized into politically effective interest groups? What if the interest group system represents well-organized, economically-powerful, producer groups, who actively seek immediate tangible benefits from the government? What if the interest group system leaves out a majority of Americans, particularly the less-organized, economically-dispersed consumers and taxpayers, who wish for broad policy goals such as fairness, simplicity, and general economic well-being? Most serious social scientists acknowledge that the interest group system in Washington fails to represent the mass public in policy making. Political scientist E.E. Schattschnieder writes: "The business or upper-class bias of the pressure system shows up everywhere."[2] Even the so-called "public interest" groups are really "models of elitism" representing a tiny group of administrators, lobbyists, and lawyers, who make their living claiming to represent the public in Washington.

There is no better illustration of the influence of organized interest groups in policy making than national tax policy. Every economics textbook tells us that the public interest is best served by a tax system which is universal, simple, and fair, and which promotes economic growth and well-being. But until recently the federal tax system was very nearly the opposite: it was complex, unfair, and nonuniversal. About *one-half* of all personal income in the United States escaped taxation through various exemptions, deductions, and special treatments in tax laws. Most of these tax breaks benefited businesses and upper-income individuals. Tax laws treated different types of income differently. They penalized work, savings, and investment, and diverted capital investment into nonproductive tax shelters and an illegal "underground economy."

The unfairness, complexity, and inefficiency of the tax laws were directly attributable to organized interest groups. The nation's elected policy makers were fully aware of this. Representative Dan Rostenkowski of

[1]Robert A. Dahl, *A Preface to Democratic Theory* (Chicago: University of Chicago Press, 1956), p. 124.

[2]E.E. Schattschnieder, *The Semi-Sovereign People* (New York: Holt, Rinehart & Winston, 1960), p. 31.

Chicago, chairman of the House Ways and Means Committee, which writes the nation's tax laws, admitted:

> We gave oil companies breaks to fuel our oil industry. We gave real estate incentives to build more housing. We sharpened our technology with research and development credits. We gave tax breaks to encourage people to save. We pile one tax benefit on top of another—each one backed with good intention.
>
> Unfortunately it didn't take too long before those with the best accountants and lawyers figured out how to beat the system . . . and the cost of government was shifted to families like those in my neighborhood who don't have the guile to play the game of hide-and-seek with the IRS. . . .
>
> In the end tax reform comes down to a struggle between the narrow interests of the few—and the broad interests of working American families.[3]

Indeed, the influence of the special interests in federal tax policy was so great that few observers expected that tax reform efforts would ever succeed. For years congressional advocates of tax reform—Representatives Jack Kemp (R.–N.Y.) and Richard Gephardt (D.–IN) and Senator Bill Bradley (D.–N.J.)—were ignored. And President Reagan's tax reform proposals were said to be doomed. But in a dramatic turnabout in the Tax Reform Act of 1986, the special interests suffered a rare but major defeat on tax policy. The president and Congress, Republicans and Democrats, joined together in a sweeping reform of the nation's tax laws.

In this chapter, we will examine the nation's tax laws and the influence of the special interest on these laws, and we will describe how reform was accomplished over the opposition of the special interests.

TAX BURDENS: DECIDING WHAT'S FAIR

The politics of taxation centers around the question of who actually bears the burden or incidence of a tax—that is, which income groups must devote the largest proportion of their income to taxes. Taxes that require high-income groups to pay a larger percentage of their incomes in taxes than low-income groups are said to be *progressive*, while taxes that take a larger share of the income of low-income groups are called *regressive*. Note that the *percentage of income* paid in taxes is the determining factor. Most taxes take more money from the rich than the poor, but a progressive or regressive tax is distinguished by the *percentages of income* taken from various income groups. The percentage of income paid in taxes is called the *effective tax rate*.

Various exemptions and deductions in tax laws can also be considered

---

[3]Text of address by U.S. Representative Dan Rostenkowski, May 28, 1985. *Congressional Quarterly Weekly Report*, June 1, 1985, p. 1077.

progressive or regressive, depending on whether they benefit the rich or the poor. For example, a personal exemption of $2,000 is considered progressive. Even though both rich and poor can claim their personal exemptions, four $2,000 exemptions for a poor family whose income is under $10,000 exempts over 80 percent of their income from taxation; whereas the same four $2,000 exemptions for a family whose income is $100,000 exempts only 8 percent of their income from taxation. In contrast, the deduction for state and local taxes is considered regressive, because wealthy taxpayers who pay heavy state and local income and property taxes are more likely to claim large deductions for these items than poorer taxpayers.

Progressive taxation is generally defended on the principle of ability to pay; the assumption is that high-income groups can afford to pay a large percentage of their incomes into taxes at no more of a sacrifice than that required of lower-income groups to devote a smaller proportion of their income to taxation. This assumption is based on what economists call *marginal utility theory* as it applies to money: Each additional dollar of income is slightly less valuable to an individual than preceding dollars. For example, a $5,000 increase in the income of an individual already earning $100,000 is much less valuable than a $5,000 increase to an individual earning only $3,000 or to an individual with no income. Hence, added dollars of income can be taxed at higher *rates* without violating equitable principles.

Opponents of progressive taxation generally assert that equity can only be achieved by taxing everyone at the *same* percentage of their income, regardless of the size of their income. A tax which requires all income groups to pay the same percentage of their income is called a *flat tax*. Progressivity penalizes initiative, enterprise, and risk, and reduces incentives to expand and develop the nation's economy. Moreover, by taking incomes of high-income groups, governments take money that would otherwise go into business—investments, stocks, bonds, loans, etc.—and thus curtailing economic growth.

Certainly the most dramatic change in federal tax laws during the Reagan years was the reduction in the progressivity of tax rates. The top marginal tax rate was reduced from 70 percent when President Reagan took office to 28 percent following enactment of tax reform in 1986. (*Marginal* is a term used by economists to mean additional; a progressive tax taxes additional increments of income at higher rates; these increments are often referred to as "brackets"; the top marginal rate refers to the rate applied to the highest tax bracket.) This reduction in progressivity in the rate structure occurred in two major tax enactments: The Economic Recovery Tax Cut Act of 1981 reduced the rate structure from 14–70 percent to 11–50 percent; the Tax Reform Act of 1986 reduced the fourteen rate brackets varying from 11–50 percent to only two rate brackets, 15 and 28 percent. These reductions in the progressivity of federal income tax rates suggests that our ideas about fairness, simplicity, and economic growth have undergone important changes in recent years.

Increasingly Americans have come to perceive *fairness* to mean that there should be no great differences in the percentages of their income people at different income levels devote to taxation. Although the federal tax laws now exempt most poor people from paying income taxes, the range of progressivity among taxpayers extends only from 13 to 28 percent, a stark contrast to rate diffferences in past eras.

Americans have also come to associate *universality* with fairness. Universality means that all types of income should be subject to the same tax rates: Income earned from stocks, bonds, and real estate, and the buying and selling of these investments, should be taxed at the same rate as income earned from wages. Moreover, Americans have become somewhat more skeptical of exemptions, deductions, and special treatment in the tax laws. It is true that most people wish to retain the widely used tax breaks—the personal exemption, charitable deductions, and home mortgage deductions. But there is a growing sentiment that tax laws should not be used to promote social policy objectives by granting a wide array of tax preferences.

Americans also appear to have a new appreciation of the effect of high tax rates on *economic growth*. Excessively high rates cause investors to seek "tax shelters"—to use their money not to produce more business and employment but rather to produce tax breaks for themselves. High tax rates discourage work, savings, and productive investment; they also encourage costly "tax avoidance" (legal methods of reducing or eliminating taxes) as well as "tax evasion" (illegal means of reducing or eliminating taxes.).

Finally, *simplicity* in taxation is now recognized both as a means of reducing the costs of paying taxes and a way of reassuring taxpayers that the tax structure is fair, reasonable, and understandable.

WHO REALLY BEARS THE TAX BURDEN?

We know that federal income tax *rates* are progressive, but we also know that most exemptions, deductions, and special treatments are regressive, benefitting the rich more than the poor. So the question arises, who really bears the burden of the federal income taxes?

Overall federal income taxes are progressive, although much less progressive than the legal rate structure. Economist Joseph Pechman estimates that the lowest income class in the nation (the lowest 10 percent or decile of income earners) pays 4.2 percent of its total income into federal income taxes. This is their effective tax rate (see Figure 10-1). Effective tax rates rise for each higher income class, to a high of 12.7 percent for the highest income class.

Note, however, that social security taxes are estimated to be regressive. The three lowest income classes (30 percent of the population) pay *more* in social security taxes than income taxes. For example, the poorest 10 percent of the population pays 9.4 percent of its income into social security

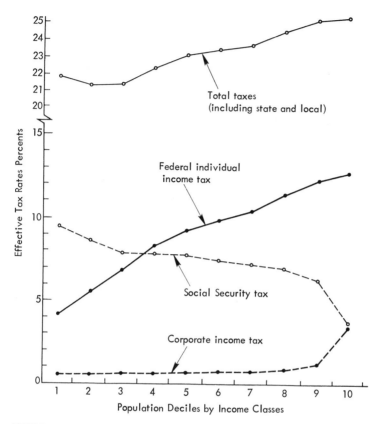

FIGURE 10-1 Effective tax rates by income class.

taxes and 4.2 percent into federal income taxes. Because of the ceiling on social security taxes, the effective rate for the highest income class falls abruptly to 3.7 percent.

If we combine all taxes—federal, state, and local—the American tax system is only very mildly progressive. The effective tax rate for the lowest income class is estimated to be 21.9 percent, compared to 25.3 percent for the highest income class. The tax system, then, does not change the distribution of income in the nation very much.

Who pays the taxes? The American middle class pays the bulk of federal income taxes. About 100 million tax returns are received by the Internal Revenue Service (IRS) each year. About 35 percent of these returns are sent by people with adjusted gross incomes under $10,000; but these low-income taxpayers account for less than 3 percent of all income taxes paid. (See Figure 10-2.) At the other end of the scale, about 8,000 people, less than 1 percent, make over $1 million *per year;* they account for about 2.5 percent of all income taxes paid. The taxpayers with adjusted gross

WHO PAYS FEDERAL TAXES?

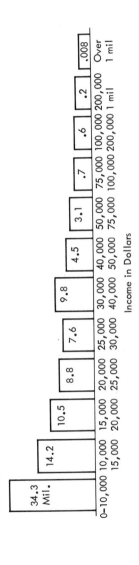

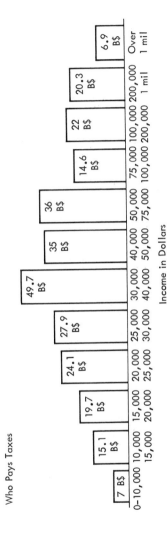

FIGURE 10-2 Who pays federal taxes?

incomes of $20,000 to $75,000 a year pay 62 percent of all the dollars collected by the federal individual income tax.

REAGANOMICS AND TAX CUTTING

The goal of any tax system is not only to raise sufficient revenue for the government to perform its assigned tasks, but also to do so simply, efficiently, and fairly, and in a way that does not impair economic growth. The Reagan administration argued on behalf of tax reform that the federal tax system failed to meet *any* of these criteria:

• It was so complex that a majority of taxpayers hired professional tax preparers; an army of accountants and lawyers made their living from the tax code.

• Tax laws were unfair in treating various sources of income differently; the many exemptions, deductions, and special treatments were perceived as "loopholes" that allowed the privileged to escape fair taxation.

• Tax laws encouraged tax avoidance, directing investment away from productive uses and into inefficient tax shelters; whenever people make decisions about savings and investment based on tax laws instead of most productive use, the whole economy suffers.

• Tax laws encouraged cheating and reduced trust in government; they encouraged the growth of an underground economy, transactions which were never reported on tax forms.

• High marginal tax rates discouraged work and investment; economic growth was diminished when individuals face tax rates of 50 percent or more on additional income they received from additional work, savings, or investment.

When the Reagan team arrived in Washington, its first priority was to reduce high marginal rates of taxation in the hope of stimulating economic growth. According to its supply-side economists, poor economic growth rates and high inflation were caused in large part by high tax rates. High tax rates were discouraging Americans from working and investing; the resulting lower production levels were causing inflation. If tax rates could be lowered, argued the supply siders, more Americans would work, save, and invest, and a larger supply of goods would be produced. This increased supply of goods would keep prices in check and reduce inflation.

The Laffer curve.   Would not tax cuts create government deficits? Not necessarily, argued the supply siders. If tax rates are reduced, the paradoxical results may be to *increase* government revenue because more people will work harder and start new businesses knowing they can keep a larger share of their earnings. Tax cuts will stimulate increased economic activity, and this increased activity will produce more government revenue even though tax rates are lower.

Economist Arthur Laffer developed the diagram shown in Figure 10-

3. If the government imposed a zero tax rate, of course, it would receive no revenue (point *A*). Initially, government revenues rise with increases in the tax rate. However, when tax rates become too high (beyond point *C*), they discourage workers and businesses from producing and investing. When this discouragement occurs, the economy declines, and government revenues fall. Indeed, if the government imposed a 100-percent tax rate (if the government confiscated everything anyone produced), then everyone would quit working and government revenues would fall to zero (point *B*).

According to the "Laffer curve," modest increases in tax rates will result in increased government revenues up to an optional point (point *C*), after which further tax increases discourage work and investment. Laffer does not claim to know exactly what the optimum rate of taxation should be. But Laffer (and the Reagan administration) clearly believe that the United States had been in the "prohibitive range" throughout the 1970s.

Bracket creep is a term used to describe a particular contribution to the adverse economic effect of high personal income tax rates. Bracket creep occurs when individuals receive higher wages due to inflation, but because of that inflation these higher wages do not add to their buying power. However, higher wages cause higher tax rates. In this way inflation gradually pushes all wage earners into higher tax brackets and increases everyone's tax burden. These tax increases occur "automatically," without a need for Congress to enact higher taxes. According to supply-side economists, this bracket creep, by increasing tax burdens, further erodes incentives to work, save, invest, and produce.

The Economic Recovery Tax Cut Act. The Economic Recovery Tax Cut Act of 1981, pushed through Congress by President Reagan, reduced per-

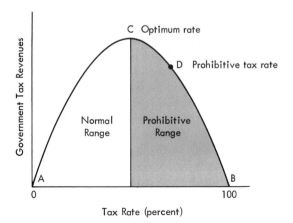

FIGURE 10-3 The Laffer curve.

sonal income taxes by 25 percent over a three-year period. Marginal tax rates were reduced from a range of 14 to 70 percent to a range of 11 to 50 percent; this was only a minor reduction at the bottom end of the income brackets but a very significant reduction in the highest income brackets. In addition, the act granted many new investment incentives for business, and "indexed" taxes against inflation in future years in order to prevent bracket creep.

The Reagan administration hoped that the tax cuts would stimulate work, productivity, investment, and economic growth. According to Reagan's budget calculations, the federal tax bite out of the nation's GNP would be reduced to less than 20 percent. Without the tax cuts, the tax bite would have climbed to nearly 25 percent of the GNP (see Figure 10-4). Moreover, the tax cuts and the indexing of taxes in future years would place the government on a reduced "allowance." Hopefully, this "allowance" would force Congress to limit the growth of federal spending.

The impact of the Reagan tax cuts.   The recession of 1981–82 was the deepest since the Great Depression of the 1930s. For the first time since the Depression, unemployment reached double-digit levels—exceeding 10 percent. Total output declined, steel and automobile plants operated at less than half of capacity, house building was brought to a standstill, and business bankruptcies reached new highs. Personal income grew very slowly and corporate profits declined, while government unemployment compensation payments soared. The result was the largest peacetime federal deficit in history.

Traditionally in American politics, the "in" party is blamed when the economy falters. Yet the recession of 1981–82 was already underway before the Economic Recovery Tax Cut Act of 1981 took effect. The recession can be traced to high interest rates which slowed capital investment, and high interest rates can be traced to runaway inflation in the 1970s. The Reagan administration claimed that the recession would have been *worse* without its tax cuts. Throughout the recession, the Reagan administration believed that its economic recovery program would eventually bring economic growth, more jobs, and stable prices, if Americans would "stay the course." The important early accomplishments of their program included a reduced rate of inflation and lower interest rates.

Critics of Reaganomics argued that: (1) the tax cuts failed to result in new investment or new employment—in other words, "trickle down" did not work; (2) the huge federal deficits created by the tax cuts (and increased military spending) kept interest rates high—in other words, government borrowing crowded out private borrowing and increased interest rates; and (3) budget reductions in social programs further reduced personal income and added to the hardship of the poor.

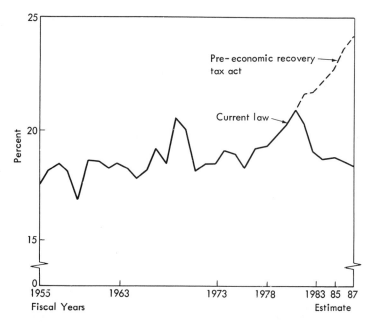

FIGURE 10-4   Federal tax claims on GNP, 1955–1987. (Source: *The Budget of the United States Government FY84,* Washington, D.C.: Government Printing Office, 1983).

THE POLITICS OF TAX REFORM

For fifty years, politicians in Washington promised to make tax laws simple and fair. Almost every year Congress tinkered with the laws, but the results of these changes only made matters worse. Or, as President Reagan observed: "They made it more like Washington itself: complicated, unfair, cluttered with gobbledygook and loopholes designed for those with the power and influence to hire high-priced legal and tax advisers."[4]

It comes as no surprise that most Americans believed that the federal tax system was unfair. Interestingly, this evaluation did *not* differ much by income class; people at all income levels believed federal taxes were unfair (see Table 10-1).

Although tax reform is popular as a general theme, most Americans want to keep their own favorite deductions. Despite these general negative views of the federal tax system, Americans consider most of the major personal deductions to be a "perfectly reasonable deduction" and not a tax loophole (see Table 10-2). Obviously, the popularity of these deductions and exemptions made it difficult for the president and Congress to fashion true tax reform.

[4]Text of Presidential Address on Tax Reform, May 28, 1985. *Congressional Quarterly Weekly Report,* June 1, 1985, p. 1074.

TABLE 10-1   Public Opinion on Federal Taxes

	PERCENT AGREE
The federal tax system is unfair.	59%
The present tax system benefits the rich and is unfair to the ordinary working man or woman.	75%
Corporations are undertaxed.	52%
The rich tend to get out of paying taxes by using accountants and lawyers.	92%
Cheating on taxes is becoming more common these days.	54%

Source: *Public Opinion,* February–March 1985.

Public opinion generally supports a shift from individual income taxes to corporate taxes and "sin" taxes on liquor and cigarettes. Other types of federal revenue raising are generally unpopular, even "to reduce the deficit" (see Table 10-3).

More importantly, there are a host of special interest groups who want to keep special provisions in the tax laws that benefit themselves. These interest groups, representing manufacturers, oil and gas companies, farmers, accountants, real estate developers, bankers, charities and foundations, and even state and local government officials, all combine to place major obstacles in Washington to comprehensive tax reform.

Congress has always had a strong distaste for the medicine of tax reform. Instead it made only incremental changes in the tax laws over the years. In the early 1960s the Kennedy administration reduced the progressivity of the federal income taxes—from the previous 20–91 percent to rates of 14–70 percent—but retained all of the traditional exemptions and deductions. In 1968, the costs of the Vietnam War moved Congress to raise personal income taxes; but instead of tampering with basic tax laws,

TABLE 10-2   Public Opinon on Various Federal Tax Deductions and Exemptions

	PERCENT SAYING PERFECTLY REASONABLE
Property taxes	93%
Interest on home mortgages	92%
State and local income taxes	88%
Interest paid on loans	87%
Child care for working parents	84%
Contributions to charity	71%
Social Security income as nontaxable	92%
Municipal bond income as nontaxable	53%

Source: *Public Opinion,* February–March 1985.

TABLE 10-3   Public Opinion on Various Deficit-reducing Measures

	PERCENT AGREEING A STEP THAT SHOULD BE CONSIDERED VERY SERIOUSLY TO REDUCE THE DEFICIT
An increase in corporate income taxes	78%
Raising taxes on liquor and cigarettes	76%
A national lottery	66%
Raising user taxes—gasoline taxes for drivers, airport taxes for passengers, etc.	38%
A value-added or national sales tax	34%
An increase in personal income taxes	24%

Source: *Public Opinion*, February–March 1985.

Congress chose to impose a "surtax"—a 10 percent increase over whatever the individual was already paying. President Reagan's Economic Recovery Tax Cut Act of 1981 was the largest tax cut in history, but it did not make any significant changes in the traditional exemptions and deductions. Its greatest change was a lowering of the top income tax bracket from 70 to 50 percent. None of these changes in tax laws could be called tax *reform.*

In 1985, President Reagan launched a campaign for sweeping tax reform:

> For the sake of fairness, simplicity, and growth, we must radically change the structure of a tax system that still treats our earnings as the personal property of the Internal Revenue Service, radically change a system that still treats similar incomes much differently. And yes, radically change a system that still causes some to invest their money, not to make a better mousetrap, but simply to avoid a tax trap.[5]

The major features of the Reagan tax reform package were:

- Reduce marginal tax rates to three brackets, 15, 25, and 35 percent (from fourteen brackets, 11–50 percent).
- Index these bracket amounts to protect taxpayers from inflation.
- Increase the personal exemption to $2,000 (from $1,000) and index it in later years for inflation.
- Raise the zero bracket amount so that the poor (families of four under $12,000) would pay no federal income tax.

[5]Text of presidential address on tax reform, May 28, 1985. *Congressional Quarterly Weekly Report,* June 1, 1985, p. 1074.

- Eliminate interest deductions except for home mortgages.
- Eliminate deductions for state and local taxes paid.
- Retain deductions for charitable contributions and medical expenses over 5 percent of income; and retain special lower rates for capital gains.
- Tax employer-paid fringe benefits including insurance.
- Tax unemployment compensation benefits, but continue to exempt welfare and social security benefits.
- End investment tax credits for business.
- Tighten rules on estimating depreciation on building and machinery.
- Reduce the number and size of many business deductions, including entertainment.
- Reduce the corporate tax rate from 46 to 33 percent.
- Impose a minimum tax of 20 percent for individuals and corporations which otherwise would pay no taxes because of depreciation and interest deductions.
- Eliminate the depletion allowance for large oil and gas companies.

STRUGGLING WITH THE SPECIAL INTERESTS

Tax reform turned out to be the most heavily lobbied legislation in the history of the Congress of the United States. The task fell first to the House Ways and Means Committee to try to shape President Reagan's tax reform proposal into law. The committee was chaired by Chicago Democrat Dan Rostenkowski, a man of extraordinary stamina and political skill and a supporter of tax reform. Yet no one knew better than Rostenkowski that a host of deals would have to be made with the powerful special interests in order to pass any tax bill. Indeed, some would argue that Rostenkowski made so many deals over tax reform that the final version of the tax reform bill had little "reform" left in it. Nonetheless, without Rostenkowski's skill and dedication, there would have been no tax bill at all.

Industry.   Opponents of tax reform were led by the U.S. Chamber of Commerce, the National Association of Manufacturers, and the Business Roundtable. Heavy manufacturing businesses strongly opposed the elimination of the investment tax credit, accelerated depreciation, and foreign tax credit provisions in existing tax laws. The lowering of the corporation tax rate from 46 to 33 percent did not really appeal to large manufacturers as few of them paid any taxes anyway because of the generous loopholes in the law.

Real estate and housing.   The National Association of Home Builders strongly opposed the elimination of interest deductions for second and vacation homes, as well as the elimination of real estate tax shelters which encouraged investors to put money into real estate projects that earned little or no income. The real estate industry also wanted to preserve deductions for property taxes.

Multinational corporations. Businesses involved in international trade opposed efforts to eliminate the foreign tax credit which allows U.S. companies to use taxes paid to other countries to reduce their U.S. tax liability.

Timber. Existing tax laws treat corporate income from timber sales as capital gains rather than ordinary income. The timber companies fought hard to retain their special treatment.

Oil and gas. The American Petroleum Institute, representing America's powerful oil companies, fought bitterly against any reductions in their "depletion allowance" or deductions for "intangible costs." Their familiar argument was that any change in their privileged status in the tax code would inhibit capital investment in energy and reduce production. But as an old Washington hand observed: "There are three reasons for keeping the oil depletion allowance—Texas, Oklahoma, and Louisiana."

Wall Street investment firms. The Securities Industries Association, the American Council for Capital Formation, and the nation's large investment firms lobbied heavily to keep preferential treatment of capital gains—profits from the sales of stocks and bonds. And the investment firms joined with banks in arguing for the retention of tax-free Individual Retirement Accounts (IRAs).

Charities and foundations. Even before President Reagan sent his tax reform proposals to Congress, the nation's leading foundations had petitioned the president to retain deductions for charitable contributions.

Restaurant and entertainment. The president proposed to limit business deductions for meals to $25 per person per meal and to eliminate entertainment deductions—night clubs, concerts, sport tickets, etc. The National Restaurant Association representing high-priced restaurants convinced Congress that business would falter without $100 meals and three-martini lunches; even the restaurant workers union appeared to plead the same case. The National Football League, the National Basketball Association, and the National Hockey League all reported that businesses purchased most of their season tickets as tax deductions.

Labor unions. The AFL-CIO was unimpressed with the notion of reducing and simplifying tax rates. Instead, it focused its opposition on the proposal to tax fringe benefits, including employer-paid health insurance and group life insurance. Unions also tried to keep the deduction for union dues.

Banks. Banking interests, led by the American Bankers Association, wished to continue unlimited deductions for all interest payments. This makes borrowing easier by shifting part of the costs of borrowing from the debtor to the government and the taxpayers who must make up the lost revenue. Interest deductions make more customers for banks.

Auto industry. The auto industry fought hard to keep deductions for interest paid on auto loans.

These special interests are powerful in Congress. An estimated one-third of all campaign contributions in congressional elections come from Political Action Committees, or PACs, which distribute these contributions on behalf of business, trade associations, and labor unions. Most of these contributions go to *incumbent* members of Congress. Seldom do PACs try to bargain on specific pieces of legislation, that is to "buy votes," because bribery is illegal. But every member of Congress knows who has contributed to his or her campaign costs in the past and who may do so in the future. When these same interests strongly urge him or her to vote with them on pending legislation, attention must at least be paid to their urgings.

Rostenkowski devoted two months of closed-door sessions of his Ways and Means Committee to writing a tax reform bill. Popular enthusiasm for tax reform appeared to waiver; even the President was unable to stir much popular interest, although he announced that tax reform was the top legislative priority of his second term. Rostenkowski hammered out innumerable compromises with the special interests, restoring many popular deductions. "We have not written a perfect law," he admitted, "but politics is an imperfect process." He argued that the House bill was nonetheless a "vast improvement over current law." It limited many tax deductions and credits (see Table 10-4), and shifted part of the burden of taxation away from individuals and toward corporations.

All participants in tax reform agreed that the new law should be *revenue neutral,* that is, it should not raise or lower overall taxes. The bill that emerged from House of Representatives restored so many exemptions and deductions, compared to the original Reagan plan, that it was necessary to place the top marginal rate at 38 percent, in order to insure that revenue would not be lost. (Even though this was higher than the President's proposed 35 percent, it was still a major reduction from the 50 percent rate in the previous law.) The Democratic-controlled House succeeded in passing the Rostenkowski tax reform bill. If tax reform failed in the Republican controlled Senate, the Democrats could blame the failure on the Republicans.

In the Senate, the principal responsibility for tax reform fell on Senate Finance Committee Chairman Robert Packwood (R.–OR). Initially Packwood was lukewarm on tax reform: "I kind of like the present tax code,"[6] he said, defending special tax breaks as a way for government to shape

[6]*Congressional Quarterly Weekly Report,* May 10, 1986, p. 101.

TABLE 10-4 The Evolution of Tax Reform

	PREVIOUS LAW	REAGAN PLAN	HOUSE BILL	SENATE PLAN	TAX REFORM ACT OF 1986
Individual Tax Rate	11–50 % 14 brackets	15, 25, 35 % 3 brackets	15, 25, 35, and 38 % 4 brackets	15 and 27 % 2 brackets	15 and 28 % 2 brackets
Personal Exemption	$1,040	$2,000	$2,000	$2,000	$2,000, but phased out for high income tax-payers.
Interest Payments	Unlimited deductions	Deductions for one home mortgage; plus $5,000 other interest	Deductions for first and second residences; plus $20,000 other interest	Deductions for first and second residences; no other interest	Deductions for first and second residences; no consumer interest deductions
Charitable Deductions	Deductible	Deductible	Deductible	Deductible	Deductible
Fringe Benefits	Not taxed	Tax as income	Not taxed	Not taxed	Not taxed
Depreciation	Short: 3–19 years; plus accelerated write-offs	Longer: 4–28 years; no accelerated write-off	Longer: 3–30 years; no accelerated write-off	Longer: 3–27½; plus accelerated write-offs	Longer: 3–31½ years; plus accelerated write-offs.
Capital gains	20 %	17.5 %	22 %	same as income: 15 and 27 %	Same as income: 15 and 28%
Corporate tax rate	46 %	33 %	36 %	33 %	34 %
Investment tax credit	10 %	Repealed	Repealed	Repealed	Repealed
Business entertainment	Unlimited deductions	Limit meals to $25; repeal entertainment deduction	Allow deductions of 80% of all meals and entertainment	Allow deductions of 80% of all meals and entertainment	Allow deductions of 80% of all meals and entertainment
Oil and gas depletion and "intangible" cost deduction	Allowed deductions	Repeal depletion allowance; keep "intangible" deduction	Repeal depletion allowance for all but small wells; keep deduction with longer write-off	Allowed deductions	Allowed deductions
State and local taxes	Fully deductible	Eliminate all deductions	Fully deductible	Full deductions for income and property taxes; 60% of sales taxes deductible where sales taxes exceed income taxes.	Full deductions for income and property taxes; no deduction for sales taxes

society. He also announced that unless tax breaks for Oregon's timber industry were retained he would oppose tax reform. Lobbyists converged on Packwood's committee in droves. Packwood initially attempted to accommodate them, writing so many special preferences into the law that little revenue remained. The result was "an orgy of special interest trading." Packwood was leading his committee through tax writing in the traditional way—by trading breaks to the special interest groups for their support. Indeed, the special interest trading became an embarrassment to members of the committee. The bill accumulated more special preferences than the existing law; tax "reform" was dying. The Presidents "top" legislative priority appeared to be a lost cause, and Democrats were prepared to blame the GOP-controlled Senate for failure to reform the nation's tax laws. When it became clear that Packwood himself would bear most of the responsibility for the failure of reform, he became a "convert" to tax reform.

The key to overcoming the opposition of the special interests was to offer a tax rate low enough that most people would be willing to give up their deductions and preferences. Packwood decided to throw out the old bill and begin anew with a "clean" bill. The new bill had fewer deductions than the House bill and lower rates than either the President's plan or the House bill. To preserve low top rates—27 percent for individuals and 33 percent for corporations—and keep the bill "revenue neutral," Senators had to reject amendments by the special interests. The strategy worked to the surprise of everyone. The Senate Finance Committee voted 20–0 to send the clean bill to the full Senate. In an atmosphere of nonpartisanship the full Senate passed the bill with a vote of 97–3. A political "miracle" had occurred: Democrats and Republicans, liberals and conservatives, had united against the special interests.

Nevertheless, the special interests succeeded in keeping many of their favorite exemptions, deductions, and special treatments (see column "Tax Reform Act" on Table 10–4). Business lost its battle to keep the investment tax credit, and depreciation schedules were generally lengthened to curtail "fast tax write-offs." The real estate industry—builders, developers, mortgage lenders—succeeded in restoring deductions for vacation homes. But depreciation of housing investments was lengthened and investors were prevented from using paper losses from real estate depreciation to "shelter" unrelated income. Indeed tax shelters of many kinds were eliminated; the Act prevents taxpayers from using "passive" losses generated from investments to be used to reduce other income for tax purposes. The oil and gas industry, however, succeeded in retaining most of their special preferences in the tax code, including "depletion allowances" and "intangible" drilling costs. But the banking and automotive industries lost their fight to retain interest deductions on auto and consumer loans. The AFL-CIO knocked out the proposal to tax employer-paid fringe benefits, but lost its fight to keep union dues deductible. The restaurant and entertainment industries restored 80 percent of their favorite deductions. State and local governments were successful in retaining the exemption from taxation of interest received from state and local government bonds, and they also succeeded in keeping the deduction for most state and local government taxes.

The final version of the Tax Reform Act of 1986 was written by the House-Senate conference committee which had the responsibility for resolving differences between the House and Senate passed bills. Many last minute compromises were arranged by Dan Rostenkowski, leading the House delegation, and Robert Packwood, leading the Senate delegation. Rostenkowski pushed the Senate to agree to eliminate many corporate tax favors and to shift more of the tax burden from individuals to corporations. The Senate succeeded in keeping its low rate structure; the top rate was set at 28 percent for individuals and 34 percent for corporations. (To ease transitions to the new tax system, many provisions will not be fully phased in until 1988 or thereafter.) The Reagan White House gave its enthusiastic approval to the final bill: "A top individual rate of 28 percent will be one of the lasting legacies of Ronald Reagan's presidency. During his time in office, he has brought the top individual rate down from 70 percent. That is an extraordinary achievement." A few old guard liberals complained about the near disappearance of progressive tax rates; and some business complained that the repeal of the investment tax credit and the end to special treatment for capital gains would depress business investment and slow economic growth. But most commentators described the bill as "a remarkable bipartisan achievement." On balance the special interest suffered their single greatest legislative defeat in many decades.

GOVERNMENT AS A SPECIAL INTEREST

One of the more controversial debates for federal tax reform focused on the elimination of the tax deduction for state and local income, sales, and property taxes. This was the largest personal deduction (aside from the personal exemption), exceeding deductions for medical and dental expenses, home mortgage interest, other interest, and charitable contributions. President Reagan argued that this deduction should be dropped because it "actually provides a special subsidy for high-income individuals in a few high-tax states. Two-thirds of Americans don't even itemize so they receive no benefit from the state and local tax deduction. But they're being forced to subsidize the high tax policies of a handful of states."[7]

The effect of the federal deduction for state and local income, sales, and property taxes is to lighten the burden of state and local government financing. The burden of these deducted taxes is reduced by the marginal value of the tax against which it is deducted. Consider, for example, a state income tax of 10 percent levied on an individual's income at the highest

[7]President Ronald Reagan, Address to the Nation on Tax Reform, May 28, 1985.

TABLE 10-5   Marginal Burden of State Income Taxes Under Federal Tax Deductibility

MARGINAL FEDERAL TAX RATE	MARGINAL STATE TAX RATE (percentages)				
(percentages)	2	3	5	7	10
11	1.78	2.67	4.45	6.23	8.90
20	1.60	2.40	4.00	5.60	8.00
30	1.40	2.10	3.50	4.90	7.00
40	1.20	1.80	3.00	4.20	6.00
50	1.00	1.50	2.50	3.50	5.00

federal rate of 50 percent. The federal deduction reduces the state tax rate to 5 percent (see Table 10-5).

Note, however, that the effect of federal deductibility is to make state and local taxes very regressive. For example, low-income taxpayers at the lowest federal marginal rate of 11 percent would pay 1.78 percent of a state tax of 2 percent. (Indeed, they would pay the full 2 percent if, like most federal taxpayers at this lowest rate, they did not itemize deductions.) In contrast, high-income taxpayers at the highest federal marginal rate of 50 percent would pay only 1 percent of a proportional state tax of 2 percent.

Federal deductibility narrows interstate differences in net tax burdens, particularly at higher income levels. Deductible per capita state-local taxes were only $443 in Alabama, but they were over $1,000 in New York, Massachusetts, and California. In short, the current state-local tax deduction is worth over three times as much in high-tax states as in low-tax states. We should note, however, that in *every* state a majority of federal income tax payers do *not* itemize and therefore would not lose anything from the elimination of the state-local tax deductibility. It is the high-income itemizers in high-tax states who would be hurt most by this reform.

Governor Mario Cuomo of New York was an outspoken opponent of the elimination of deductibility. He argued that reductions to low-income families from proposed cuts in tax rates would be more than offset by higher taxes paid by former "itemizers" who could no longer claim deductibility of taxes paid to New York. White House Chief of Staff Donald T. Regan countered: "New York has a problem. But I submit that New York's problem has always been that it is a high-tax state." If federal tax reform eliminated deductibility, then New York would be forced to lower its taxes. Mr. Regan counted this a favorable side-effect of federal tax reform. When he was chairman of the New York-based investment firm of Merrill Lynch & Co., Mr. Regan moved from New York to New Jersey to escape New York's taxes.

Opposition to the elimination of deductibility came from high-income taxpayers in high-tax states. This opposition was informed, active, skilled, and well-positioned to influence policy discussion. The deductibility question is the type of policy issue on which everyone loses something, but some lose more than others. The people who will lose most—the high-income taxpayers in high-tax states—have more reason to inform and activate themselves politically, and by so doing, weigh the outcome of the collective choice process in their own favor.

These taxpayers were joined by state and local officials throughout the country who understood that federal deductibility would reduce the direct costs of their own taxing decisions. In other words, when these state and local officials vote for higher taxes in their states, they know that their higher income taxpayers can deduct these taxes from their federal income tax liability, in effect shifting the cost to the federal government.

So lobbyists from state, county, and city governments, particularly those with high taxes, convened in Washington to lobby against tax reform. The leading state and local government lobbying organizations were the National Governors' Association, the National League of Cities, the National Conference of State Legislatures, the U.S. Conference of Mayors, the Council of State Governments, the International City Managers Association, and the American Federation of State, County, and Municipal Employees. They were joined by labor unions representing public employees.

The governmental lobby triumphed over the president and tax reform. Deductions for state and local income and property taxes were retained by Congress. Only the deduction for sales taxes was eliminated.

THE FEDERAL TAX SYSTEM TODAY

Federal taxes are derived from five major sources:

Individual income taxes. The personal income tax is the federal government's largest source of revenue; it accounts for 49 percent of the federal government's income (see Figure 10–5).

Individual income is now taxed at two rates: 15 and 28 percent. For married couples, taxable income up to $29,750 is taxed at 15 percent with income over that amount taxed at 28 percent. This amount will be indexed annually to reflect inflation. A personal exemption of $2,000 for each taxpayer and dependent, together with a standard deduction of $5,000 for married couples, insures that poor working families will pay no income tax. (However, they still must pay social security taxes.) The personal exemption and standard deduction will also be indexed to protect against inflation.

The federal individual income tax was adapted in 1913, but for many years it was very modest and it applied only to a small number of high-income people. But during the Second World War, rates were increased and revenue collected by this tax rose dramatically. Since then, inflation has increased the yield of the tax many times over.

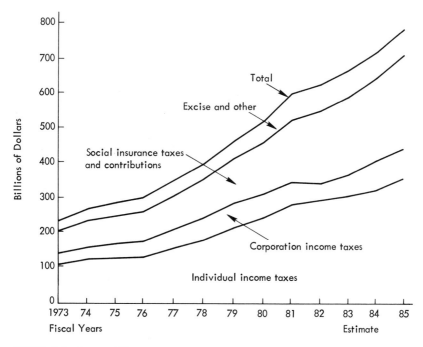

FIGURE 10-5 Sources of Federal Revenue.

The income tax is automatically deducted from the paychecks of all employees except farm and domestic workers. This "withholding" system is the backbone of the individual income tax. There is no withholding of nonwage income, but taxpayers with such income must file a "Declaration of Estimated Taxes" and pay this estimate in quarterly installments. Before April 15th of each year, all income-earning Americans must report their taxable income to the Internal Revenue Service on its 1040 Form.

Americans are usually surprised to learn that half of all personal income is *not* taxed. To understand why, we must know how the tax laws distinguish between *adjusted gross income* (which is an individual's total money income minus expenses incurred in earning that income) and *taxable income* (that part of adjusted gross income suject to taxation). Federal tax rates apply only to *taxable* income. Federal tax laws allow many reductions in adjusted gross income in the calculation of taxable income. For example, tax laws, both before and after reform, allow deductions from gross personal income for such items as:

BEFORE REFORM	**AFTER REFORM**
• Charitable contributions.	• Charitable contributions.
• Home mortgage and other interest paid including auto loans and consumer credit.	• Home mortgage on first and second residences but no other consumer credit.

- All state and local taxes.
- Medical costs over 5 percent of income.
- Social Security benefits.
- Welfare and unemployment benefits.
- Personal exemptions of $1,000 for each dependent; double exemptions for the aged and blind.
- Interest received from state and local bonds.
- Contributions to individual retirement accounts (IRAs).
- Fringe benefits, including employer payments for retirement and insurance.

- State and local income and property taxes.
- Medical costs over 7.5 percent of income.
- Social Security benefits.
- Welfare but not unemployment benefits.
- Personal exemptions of $2,000 for each dependent; no additional exemptions for aged or blind.
- Interest received from state and local bonds.
- Limit IRAs to only those not covered by other pension plans.
- Fringe benefits including employer payments for retirement and insurance.

Most Americans fail to itemize their deductions: Only 35 percent of the nation's taxpayers itemize their deductions. These are mostly middle- and upper-income taxpayers. Lower-income taxpayers seldom itemize (only 5 percent of taxpayers with income under $10,000), while upper-income taxpayers almost always itemize their deductions (over 90 percent of taxpayers with income over $50,000). Itemizing deductions reduces the progressivity of the federal income tax.

Income which is derived from profit on the sale of an asset originally purchased at a lower cost is called a *capital gain*. Capital gains are commonly made on the sale of stocks, bonds, and real estate. Prior to tax reform they were taxed at a maximum rate of only 20 percent, compared to the maximum of 50 percent on wage income. This preferential treatment of capital gains clearly favored wealthier taxpayers whose income was derived in whole or in part from capital investments. But in a major reform, Congress ended the favorable treatment given capital gains; today capital gains are taxed at the same rate as all other income.

All of these exemptions and deductions add up to over half of the nation's personal income![8] In other words, about 52 percent of total personal income in the nation escapes taxation.

Corporate income tax. The corporate income tax provides only 8 percent of the federal government's total income. The Tax Reform Act of 1986 reduced the top corporate income tax rate from 46 to 34 percent. However, prior to this Act, corporations had many ways of reducing their

[8]Joseph A. Pechman, *Federal Tax Policy,* 4th ed. (Washington, D.C.: Brookings Institution, 1984).

"taxable income," often to zero. The result was that many very large and profitable corporations paid little or no taxes.

Moreover, corporate America has been successful over the years in lobbying for a variety of special exemptions and deductions in the tax code. Some of the most notorious of these corporate tax breaks were modified or eliminated in the Tax Reform Act of 1986:

BEFORE REFORM	AFTER REFORM
• Depreciation write-offs for plant and equipment much faster than their actual depreciation.	• Depreciation write-offs slowed but many continue faster than actual depreciation.
• An investment tax credit of 10 percent for purchases of new equipment.	• Investment tax credit repealed.
• Special deductions for the costs of exploration and development of minerals, oil and gas, which greatly exceed the actual costs. A special write-off for "intangible" costs of exploration up to 100 percent above actual costs.	• Oil and gas preferences retained.
• Special "depletion allowances" for oil and gas companies.	• Depletion allowances retained.
• Tax credit for research and development outlays.	• Research and development tax credit retained.
• Credit against U.S. corporate taxes for foreign taxes paid abroad.	• Revised but retained foreign tax credit.

Tax reform succeded in shifting some of the overall federal tax burden from individuals to corporations. In future years the corporate share of federal revenues (8 percent) should rise somewhat and the individual share (49 percent) should decline. Such change would reverse trends in the previous twenty years which saw corporate taxes decline from 20 percent of total federal revenue to 8 percent.

Who pays the corporate income tax? Economists differ over whether this tax is "shifted" to consumers or whether corporations and their stockholders bear its burden. The evidence on the *incidence*—that is, who actually bears the burden—of the corporate income tax is inconclusive.[9]

Religious, charitable, and educational organizations, as well as labor unions, are exempt from corporate income taxes, except for income they may derive from "unrelated business activity."

Social security taxes. The second largest, and fastest growing, source of federal revenue is the social security tax; it now provides 39 percent of

[9]Pechman, *Federal Tax Policy,* chapter 5.

TABLE 10-6   Employer-Employee Tax Rate

	1978	1979	1980	1981	1982	1983	1984
Tax rate	12.1	12.26	12.26	13.3	13.4	13.4	14.0
Earnings base	17,000	22,900	25,900	29,700	32,100	34,500	37,800

the federal government's income. It is withheld from paychecks as the "FICA" deduction, an obscure acronym which helps to hide the true costs of social security from wage earners. To keep up with the rising number of beneficiaries and the higher levels of benefits voted by Congress, the social security tax has risen incrementally each year in two ways: (1) a gradual increase in the combined employer-employee tax rate (percent); and (2) a gradual increase in the taxable earnings base.

The taxes collected under social security are earmarked (by social security number) for the account of each taxpayer. Workers, therefore, feel they are receiving benefits as a right rather than as a gift of the government. However, benefits are only slightly related to the earnings record of the individual worker; there are both minimum and maximum benefit levels which prevent benefits from corresponding to payments. Indeed, for current recipients of social security, less than 15 percent of the benefits can be attributed to their prior contributions. Current taxpayers are paying over 85 percent of the benefits being received by current retirees.

Because of the top limit on the amount of earnings subject to the social security tax (currently $37,800), the tax is considered regressive in its treatment of incomes above that level. In other words, income above the top level is not subject to the social security tax; once the top payment is reached in any year, no social security taxes are levied on additional income. However, benefits are also capped. High-income earners cannot expect high social security benefits upon retirement. This is the traditional justification for the regressivity of the tax.

Estate and gift taxes.   Taxes on property left to heirs is one of the oldest forms of taxation in the world. Federal estate taxes begin on estates of $600,000 and levy a tax of 37 percent on amounts above this level. Because taxes at death could be easily avoided by simply giving estates to heirs while still alive, a federal gift tax is also levied. There is an annual exclusion of $10,000 in gifts per donee.

Excise taxes and custom duties.   Federal taxes on liquor, tobacco, gasoline, telephones, air travel, and other so-called luxury items account for only about 1 to 2 percent of total federal revenue. Taxes on imports provide another 1 to 2 percent of total federal revenues.

SUMMARY

Modern pluralism praises the virtues of an interest group system in which public policy represents the equilibrium in the group struggle and the best approximation of the public interest. Yet it is clear that the interest group system disadvantages broad segments of the American public, especially individual taxpayers.

1. Over half of the nation's total personal income escapes taxation through exemptions, deductions, and special treatments.

2. Most individual taxpayers fail to itemize their deductions. Only 35 percent of the nation's taxpayers are "itemizers," mostly middle- and upper-income taxpayers.

3. The corporate income tax has declined to only 8 percent of total federal revenues. The individual income tax and the social security payroll tax provide most of the federal government's revenue.

4. Most federal tax revenues are derived from the middle classes—married taxpayers with incomes between $25,000 and $75,000 per year.

5. Supply-side economists are concerned about the impact of high marginal tax rates on economic behavior, including disincentives to work, save, and invest, and inefficiencies created by tax avoidance activity. According to the Laffer curve, reducing high marginal tax rates will increase government revenues by encouraging productivity.

6. But the Economic Recovery Tax Cut Act of 1981, reducing individual income taxes by 25 percent and lowering the top marginal rate from 70 to 50 percent, did not result in increased government revenue. These tax cuts, unaccompanied by spending cuts, created the largest deficits in the nation's history.

7. Tax reform to achieve fairness, simplicity, and economic growth is an elusive goal. The interest group system, designed to protect special privileges and treatments, especially in the tax code, will not permit true tax reform.

8. President Reagan's tax reform proposal has been the most heavily lobbied piece of legislation in the history of Congress. Powerful interests opposing significant tax reform include the nation's largest manufacturers, the real estate and housing industries, multinational corporations, timber, oil, and gas companies, labor unions, banks, the restaurants and entertainment industries, and even many state and local governments. While these special interests won some important battles, on balance they lost the war over tax reform.

BIBLIOGRAPHY

JOSEPH A. PECHMAN, *Federal Tax Policy*, 4th ed. Washington, D. C.: The Brookings Institution, 1984.

———, *Who Paid the Taxes 1966–85*. Washington, D.C.: The Brookings Institution, 1985.

AMERICAN FEDERALISM
institutional arrangements
and public policy

The U.S. Conference of Mayors frequently urges Congress to increase federal aid to the nation's cities.
(AP/Wide World Photos)

HOW MANY GOVERNMENTS?

The U.S. Constitution divides power between two separate authorities, the national government and the states. Both the national government and the states can levy taxes, spend money, and directly enforce their own laws on individuals through their own courts. The national government has no constitutional authority to determine, alter, or abolish the powers of the states. The Constitution is the "supreme law of the land" and it cannot be changed without the approval of the national government and three-fourths of the states. This institutional arrangement is labeled American "federalism" and it has a profound impact on public policy.

There are nearly eighty thousand separate governments in the United States, over sixty thousand of which have the power to levy their own taxes. There are states, cities, counties, towns, boroughs, villages, special districts, school districts, and public authorities (see Table 11-1). However, only the national government and the states are recognized in the U.S. Constitution; all other governments are subdivisions of states. States may create, alter, or abolish these other governments by amending state laws or constitutions.

THE POLICY IMPLICATIONS OF FEDERALISM

What are the general policy implications of the institutional arrangements we call "federalism"? Throughout American history, from the earliest debates between Alexander Hamilton and his "Federalists" on one side and Thomas Jefferson and his "Anti-Federalists" on the other, the advantages and disadvantages of federalism have been argued. Over the years the general lines of this argument have remained the same.

Among the advantages of federalism:

1. Federalism permits policy diversity. The entire nation is not "straitjacketed" with a uniform policy that every state and community must conform to. State and local governments may be better suited to deal with specific state and

TABLE 11-1   How Many Governments in the United States?

U.S. government		1
State governments		50
Local governments		79,862
Counties	3,042	
Municipalities	18,862	
Townships	16,822	
School districts	15,174	
Special districts	25,962	
Total		79,913

local problems. Washington bureaucrats do not always know best about what to do in Commerce, Texas.

2. Federalism helps manage policy conflict. Permitting states and communities to pursue their own policies reduces the pressures that would build up in Washington if the national government had to decide everything. Federalism permits citizens to decide many things at the state and local levels of government and avoid battling over single national policies to be applied uniformly throughout the land.

3. Federalism disperses power. The widespread distribution of power is generally regarded as a protection against tyranny. To the extent that pluralism thrives in the United States, state and local governments have contributed to its success. State and local governments also provide a political base for the survival of the opposition party when it has lost national elections.

4. Federalism increases political participation. It allows more people to run for and hold political office. Nearly a million people hold some kind of political office in counties, cities, townships, school districts, and special districts. These local leaders are often regarded as "closer to the people" than Washington officials. Public opinion polls show that Americans believe that their local governments are more manageable and responsive than the national government.

5. Federalism improves efficiency. Even though we may think of having eighty-thousand governments as inefficient, governing the entire nation from Washington would be even worse. Imagine the bureaucracy, red tape, delays, and confusion if every government activity in every community in the nation—police, schools, roads, firefighting, garbage collection, sewage disposal, street lighting, and so on—were controlled by a central government in Washington. Moreover, federalism encourages experimentation and innovation in public policy in the states.

However, federalism has its drawbacks:

1. Federalism allows special interests to protect their privileges. For many years segregationists used the argument of "states' rights" to avoid federal laws designed to guarantee equality and prevent discrimination. Indeed, the states' rights argument has been used so often in defense of racial discrimination that it has become a "code word" or symbol for racism.

2. Federalism allows local leaders to frustrate national policy. They can obstruct not only civil rights policies but also those in areas as diverse as energy, poverty, and pollution.

3. Federalism allows the benefits and costs of government to be spread unevenly. Some states spend more than twice as much per capita as other states on education. Even in the same state, some wealthy school districts spend two or three times as much as poorer districts. The taxes in some states are much higher than in other states, while five states have no state income tax at all.

4. Federalism puts poorer states and communities at a disadvantage; they must generally provide lower levels of education, health and welfare services, police protection, environmental protection, and so on than wealthier states and communities.

5. Federalism obstructs action on national issues. Although decentralization may reduce conflict at the national level, the result may be one of "sweeping under

the rug" some very serious national issues. For many years, decentralizing the issue of civil rights allowed segregation to flourish. Only when the issue was nationalized in the 1960s by the civil rights movement was there any significant progress. Minorities can usually expect better treatment by national agencies than by state or local authorities.

AMERICAN FEDERALISM: VARIATIONS ON THE THEME

American federalism has undergone many changes over the two hundred years since the Constitution of 1787. The original constitutional rules have stayed the same, but their use and interpretation over the years have changed dramatically.

Dual Federalism (1787–1913)

For the nation's first hundred years, the pattern of federal-state relations has been described as "dual federalism." Under this pattern, the states and the nation divided most governmental functions. The national government concentrated its attention on the "delegated" powers—national defense, foreign affairs, tariffs, commerce crossing state lines, coining money, establishing standard weights and measures, maintaining a post office and building post roads, and admitting new states. State governments decided the important domestic policy issues—slavery (until the Civil War), education, welfare, health, and criminal justice. This separation of policy responsibilities was once compared to a "layer cake"[1] with local governments at the base, state governments in the middle, and the national government at the top. This view implied that state and local governments were "closer" to people than the national government, that the national government did not serve the people directly, and that governmental responsibility was parceled out to *either* states or localities, or to the national government.

The national government was not completely divorced from local concerns.[2] The national government financed state militias, which eventually became the National Guard. The U.S. Army Corps of Engineers helped build roads and canals. The national government appropriated money for various "internal improvements"—these expenditures for roads, rivers, and harbors were the forerunners of what we call pork-barrel legislation today. Nonetheless, most important policy decisions were made by the states.

The greatest crisis in American federalism occurred during this period—the struggle over slavery, the attempted secession of eleven Southern

---

[1]Morton Grodzins, *The American System* (Chicago: Rand McNally, 1966), pp. 8–9.

[2]See Daniel Eldzar, *The American Partnership* (Chicago: University of Chicago Press, 1962.

states, and the Civil War, 1861–1865. The national government intervened forcefully in what had been a state affair to end slavery. During the reconstruction period, 1865–1877, Congress and the national military occupation governments in the Southern states also tried to guarantee black voting rights and end many forms of racial discrimination. But this national effort failed when "states' rights" were restored; the national government waited until the 1960s before reasserting its authority in civil rights.

Dual federalism came to an end in the twentieth century. With the emergence of a national industrial economy, Congress began to intervene in economic affairs—with the Interstate Commerce Commission in 1887 and the Sherman Anti-Trust Act in 1889. But it was the passage of the Sixteenth Amendment in 1913 giving the national government the power to levy the income tax that brought the era of dual federalism to an end. The income tax shifted the balance of financial power to the national government and paved the way for national intervention in many fields once "reserved" to the states.

Cooperative Federalism (1913–1964)

The Industrial Revolution and the development of a national economy, the shift in financial resources to the national government, and the challenges of two world wars and the Great Depression, all combined to end the distinction between national and state concerns. The new pattern of federal-state relations was labeled "cooperative federalism." Both the nation and the states exercised responsibilities for welfare, health, highways, education, and criminal justice. This merging of policy responsibilities was compared to a "marble cake." "As the colors are mixed in a marble cake, so functions are mixed in the American federal system."[3]

The Great Depression of the 1930s forced states to ask for federal financial assistance in dealing with poverty, unemployment, and old age. Governors welcomed massive federal public works projects. In addition, the federal government intervened directly in economic affairs, labor relations, business practices, and agriculture. Through the grant-in-aid device, the national government cooperated with the states in public assistance, employment services, child welfare, public housing, urban renewal, highway building, and vocational education.

Yet even in this period of shared national-state responsibility, the national government emphasized cooperation in achieving common national and state goals. Congress generally acknowledged that it had no direct constitutional authority to regulate public health, safety, or welfare. Congress relied primarily on its powers to tax and spend for the general welfare to provide financial assistance to state and local governments to

[3]Grodzins, *The American System*, p. 265.

achieve shared goals. Congress did not usually legislate directly on local matters. For example, Congress did not require the teaching of vocational education in public high schools because public education was not an "enumerated power" of the national government in the U.S. constitution. But Congress could offer money to states and school districts to assist in teaching vocational education, and even threaten to withdraw the money if federal standards were not met. In this way the federal government involved itself in fields "reserved" to the states.

Centralized Federalism (1964 to the Present)

Over the years it became increasingly difficult to maintain the fiction that the national government was merely assisting the states in performing their domestic responsibility. By the time President Lyndon B. Johnson launched the "Great Society" in 1964, the federal government had clearly set forth its own "national" goals. Virtually all problems confronting American society—from solid waste disposal and water and air pollution, to consumer safety, home insulation, noise abatement, and even metric conversion—were declared to be national problems. Congress legislated directly on any matter it chose, without regard to its "enumerated powers" and without pretense to financial assistance. The Supreme Court no longer concerned itself with the "reserved" powers of the states; the Tenth Amendment lost most of its meaning. The pattern of national-state relations became centralized. As for the cake analogies, one commentator observed: "The frosting had moved to the top, something like a pineapple upside-down cake."[4]

The states' role is now often one of carrying out federal mandates. The administrative role of the states remains important; states help to implement federal policies in public assistance, Medicaid, energy conservation, employment training, elementary and secondary education, and so on. But the states' role is determined not by the states themselves but by the national government.

Bureaucracies at the federal, state, and local levels are increasingly indistinguishable. Coalitions of professional bureaucrats—whether in education, public assistance, employment training, rehabilitation, natural resources, agriculture, or whatever—work together on behalf of shared goals, whether they are officially employed by the federal government, the state government, or a local authority. One commentator refers to this type of policy making as "functional federalism."[5] State and local officials in agencies receiving a large proportion of their funds from the federal government feel very little loyalty to their governor or state legislature.

[4]Charles Press, *State and Community Governments in the Federal System* (New York: John Wiley, 1979), p. 78.

[5]Michael D. Reagan, *The New Federalism* (New York: Oxford University Press, 1972).

THE GROWTH OF POWER IN WASHINGTON

Over time governmental power has been centralized in Washington. While the formal constitutional arrangements of federalism remain in place, power has flowed relentlessly toward the national government since the earliest days of the nation. Perhaps the most important developments over time are (1) the broad interpretation of the necessary and proper clause of the Constitution to obscure the notion of "delegated powers" and allow the national government to do anything not specifically prohibited by the Constitution; (2) the victory of the national government in the Civil War, demonstrating that the states could not successfully resist federal power by force of arms; (3) the establishment of a national system of civil rights based upon the Fourteenth Amendment, which brought federal government into the definition and enforcement of civil rights; (4) the growth of federal power within the scope of the interstate commerce clause as a national industrial economy emerged; and (5) the growth of federal grants-in-aid to state and local governments as a major source of revenues for these governments and a major source of federal intervention into state and local affairs.

Consider overall changes in state versus local financial resources and manpower levels. Table 11-2 shows the percentage distribution of federal, state, and local revenues, expenditures, and manpower, for 1902, 1970, and 1980. Early in the twentieth century, local governments raised the bulk of governmental revenue, spent the most money, and employed the most

TABLE 11-2   Federal, State, and Local Revenues, Expenditures, and Manpower, 1902–1980

	PERCENTAGE DISTRIBUTIONS		
	1902	1970	1980
Revenues from Own Sources			
Federal	38	62	58
State	11	20	23
Local	51	18	19
Total Direct Expenditures			
Federal	34	55	51
State	8	17	20
Local	58	28	29
Public Employment			
Federal	32	39	20
State	10	16	21
Local	58	44	59

Source: U.S. Bureau of the Census, *Historical Statistics of the United States* (Washington, D.C.: Government Printing Office, 1960); updated from *Statistical Abstract of the United States*, and *Budget of the United States Government, 1980.*

people. Today, the nation's eighty thousand local governments raise less money than the nation's fifty state governments, and a great deal less than the national government. However, because of grants-in-aid from both state and federal governments, local governments still spend more than state governments, and they still employ more people in "labor-intensive" fields such as police and fire protection, sanitation, and so on. However, the direction of change is clear.

Today grant-in-aid programs are the single most important source of federal influence over state and local affairs. The growth of federal grants is depicted in Figure 11-1. Approximately one-fifth of all state and local government revenues are from federal grants. This money is paid out through a staggering number and variety of programs. Federal grants may be obtained to assist in everything from the preservation of historic buildings, the development of minority-owned businesses, and aid for foreign refugees, to the drainage of abandoned mines, riot control, and school milk. However, federal aid for welfare, Medicaid, food stamps, and highways accounts for over two-thirds of total federal aid money.

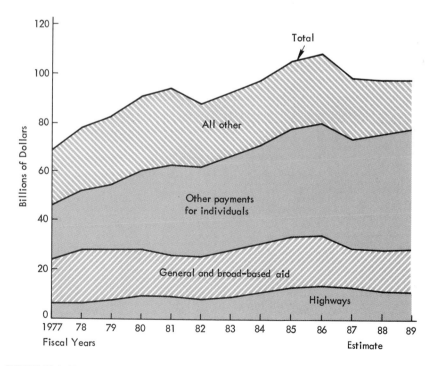

FIGURE 11-1 Federal aid to state and local governments. *(Source: The Budget of the United States Government FY 1987.)*

THE DEBATE OVER GOVERNMENTAL CENTRALIZATION

There are several reasons for this growth of federal aid.[6] First, these grants permit the federal government to single out and support those state and local government services in which it has a particular interest. Grants permit the national government to set national goals and priorities in all levels of government without formally altering the federal structure. Thus, as problems of public assistance, community development, highway construction, education, poverty, and so on, acquire national significance, they can be dealt with by the application of national resources.

Second, the grant-in-aid system helps to overcome the inadequacies of state-local revenue resources. States and communities must raise revenues and at the same time carry on interstate and interlocal competition for industry and wealth. Although the influence of tax considerations on industrial locations decisions may be overstated by most lawmakers, this overstatement itself is part of the political lore at statehouses and courthouses that operates to impede revenue raising. Not only do competitive considerations inhibit state-local taxing efforts, but they also tend to push them in regressive directions.

Debates over finances in state capitals invariably include references to the "preemption" of income taxes by the national government. There are no compelling economic reasons for the argument that the federal income tax preempts this source of revenue for the states (particularly because the federal government permits the deduction of state income taxes from total taxable income). Nonetheless, in the minds of most state lawmakers, and probably in the minds of their constituents as well, there is the belief that the federal government already takes all the income taxes they wish to pay. This means states are stuck with sales taxes and localities with property taxes, and, in contrast to income taxes, these taxes respond sluggishly to rises in the GNP.

Finally, grants-in-aid provide an opportunity for the national government to insure a uniform level of public service throughout the nation as a minimum or foundation program—for example, federal grants-in-aid help achieve equality in educational opportunity in all parts of the nation, or help insure a minimum level of existence for the poverty-stricken regardless of where they live. This aspect of federal policy assumes that in some parts of the nation, state and local governments are unable, or perhaps unwilling, to devote their resources to raising public service levels to minimum national standards.

Whenever the national government contributes financially to state or local programs, state and local officials have less freedom of choice than they would have without federal aid. They must adhere to federal standards

[6]See George F. Break, *Intergovernmental Fiscal Relations in the United States* (Washington, D.C.: Brookings Institution, 1967); Deil S. Wright, *Federal Grants-in-Aid: Perspectives and Alternatives* (Washington, D.C.: American Enterprise Institute, 1968).

or "guidelines," which invariably accompany federal grants-in-aid, if they are to receive their federal money. The national government gives money to states and communities only if they are willing to meet conditions specified by Congress. Often Congress delegates to federal agencies the power to establish the "conditions" that are attached to grants.

No state is required to accept a federal grant-in-aid. In other words, states are not required to meet federal standards or guidelines that are set forth as conditions for federal aid because they have the alternative of rejecting the federal money—and they have sometimes done so. But it is very difficult for states and communities to resist the pressure to accept federal money.

In short, through the power to tax and spend for the general welfare, and through "conditions" attached to federal grants-in-aid, the national government has come to exercise great powers in many areas originally "reserved" to the states—highways, welfare, education, housing, natural resources, employment, health, and so on. Of course, federal grants-in-aid have enabled many states and communities to provide necessary and desirable services that they could not have afforded otherwise. Federal guidelines have often improved the standard of administration, personnel policies, and fiscal practices in states and communities. More important, federal guidelines have helped to insure that states and communities will not engage in racial discrimination in federally aided programs.

The centralization of power in Washington has also created some serious problems in the implementation of public policy. First of all, federal grant programs frequently work at cross-purposes, reflecting fragmentation of federal programs. For example, community development grants attempt to save central cities from deterioration and population loss, while federal highway grants have built expressways to make possible the suburban exodus. The federal public housing programs have tried to increase the supply of low-rent housing for the poor, but federally funded urban renewal and highway programs have torn down low-rent housing.

Second, the federal government has never set any significant priorities among its hundreds of grant programs. The result is that too few dollars chase too many goals. Cities are pressured to apply for funds for projects they do not really need, simply because federal funds are available, although they may receive little or no federal assistance for more vital programs. Federal grant money is frequently provided for "new" or "innovative" or "demonstration" programs, when the real crisis facing states and communities may be in traditional public services, such as police, sewage, sanitation, and so forth.

Third, the administrative quagmire created by the maze of separate federal grant programs threatens to drown state and local officials in red tape. The five hundred separate federal grant programs with separate purposes and guidelines are uncoordinated and bureaucratic. State and local officials spend a great deal of their time in "grantmanship," that is, learning where to find federal funds, how to apply, and how to write applications in such a way as to appear to meet purposes and guidelines.

Finally, the current grant-in-aid system assumes that federal officials are better judges of goals and priorities at all levels of government than state or local officials. State and local officials do not determine what activities in their states and communities will receive federal money; federal officials determine these priorities. Whether federal officials or state and local officials are better judges of public goals and priorities is, of course, a political question.

DECENTRALIZATION: THE "NEW FEDERALISM"

Efforts to reverse the flow of power to Washington and return responsibilities to state and local government have been labeled the "New Federalism." The phrase originated in the administration of President Richard M. Nixon, who used it to describe General Revenue Sharing, that is, federal sharing of tax revenues with state and local governments, with few strings attached. More recently, however, the phrase "New Federalism" has been used by President Ronald Reagan to describe a series of proposals designed to reduce federal involvement in domestic programs and encourage states and cities to undertake greater policy responsibilities themselves. These efforts include (1) the consolidation of many categorical grant programs into fewer block grants; (2) the turnback of many social service, transportation, educational, and community development programs to the states; and (3) an end to General Revenue Sharing.

General Revenue Sharing.   Although the Reagan administration ended General Revenue Sharing (GRS) in implementing *its* definition of "New Federalism," the original GRS legislation in 1972 was designed as a conservative alternative to categorical grants by federal agencies for specific projects. It was argued that unrestricted federal money grants to state and local government were preferable to centralized bureaucratic decision making in Washington. GRS promised to reverse the flow of power to federal bureaucrats, end excessive red tape, and revitalize state and local governments. GRS was strongly supported by state and local government officials, who were happy to have the federal government collect tax money and then turn it over to them to spend. The history of GRS shows that these monies were used for common state and local government functions—police, fire, sewage, waste disposal, transportation, etc. But revenue sharing never really replaced any of the hundreds of categorical grant programs; it was simply an added source of state and local government revenue.

The Reagan administration, confronting high federal deficits and wanting to reduce Washington's role in domestic policy, undertook a long and eventually successful effort to end General Revenue Sharing. The president argued that it was unreasonable to expect the federal government, which is running deep deficits, to turn over revenues to state and local governments, which have no deficits. (Most state and local governments are prohibited by their own constitutions and charters from having deficits in their operating budgets; bond issues for capital improvement must usually be approved by local residents in referenda.) Most GRS funds, the argument ran, went for traditional services which local taxpayers should fund themselves. For several years, state and local government officials successfully lobbied Congress to restore GRS funds cut from the president's budget. But deficit pressures finally ended GRS in 1986.

Block Grants.   Another approach to cutting federal strings in grant-in-aid programs is the "block grant." Block grants may be used by states and communities for specific projects decided upon at the local level within a broad category—"community development" or "law enforcement," for example. Federal agencies still supervise "block grants," but specific projects are supposed to be decided upon at the local level. Obviously, block grants do not give states and communities the same freedom as revenue sharing money. But block grants provide greater flexibility than traditional project grants.

The Reagan administration succeeded in consolidating many categorical grant programs into nine large block grant programs (see Table 11-3). A block grant is a payment to a state or local government for a general function, such as community development or education. State and local officials may use block grant funds for their stated purposes without seeking the approval of federal agencies for specific projects. Congress endorsed these block grants, but the struggle between categorical grant interests (liberals and Democrats) and the consolidationists (Reagan and the Republicans) was really a draw. Many categorical grant programs were merged, but many others remained independent. Under President Reagan, the total amounts budgeted for the block grants were smaller than the total of the categorical programs that were consolidated. Officials in the Reagan administration argued that cities and states could get along with less money under block grants because such grants eliminate the costs of "people-processing paper" and allow local officials to use the money for the most urgent needs. Critics of Reagan's approach argued that block grants were just another way of cutting domestic spending.

Turnbacks.   President Reagan also proposed to turn back to the states a variety of other federal grant-in-aid programs, including child nutrition, social services, mental health, family planning, airports, highways, urban mass transit, vocational rehabilitation, adult education, community facili-

TABLE 11-3   Consolidation of Federal Aid Programs through Block Grants

NEW BLOCK GRANTS, 1982	OLD CATEGORICAL GRANTS CONSOLIDATED, 1981
Preventive health care and health services	Home health, rodent control, emergency medical services, fluoridation, rape crisis, hypertension control, health incentive, health education
Alcohol, drug abuse, and mental health services	Community Health Centers Act, Mental Health Systems Act, Comprehensive alcohol abuse and alcoholism prevention, drug abuse prevention
Social services	Title XX of the Social Security Act
Maternal and child health	Maternal and child health grants, supplemental security income for children, lead poisoning prevention, genetic disease, sudden infant death, hemophilia screening, adolescent health services
Home energy assistance	Low-income energy assistance
Community services	Various programs of the Economic Opportunity Act of 1984, including senior opportunities and services, community food and nutrition, energy conservation and training
Community development	Small cities community development program (cities under 50,000 population); 701 planning grant; neighborhood self-help development; territories program
Primary health care	Community health centers; primary care research and demonstration grants
Education	37 elementary and secondary school categorical programs (such as desegregation aid, National Teachers Corp., metric education, consumer education, education of the handicapped, migrant education, education of deprived, neglected or delinquent children, education of gifted children)

ties, waste-water treatment, and community development. It was argued that these programs ought to be state and local programs and not federal responsibilities. By gradually reducing federal aid for the programs in each federal budget, the Reagan administration hoped to achieve the turnbacks. But opposition in the Congress has succeeded in retaining most of these federal programs.

The response of the nation's governors and mayors to these "New Federalism" proposals was less than enthusiastic. State and local officials generally want relief from federal guidelines, regulations, and conditions associated with federal grants. They usually want control over welfare, health, transportation, and community development programs in their states and cities. But they fear the financial burdens of these programs. Indeed, if a choice must be made, most state and local government officials would prefer to see the federal government take over the burdens of these programs even if it means the loss of local authority.

INSTITUTIONAL POLITICS AND PUBLIC POLICY

In recent years political conflict over federalism—over the division of responsibilities and finances between national and state/local governments—has tended to follow traditional liberal and conservative political cleavages. Generally, liberals seek to enhance the power of the *national* government. Liberals believe that people's lives can be changed by the exercise of governmental power to end discrimination, abolish poverty, eliminate slums, ensure employment, uplift the downtrodden, educate the masses, and cure the sick. The government in Washington has more power and resources than state and local governments have, and liberals have turned to it rather than to state and local governments to cure America's ills. State and local governments are regarded as too slow, cumbersome, weak, and unresponsive. The government in Washington is seen as the principal instrument for liberal social and economic reform. Thus, liberalism and centralization are closely related in American politics.

The liberal argument for national authority can be summarized as follows:

1. State and local governments have insufficient awareness of social problems. The federal government must take the lead in civil rights, equal employment opportunities, care for the poor and aged, the provision of adequate medical care for all Americans, and the elimination of urban poverty and blight.

2. It is difficult to achieve change when reform-minded citizens must deal with fifty state governments or eighty thousand local governments. Change is more likely to be accomplished by a strong central government.

3. State and local governments contribute to inequality in society by setting different levels of services in education, welfare, health, and other public functions. A strong national government can ensure uniformity of standards throughout the nation.

4. A strong national government can unify the nation behind principles and ideals of social justice and economic progress. Extreme decentralization can foster local or regional special interests at the expense of the general public interest.

Generally, conservatives seek to return power to *state and local* governments. Conservatives are more skeptical about the good that government can do. Adding to the power of the national government is not an effective way of resolving society's problems. On the contrary, conservatives argue that "government is the problem, not the solution." Excessive governmental regulation, burdensome taxation, and inflationary government spending combine to restrict individual freedom, penalize work and saving, and destroy incentives for economic growth. Government should be kept small, controllable, and close to the people.

The conservative argument for state and local autonomy can be summarized as follows:

1. "Grassroots" government promotes a sense of state and community self-responsibility and self-reliance.
2. State and local governments can better adapt public programs to local needs and conditions.
3. State and local governments promote participation in politics and civic responsibility by allowing more people to become involved in public questions.
4. Competition between states and cities can result in improved public programs and services.
5. The existence of multiple state and local governments encourages experimentation and innovation in public policy, from which the whole nation may gain.
6. State and local governments reduce the administrative workload on the national government, as well as reducing the political turmoil that results when one single policy must govern the entire nation.

There is no way to settle the argument over federalism once and for all. Debates over federalism are part of the fabric of American politics.

SUMMARY

American federalism creates unique problems and opportunities in public policy. For nearly two hundred years, since the classic debates between Alexander Hamilton and Thomas Jefferson, Americans have argued the merits of centralized versus decentralized policy making. The debate continues today over the "New Federalism."

1. Eighty thousand separate governments—states, counties, cities, towns, boroughs, villages, special districts, school districts, and authorities—make public policy.

2. Proponents of federalism since Thomas Jefferson have argued that it permits policy diversity in a large nation, helps to reduce conflict, disperses power, increases political participation, encourages policy innovation, and improves governmental efficiency.

3. Opponents of federalism argue that it allows special interests to protect positions of privilege, frustrates national policies, distributes the burdens of government unevenly, disadvantages poorer states and communities, and obstructs action toward national goals.

4. American federalism has evolved over two centuries from "dual federalism" with a fairly clear division of responsibilities; to "cooperative

federalism" with federal financial assistance going to the states to achieve shared goals; to "centralized federalism" with the federal government assigned the dominant role in determining national policy.

5. The growth of power in Washington is revealed in figures showing that the federal government collects nearly 60 percent of all governmental revenues. About one-fifth of all state and local government revenues comes from federal grants.

6. The Reagan "New Federalism" proposals are designed to return power over many domestic programs to the states. This is to be accomplished through greater use of block grants, turnbacks of program responsibility to the states, and an end to General Revenue Sharing.

7. Conflict over federalism currently follows the liberal and conservative cleavage in American politics. Liberals favor social and economic interventions with the power and resources of the federal government. Conservatives are more skeptical about government interventions and prefer "grassroots" programs and decentralized decision making.

BIBLIOGRAPHY

ELAZAR, DANIEL J., *American Federalism: A View from the States.* New York: Harper & Row, 1972.

GLENDENING, PARRIS N., and MAVIS M. REEVES, *Pragmatic Federalism: An Intergovernmental View of American Government.* Pacific Palisades: Palisades Publishers, 1977.

HANUS, JEROME J., *The Nationalization of State Government.* Lexington, Ma.: D.C. Health, 1981.

JEWELL, MALCOLM E., and DAVID M. OLSON, *American State Political Parties and Elections.* Homewood, Ill.: Dorsey Press, 1982.

REAGAN, MICHAEL D., *The New Federalism.* New York: Oxford University Press, 1972.

SHARKANSKY, IRA, *The Maligned States.* New York: McGraw-Hill, Inc., 1972.

WALKER, DAVID B., *Toward a Functioning Federalism.* Cambridge: Winthrop Press, 1981.

WRIGHT, DEIL S., *Understanding Intergovernmental Relations.* Boston: Duxbury, 1978.

12

INPUTS, OUTPUTS, AND BLACK BOXES

a systems analysis of state policies

Political activity in state capitols: abortion rights activists. (UPI/Bettmann Newsphotos)

COMPARING PUBLIC POLICIES OF THE AMERICAN STATES

The American states provide an excellent setting for comparative analysis and the testing of hypotheses regarding the determinants of public policy. Fortunately, if only for the sake of analysis, public policies in education, welfare, health, transportation, natural resources, and public safety, and many other areas, vary considerably from state to state. These differences are important in systems analysis because they enable us to search for relationships between different socioeconomic conditions, political system characteristics, and public policies.

By way of example, we might ask *why* some states spend over twice as much for the education of a single pupil in public schools as other states (see Figure 12-1). Of course, policy differences among the states might be attributed to a wide variety of socioeconomic conditions in the states—income and wealth, growth rates, racial composition and ethnic diversity, political competition or partisanship, interest group strength, public opinion, historical experiences, and so on. From an almost unlimited number of variables which might influence educational policy in the states, we must choose only a limited number for inclusion in systematic research. We are always obliged to reduce our studies to manageable proportions by making choices about what forces *might* shape public policy, that is, by making a selection of hypotheses for testing.

THE "NATIONALIZATION" OF THE STATES

We know that states differ in their histories, economies, growth rates, and ethnic and racial compositions. Yet over time these differences are diminishing—a process that has been labeled the "nationalization" of the states.

Over time the states have become more similar in levels of economic development. Income differences among the states are diminishing, although only very slowly. (Between 1950 and 1980 the *coefficient of variation* for per capita personal income among the states declined from 24.4 to 12.1.[1]) As industry, people, and money move from the Northeast and Midwest to the South, the historic disadvantage of the South gradually diminishes.

As people move about the country, the distinct cultural and ethnic differences of the regions also diminish. Even regional accents become less pronounced. The impact of national television, motion pictures, and the record industries adds to the "homogenization" of state and regional cultures.

---

[1] The *coefficient of variation* is the mean divided by the standard deviation; it is a common way to measure the extent of variation among any units of observation.

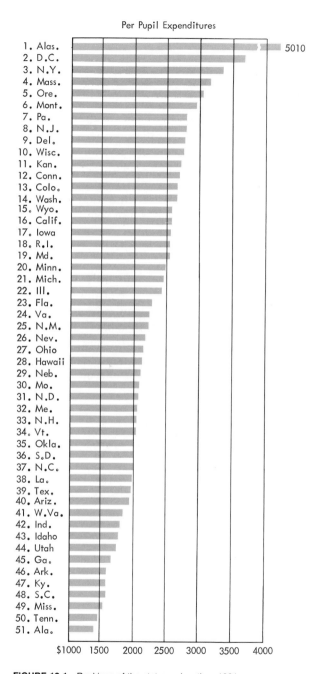

Per Pupil Expenditures

1. Alas.   5010
2. D.C.
3. N.Y.
4. Mass.
5. Ore.
6. Mont.
7. Pa.
8. N.J.
9. Del.
10. Wisc.
11. Kan.
12. Conn.
13. Colo.
14. Wash.
15. Wyo.
16. Calif.
17. Iowa
18. R.I.
19. Md.
20. Minn.
21. Mich.
22. Ill.
23. Fla.
24. Va.
25. N.M.
26. Nev.
27. Ohio
28. Hawaii
29. Neb.
30. Mo.
31. N.D.
32. Me.
33. N.H.
34. Vt.
35. Okla.
36. S.D.
37. N.C.
38. La.
39. Tex.
40. Ariz.
41. W.Va.
42. Ind.
43. Idaho
44. Utah
45. Ga.
46. Ark.
47. Ky.
48. S.C.
49. Miss.
50. Tenn.
51. Ala.

$1000   1500   2000   2500   3000   3500   4000

FIGURE 12-1   Rankings of the states: education, 1981.

The political systems of the states are no longer as distinct as they were historically. Years ago the Democratic party could count on "the Solid South" in national elections. The Democrats can still count on winning most state and local offices in Southern and border states, but these states are now "swing" states in presidential elections and occasionally elect Republican governors and U.S. senators. (Between 1950 and 1980 the coefficient of variation for party competition in gubernatorial elections declined from 41.6 to 18.4.) Historically, voter participation in the Southern states has been very low and it is still lower there than in the rest of the nation. However, one important effect of the civil rights movement was to increase black voter participation in the South. Today, voter turnout in the South is both higher than in previous decades and closer to the national average. (Between 1950 and 1980 the coefficient of variation for voter turnout in congressional elections declined from 42.5 to 27.0.)

Nonetheless, even though the states are gradually becoming more similar over time in many respects, there is still enough variation to merit comparative analysis.[2] Interestingly, *policy* variation among the states does *not* appear to be declining over time. There is no reliable evidence that the policy preferences of the states are becoming homogenized, or even that federal intervention is forcing uniform policies on the states. Table 12-1 shows coefficients of variation over time for personal income, interparty competition, voter participation, and welfare and education benefits from 1950 to 1980. Variations in public policy measures show no consistent decrease over time.

TABLE 12-1   Variation among the States over Time: Income, Competition, Welfare, and Education Benefits

	INC	COMP	AFDC	PUPIL
1980	14.1	18.4	34.1	26.9
1975	15.7	19.0	34.1	20.7
1970	15.5	26.4	35.8	21.5
1965	18.3	27.8	31.6	21.0
1960	20.0	38.4	31.0	22.8
1955	21.7	37.3	30.7	23.9
1950	24.4	41.6	29.3	25.3

Note: All figures are coefficients of variation: standard deviation divided by the mean. INC = per capita personal income; COMP = one minus winning percentage in gubernatorial elections; AFDC = average monthly AFDC benefits per family; PUPIL = educational expenditures per pupil in average daily attendance.

[2]See Kathleen A. Kemp, "Nationalization of American States," *American Politics Quarterly*, 6 (April 1978), 237–47; Harvey J. Tucker, "Interparty Competition in the American States," *American Politics Quarterly*, 10 (January 1982), 93–116; Philip W. Roeder, *Stability and Change in the Determinants of Public Expenditures* (Beverly Hills, Calif.: Sage Publications, Inc., 1976).

ECONOMIC RESOURCES AND PUBLIC POLICY

Economists have contributed a great deal to the systematic analysis of public policy. Economic research very early suggested that government activity was closely related to the level of economic resources in a society.[3] Economic development was broadly defined to include levels of wealth, industrialization, urbanization, and adult education.

We can picture the relationship between economic resources and public policy by viewing a "plot" of the relationship between median family

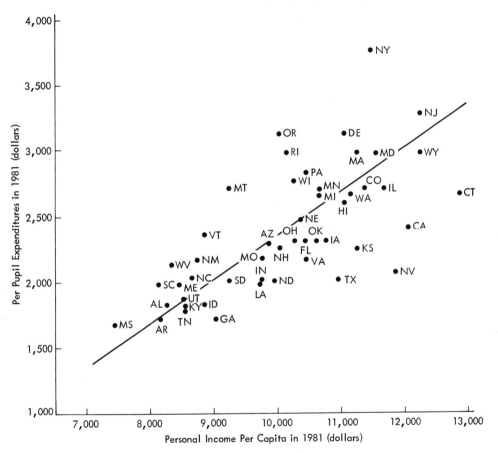

FIGURE 12-2   The Fifty States Arranged According to Per Capita Personal Income and Per Pupil Educational Expenditures.

[3]See Solomon Fabricant, *Trend of Government Activity in the United States Since 1900* (New York: National Bureau of Economic Research, 1952); Glenn F. Fisher, "Interstate Variation in State and Local Government Expenditures," *National Tax Journal*, 17 (March 1964), 57–74; Seymour Sachs and Robert Harris, "The Determinants of State and Local Government Expenditures and Intergovernmental Flow of Funds," *National Tax Journal*, 17 (March 1964), 78–85.

income and per pupil spending in public schools as in Figure 12-2. Median family income is measured on the horizontal or X axis, while per pupil spending is measured on the vertical or Y axis. Each state is plotted in the graph according to its values on these two measures. The resulting pattern—states arranged from the lower left to the upper right—shows that increases in income are associated with increases in educational spending. The broken line is a representation of the hypothesis that income determines educational spending. To the extent that states cluster around this line, they conform to the hypothesis. States which are above the line spend more for education than their income level predicts; states which are below the line spend less than their income predicts. In general, states tend to cluster around the line, indicating considerable support for the hypothesis.

Governmental Resources and Public Policy: The Federal Effect

While a state's economic resources are very important in determining levels of public taxing and spending, nonetheless, the *relationship* between economic resources and public spending among the states has diminished over time. A state's own economic resources are not *as* important in determining spending levels for education highways, welfare, and health, as in the past (see Table 12-2).

TABLE 12-2   The Linkages Between Economic Resources, Federal Aid, and State-Local Spending

	PERCENT OF STATE-LOCAL SPENDING DETERMINED BY:						
STATE-LOCAL EXPENDITURES	ECONOMIC RESOURCES[a]					ECONOMIC DEVELOPMENT PLUS FEDERAL AID[b]	
	1942	1957	1960	1970	1980	1970	1980
Total Expenditures	72	53	53	62	41	72	89
Education	59	62	60	52	36	67	71
Highways	29	34	37	50	32	86	68
Public Welfare	45	14	11	17	25	48	56
Health and Hospitals	72	46	44	37	6	38	31

Note: Figures are coefficients of multiple determination (R^2) for 48 states in 1942, 1957, and 1960, and 50 states in 1970 and 1980.
[a]*Economic resources* are defined as per capita income, population density, and percent urbanization.
[b]Three economic development variables plus per capita federal aid.

Source: Figures for 1942, 1957, and 1960 from Seymour Sachs and Robert Harris, "The Determinants of State and Local Government Expenditures and Intergovernmental Flow of Funds, *National Tax Journal,* 17 (March 1964), 78–85. Figures for 1970 and 1980 calculated by the author.

The decline in the explanatory power of economic resources may be attributed to the intervening effect of federal grants-in-aid, particularly in the welfare and health fields. Federal grants free the states from the constraints of their own economic resources. Federal grants are "outside money" to state and local government officials, which permits them to fund programs at levels beyond their own resources. Hence the decline in the closeness of the relationship between economic resources and state-local spending, particularly in the fields with the heaviest federal involvement: welfare and health.

Table 12-2 shows some decline over time in the importance of economic resources in explaining state-local spending. But it also shows what happens when federal grants-in-aid are included among the explanatory variables: federal grants add considerably to the explanation of state-local spending. For example, in 1980 the proportion of total state-local spending explained by economic resources alone is 41 percent; but by considering federal grants-in-aid in addition to economic resources, 89 percent of total state-local spending can be explained. Indeed, in recent years federal aid has become one of the most important determinants of state-local spending for many functions. A state's own income, together with federal aid, largely determines what services it can provide.

In summary, there is little doubt that levels of government revenue, expenditures, and services are closely linked to economic resources. Although there are some notable exceptions, virtually all the systematic evidence points to this fact: economic resources (particularly income) are the most important determinants of *levels* of government taxing, spending, and service. Socioeconomic measures, such as per capita income, adult education, and urbanization, together with federal grant-in-aid money, consistently turn out to be the most influential variables in systematic analysis of public policies when public policies are defined as levels, amounts, or averages of taxes, expenditures, or services.

POLITICS AND PUBLIC POLICY

The political system functions to transform demands generated in the environment into public policy. The traditional literature in American politics instructed students that characteristics of the political system, particularly two-party competition, voter participation, and apportionment had direct bearing on public policy.[4] Because political scientists devoted most

---

[4]V. O. Key, Jr., *American State Politics: An Introduction* (New York: Knopf, 1956); also his *Southern Politics in State and Nation* (New York: Knopf, 1951); Duane Lockard, *New England State Politics* (Princeton, N.J.: Princeton University Press, 1959); Malcolm Jewell, *The State Legislature* (New York: Random House, 1962); Duane Lockard, *The Politics of State and Local Government* (New York: Macmillan, 1963); John H. Fenton, *People and Parties in Politics* (Glenview, Ill.: Scott, Foresman, 1966).

of their time to studying what happened *within* the political system, it was easy for them to believe that the political processes and institutions which they studied were important determinants of public policies. Moreover, the belief that competition, participation, and equality in representation had important consequences for public policy squared with the value placed upon these variables in the prevailing pluralist ideology.

The assertion that political variables such as party competition and voter participation affected public policy rested more upon a priori reasoning than upon systematic research. It seemed reasonable to *believe* that an increase in party competition would increase educational spending, welfare benefits, numbers of welfare recipients, highway spending, health and hospital care, and so on, because competitive parties would try to outbid each other for public favor by offering such inducements, and the overall effect of such competition would be to raise levels of spending and service. It also seemed reasonable to believe that increased voter participation would influence public policy, presumably in a more liberal direction.

The earliest systems model in the state policy field was a "competition-participation" model:

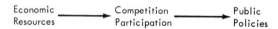

Economic Resources ⟶ Competition Participation ⟶ Public Policies

where economic resources determined political competition and participation and these political factors in turn determined public policies in welfare, education, health, highway, taxation,and spending. The early work of V. O. Key, Jr., Duane Lockard, John Fenton, and others, asserted the central place of political factors in shaping state policy.[5] For many years there was no empirical evidence to contradict this model: poor, rural, agrarian states tended to have less competitive parties ("one-party" or "modified one-party" systems, in contrast to "two-party" systems), and these same states spent less per capita for education, welfare, health, and other social services.

However, in order to assess the *independent* effect of politics on public policy, it is important to control for the intervening effects of socioeconomic variables. For example, if it is shown that, in general, wealthy states have more party competition than poor states, it might be that differences in the level of welfare benefits of competitive and noncompetitive states are really a product of the fact that the former are wealthy and the latter are poor. If this is the case, policy differences between the states might be attributable to wealth rather than to party competition. In order to isolate the effect of party competition on education and welfare policies from the effect of economic resources, it is necessary to control for these variables.

---

[5]Key, *American State Politics;* Lockard, *The Politics of State and Local Government;* Fenton, *People and Parties in Politics.*

The first hint that political variables might not be as influential in determining levels of public taxing, spending, and service as commonly supposed came in an important research effort by Richard E. Dawson and James A. Robinson in 1963.[6] These political scientists examined the linkages between socioeconomic variables (income, urbanization, industrialization), the level of interparty competition, and nine public welfare policies. They concluded that "high levels of interparty competition are highly interrelated both to socioeconomic factors and to social welfare legislation, but the degree of interparty competition does not seem to possess the important intervening influence between socioeconomic factors and the liberal welfare programs that our original hypothesis and theoretical schemes suggested."

A comprehensive analysis of public policy in the American states was published in 1965 by Thomas R. Dye.[7] Employing a systems model, the linkages between the four economic development variables, four political system characteristics, and over ninety separated policy output measures in education, health, welfare, highways, corrections, taxation, and public regulation were described. This research produced some findings that were very unsettling for many political scientists. Four of the most commonly described characteristics of political systems—(1) Democratic or Republican control of state government, (2) the degree of interparty competition, (3) the level of voter turnout, and (4) the extent of malapportionment—were found to have less effect on public policy than environmental variables reflecting the level of economic development—urbanization, industrialization, wealth, and education. The conclusion: "The evidence seems conclusive: economic development variables are more influential than political system characteristics in shaping public policy in the states." This reasoning was similar to that of Dawson and Robinson; most of the associations that occur between political variables and policy outcomes are really a product of the fact that economic development influences both political system characteristics and policy outcomes. When political factors are controlled, economic development continues to have a significant impact on public policy. But when the effects of economic development are controlled, political factors turn out to have little influence on policy outcomes. Several policy areas were pointed out where political factors remained important, and certain policy areas were also identified in which federal programs tended to offset the impact of economic development levels on state policies. Yet in an attempt to generalize about the determinants of public policy, it was concluded that, on the whole, economic development was more influential in shaping state policies than any of the political variables previously thought to be important in policy determination.

---

[6]Richard E. Dawson and James A. Robinson, "Inter-Party Competition, Economic Variables, and Welfare Policies in the American States," *Journal of Politics*, 25 (May 1963), 265–89.

[7]Thomas R. Dye, *Politics, Economics, and the Public* (Chicago: Rand McNally, 1966).

The resulting "economic resources" model may be viewed as follows:

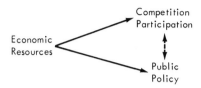

In this view, economic resources shape both the political system characteristics (competition and participation) and public policy, but characteristics of the political system have no direct causal effect on public policy.

These findings—regarded as commonplace by economists—were very disturbing to political scientists who were committed to a pluralist ideology which asserted the importance of competition and participation in politics. Now of course most of us would prefer to live in a political system in which there are high levels of competition and participation, since these conditions are highly valued in any democracy. But it remains a scientific question whether these political conditions produce different kinds of policies than noncompetitive, nonparticipating political systems. We cannot *assume* that competition and participation will produce "better" public policies simply because we prefer a competitive, participating political system.

Nonetheless, the challenge to political scientists to prove that "politics count" in shaping public policy inspired a new systematic reexamination of the determinants of public policy. A number of scholars were stimulated to reexamine systematically the traditional wisdom in the state politics field. New and more sophisticated methods were introduced;[8] additional political variables were tested for their policy impact,[9] some policy variables other than levels of public expenditures and sources were examined;[10] changes over time were described and analyzed;[11] some more sophisticated con-

---

[8]Ira Sharkansky and Richard Hofferbert, "Dimensions of State Politics, Economics, and Public Policy," *American Political Science Review*, 63 (September 1969), 867–79; James C. Strouse and Oliver J. Williams, "A Non-Additive Model for State Policy Research," *Journal of Politics*, 35 (May 1972), 648–57.

[9]Ira Sharkansky, "Agency Requests, Gubernatorial Support, and Budget Success in State Legislatures," *American Political Science Review*, 62 (December 1968), 926–39; Thomas R. Dye, "Executive Power and Public Policy in the States," *Western Political Quarterly*, 22 (December 1969), 926–39.

[10]Bryan R. Fry and Richard Winters, "The Politics of Redistribution," *American Political Science Review*, 64 (June 1970), 508–22; Ronald E. Weber and William R. Schaffer, "Public Opinion and American State Policy-Making," *Midwest Journal of Political Science*, 16 (November 1972), 683–99; Anne H. Hopkins, "Public Opinion and Support for Public Policy in the American States," *American Journal of Political Science*, 18 (February 1974), 167–78.

[11]Virginia Gray, "Models of Comparative State Politics: A Comparison of Cross-Sectional and Time Series Analyses," *American Journal of Political Science*, XX, 2 (May 1976), 235–56; Richard Hofferbert, "Socioeconomic Dimensions of the American States, 1890–1960," *Midwest Journal of Political Science*, 2 (August 1968), 401–18; Richard Hofferbert, "Ecological Development and Policy Change," *Midwest Journal of Political Science*, 10 (November 1966), 464–83.

ceptual notions were explored;[12] and policy innovation became an important topic itself.[13] In short, a whole subfield grew to maturity in a short period of time.

Implicit in much of this literature, however, was a reluctance to accept the view that political system characteristics, particularly those reflecting the pluralist values of competition and participation, possessed less policy relevance than economic resources. Indeed, there seemed to be a great deal of scrambling about by political scientists ideologically committed to proving that party competition, voter participation, partisanship, and apportionment did indeed influence public policy.[14] Of course, there is nothing wrong with trying to find the policy relevance of differing governmental structures or political processes, but we should not insist that political variables *must* influence public policy simply because our traditional training in political science has told us that political variables should be important.

One interesting model of policy determination to emerge from this research was a "hybrid model" suggested by political scientists Charles F. Cnudde and Donald J. McCrone, illustrated in the following diagram:[15]

In this model, economic resources shape public policy both *directly* and *indirectly* by affecting competition and participation, which in turn affect public policy. This study focused on only one policy field—welfare—rather than on the broader array of policies in education, health, highways, spending, taxation, and so on. Welfare policy was thought to magnify the conflict between "haves" and "have nots" and therefore to magnify the effect of competition and participation.

Cnudde and McCrane reported that both economic resources and political competition and participation independently affected welfare policies in the States. Similar findings were reported by political scientist Mi-

---

[12]Ira Sharkansky, "Environment, Policy, Output and Input: Problems of Theory and Method in the Analysis of Public Policy," in *Policy Analysis in Political Science*, Ira Sharkansky, ed. (Chicago: Markham, 1970); Strouse and Williams, "A Non-Additive Model for State Policy Research."

[13]Jack L. Walker, "The Diffusion of Innovation Among the American States," *American Political Science Review*, 63 (September 1969), 880–89; Virginia Gray, "Innovation in the States," *American Political Science Review*, 67 (December 1973), 1174–85.

[14]John Crittenden, "Dimensions of Modernization in the American States," *American Political Science Review*, 61 (December 1967), 982–1002; Alan G. Pulsipher and James L. Weatherby, "Malapportionment, Party Competition, and the Functional Distribution of Government Expenditures," *American Political Science Review*, 62 (December 1968), 1207–20; Guenther F. Schaefer and Stuart Rakoff, "Politics, Policy, and Political Science," *Politics and Society*, 1 (November 1970), 52.

[15]Charles F. Cnudde and Ronald J. McCrone, "Party Competition and Welfare Policies in the American States," *American Political Science Review*, 62 (December 1968), 1220–31.

chael Lewis-Beck, using a statistical model based on the hybrid model described above.[16] Both studies acknowledged that economic resources were stronger determinants of welfare policies than party competition or voter turnout.

THE POLITICAL SYSTEM AS A CONVERSION PROCESS

The general failure of political variables to be influential determinants of public policy raises the question of whether we should view politics as a conversion system, rather than a direct cause of public policy. In other words, politics does not *cause* public policy, but rather, it *facilitates* the conversion of demands and resources into public policy.

If we accept this view, we would not really expect variations in political systems—variations in competition, participation, partisanship, and reformism—to directly cause public policy. Instead, we would expect variations in political systems to affect *relationships* between demands and resources and public policies. For example, we would not expect highly competitive political systems to produce policies different from noncompetitive systems, but instead we might inquire whether the relationships between population characteristics and public policy are closer in competitive than in noncompetitive systems. Our focus would shift to the impact of political system variables on *relationships* between environmental conditions (measures of demands and resources) and public policies.

As a hypothetical example, we might portray relationships between economic resources and educational policies in two different kinds of political systems—competitive and noncompetitive. Among the competitive political systems (cities or states), it may turn out that per pupil expenditures rise in direct proportion to increases in economic resources. (See left drawing in Figure 12-3.) However, among the noncompetitive political systems, it may turn out that there is *no* relationship between economic resources and per pupil expenditures. (See right drawing in Figure 12-3.) In other words, competition may *facilitate* relationships between resources and public policy, but noncompetitive systems *obstruct* relationships between economic resources and public policy. This would suggest that competitive political systems are more *responsive* to socioeconomic conditions of the population than noncompetitive political systems.

Not enough research has been completed to really tell us whether our hypothetical example applies to the real world, that is, to cities, states, or

[16]Michael Lewis-Beck, "The Relative Importance of Socioeconomic and Political Variables in Public Policy," *American Political Science Review*, 71 (June 1977), 559–66.

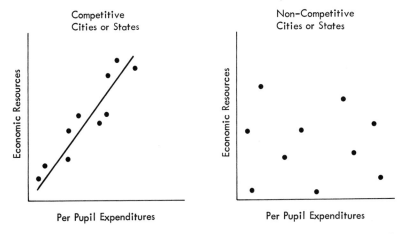

FIGURE 12-3 Possible relationships between economic resources and educational expenditures in competitive and noncompetitive political systems.

nations, and to policies in education, welfare, health, housing, and so on.[17] However, an early study on "reformism" in American city governments suggested that the type of government could indeed affect the responsiveness of public policy to characteristics of city populations.

In a study of 200 American cities, Robert L. Lineberry and Edmund D. Fowler found that reformed cities tended to tax and spend less than unreformed cities.[18] Cities with manager governments and at-large council constituencies were less willing to spend money for public purposes than cities with mayor-council governments and ward constituencies. In short, reformism does save tax money.

Lineberry and Fowler also found that environmental variables had an important impact on tax and spending policies. For example, they found that

1. the more middle class the city (measured by income, education, and occupation), the lower the general tax and spending levels
2. the greater the homeownership in a city, the lower the tax and spending levels

[17]However, there is some evidence that "professional" state legislatures produce welfare policies more closely linked to their states' resources than "nonprofessional" state legislatures. See Edward C. Carmines, "The Mediating Influence of State Legislatures on the Link Between Interparty Competition and Welfare Policies," *American Political Science Review*, 68 (September 1974), 1118–24. There is also some evidence that elected officials and the general public "concur" on policy issues more often in politically competitive cities than in noncompetitive cities. See Susan B. Hansen, "Participation, Political Structure and Concurrence," *American Political Science Review*, 69 (December 1975), 1181–99.

[18]Robert L. Lineberry and Edmund D. Fowler, "Reformism and Public Policies in American Cities," *American Political Science Review*, 61 (September 1967), 701–17.

3. the larger the percentage of religious and ethnic minorities in the population, the higher the city's taxes and expenditures.

What turned out to be an even more important finding in the Lineberry and Fowler study was the difference in *responsiveness* of the two kinds of city governments—reformed and unreformed—to the socioeconomic composition of their populations. These researchers simply grouped their cities into subsamples—reformed cities (cities with manager governments, nonpartisan elections, and at-large constituencies) and unreformed cities (cities with mayor-council governments, partisan elections, and ward constituencies). Among reformed cities there were no significant correlations between tax and spending policies and income and educational, occupational, religious, and ethnic characteristics of their populations (as on the right side of Figure 12-3). In contrast, among unreformed cities there were many significant correlations between taxing and spending policies and these socioeconomic characteristics of the population (as on the left side of Figure 12-3).

In short, "reformism" tended to reduce the importance of class, homeownership, ethnicity, and religion in city politics. It tended to minimize the role that social conflicts play in public decision making. In contrast, mayor-council governments, ward constituencies, and partisan elections permitted social cleavages to be reflected in city politics and public policy to be responsive to socioeconomic factors. Thus, political systems seem to play an important role in policy formation:

> . . . a role substantially independent of a city's demography. . . . Nonpartisan elections, at-large constituencies, and manager governments are associated with a lessened *responsiveness* of cities to the enduring conflicts of political life.[19] (Italics added)

Parties and Policy in the States

Political scientists have long placed great faith in party government. E. E. Schattschneider expressed this faith when he wrote: "The rise of political parties is undoubtedly one of the principal distinguishing marks of modern government . . . political parties created modern democracy and modern democracy is unthinkable save in terms of parties."[20] Recently Sarah McCally Morehouse reaffirmed faith in the centrality of political parties in the American states: "The single most important factor in state politics is the political party. It is not possible to understand the differences in the way sovereign states carry out the process of government without

[19]Ibid., p. 717.
[20]E.E. Schattschneider, *Party Government* (New York: Rinehart, 1942), p. 1.

understanding the type of party whose representatives are making decisions that affect the health, education, and welfare of its citizens."[21]

Yet other "spatial" theories of parties suggest that parties have little policy relevance given a normal unimodal distribution of opinion on most policy questions. Anthony Downs explained: "In the middle of the scale where most voters are massed, each party scatters its policies on both sides of the midpoint. It attempts to make each voter in this area feel that it is centered right at his position. Naturally this causes an enormous overlapping of moderate positions." Downs acknowledged that a left or right party may "sprinkle these moderate policies with a few extreme stands in order to please its far-out voters," but overall "both parties are trying to be as ambiguous as possible" about policy positions. "Political rationality leads parties in a two-party system to becloud their policies in a fog of ambiguity."[22]

For example, if most voters in a state were found in the middle of an opinion scale on a policy issue, the parties in that state would be encouraged to take moderate policy positions not very different from each other. Both parties would be competing for the many voters in the center. Since both parties took moderate positions on the issue, a change in party control of state government (the governor's office, the state legislature, or both) would *not* result in any significant shift in public policy (see top of Figure 12-4). Only if the voters were divided on a policy issue into a bimodal distribution would we expect the parties to take significantly different policy positions (see bottom of Figure 12-4). The parties would be constrained by the large number of voters on each side of the issue from moving toward the center. In this case, a change in party control of state government might result in a significant shift in public policy.

A careful specification of the conditions under which party competition and Democratic or Republican control of state government would directly affect public policy was provided by Edward T. Jennings.[23] He correctly observed that the early assumption that party competition would always assist the "have nots" is not theoretically valid. He reasoned that party competition would increase policy benefits to "have nots" only when: (1) parties in the states reflected class divisions; and (2) the party associated with the lower- or working-class gains control of government.

The distinction between competitive parties and policy-relevant par-

---

[21]Sarah McCally Morehouse, *State Politics, Parties, and Policy* (New York: Holt, Rinehart Winston, 1981), p. 29.

[22]Anthony Downs, *An Economic Theory of Democracy* (New York: Harper & Row, 1957), pp. 135, 136.

[23]Edward T. Jennings, "Competition, Constituencies, and Welfare Policies in the American States," *American Political Science Review* Vol. 73 (1979), 414–29.

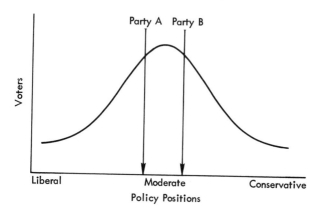

A Unimodal Distribution of Opinion

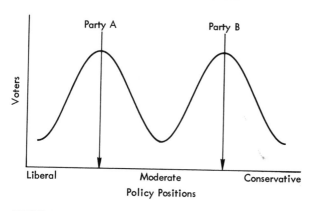

A Bimodal Distribution of Opinion

FIGURE 12-4 Parties, opinions, and policies.

ties is an important one. Competitive parties do not by themselves ensure that the "have-nots" will succeed in politics. Competition itself is not a cause of increased welfare spending. Nor is there any theoretical reason to believe competitive parties will necessarily offer alternative policies. Indeed if Downs is correct and if many state electorates cluster at the midpoints of their respective opinion distributions on policy issues, then competitive parties will have no incentive to offer significantly different policies. Only if the parties reflect different class constituencies, the party activists are concerned with policy issues, and the party of the "have-nots" gains control of state government, can we then expect party politics to influence public policy.

TABLE 12-3   The Policy Relevance of the Parties in the States

FIFTY STATES CLASSIFIED BY PARTY COMPETITION
AND POLICY RELEVANCE OF THEIR PARTY SYSTEMS

	Policy Relevant	Non-Policy Relevant
Competitive Parties	CA, HI, IA, ME, MI, MN, NE ND, OR, WI, WY, NJ, OH, PA	AK, CT, IL, NI, NY, SD
Less Competitive Parties	ID, MA, MT, NV, UT	CO, KS, NH, VT, WA
Noncompetitive Parties	RI	AL, AZ, AR, DE, FL, GA, KY, LA, MD, MS, NO, NM, NC, OK, SC, TN, TX, VA, WV

Source: Thomas R. Dye, "Party and Policy in the States," *Journal of Politics* vol. 46, November 1984, 1097–1116.

A classification of state political systems based on *both* the *competitiveness* of their parties and the *policy relevance* of their parties is shown in Table 12-3. The determination of whether their party systems are policy relevant or non–policy relevant is based upon observations of changes in welfare spending and changes in party control of state government over thirty years.[25] If welfare spending in a state increased more under Democratic administrations than under Republican administrations, then the party system is classified as policy relevant. But if there were no significant differences in welfare spending in Democratic or Republican state administrations, then the party system is classified as non–policy relevant. Some Southern states' party systems are also classified as non–policy relevant because Republicans have never gained control of state government and therefore never had the opportunity to change policy.

Note that thirty of the fifty states are adjudged to have non–policy-relevant party systems. Some of these states (e.g., New York) have *competitive* party systems, but the election of Democratic or Republican governors or state legislatures does not significantly affect welfare spending in these states (e.g., welfare spending increased as rapidly in New York under Republican governor Rockefeller as under Democratic governor Carey). Hence, their party systems are adjudged to be non–policy relevant. Of course, most

[25]See Thomas R. Dye, "Party and Policy in the States," *Journal of Politics* Vol. 46 (1984), 1097–1116.

non–policy-relevant party systems are found in noncompetitive states, especially in the South. But even when one of these states elects a Republican governor, welfare spending is unaffected, that is, it rises no more slowly than under Democratic governors. Rhode Island, with its long history of Democratic party domination of state politics, is the only noncompetitive state where the parties are clearly distinguished along liberal and conservative lines. The pluralist ideal—competitive parties offering clear policy alternatives to the voters—occurs in only fourteen states.

SUMMARY

We have employed a systems model, and variations based on this model, to describe linkages between economic resources, political system characteristics, and public policies in the American states. Some general propositions about public policy which are suggested by our systems model might include:

1. Economic resources are an important determinant of overall levels of government taxing, spending, and service in the states. Economic differences among the states have narrowed somewhat over time, but significant policy differences remain.

2. Federal grants-in-aid, considered "outside" money to state and local governments, help to free these governments from their dependence upon economic conditions within their jurisdictions and permit them to spend at higher levels than they would otherwise be able to do. Federal grants reduce the impact of a state's own economic resources on its level of spending and service.

3. The traditional literature in American politics asserted that characteristics of political systems—particularly party competition and voter participation—had an important impact on the content of public policy. But systematic research suggests that the characteristics of political systems are not as important as economic resources in shaping public policy. Most of the correlations between political system variables and public policy measure are a product of the fact that economic resources shape both the political system and public policy.

4. The testing of alternative causal models in policy determination leads us to reject the proposition that economic resources shape public policy only through changes which are made in the political system. We must also reject the idea that the character of the political system must be changed in order to change public policy. Economic resources can affect public policy directly regardless of the character of the political system. However, in some policy areas, especially welfare, economic resources shape public policy both directly and indirectly through political variables.

5. Rather than think of the political system as causing public policy,

perhaps we should think of it as facilitating public policy. Competition and participation may not affect public policy itself, but these political variables may affect the relationship between environmental demands and resources and public policies.

6. Competition and participation may increase the *responsiveness* of public policies to environmental conditions.

7. State political systems may be classified by both the competitiveness and the policy relevance of their parties. By observing whether welfare expenditures change significantly with changes in party control of state government, we can estimate the policy relevance of state party systems.

8. In twenty of the fifty states a change in party control of state government results in significant changes in welfare expenditures. Thus, in most states the party system is non–policy relevant.

BIBLIOGRAPHY

DOWNS, ANTHONY. *An Economic Theory of Democracy*. New York: Harper & Row, 1957.

———, *Inside Bureaucracy*. Boston: Little, Brown, 1967.

DUNN, WILLIAM N., *Public Policy Analysis: An Introduction*. Englewood Cliffs, N.J.: Prentice-Hall, 1981.

DYE, THOMAS R., *Politics, Economics, and the Public: Policy Outcomes in the American States*. Chicago: Rand McNally, 1966.

DYE, THOMAS R., and VIRGINIA GRAY, *Determinants of Public Policy*. Boston: Lexington, 1980.

EDELMAN, MURRAY. *The Symbolic Uses of Politics*. Urbana: University of Illinois Press, 1964.

KEY, V.O. Jr., *American State Politics: An Introduction*. New York: Knopf, 1956.

———, *Southern Politics in State and Nation*. New York: Knopf, 1951.

LINEBERRY, ROBERT L., *American Public Policy*. New York: Harper & Row, 1977.

LOWI, THEODORE. *The End of Liberalism*. New York: Norton, 1969.

MOREHOUSE, SARAH MCCALLY. *State Politics, Parties and Policy*. New York: Holt Rinehart Winston, 1981.

SHARKANSKY, IRA, *Spending in the American States*. Chicago: Rand McNally, 1968.

THE POLICY-MAKING
PROCESS
getting inside the system

Inside the policy-making process: the President's Commission on Social Security worked out compromises later enacted by Congress. (Art Stein/Photo Researchers)

THE BLACK BOX PROBLEM

It is important that we understand what goes on in the little black box labeled "political system." The systems approach employed in the previous chapter deals with aggregate characteristics of *whole* political systems; this model does not say much about what goes on *within* political systems. Our comparative analysis focused attention on the linkages between environmental resources, system characteristics, and public policy, and dealt with whole political systems. But we also want to know what happens *within* political systems. We want to know how public policy is generated within the political system, how institutions and processes function to handle demands generated in the environment, and how parties, interest groups, voters, governors, legislators, and other political actors behave in the policy-making process.

Let us try to illustrate the differences between a *comparative systems* approach and a *within-system* approach. Finding a high correlation between cigarette smoking and the incidence of cancer among human systems is important. But this correlation does not in itself reveal the functioning of cells within the human body: we still want to know *how* cancers are formed and how they behave. So also, finding a high correlation between urbanization and police protection does not in itself reveal the functioning of political systems; we will want to know *how* a political system goes about transforming demands arising from the socioeconomic environment into public policy.

The process model of public policy assists in identifying various processes occurring *within* the political system. They are:

- the *identification* of policy problems through public demands for government action;
- the *formulation* of policy proposals through the initiation and development of policy proposals by policy-planning organizations, interest groups, government bureaucracies, and the president and Congress;
- the *legitimation* of policies through political actions by parties, interest groups, the president, and Congress;
- the *implementation* of policies through organized bureaucracies, public expenditures, and the activities of executive agencies;
- the *evaluation* of policies by government agencies themselves, outside consultants, the press, and the public.

We have already talked about these processes in the chapters covering specific policy fields: civil rights, criminal justice, poverty and welfare, health, education, government spending, taxation, and national defense. In the final chapter of this book, "Policy Evaluation: Finding Out What Happens after a Law is Passed," we will examine more closely the "policy evaluation" phase of the policy process model. In this chapter, we shall add a few general comments about the influence of mass opinion, elite attitudes, the mass media, interest groups, and political parties in the policy-making process.

In describing these political processes, however, it is important to remember that the activities of the various political actors are greatly constrained by environmental conditions. We have already described the great influence environmental resources have on the character of the political system and the content of public policy. It is true that not *all* the variance in public policy can be explained by environmental resources. However, the activities of parties, groups, and individuals *within* the political system are heavily influenced by the nature of the environment. So our systems model has warned us not to expect the activities of individuals, groups, parties, or decision makers to produce policies at variance with environmental resources and constraints.

IDENTIFYING POLICY ISSUES: PUBLIC OPINION

The influence of public opinion over government policy has been the subject of great philosophical controversies in the classic literature on democracy. Edmund Burke believed democratic representatives should serve the *interest* of the people but not necessarily conform to their *will* in deciding questions of public policy. In contrast, some democratic theorists have evaluated the success of democratic institutions by whether or not they facilitate popular control over public policy.

The philosophical question of whether public opinion *should* be an important independent influence over public policy may never be resolved. But the empirical question of whether public opinion *does* constitute an important independent influence over public policy can be tackled by systematic research. However, even this empirical question has proved very difficult to answer.

The problem in assessing the independent effect of mass opinion on the actions of decision makers is that their actions help to mold mass opinion. Public policy may be in accord with mass opinion but we can never be sure whether mass opinion shaped public policy or public policy shaped mass opinion.

In V. O. Key's most important book, *Public Opinion and American Democracy,* he wrote:

> Government, as we have seen, attempts to mold public opinion toward support of the programs and policies it espouses. Given that endeavor, perfect congruence between public policy and public opinion could be government *of* public opinion rather than government *by* public opinion.[1]

[1]V. O. Key, Jr., *Public Opinion and American Democracy* (New York: Knopf, 1967), pp. 422–23.

Although Key himself was convinced that public opinion did have some independent effect on public policy, he was never able to demonstrate this in any systematic fashion. He lamented:

> Discussion of public opinion often loses persuasiveness as it deals with the critical question of how public opinion and governmental action are linked. The democratic theorist founds his doctrines on the assumption that an interplay occurs between mass opinion and government. When he seeks to delineate that interaction and to demonstrate the precise bearing of the opinions of private citizens on official decision, he encounters almost insurmountable obstacles. In despair he may conclude that the supposition that public opinion enjoys weight in public decision is a myth and nothing more, albeit a myth that strengthens a regime so long as people believe it.[2]

Yet Key compiled a great deal of circumstantial evidence supporting the notion that elections, parties, and interest groups do institutionalize channels of communication from citizens to decision makers. But there is very little *direct* evidence in the existing research literature to support the notion that public opinion has an important influence over public policy.

Public policy shapes public opinion more often than opinion shapes policy. There are several reasons why policies are relatively unconstrained by public opinion. First, few people have opinions on the great bulk of policy questions confronting the nation's decision makers. Second, public opinion is very unstable. It can change in a matter of weeks in response to news events precipitated by leaders. Third, leaders do not have a clear perception of mass opinion. Most communications received by decision makers are from other elites—newsmakers, interest group leaders, and other influential persons—and not from ordinary citizens.

We must not assume that the opinions expressed in the news media are public opinion. Frequently, this is a source of confusion. Newspersons believe *they* are the public, often confusing their own opinions with public opinion. They even tell the mass public what its opinion is, thus actually helping to mold it to conform to their own beliefs. Decision makers, then, may act in response to news stories or to the opinions of influential newsmakers in the mistaken belief that they are responding to "public opinion."

Most people do not have opinions on most policy issues. Public opinion polls frequently create opinions by asking questions that respondents never thought about until they were asked.[3] Few respondents are willing to admit they have no opinion; they believe they should provide some sort of answer, even if their opinion is weakly held or was nonexistent before the question was asked. Thus pollsters produce "doorstep" opinions. But it is unlikely

---

[2] Ibid., p. 411.

[3] Robert S. Erikson and Norman R. Luttbeg, *American Public Opinion* (New York: John Wiley, 1973).

that many Americans have seriously thought about, or gathered much information on, such specific issues as AFDC eligibility, Medicaid cost containment, Gramm-Rudman deficit reduction ceilings, the B-1 bomber, investment tax credits, and similar specific questions; nor do many Americans have information on these topics.

Public opinion is also very unstable. Mass opinion on a particular issue is often very weakly held. Asked the same question at a later date, many respondents fail to remember their earlier answers and give the pollster the opposite reply. These are not real changes in opinion, yet they register as such. One study estimates that less than 20 percent of the public holds meaningful, consistent opinions on most issues, even though two-thirds or more will respond to questions asked in a survey.[4]

Opinions also vary according to the wording of questions. It is relatively easy to word almost any public policy question in such a way as to elicit mass approval or disapproval. Thus, differently worded questions on the same issue can produce contradictory results. For example, in a California poll about academic freedom,[5] a majority of respondents (52 to 39) agreed with the statement: "Professors in state-supported institutions should have freedom to speak and teach the truth as they see it." However, a majority of respondents (by the same 52 to 39 ratio) also agreed with the statement: "Professors who advocate controversial ideas or speak out against official policy have no place in a state-supported college or university."

Opinion polls that ask the exact same question over time are more reliable indicators of public opinion than one-shot polls. Respondents in a one-shot poll may be responding to the wording of the question. But if the same wording is used over time, the bias in the wording remains constant and changes in opinion may be observed. This is why only verbatim wording used continuously over time produces reasonably accurate information about the public mood.

Finally, decision makers can easily misinterpret public opinion because the communications they receive have an upper-class bias. Members of the masses seldom call or write their senators or representatives, much less converse with them at dinners, cocktail parties, or other social occasions. Most of the communications received by decision makers are *intra-elite* communications—communications from newspersons, organized group leaders, influential constituents, wealthy political contributors, and personal friends—people who, for the most part, share the same views. It is not surprising, therefore, that members of Congress say that most of their mail is in agreement with their own position; their world of public opinion is self-reinforcing. Moreover, persons who initiate communication with de-

---

[4]Phillip Converse, "Attitudes and Non-attitudes," in Edward R. Tufte, ed., *Quantitative Analysis of Social Problems* (Reading, Mass.: Addison-Wesley, 1970).

[5]Erikson and Luttbeg, *American Public Opinion*, p. 38.

cision makers, by writing or calling or visiting their representatives, are decidedly more educated and affluent than the average citizen.

In a careful study of the relationship between mass opinion and congressional voting on public issues, Warren E. Miller and Donald Stokes found very low correlations between the voting records of members of Congress and the attitudes of their constituents on social welfare issues, and even lower correlations on foreign policy issues.[6] Only in the area of civil rights did members of Congress appear to vote according to the views of a majority of their constituents. In general, "the representative has very imperfect information about the issue preferences of his constituency, and constituency's awareness of the policy stands of the representative is ordinarily slight." With the possible exception of civil rights questions, most members of Congress are free from the influence of popular preferences in their legislative voting.

This is not to say that policy makers are completely free from the influence of mass opinion. On the contrary, the voting behavior of members of Congress on roll call votes correlates very closely with characteristics of their constituencies. Districts of different social and economic makeup produce different political orientations and voting records for members of Congress. For example, members from urban-industrial districts are more likely to vote "liberal" than are those from rural, agricultural districts, regardless of party affiliation. Members of Congress from suburban, high-income, white-collar districts have voting records different from those from big-city, low-income, political-machine-dominated districts. Because members of Congress are products of the social systems of their constituencies, they share the dominant goals and values of those constituencies. They have deep roots in the constituency—many organizational memberships, many overlapping leadership positions, lifetime residency, close ties with social and economic elites, shared religious affiliations, and so on. Members of Congress are so much "of" their constituencies that conflicts seldom occur between their own views and the dominant views in their constituencies.

IDENTIFYING POLICY ISSUES: ELITE OPINION

When V. O. Key wrestled with the same problem confronting us—namely, the determination of the impact of popular preferences on public policy— he concluded that "the missing piece of the puzzle" was "that thin stratum

---

[6]Miller and Stokes, "Constituency Influence in Congress," *American Political Science Review*, 57 (March 1963), 55–65; see also Charles F. Cnudde and Donald J. McCrone, "The Linkage Between Constituency Attitudes and Congressional Voting Behavior," *American Political Science Review*, 60 (March 1966), 66–72.

of persons referred to variously as the political elite, the political activists, the leadership echelons, or the influentials."

> The longer one frets with the puzzle of how democratic regimes manage to function, the more plausible it appears that a substantial part of the explanation is to be found in the motives that activate the *leadership echelon*, the values that it holds, the rules of the political game to which it adheres, in the expectations which it entertains about its own status in society, and perhaps in some of the objective circumstances, both material and institutional, in which it functions.[7]

In view of our inability to find any direct links between public policy and popular preferences, it seems reasonable to ask whether the preferences of elites are more directly reflected in public policy than the preferences of masses. Do elite attitudes independently affect public policy? Or are elite attitudes so closely tied to environmental conditions that elites have relatively little flexibility in policy making and therefore little independent influence over the content of public policy?

Elite preferences are more likely to be in accord with public policy than mass preferences. This finding is fairly well supported in the existing research literature. Of course this does not *prove* that policies are determined by elite preferences. It may be that government officials are acting rationally in response to events and conditions, and well-educated, informed elites understand the actions of government better than masses. Hence, it might be argued that elites support government policies because they have greater understanding of and confidence in government, and they are more likely to read about and comprehend the explanations of government officials. On the other hand, the correspondence between elite opinion and public policy may also indicate that elite opinion determines public policy.

Elite Opinion and the War in Vietnam

Let us consider, for example, the relationship between elite and mass opinion and the Vietnam War. Early in the war, well-educated Americans gave greater support to the war than less-educated Americans. The masses had greater doubts about the advisability of the war than the elites. However, the Johnson administration went ahead with a policy of escalation, increasing U.S. combat forces in Vietnam. By 1968 elite opinion was divided, and in the 1968 elections both Democratic and Republican presidential candidates gave only guarded support for the policy of the administration. By 1969, elite opinion had shifted dramatically; nearly two out of every three well-educated Americans had come to believe that U.S.

---

[7]Key, *Public Opinion and American Democracy*, p. 537.

involvement in Vietnam was a "mistake." Mass opposition to the war had also grown to a point where a majority now felt U.S. policy was a mistake. But mass opinion never shifted as dramatically as elite opinion. It was at this point that the policy of escalation was reversed, and President Nixon began his policy of gradual U.S. combat troop withdrawal and "Vietnamization" of the war. Figure 13-1 shows that the greatest *shift* in opinion on the Vietnam War occurred among college-educated groups—the groups from which elites are largely drawn. These groups gave the greatest *support* for the war in 1966 and the greatest *opposition* in 1969. In 1966 the U.S. government was escalating the war; in 1969 the government began withdrawing U.S. troops.

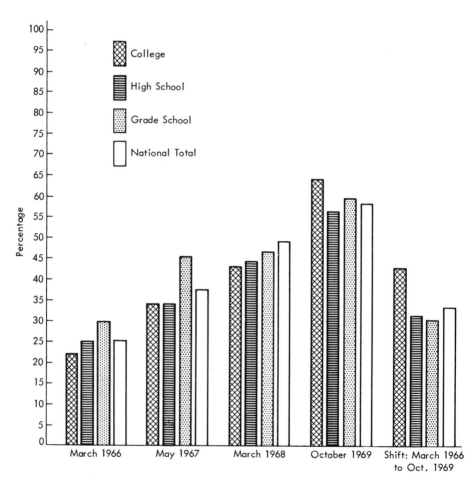

FIGURE 13-1 Agreement that U.S. involvement in Vietnam was a mistake, by education levels. (Source: *Gallup Opinion Index*, October 1969, p. 15.)

Nothing arouses patriotism more than decisive military victory; and nothing loses support for war efforts more than military defeat. When the United States was forced to retreat from North Korea after the Chinese invaded it in December 1950, popular support for the Korean War plunged. Likewise, after the successful communist Tet offensive in 1968, support of the Vietnam War by college-educated Americans declined and President Lyndon Johnson announced that he would not seek reelection and would open peace negotiations in Paris with the North Vietnamese. Support for both wars lasted a little over two years after the introduction of American combat ground troops. Analysis reveals that support for these two wars declined in direct relationship to the numbers of casualties and the length of the war. "To summarize, then, when one takes support or opposition for the wars in Korea or Vietnam and correlates them with (1) the casualties suffered at the time of the poll or (2) the direction of the war at the time of the poll, one gets a reasonably good fit."[8] The initial support of all population groups for the military action indicates that the masses will support the military adventures of the leadership. But this support will evaporate when military actions fail to bring a speedy victory.

Perhaps more importantly, policy making in both wars followed elite, not mass, opinion. Mass opinion never supported the Vietnam War. When elites supported these wars in their early stages, the United States "escalated" its participation—despite little enthusiastic support by less-educated groups. The United States withdrew from both wars and sought negotiated settlements after elites, not masses, made a dramatic shift in opinion. Elites agreed on escalation in the early phases of the Vietnam War, and they agreed on withdrawal in its later phases. The only disagreements occurred over how quickly we should withdraw. The student antiwar protesters had no significant effect on the course of the war. Indeed, if anything, the protestors strengthened the war effort. After a careful analysis of change in elite and mass opinion on the war, John E. Mueller concludes: " . . . the protest against the war in Vietnam may have been counterproductive in its impact on public opinion: that is, the war might have been somewhat more unpopular if protest had not existed."[9] Disagreement over the speed of withdrawal occurred *within* elite circles. Elites were not responding to mass opinion in their decision to withdraw.

Finally, elites can initiate events that profoundly shape public opinion. Any successful use of force will win widespread public approval in its initial phases. Indeed, even a crisis will strengthen the support of national leaders. Polls showed dramatic increases in support for Truman after the beginning of the Korean War, for Eisenhower after the invasion of Lebanon, for

[8]John Mueller, *War, Presidents and Public Opinion* (New York: John Wiley, 1973), p. 61.
[9]Ibid., p. 164.

Johnson after committing U.S. combat troups to Vietnam, for Nixon after the Cambodian invasion, for Ford after the Mayaguez Attack, for Carter after the Iranian kidnapping of the U.S. embassy staff, and for Reagan after the U.S. invasion of Grenada. Thus, the president's ability to "make something happen" is an important tool in shaping mass opinion.

Many other policy areas display the same elite-mass opinion linkages. It is usually the most highly educated, prestigiously employed, wealthy people who are highly supportive of government policies. Policy change more closely corresponds to changes in elite opinion than to changes in mass opinion.

AGENDA SETTING AND "NONDECISIONS"

Who decides what will be decided? Defining the problems of society, and suggesting alternative solutions, is the most important stage of the policy-making process. We can refer to this stage as "agenda setting." Conditions in society which are not defined as a problem, and for which alternatives are never proposed, never became policy issues. They never get on the "agenda" of decision makers. Government does nothing and conditions remain the same. On the other hand, if certain conditions in society are defined as problems and alternative solutions put forward, the conditions become policy issues. Governments are forced to decide what to do.

Clearly then, the power to decide what will be a policy issue is crucial to the policy-making process. Deciding what will be the problems is even more important than deciding what will be the solutions. Political scientist E. E. Schattschneider once wrote:

> . . . As a matter of fact, the definition of the alternative is the supreme instrument of power; the antagonists can rarely agree on what the issues are because power is involved in the definition. He who determines what politics is about runs the country, because the definition of the alternatives is the choice of conflicts, and the choice of conflicts allocates power.[10]

Many civics textbooks imply that agenda setting just "happens." It is sometimes argued that in an open plural society such as ours, channels of access and communication to government are always open, so that any problem can be discussed and placed on the agenda of national decision making. Individuals and groups, it is said, can organize themselves to assume the tasks of defining problems and suggesting solutions. People can define their own interests, organize themselves, persuade others to support their cause, gain access to government officials, influence decision making,

[10]E. E. Schattschneider, *The Semisovereign People* (New York: Holt, Rinehart & Winston, 1961), p. 68.

and watch over the implementation of government policies and programs. Indeed, it is sometimes argued that the absence of political activity such as this is an indicator of "satisfaction."

But, in reality, policy issues do not just "happen." Creating an issue, dramatizing it, calling attention to it, and pressuring government to do something about it are important political tactics. These tactics are employed by influential individuals, organized interest groups, policy planning organizations, political candidates and officeholders, and perhaps most importantly, the mass media. These are the tactics of "agenda setting."

On the other hand, *preventing* certain conditions in society from becoming policy issues is also an important political tactic. "Nondecision making" occurs when influential individuals or groups, or the political system itself, operate to prevent the emergence of challenges to the dominant values or interests in society. According to political scientists Peter Bachrach and Morton Baratz:

> A nondecision, as we define it, is a decision that results in the suppression or thwarting of a latent or manifest challenge to the values and interests of the decision-maker. To be more clearly explicit, non-decision-making is a means by which demands for change in the existing allocation of benefits and privileges in the community can be suffocated before they are even voiced; or kept covert; or killed before they gain access to the relevant decision-making arena; or failing all these things, maimed or destroyed in the decision-implementing stage of the policy process.[11]

Nondecision making may occur when dominant elites act openly or covertly to suppress an issue because they fear that if public attention is focused on it something will be done and what is done will not be in their interest.

Nondecision making may also occur when political candidates or officeholders or administrative officials anticipate that elites will not favor a particular idea and therefore these officeholders and officials drop the idea. They do not want to "rock the boat." Elites do not have to *do* anything. Officials are acting in anticipation of what they *might* do.

Finally, and perhaps most importantly, nondecision making occurs because the political system itself is structured in such a way as to facilitate the resolution of some kinds of issues and to obstruct the resolution of others. There is a "mobilization of bias" within the political system itself, that is, "a set of predominant values, beliefs, rituals, and institutional procedures . . . that operate systematically and consistently to the benefit of others."[12] For example, many scholars believe that the interest group system

---

[11]Peter Bachrach and Morton S. Baratz, *Power and Poverty* (New York: Oxford University Press, 1979), p. 7.

[12]Ibid., p. 43.

is the key to understanding how issues are identified, solutions proposed, and policies adopted. However, we know that the political system responds well to large-scale, well-organized, wealthy, active interest groups with good access to government officials. It responds less well to smaller, unorganized, poorer, inactive interest groups with few available channels of communication to government officials. According to Schattschneider the interest group system "has an upper-class bias":

> The business or upper class bias of the pressure system shows up everywhere. . . . The data raise a serious question about the validity of the proposition that special interest groups are a universal form of political organization reflecting all interests.[13]

The same observations might be made for the party system—that parties respond to well-organized, wealthy, skilled, active, and knowledgeable individuals and groups rather than to the disorganized, poor, unskilled, inactive, or unknowledgeable. Indeed, all governmental bodies—elected and appointed; legislative, executive, and judicial; federal, state, and local—contain this same bias.

Thus, it is difficult to maintain the fiction that anyone in a democracy can raise any policy issue anytime he or she wishes. Who, then, is responsible for "agenda setting"? Who decides what will be decided?

AGENDA SETTING AND MOBILIZING OPINION: THE MASS MEDIA

Television is the major source of information for the vast majority of Americans. Over two-thirds of Americans report that they receive all or most of their news from television. The importance of television in transmitting information is a relatively recent occurrence: In 1952 only 19.8 percent of all American homes had TV sets, compared to 99.8 percent in 1972. Newspapers had always reported wars, riots, scandals, and disasters, just as they do today, but the masses of Americans did not always read the news sections of their daily paper—and fewer still chose to read the editorials on these topics. But today television is really the first form of *mass* communication, that is, communication which reaches nearly everyone, including children. The television viewer *must* see the news or else turn off the set; the newspaper reader can turn quickly to the sports and comics without confronting the political news. More importantly, television presents a *visual* image, not merely a printed word. The visual quality of television—the emotional impact that is conveyed by pictures—enables the television networks to convey emotions as well as information.

[13]Schattschneider, *The Semisovereign People*, p. 31.

What the American people will see and hear about their world is largely determined by three private corporations—the American Broadcasting Company (ABC), the National Broadcasting Corporation (NBC) which is owned by RCA Inc., and the Columbia Broadcasting System Inc. (CBS). Despite new competition from cable and satellite technology (e.g., CNN cable news and the WTBS Turner Broadcasting "superstation"), these networks still dominate television news and entertainment. Individual television stations are privately owned and licensed to use public broadcast channels by the Federal Communications Commission. But these stations are forced to receive news and programming from the networks because of the high costs involved in producing news or entertainment at the local station level. The top officials of these corporate networks, particularly the people in charge of the news, are indeed "a tiny, enclosed fraternity of privileged men."[14] Nicholas Johnson, a member of the Federal Communications Commission and self-professed liberal, has said:

> The networks in particular . . . are probably now beyond the check of any institution in our society. The President, the Congress of the United States, the FCC, the foundations, and universities are reluctant even to get involved. I think they may now be so powerful that they're beyond the check of anyone.[15]

The news media generally credit themselves with the success of the civil rights movement: The dramatic televised images of nonviolent civil rights demonstrators of the early 1960s being attacked by police with nightsticks, cattle prods, and vicious dogs helped to awaken the nation and its political leadership to the injustices of segregation. These leaders also credit TV with "decisively changing America's opinion of the Vietnam War," and forcing Lyndon Johnson out of the presidency. Television news, together with the Washington press corps, also lays claim, of course, to the expulsion of Richard Nixon from the presidency. The *Washington Post* conducted the investigative reporting that produced a continuous flow of embarrassing and incriminating information about the president and his chief advisers. But it was the television networks that maintained the continuous nightly attack on the White House for nearly two years and kept Watergate in the public eye. Richard Nixon's approval rating in public opinion polls dropped from an all-time high of 68 percent in January 1973 following the Vietnam Peace Agreement to a low of 24 percent less than one year later.

Yet the leadership of the mass media frequently claim that they do

---

[14]The phraseology is courtesy of former vice president Spiro Agnew, who also used a more colorful description of the network top brass—"supersensitive, self-anointed, supercilious electronic barons of opinion." See *Newsweek*, November 9, 1970, p. 22.

[15]Quoted by Edward Jay Epstein, *News from Nowhere* (New York: Random House, 1973), p. 6.

no more than "mirror" reality. Although the "mirror" argument contradicts many of their more candid claims to having righted many of America's wrongs (segregation, Vietnam, Watergate), the leadership of the three television networks claim that television "is a mirror of society." Of course, the mirror analogy is nonsense. Newsmen decide what the news will be, how it will be presented, and how it will be interpreted. As David Brinkley explained, "News is what I say it is. It's something worth knowing by my standards."[16]

The power of television is not really in persuading viewers to take one side of an issue or another. Instead, *the power of television is in setting the agenda for decision making*—deciding what issues will be given attention and what issues will be ignored. Systematic research has shown that issues which receive greatest attention in the media are more likely to be viewed by voters as important.[17]

The television network executives and producers who decide which issues and events will be covered interact daily with their counterparts in the national press—the executives and editors of the *New York Times,* the *Washington Post, Time, Newsweek,* and so on. Even at the working level, the television and newspaper reporters interact in the "Washington press corps." This interaction reinforces decisions about what the "news" should be. As a result, there is not much diversity in news reporting. All three networks, as well as the major newspapers and news magazines, will carry stories on the same topics at the same time.

In exercising their judgment regarding which stories should be given television time or newspaper space, the media executives must rely on their own political values and economic interests as guidelines in determining what will be "news." In general, the media executives are more "liberal" in their views than other segments of the nation's leadership. Topics selected weeks in advance for coverage reflect, or often create, current liberal issues: concern for the poor and blacks, women's liberation, opposition to defense spending and the CIA, ecology, migrant farm labor, tax loopholes, Indian rights, and for nearly two years, Watergate. But liberalism is *not* the major source of bias in the news.

The principal source of distortion in the news is caused by the need for drama, action, and confrontation to hold audience attention. NBC news

[16]*TV Guide,* April 11, 1964.

[17]J. M. McCleod, L. B. Becker, and J. E. Byrne, "Another Look at the Agenda-Setting Function of the Press," *Communications Research* (April 1974), 131–66; "The Political Consequences of Agenda-Setting," *Mass Communication Review* (Spring 1976), 8–15; M. E. McCombs, "Agenda-Setting Research: A Bibliographic Essay," *Political Communication Review* (March 1976), 1–7; and D. L. Shaw and M. E. McCombs, eds., *The Emergence of American Political Issues* (New York: West, 1977).

executive producer Reuben Frank advised his producers in a memorandum: "The highest power of television journalism is not in the transmission of information but in the transmission of experience—joy, sorrow, shock, fear—these are the stuff of news."[18]

Television must entertain. To capture the attention of jaded audiences, news must be selected which includes emotional rhetoric, shocking incidents, dramatic conflict, overdrawn stereotypes. Race, sex, violence, and corruption in government are favorite topics because of popular interest. More complex problems such as inflation, government spending, and foreign policy must either be simplified and dramatized or ignored. To dramatize an issue the newsmakers must find or create a dramatic incident; film it; transport, process, and edit the film; and write a script for the introduction, the "voice-over," and the "recapitulation." All this means that "news" must be created well in advance of scheduled broadcasting.

However, the networks' concentration on scandal, abuse, and corruption in government has not always produced the desired liberal, reformist notions in the minds of the mass viewers. Contrary to the expectations of network executives, their focus on governmental scandals—Watergate, illicit CIA activities, FBI abuses, congressional scandals, and power struggles between Congress and the executive branch—has produced feelings of general political distrust and cynicism toward government and "the system." These feelings have been labeled "television malaise"—a combination of social distrust, political cynicism, feelings of powerlessness, and disaffection from parties and politics which seem to stem from television's emphasis on the negative aspects of American life.[19]

Network executives do not intend to create "television malaise" among the masses. But scandal, sex, abuse of power, and corruption attract large audiences and increase ratings. "Bad" news is placed up front in the telecast, usually with some dramatic visual aids. Negative television journalism ". . . is concerned with what is wrong with our governmental system, our leaders, our prisons, schools, roads, automobiles, race relations, traffic systems, pollution laws, every aspect of our society. In Europe, there is much less emphasis on exposing what is wrong, much more satisfaction with the status quo."[20] The effect of negative television coverage of the American political system is to "turn off" the masses from participation in government.

---

[18]Epstein, *News from Nowhere*, p. 39.

[19]Michael J. Robinson, "Public Affairs Television and the Growth of Political Malaise," *American Political Science Review*, 70 (June 1976), 409–32; and "Television and American Politics," *The Public Interest* (Summer 1977), pp. 3–39.

[20]Merrit Panitt, "America Out of Focus," *TV Guide*, January 15, 1972, p. 6.

FORMULATING POLICY:
THE POLICY-PLANNING ORGANIZATIONS

It is the policy-planning organizations which are central coordinating points in the policy-making process. Certain policy-planning groups—for example, the Council on Foreign Relations, the Committee on Economic Development, and the Brookings Institution—are influential in a wide range of key policy areas. Other policy-planning groups—the Urban Institute, Resources for the Future, the Population Council, for example—specialize in a particular policy field.

These organizations bring together the leadership of corporate and financial institutions, the foundations, the mass media, the leading intellectuals, and influential figures in the government. They review the relevant university and foundation-supported research on topics of interest, and more important, they try to reach a consensus about what action should be taken on national problems under study. Their goal is to develop action recommendations—explicit policies or programs designed to resolve national problems. These policy recommendations of the key policy-planning groups are distributed to the mass media, federal executive agencies, and the Congress. The purpose is to lay the groundwork for making policy into law. Soon the results of elite decision making and consensus building will be reflected in the actions of elected officials—the "proximate policy makers."

Let us illustrate these propositions by examining one of the nation's leading policy-planning organizations, the Council on Foreign Relations. The CFR is the most influential private policy-planning organization in foreign affairs. It was founded in 1921 and supported by grants from the Rockefeller and Carnegie foundations and later by the Ford Foundation. Its early directors were internationally minded Wall Street corporation lawyers: Elihu Root, also secretary of state; John W. Davis, also 1924 Democratic presidential nominee; Paul Cravath, founder of the prestigious New York law firm of Cravath, Swaine, and Moore.

The history of the CFR accomplishments is impressive: it developed the Kellogg Peace Pact in the 1920s, stiffened U.S. opposition to Japanese Pacific expansion in the 1930s, designed major portions of the United Nations Charter, and devised the "containment" policy to halt Soviet expansion in Europe after World War II. It laid the groundwork for the NATO agreement and devised the Marshall Plan for European recovery.[21] When top elites began to suspect that the United States was overreliant upon nuclear weapons in the late 1950s, the CFR commissioned a young

---

[21]See Joseph Kraft, "School for Statesmen," *Harper's*, July 1958, pp 64–68.

Harvard professor to look into the matter. The result was Henry Kissinger's influential book *Nuclear Weapons and Foreign Policy*, which challenged the "massive retaliation" doctrine of John Foster Dulles and urged greater flexibility in response to aggression.[22]

Political scientist Lester Millbraith once observed that the influence of the CFR throughout the government is so pervasive that it is difficult to distinguish CFR from government programs. "The Council on Foreign Relations, while not financed by government, works so closely with it that it is difficult to distinguish Council actions stimulated by government from autonomous actions."[23]

When the CFR changes *its* policy position, we can expect a change in official U.S. policy. In 1980, the CFR acknowledged the crumbling of foreign and military policies of the United States in the previous decade. The CFR issued a stern report citing "sharp anguish over Americans held hostage by international outlaws" (in Iran) and "the brutal invasion of a strategic nation" (Afghanistan).[24] It described the U.S. military posture as "a troubling question." More importantly, the CFR announced the end of its "1980 Project," with its concern for "human rights," and started a new study program—on Soviet military strength and expansionism. Even before Carter left office, leading CFR members had decided that the "human rights" policy was crippling U.S. relations with allies but was not relieving repression in communist countries. The CFR recognized "the relentless Soviet military buildup and extension of power by invasion, opportunism, and proxy," and recommended that the U.S.-Soviet relationship "occupy center stage in the coming decade." Thus, elite support for a harder line in foreign and defense policy developed through CFR even before Ronald Reagan took office.

The Reagan administration relied on the CFR for both policy advice and personnel. The United States began a comprehensive long-term military buildup recommended in a CFR 1981 report, *The Soviet Challenge: A Policy Framework for the 1980s*. CFR members on the Reagan team did not publicize their membership, but they included Secretary of State Alexander Haig, Secretary of Defense Caspar Weinberger, Vice President George Bush, Secretary of Treasury Donald Regan, and CIA Director William Casey.[25]

[22]Henry Kissinger, *Nuclear Weapons and Foreign Policy* (New York: Council on Foreign Relations, 1957).

[23]Lester Millbraith, "Interest Groups in Foreign Policy," in *Domestic Sources in Foreign Policy*, James R. Rosenau, ed. (New York: Free Press, 1967), p. 247.

[24]Council on Foreign Relations, *Annual Report 1979–1980*, p. 11.

[25]See Thomas R. Dye, *Who's Running America: The Conservative Years* (Englewood Cliffs, N.J.: Prentice-Hall, 1986).

POLICY LEGITIMATION: THE "PROXIMATE POLICY MAKERS"

What is the role of the proximate policy makers?[26] The activities of the "proximate policy makers"—the president, Congress, federal agencies, congressional committees, White House staff, and interest groups—in the policy-making process have traditionally been the central focus of political science. Political scientists usually portray the activities of the proximate policy makers as the whole of the policy-making process. But our notion of public policy making views the activities of the proximate policy makers as only the *final phase* of a much more complex process. This final stage is the open, public stage of the policy-making process, and it attracts the attention of the mass media and most political scientists. The activities of the "proximate policy makers" are much easier to study than the private actions of corporations, foundations, the mass media, and the policy-planning organizations.

Many scholars concentrate their attention on this final phase of public policy making and conclude that policy making is a process of bargaining, competition, persuasion, and compromise among interest groups and governmental officials. Undoubtedly, bargaining, competition, persuasion, and compromises over policy issues continue throughout this final "law-making" phase of the policy-making process. Conflict between the president and Congress, or between Democrats and Republicans, or liberals and conservatives, and so forth, may delay or alter somewhat the final actions of the "proximate policy makers."

But the agenda for policy consideration has been set before the "proximate policy makers" become actively involved in the policy-making process—the major directions of policy change have been determined, and the mass media have prepared the public for new policies and programs. The formal law-making process concerns itself with details of implementation: who gets the "political" credit; what agencies get control of the program; and exactly how much money will be spent. These are not unimportant questions, but they are raised and decided within the context of policy goals and directions which have already been determined. The decisions of the "proximate policy makers" tend to center around the *means* rather than the *ends* of public policy.

[26]The phrase "proximate policy maker" is derived from political scientist Charles E. Lindbloom who uses the term to distinguish between citizens and elected officials: "Except in small political systems that can be run by something like a New England town meeting, not all citizens can be the immediate, or proximate, makers of policy. They yield the immediate (or proximate) task of decision to a small minority." See Charles E. Lindbloom, *The Policy-Making Process* (Englewood Cliffs, N.J.: Prentice-Hall, 1968), p. 30.

PARTY INFLUENCE ON PUBLIC POLICY

Parties are important institutions in the American political system, but it would be a mistake to overestimate their impact on public policy. It makes relatively little difference in the major direction of public policy whether Democrats or Republicans dominate the political scene. American parties are largely "brokerage" organizations, devoid of ideology and committed to winning public office rather than to advancing policy positions. Both the Democratic and Republican parties and their candidates tailor their policy positions to societal conditions. The result is that the parties do not have much independent impact on policy outcomes.

Both American parties subscribe to the same fundamental political ideology. Both share prevailing democratic consensus about the sanctity of private property, a free enterprise economy, individual liberty, limited government, majority rule, and due process of law. Moreover, since the 1930s both parties have supported the same major domestic programs—social security, unemployment compensation, a national highway program, a federally aided welfare system, and countercyclical fiscal and monetary policies. Finally, both parties have supported the basic outlines of American foreign and military policy since World War II—international involvement, anticommunism, the cold war, European recovery, NATO, military preparedness, and even the Korean and Vietnam wars. A change in party control of the presidency or Congress has not resulted in any significant shifts in the course of American foreign or domestic policy.

Yet there are nuances of differences between the parties that can be observed in the policy-making process. The social bases of the Democratic and Republican parties are slightly different. Both parties draw support from all social groups in America, but the Democrats draw disproportionately from labor, big-city residents, ethnic voters, blacks, Jews, and Catholics; while Republicans draw disproportionately from rural, small-town, and suburban Protestants, businessmen, and professionals. To the extent that the policy orientations of these two broad groups differ, the thrust of party ideology also differs. However, the magnitude of this difference is not very great.

Conflict between parties occurs most frequently over issues involving social welfare programs, housing and urban development, Medicare, antipoverty programs, and the regulation of business and labor. On some issues, such as civil rights and appropriations, voting will follow party lines during roll calls on preliminary motions, amendments, and other preliminary matters, but swing to a bipartisan vote on passage of the final legislation. This means that the parties have

TABLE 13-1   **Party Division on Selected Votes in Congress**

	HOUSE VOTES			
	REPUBLICANS		DEMOCRATS	
	YES	NO	YES	NO
Medicare (1965)	65	73	248	42
Establish Department of Housing and Urban Development (1965)	9	118	208	66
Turnover Poverty Program to states (1970)	103	63	60	168
Make Martin Luther King Jr.'s birthday a holiday	39	101	213	32
Chrysler loan guarantee (1979)	62	88	209	48
No abortion funds under Medicaid (1979)	119	23	116	132
Implement Panama Canal Treaty (1979)	19	125	173	78
Reagan domestic program budget cuts (1981)	191	0	62	182
Reagan income tax cuts (1981)	189	1	48	196
MX missile production (1985)	158	24	61	189

	SENATE VOTES			
	REPUBLICANS		DEMOCRATS	
	YES	NO	YES	NO
Medicare (1965)	13	14	55	7
Repeal Taft-Hartley "right to work" (1965)	5	26	40	21
Antiballistic missile (ABM) system (1970)	29	14	21	36
Increase food stamps (1976)	13	18	39	4
Delay production of B-1 bomber (1976)	7	22	37	15
Establish new cabinet-level Department of Education (1979)	18	17	51	5
Index income tax to prevent "bracket creep" (1981)	43	8	14	32
Reagan income tax cuts (1981)	51	0	20	26
Reduce "Star Wars" funding (1985)	6	45	32	12

Source: *Congressional Quarterly,* "Key votes" in various issues, 1965–1986.

disagreed on certain aspects of the bill, but compromised on its final passage.

What are the issues that cause conflict between the Democratic and Republican parties? In general, Democrats have favored federal action to assist low-income groups through public assistance, housing, and anti-poverty programs; and generally a larger role for the federal government in launching new projects to remedy domestic problems. Republicans, on the other hand, have favored less government involvement in domestic affairs, and greater reliance on private action (see Table 13-1).

POLICY INNOVATION

Policy innovation has been a central concern of students of the policy processes.[27] Policy innovation is simply the readiness of a government to adopt new programs and policies. Several years ago, political scientist Jack L. Walker constructed an "innovation score" for the American states based upon elapsed time between the first state adoption of a program and its later adoption by other states. Walker monitored eighty-eight different programs adopted by twenty or more states, and he averaged each state's score on each program adoption to produce an index of innovation for each state. The larger the innovation score, the faster the state has been on the average in responding to new ideas or policies.[28] Walker proceeded to explore relationships between innovation scores in the fifty states and socioeconomic, political, and regional variables. It turned out that innovation was more readily accepted in urban, industrialized, wealthy states.

However, in a subsequent study of policy innovation in the American states, Virginia Gray argued persuasively that no general tendency toward "innovativeness" really exists—that states which are innovative in one policy area are not necessarily the same states which are innovative in other policy areas. She examined the adoption of twelve specific innovations in civil rights, welfare, and education, including the adoption of state public accommodations, fair housing and fair employment laws, and merit systems and compulsory school attendance. States that were innovative in education were not necessarily innovative in civil rights or welfare. Nonetheless, she discovered that "first adopters" of most innovations tended to be wealthier states.[29]

Let us try to explain why wealth, urbanization, and education are associated with policy innovation. First of all, *income* enables a state to afford the luxury of experimentation. Low incomes place constraints on the ability of policy makers to raise revenues to pay for new programs or policies; high incomes provide the *tax resources* necessary to begin new undertakings. We can also imagine that *urbanization* would be conducive to policy innovation. Urbanization involves social change and creates demands for new programs and policies, and urbanization implies the concentration of cre-

[27]Victor Thompson, *Bureaucracy and Innovation* (Tuscaloosa: University of Alabama Press, 1969); Lawrence B. Mohr, "Determinants of Innovation in Organizations," *American Political Science Review*, 63 (March 1969), 111–26; Michael Aiken and Robert R. Alford, "Community Structure and Innovation: The Case for Public Housing," *American Political Science Review*, 64 (September 1970), 843–64; Jack L. Walker, "The Diffusion of Innovations Among the American States," *American Political Science Review*, 63 (September 1969), 880–99.

[28]Walker, "Diffusion of Innovations Among the American States," p. 883.

[29]Virginia Gray, "Innovation in the States," *American Political Science Review*, 67 (December 1973), 1174–85.

ative resources in large cosmopolitan centers. Rural societies change less rapidly and are considered less adaptive and sympathetic to innovation. Finally, it is not unreasonable to expect that *education* should facilitate innovation. An educated population should be more receptive toward innovation in public policy, and perhaps even more demanding of innovation in its appraisal of political candidates. In summary, wealth, urbanization, and education, considered together, should provide a socioeconomic environment conducive to policy innovation.

We might also expect both party competition and voter participation to affect policy innovation. Closely contested elections should encourage parties and candidates to put forward innovative programs and ideas to capture the imagination and support of the voter. Competitive states are more likely to experience turnover in party control of state government. Innovations in policy are more likely when a new administration takes office. An increase in political participation should also encourage policy innovation.

The decision-making milieu itself—characteristics of the legislative and executive branches of state government—can also be expected to influence policy innovation. Specifically, we expect that the ethic of "professionalism" among legislators and bureaucrats is a powerful stimulus to policy innovation. Professionalism involves, among other things, acceptance of professional reference groups as sources of information, standards, and norms. The professional bureaucrat attends national conferences, reads national journals, and perhaps even aspires to build a professional reputation that extends beyond the boundaries of a home state. Thus, he or she constantly encounters new ideas, and he or she is motivated to pursue innovation for the purpose of distinction in a chosen field. Moreover, one might argue that professional bureaucrats are also moved to propose innovative programs in order to expand their authority within the bureaucracy—"empire building."

All these factors—income, urbanization, education, tax revenue, party competition, voter participation, civil service coverage, and legislative professionalism—are *related* to policy innovation. Table 13-2 shows the

TABLE 13-2   Correlates of Policy Innovation in the American States

FIGURES ARE SIMPLE CORRELATION COEFFICIENTS
FOR RELATIONSHIPS WITH THE INNOVATION INDEX

Income	.56	Party Competition	.34
Urbanization	.54	Voter Participation	.28
Education	.32	Civil Service Coverage	.53
Tax Revenue	.28	Legislative Professionalism	.62

simple correlation coefficients between each of these explanatory variables and the policy innovation scores.

Further causal analysis reveals that "professionalism" in the legislative and executive branches of state government appears to be the most direct source of policy innovation. We might speculate that professionalism among both legislators and bureaucrats encourages the development of national standards for governmental administration. Professionals know about programmatic developments elsewhere through professional meetings, journals, newsletters, etc. More importantly, they view themselves as professional administrators and governmental leaders and they seek to adopt the newest reforms and innovations for their own states. As Jack Walker comments, "They are likely to adopt a more cosmopolitan perspective and to cultivate their reputations within a national professional community rather than merely within their own state or agency."[30] Even if individual legislators themselves do not think in professional terms, legislatures with professional staffs may be influenced by these values.

Education, participation, and innovation appear to be linked in a causal fashion. This lends some limited support to the pluralist contention that an educated and active political constituency can have an impact on public policy—at least to the extent that such a constituency seems to promote novelty and experimentation in programs and policies. In summary, the explanation of policy innovation turns out to be one that emphasizes professionalism in legislature and bureaucracies, and an educated and politically active population.

SUMMARY

Systems theory helps us to conceptualize the linkages between the environment, the political system, and public policy, but it does not really describe what goes on inside the "black box" labeled "political system." The *process model* identifies a variety of activities which occur *within* the political system, including identification of problems and "agenda setting," formulating policies proposals, legitimating policies, implementing policies, and evaluating their effectiveness. Although political science has traditionally concerned itself with describing political institutions and processes, seldom has it systematically examined the impact of political processes on the *content* of public policy. Let us try to set forth some general propositions about the impact of political processes on policy content.

1. It is difficult to assess the independent effect of public opinion on public policy. Public policy may accord with mass opinion but we can never

---

[30]Walker, "Diffusion of Innovations Among the American States."

be certain whether mass opinion shaped public policy or public policy shaped mass opinion. The "public" does not have opinions on many major policy questions; public opinion is unstable; and decision makers can easily misinterpret as well as manipulate public opinion.

2. Public policy is more likely to conform to elite opinion than mass opinion. Elite opinion has been particularly influential in the determination of foreign policy. However, it is unlikely that elites can operate independently of environmental resources and demands for very long.

3. Deciding what will be decided—agenda setting—is a crucial stage in the policy process. Policy issues do not just "happen." Preventing certain conditions in society from becoming policy issues—"nondecision making"—is an important political tactic of dominant interests.

4. The mass media, particularly the three television networks, play a major rule in agenda setting. By deciding what will be "news," the media set the agenda for political discussion, whether or not the media can persuade voters to support one candidate or another. The continuing focus on the dramatic, violent, and negative aspects of American life may unintentionally create apathy and alienation—"television malaise."

5. A great deal of policy formulation occurs outside the formal governmental process. Prestigious, private, policy-planning organizations—such as the Council on Foreign Relations—explore policy alternatives, advise governments, develop policy consensus, and even supply top governmental leaders. The policy-planning organizations bring together the leadership of the corporate and financial worlds, the mass media, the foundations, the leading intellectuals, and top government officials.

6. The activities of the "proximate policy makers"—the president, Congress, executive agencies, etc.—attract the attention of most commentators and political scientists. But nongovernmental leaders, in business and finance, foundations, policy-planning organizations, the mass media, and other interest groups, may have already set the policy agenda and selected major policy goals. The activities of the "proximate policy makers" tend to center around the *means,* rather than the *ends,* of public policy.

7. The Democratic and Republican parties have agreed on the basic outlines of American foreign and domestic policy since World War II. Thus, partisanship has not been a central influence on public policy. However, there have been some policy differences between the parties. Differences have occurred most frequently over questions of welfare, housing and urban development, antipoverty efforts, health care, and the regulations of business and labor.

8. Most votes in Congress and state legislatures show the Democratic and Republican party majorities to be in agreement. However, when conflict occurs it is more likely to occur along party lines than any other kind of division.

9. Policy innovation—the readiness of a government to adopt new programs and policies—is linked to urbanization, education, and wealth, as well as competition, participation, and professionalism. Specifically, policy innovation appears to be a product of professionalism in legislatures and bureaucracies, and an educated and politically active population.

BIBLIOGRAPHY

DYE, THOMAS R., *Who's Running America: The Conservative Years.* Englewood Cliffs, N.J.: Prentice-Hall, 1986.

EDELMAN, MURRAY, *The Symbolic Uses of Politics.* Urbana: University of Illinois Press, 1964.

EYESTONE, ROBERT, *From Social Issues to Public Policy.* New York: John Wiley, 1978.

KEY, V. O., JR., *Public Opinion and American Democracy.* New York: Knopf, 1967.

LIPSET, SEYMOUR MARTIN, *Political Man.* New York: Doubleday, 1963.

SCHATTSCHNEIDER, E. E., *The Semisovereign People.* New York: Holt, Rinehart & Winston, 1960.

ZEIGLER, HARMON, *Interest Groups in American Society.* Englewood Cliffs, N. J.: Prentice-Hall, 1964.

POLICY EVALUATION

finding out what happens after a law is passed

Policy Evaluation: Does the government know what it is doing? (Mary Anne Fackelman, The White House)

DOES THE GOVERNMENT KNOW WHAT IT IS DOING?

Americans generally assume that once we pass a law, create a bureaucracy, and spend money, the purpose of the law, the bureaucracy, and the expenditure should be achieved. We assume that when Congress adopts a policy and appropriates money for it, and when the executive branch organizes a program, hires people, spends money, and carries out activities designed to implement the policy, the effects of the policy will be felt by society and will be those intended by the policy. Unfortunately, these assumptions are not always warranted. The national experiences with many public programs indicate the need for careful appraisal of the real impact of public policy. America's problems cannot always be resolved by passing a law, creating a new bureaucracy, and throwing a few billion dollars in the general direction of the problem in the hope that it will go away.

Does the government really know what it is doing? Generally speaking, no. Governments usually know how much money they spend, how many persons ("clients") are given various services, how much these services cost, how their programs are organized, managed, and operated, and perhaps how influential interest groups regard their programs and services. But even if programs and policies are well-organized, efficiently operated, widely utilized, adequately financed, and generally supported by major interest groups, we may still want to ask: "So what?"; "Do they work?"; "Do these programs have any beneficial effects on society?"; "Are the effects immediate or long-range? positive or negative?"; "What about persons *not* receiving these services?"; "What is the relationship between the costs of the program and the benefits to society?"; "Could we be doing something else with more benefit to society with the money and manpower devoted to these programs?" Unfortunately, governments have done very little to answer these more basic questions.

A candid report on federal evaluation effort is worth quoting at length:

> The most impressive finding about the evaluation of social programs in the federal government is that substantial work in this field has been almost nonexistent.
>
> Few significant studies have been undertaken. Most of those carried out have been poorly conceived. Many small studies around the country have been carried out with such lack of uniformity of design and objective that the results rarely are comparable or responsive to the questions facing policy makers.
>
> There is nothing akin to a comprehensive federal evaluation system. Even within agencies, orderly and integrated evaluation operations have not been established. Funding has been low. Staffing has been worse, forcing undue reliance on outside contractors by agencies that lack the in-house capacity to monitor contract work. The most clear-cut evidence of the primitive state of federal self-evaluation lies in the widespread failure of agencies even to spell out program objectives. Unless goals are precisely stated, there is no standard against which to measure whether the direction of a program or its rate of progress is satisfactory.

The impact of activities that cost the public millions, sometimes billions, of dollars has not been measured. One cannot point with confidence to the difference, if any, that most social programs cause in the lives of Americans.[1]

This is a damning appraisal. It is just as true today as it was many years ago. The government does not know how to tell whether or not most of the things it does are worth doing at all.

POLICY EVALUATION: ASSESSING THE IMPACT OF PUBLIC POLICY

Policy evaluation is learning about the consequences of public policy. Other more complex, definitions have been offered: "Policy evaluation is the assessment of the overall effectiveness of a national program in meeting its objectives, or assessment of the relative effectiveness of two or more programs in meeting common objectives."[2] "We should reserve the name 'program evaluation' for when we are referring to a comprehensive evaluation of the entire system under consideration, and call it 'problem or procedure evaluation' when we refer to some segment within that system."[3] "Policy evaluation research is the objective, systematic, empirical examination of the effects ongoing policies and public programs have on their targets in terms of the goals they are meant to achieve."[4]

Note that some of these definitions tie evaluation to the stated "goals" of a program or policy. But since we do not always know what the "goals" of a program or policy really are, and because we know that some programs and policies pursue conflicting "goals," we will not limit our notion of policy evaluation to the achievement of goals. Instead, we will concern ourselves with the *all* of the consequences of public policy, that is, with "policy impact."

The impact of a policy is all its *effects on real-world conditions*. The impact of a policy includes:

1. Its impact on the target situation or group
2. Its impact on situations or groups other than the target ("spillover effects")
3. Its impact on future as well as immediate conditions
4. Its direct costs, in terms of resources devoted to the program
5. Its indirect costs, including loss of opportunities to do other things.

[1] Joseph S. Wholey et al., *Federal Evaluation Policy* (Washington, D.C.: Urban Institute, 1970), p. 15.
[2] Ibid., p. 25.
[3] Paul R. Binner, cited in Jack L. Franklin and Jean H. Thrasser, *An Introduction to Program Evaluation* (New York: John Wiley, 1976), p. 22.
[4] David Nachmias, *Public Policy Evaluation* (New York: St. Martin's Press, 1979), p. 4.

All the benefits and costs, both immediate and future, must be measured in terms of both *symbolic* and *tangible* effects.

Identifying the *target groups* means defining the part of the population for whom the program is intended—e.g., the poor, the sick, the ill-housed. Then the desired effect of the program on the target group must be determined. Is it to change their physical or economic circumstances—for example, the percentage of blacks or women employed in professional or managerial jobs, the income of the poor, the housing conditions of ghetto residents? Or is it to change their knowledge, attitudes, awareness, interests, or behavior? If multiple effects are intended, what are the priorities among different effects—for example, is a high payoff in terms of positive attitudes toward the political system more valuable than tangible progress toward the elimination of black-white income differences? What are the possible unintended effects (side effects) on target groups—for example, does public housing achieve better physical environments for many urban blacks at the cost of increasing their segregation and alienation from the white community? What is the impact of a policy on the target group in proportion to that group's total need? Accurate data describing the unmet needs of the nation are not generally available, but it is important to estimate the denominator of total need so that we know how adequate our programs are. Moreover, such an estimate may also help in estimating symbolic benefits or costs; a program that promises to meet a national need but actually meets only a small proportion of it may generate great praise at first but bitterness and frustration later when it becomes known how small its impact is relative to the need.

"Policy impact" is not the same as "policy output." In assessing policy impact, we cannot be content simply to measure government activity. For example, the number of dollars spent per member of a target group (per pupil educational expenditures, per capita welfare expenditures, per capita health expenditures) is not really a measure of the *impact* of a policy on the group. It is merely a measure of government activity—that is to say, a measure of *policy output*. We cannot be satisfied with measuring how many times a bird flaps its wings, we must know how far the bird has flown. In *describing* public policy, or even in *explaining* its determinants, measures of policy output are important. But in assessing the *impact* of policy, we must find changes in the environment that are associated with measures of government activity.

All programs and policies have differential effects on various segments of the population. Identifying important *nontarget groups* for a policy is a difficult process. For example, what is the impact of the welfare reform on groups other than the poor—government bureaucrats, social workers, local political figures, working-class families who are not on welfare, taxpayers, others? Nontarget effects may be expressed as benefits as well as costs, such as the benefits to the construction industry of public housing projects. And these effects may be symbolic as well as tangible—for example, wealthy liberals enjoy a good feeling from supporting antipoverty programs, whether the programs help the poor or not.

When will the benefits or costs be felt? Is the program designed for short-term, emergency situations? Or is it a long-term, developmental effort? If it is short-term, what will prevent the processes of incrementalism and bureaucratization from turning it into a long-term program, even after immediate need is met? Many impact studies show that new or innovative programs have short-term positive effects—for example, Operation Head Start and other educational programs. However, the positive effects frequently disappear as the novelty and enthusiasm of new programs wear off. Other programs experience difficulties at first, as in the early days of social security and Medicare, but turn out to have "sleeper" effects, as in the widespread acceptance of social security today. Not all programs aim at the same degree of permanent or transient change.

Programs are frequently measured in terms of their direct costs. We generally know how many dollars go into program areas, and we can even calculate (as in Chapter 9) the proportion of total governmental dollars devoted to various programs. Government agencies have developed various forms of cost-benefit analysis, such as Program, Planning, and Budgeting Systems (PPBS) and operations research, to identify the direct costs (usually, but not always, in dollars) of government programs.

But is is very difficult to identify the indirect and symbolic costs of public programs. Rarely can all these cost factors be included in a formal decision-making model. Often political intuition is the best guide available to the policy maker in these matters. What are the symbolic costs for the working poor of large numbers of welfare recipients? What were the costs of the Vietnam War in terms of American morale and internal division and strife?

Moreover, it is very difficult to measure benefits in terms of general social well-being. Cost accounting techniques developed in business were designed around units of production—automobiles, airplanes, tons of steel, etc. But how do we identify and measure units of social well-being? In recent years, some social scientists have begun the effort to develop "social indicators"—measures of social well-being of American society.[5] But we are still a long way from assessing the impact of public policy on general social indicators or rationally evaluating alternative public policies by weighing their costs against gains in social indicators.

All these aspects of public policy are very difficult to identify, describe, and measure. Moreover, the task of calculating *net* impact of a public policy

---

[5]See U.S. Department of Health, Education and Welfare, *Toward A Social Report* (Washington, D.C.: Government Printing Office, 1969); and Bertram M. Gross, ed., *Social Intelligence for America's Future* (Boston: Allyn & Bacon, 1969).

TABLE 14-1   Assessing Policy Impact

	BENEFITS			COSTS	
	PRESENT	FUTURE		PRESENT	FUTURE
Target Groups and Situations	Symbolic Tangible	Symbolic Tangible		Symbolic Tangible	Symbolic Tangible
Nontarget Groups and Situations (Spillover)	Symbolic Tangible	Symbolic Tangible		Symbolic Tangible	Symbolic Tangible
	Sum Present Benefits	Sum Future Benefits		Sum Present Costs	Sum Future Costs
	Sum All Benefits		minus	Sum All Costs	
		Net Policy Impact			

is truly awesome. The *net* impact would be all the symbolic and tangible benefits, both immediate and long range, minus all the symbolic and tangible costs, both immediate and future (see Table 14-1). Even if all the immediate and future and symbolic and tangible costs and benefits are *known* (and everyone *agrees* on what is a "benefit" and what is a "cost"), it is still very difficult to come up with a net balance. Many of the items on both sides of the balance would defy comparison—for example, how do you subtract a tangible cost in terms of dollars from a symbolic reward in terms of the sense of well-being felt by individuals or groups?

THE SYMBOLIC IMPACT OF POLICY

The impact of a policy includes both its *symbolic* and *tangible* effects. Its symbolic impact deals with the perceptions that individuals have of government action and their attitudes toward it. Even if government policies do not succeed in reducing dependency, or eliminating poverty, or preventing crime, and so on, this may be a rather minor objection to them if the failure of government to *try* to do these things would lead to the view that society is "not worth saving." Individuals, groups, and whole societies frequently judge public policy in terms of its good intentions rather than its tangible accomplishments. The general popularity and public appraisal of a program may be unrelated to the real impact of a program in terms of desired results. The implication is that very popular programs may have little positive impact, and vice versa.

The policies of government may tell us more about the aspirations of a society and its leadership than about actual conditions. Policies do more than effect change in societal conditions; they also help hold people together and maintain an orderly state. For example, a government "war on poverty" may not have any significant impact on the poor, but it reassures moral persons, the affluent as well as the poor, that government "cares" about poverty. Whatever the failures of the antipoverty programs in tangible respects, their symbolic value may be more than redeeming. For example, whether the fair housing provisions of the Civil Rights Act of 1968 can be enforced or not, the fact that it is national policy to forbid discrimination in the sale or rental of housing reassures people of all races that their government does not condone such acts. There are many more examples of public policy serving as a symbol of what society aspires to be.

The subjective condition of the nation is clearly as important as the objective condition. For example, white prejudices about blacks in schools, in public accommodations, or in housing may be declining over time. But this may not reduce racial tension if blacks *believe* that racism is as prevalent as it ever was.

Once upon a time "politics" was described as "who gets what, when, and how." Today it seems that politics centers about "who *feels* what, when, and how." The smoke-filled room where patronage and pork were dispensed has been replaced with the talk-filled room where rhetoric and image are dispensed. What governments *say* is as important as what governments *do.* Television has made the image of public policy as important as the policy itself. Systematic policy analysis concentrates on what governments *do,* why they do it, and what difference it makes. It devotes less attention to what governments *say.* Perhaps that is a weakness in policy analysis. Our focus has been primarily upon activities of governments rather than the rhetoric of governments.

PROGRAM EVALUATION: WHAT GOVERNMENTS USUALLY DO

Most government agencies make some effort to review the effectiveness of their own programs. These reviews usually take one or another of the following forms:

Hearings and Discussions

This is the most common type of program review. Government administrators are asked by chief executives or legislators to give testimony (formally or informally) regarding the accomplishments of their own programs. Frequently, written "annual reports" are provided by program administrators. But testimonials and reports of administrators are not very objective means of program evaluation. They frequently magnify the benefits and minimize the costs of programs.

Site Visits

Occasionally teams of high-ranking administrators, or expert consultants, or legislators, or some combination of these people, will decide to visit agencies or conduct inspections in the field. These teams can pick up impressionistic data about how programs are being run, whether programs are following specific guidelines, whether they have competent staffs, and sometimes whether or not the "clients" (target groups) are pleased with the services.

Program Measures

The data developed by government agencies themselves generally cover policy *output* measures: The number of recipients in various welfare programs; the number of persons in manpower training programs; the number of public hospital beds available; the tons of garbage collected; or the number of pupils enrolled. But these program measures rarely indicate what *impact* these numbers have on society: the conditions of life confronting the poor; the success of manpower trainees in finding and holding skilled jobs; the health of the nation's poor; the cleanliness of cities; and the ability of graduates to read and write and function in society.

Comparison with Professional Standards

In some areas of government activity, professional associations have developed standards of excellence. These standards are usually expressed as a desirable level of output: For example, the number of pupils per teacher, the number of hospital beds per 1,000 people, the number of cases for each welfare worker. Actual governmental outputs can be compared with "ideal" outputs. While such an exercise can be helpful, it still focuses on government outputs and not the *impact* of governmental activities on the conditions of target or nontarget groups. Moreover, the standards themselves are usually developed by professionals who are really guessing at what ideal levels of benefits and services should be. There is rarely any hard evidence that ideal levels of governmental output have any significant impact on society.

Evaluation of Citizen Complaints

Another common approach to program evaluation is the analysis of citizen complaints. But not all citizens voluntarily submit complaints or remarks regarding governmental programs. Critics of governmental programs are self-selected and they are rarely representative of the general public or even of the target groups of government programs. There is no way to judge whether the complaints of a vocal few are shared by the many more who have not spoken up. Occasionally, administrators develop questionnaires to give to participants in their program in order to learn what their complaints may be and whether they are satisfied or not. But these questionnaires really test *public opinion* toward the program and not its real impact on the lives of participants.

PROGRAM EVALUATION: WHAT GOVERNMENTS CAN DO

None of the common evaluative methods mentioned above really attempts to weigh *costs* against *benefits*. Indeed, administrators seldom calculate the ratio of costs to services—the dollars required to train one worker, to provide one hospital bed, to collect and dispose of one ton of garbage. It is even more difficult to calculate the costs of making specific changes in society—the dollars required to raise student reading levels by one grade, to lower the infant death rate by one point, to reduce the crime rate by one percent. To learn about the real *impact* of governmental programs on society, more complex and costly methods of program evaluation are required.

Systematic program evaluation involves *comparisons*—comparisons designed to estimate what changes in society can be attributed to the program rather than nonprogram factors. Ideally, this means comparing what "actually happened" to "what would have happened if the program had never been implemented." It is not difficult to measure what happened; unfortunately too much program evaluation stops here. The real problem is to measure what would have happened without a program, and then compare the two conditions of society. The difference must be attributable to the program itself and not to other changes which are occurring in society at the same time.

Before versus After Comparisons

There are several common research designs in program evaluation.[6] The most common is the "before-and-after" study which compares results in a jurisdiction at two points in time—one before the program was implemented and the other some time after implementation. Usually it is only target groups that are examined. These before and after comparisons are

---

[6]The following discussion relies upon Harry P. Hatry, Richard E. Winnie, and Donald M. Fisk, *Practical Program Evaluation* (Washington, D.C.: Urban Institute, 1973).

Design 1
Before vs. After

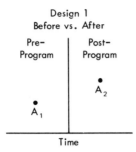

Pre-
Program

Post-
Program

• A_2

•
A_1

Time

■ $A_2 - A_1$ = Estimated Program Effect.

Design 2
Projected vs. Post-Program

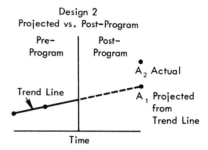

Pre-
Program

Post-
Program

•
A_2 Actual

Trend Line A_1 Projected from Trend Line

Time

■ $A_2 - A_1$ = Estimated Program Effect.

Design 3
With vs. Without Program

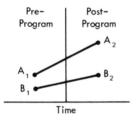

Pre-
Program

Post-
Program

A_2

A_1 •

B_1 •

• B_2

Time

■ A has Program; B does not.
■ $(A_2 - A_1) - (B_2 - B_1)$ = Estimated Program Effect.
■ Or difference between A and B in rate of change equals Estimated Program Effect.

Design 4
The Classic Research Design:
Control vs. Experimental Groups

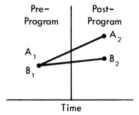

Pre-
Program

Post-
Program

• A_2

A_1

B_1

• B_2

Time

■ A has Program; B does not.
■ A and B identical in pre-program period.
■ $A_2 - B_2$ = Estimated Program Effect.

FIGURE 14-1   Policy evaluation research designs.

designed to show program impacts, but it is very difficult to know whether the changes observed, if any, came about as a result of the program or as a result of other changes which were occurring in society at the same time (see Design 1, Figure 14-1).

Projected-Trend-Line versus Postprogram Comparisons

A better estimate of what would have happened without the program can be made by projecting past (preprogram) trends into the postprogram time period. Then these projections can be compared with what actually happened in society after the program was implemented. The difference between the projections based on preprogram trends and the actual post-program data can be attributed to the program itself. Note that data on target groups or conditions must be obtained for several time periods before the program was initiated, so that a trend line can be established (see Design 2, Figure 14-1). This design is better than the before-and-after design, but it requires more effort on the part of program evaluators.

Comparisons Between Jurisdictions With and Without Programs

Another common program evaluation design is to compare individuals who have participated in programs with those who have not; or to compare cities, states, or nations which have programs with those which do not. Comparisons are sometimes made in the postprogram period only; for example, comparisons of the job records of those who have participated in manpower training programs with those who have not, or comparisons of homicide rates in states which have the death penalty with the homicide rates in states without the death penalty. But there are so many other differences between individuals or jurisdictions, that it is difficult to attribute differences in their conditions to differences in government programs. For example, persons who voluntarily enter a manpower training program may have greater motivation to find a job or different personal characteristics from those who do not. States with the death penalty may tend to be rural states which have lower homicide rates than urban states regardless of whether they have the death penalty or not.

Some of the problems involved in comparing jurisdictions with and without programs can be resolved if we observe both kinds of jurisdictions before and after the introduction of the program. This enables us to estimate differences between jurisdictions before program efforts are considered. After the program is initiated, we can observe whether the differences between jurisdictions have widened or not (see Design 3, Figure 14-1). This design provides some protection against attributing differences to a particular program when underlying socioeconomic differences between jurisdictions are really responsible for different outcomes.

Comparisons Between Control and Experimental Groups Before and After Program Implementation

The "classic" research design involves the careful selection of control and experimental groups which are identical in every way, the application of the policy to the experimental group only, and the comparison of changes in the experimental group with changes in the control group after the application of the policy. Initially, control and experimental groups must be identical, and the preprogram performance of each group must be measured and found to be the same. The program must be applied only to the experimental group. The postprogram differences between the experimental and control groups must be carefully measured (see Design 4, Figure 14-1). This classic research design is preferred by scientists because it provides the best opportunity of estimating changes which can be from the effects of other forces affecting society.

TIME-SERIES POLICY RESEARCH: GUN CONTROL

One interesting example of a "classic" before-and-after policy evaluation, with both experimental and control groups, was a study of the impact of handgun controls in New York and Boston. For many years these two large cities had the most restrictive handgun licensing laws in the United States. Despite these laws, handgun-related deaths in these cities were very high. "Experts" decided that this fact reflected the ease with which handguns could be brought into these cities from other areas with less restrictive laws. The policy solution, they said, was to limit the interstate transportation of handguns into states which restricted their sale. So, in the federal Gun Control Act of 1968, interstate traffic in firearms and ammunition to states which restricted or prohibited ownership of guns was prohibited by federal law.

Time series trends in handgun homicides are shown for New York and Boston (the experimental cities) and an average for fifty-seven other large cities (the control cities) both before and after the 1969 federal legislation (see Figure 14-2). Note that handgun homocides grew in *all* cities both before and after federal legislation. But handgun homicides grew faster in New York and Boston, the cities with restrictive laws, than the average of the fifty-seven control cities. These increases in handgun violence in the particular cities with the most restrictive legislation clearly indicate that neither local nor federal laws were working. If anything, the Gun Control Act of 1968 was having just the opposite effect intended. Based on these and other measures, the author of the study was forced to conclude:

> the data suggest that the Gun Control Act of 1968 did not result in a palpable disruption of interstate handgun traffic.[7]

PROGRAM EVALUATION: WHY IT FAILS

Occasionally governments attempt their own policy evaluations. Government analysts and administrators report on the conditions of target groups before and after their participation in a new program and some effort is

[7]Franklin E. Zimring, "Firearms and Federal Law," *Journal of Legal Studies*, 4 (January 1975), 133–98; also cited by Nachmias, *Public Policy Evaluation*.

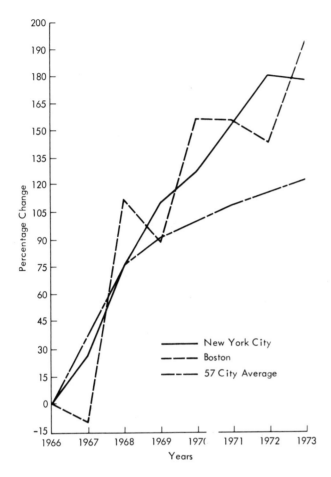

FIGURE 14-2 Trends in handgun homicides, New York, Boston, and other cities. (Source: Franklin E. Zimring, "Firearms and Federal Law: The Gun Control Act of 1968," *Journal of Legal Studies,* 4, January 1975, 177. Copyright 1975 The University of Chicago Press.) By permission of The University of Chicago.

made to attribute observed changes to the new program itself. Policy experimentation is less frequent; seldom do governments systematically select experimental and control groups of the population, introduce a new program to the experimental group only, and then carefully compare changes in the conditions of the experimental group with a control group that has not benefited from the program. Let us turn first to some of the problems confronting policy evaluation studies; later we will describe policy experimentation.[8]

[8]For an excellent discussion of policy evaluation, see Edward A. Suchman, *Evaluative Research* (New York: Russell Sage Foundation, 1967).

1. The first problem confronting anyone who wants to evaluate a public program is to determine what the goals of the program are. What are the target groups and what are the desired effects? But governments often pursue imcompatible goals to satisfy very diverse groups. Overall policy planning and evaluation may reveal inconsistencies of public policy and force reconsideration of fundamental societal goals. Where there is little agreement on the goals of a public program, evaluation studies may engender a great deal of political conflict. Government agencies generally prefer to avoid conflict, and hence to avoid studies that would raise such questions.

2. Many programs and policies have primarily symbolic value. They do not actually change the conditions of target groups but merely make these groups feel that government "cares." A government agency does not welcome a study that reveals that its efforts have no tangible effects; such a revelation itself might reduce the symbolic value of the program by informing target groups of its uselessness.

3. Government agencies have a strong vested interest in "proving" that their programs have a positive impact. Administrators frequently view attempts to evaluate the impact of their programs as attempts to limit or destroy their programs, or to question the competence of the administrators.

4. Government agencies usually have a heavy investment—organizational, financial, physical, psychological—in current programs and policies. They are predisposed against finding that these policies do not work.

5. Any serious study of policy impact undertaken by a government agency would involve some interference with ongoing program activities. The press of day-to-day business generally takes priority over study and evaluation in a governmental agency. More importantly, the conduct of an experiment may necessitate depriving individuals or groups (control groups) of services to which they are entitled under law; this may be difficult, if not impossible, to do.

6. Program evaluation requires funds, facilities, time, and personnel which government agencies do not like to sacrifice from ongoing programs. Policy impact studies, like any research, cost money. They cannot be done well as extracurricular or part-time activities. Devoting resources to study may mean a sacrifice in program resources that administrators are unwilling to make.

Government administrators and program supporters are ingenious in devising reasons why negative findings about policy impact should be rejected. Even in the face of clear evidence that their favorite programs are useless or even counterproductive, they will argue that:

1. The effects of the program are long range and cannot be measured at the present time.

2. The effects of the program are diffuse and general in nature; no single criterion or index adequately measures what is being accomplished.

3. The effects of the program are subtle and cannot be identified by crude measures or statistics.

4. Experimental research cannot be carried out effectively because to withhold services from some persons to observe the impact of such withholding would be unfair to them.

5. The fact that no difference was found between persons receiving the services and those not receiving them means that the program is not sufficiently intensive and indicates the need to spend *more* resources on the program.

6. The failure to identify any positive effects of a program is attributable to inadequacy or bias in the research itself, not in the program.

Harvard professor James Q. Wilson formulated two general laws to cover all cases of social science research on policy impact:

Wilson's First Law: All policy interventions in social problems produce the intended effect—if the research is carried out by those implementing the policy or their friends.

Wilson's Second Law: No policy intervention in social problems produces the intended effect—if the research is carried out by independent third parties, especially those skeptical of the policy.

Wilson denies that his laws are cynical. Instead he reasons that

> Studies that conform to the First Law will accept an agency's own data about what it is doing and with what effect; adopt a time frame (long or short) that maximizes the probability of observing the desired effect; and minimize the search for other variables that might account for the effect observed. Studies that conform to the Second Law will gather data independently of the agency; adopt a short time frame that either minimizes the chance for the desired effect to appear or, if it does appear, permits one to argue that the results are "temporary" and probably due to the operation of the "Hawthorne Effect" (i.e., the reaction of the subjects to the fact that they are part of an experiment); and maximize the search for other variables that might explain the effects observed.[9]

PPBS, SOCIAL INDICATORS, AND OTHER EVALUATIVE TOOLS

Despite these difficulties, however, there has been substantial progress in recent years in policy evaluation research. Increasingly, decision makers are turning to analysts to ask questions about the effectiveness of ongoing and proposed programs: What is it doing? Why do we need it? What does it cost? They do not always get good answers yet, but the need for systematic policy research is now recognized.

For example, variations of PPBS—Planning, Programming, Budgeting Systems—have been widely adopted by government agencies in recent

[9]James Q. Wilson, "On Pettigrew and Armor," *The Public Interest,* 31 (Spring 1973), 132–34.

years. Despite an elaborate terminology, PPBS is merely an attempt to rationalize decision making in a bureaucracy. It is part of the budgetary process—but the focus is on the *uses* of expenditures and the *output* provided for rather than on dollar amounts allocated by agency or department. The aim of PPBS is to specify, and hopefully to quantify, the output of a government program, and then to measure the cost of achieving this output and to learn whether benefits exceed the cost. The first step in PPBS is to define program objectives. The next, and perhaps critical step, is to develop indices or measures of the level of accomplishment under each program— the "output." Then the costs of the program can be calculated *per unit of output.* Presumably this enables the decision maker to view the real cost-benefit ratio of a program (e.g., how much it costs to teach one pupil to read, or train one worker in a manpower program, or keep one child in a daycare center, etc.). This also provides a basis for more elaborate comparisons of the costs and benefits of alternative programs or to analyze the "cost effectiveness" of alternative programs (to see which achieves a given goal at least cost).

However, it is difficult to establish prices for certain social outcomes, which are not usually sold and therefore have no price. How can we establish the value of finding a cure for cancer? How can we compare the value of finding a cure for cancer with the value of teaching poor children to read and write? A strict cost-benefit comparison would require that we add up the costs and benefits of each and choose the program with the higher excess of benefits over costs. But the benefits of certain programs may be of inestimable value. How do we set values on freedom from fear, good health, the pleasures of clean air, the joys of outdoor recreation, and so forth?

Moreover, different programs benefit different people. Public funds for higher education benefit middle-class groups more than public funds for literacy training. How do we calculate the benefits of college education for some groups in relation to the benefits of literacy training for other groups, even if costs were the same?

Finally, decision makers are constrained by the political process. They and their constituents have intuitive notions about the relative benefits of health, education, housing, or welfare programs, which are not likely to be changed by cost-benefit estimates.

A number of social scientists have advocated the development of a set of indicators to show social progress (or retrogression). They have urged the preparation of an annual "social report" similar to the President's Economic Report but designed to assess the social condition of the nation. Most Americans can agree on the values of a healthy, well-educated, adequately housed, and affluent population, even if they cannot agree on public policies designed to achieve these values. Perhaps a general assessment of the nation's progress toward these goals would be helpful in an overall evaluation of the effectiveness of public policy. At least that is the idea behind this "social indicator" movement. "Social indicators" are defined simply as quantitative data that serve as indices to socially important conditions of a society.

Presumably a set of social indicators and a social report would accomplish two things: First, it would focus attention on certain social conditions and thus make possible more informed judgments about national priorities, and second, by showing how different measures of social well-being change over time, it might help evaluate the success of public programs. In exploring the feasibility of social reporting, a team of social scientists working for the Department of Health, Education and Welfare suggested the development of a variety of measures similar to those shown in Table 14-2. Some of these social measures deal with health, education, and welfare; others with social trends such as women in the labor force, voter turnout, and vacations and leisure time.

TABLE 14-2 Suggested Social Indicators

INDICATOR
1. Infant Mortality (per 1,000 live births)
2. Maternal Mortality (per 100,000 live births)
3. Family Planning Services (for Low-Income Women 15–44)
4. Deaths from Accident (per 100,000 population)
5. Number of Persons in State Mental Hospitals
6. Expectancy of Healthy Life
7. Three- to five-year-olds in School or Preschool
8. Persons 25 and Older Who Graduate from High School
9. Persons 25 and Older Who Graduate from College
10. Persons in Learning Force
11. Percent of Major Cities with Public Community Colleges
12. Number of First-year Students in Medical Schools
13. Handicapped Persons Rehabilitated
14. Average Weekly Hours of Work—Manufacturing
15. Labor Force Participation Rate for Women Aged 35–64
16. Average Annual Paid Vacation—Manufacturing
17. Housing Units with Bathtub or Shower
18. Percent of Population Illiterate
19. Voters as a Percentage of Voting Age Population
20. Private Philanthropy as a Percent of GNP
21. Public and Private Expenditures for Health, Education and Welfare as a Percent of GNP
22. Percent of Population in Poverty
23. Income of Lowest Fifth of Population
24. Persons Who Work during the Year
25. Life Expectancy

Source: U.S. Department of Health, Education and Welfare, *Toward a Social Report* (Ann Arbor: University of Michigan Press, 1970).

But the task of choosing social indicators raises many *political* questions.[10] First of all, the choice of a particular indicator suggests a societal goal. Most people agree on the value of a longer life span and lower infant mortality rates. But should everyone graduate from college? Should every community have a community college? Should a large female labor force be a national goal? Should the government provide free family planning services to low-income families? And how do we set priorities among these goals?

There is a hidden political bias in the social indicators movement itself—a bias on behalf of liberal reform and social welfare. Proponents of social indicators and a Social Report are generally committed to long-range government planning, bettering the lot of the poor and of minorities, and using government power to ensure social welfare. Conservatives have reason to be suspicious of a movement which assumes that government can select society's goals and monitor progress toward these goals. Moreover, there is the assumption behind the social indicators idea that social measures can and should be effected by government policies. Government monitoring of social indicators *implies* government responsibility for social conditions. Finally, there is a concern that social accounting will lead to a totalitarian society in which every aspect of life is monitored and controlled by government. Even a supporter of social reporting writes:

> Any kind of Social Report would, in the eyes of many, entail a danger: it could involve government in making the kinds of judgments of value that, in our political order, are the prerogatives of the individual citizen or of the organizations of which he is a voluntary member. This danger is not imaginary. If—perhaps one should say when—we do have a Social Report, it will be necessary to subject it to rigorous and skeptical criticism.[11]

There is also an implicit political elitism in the notion of social indicatiors—the view that social scientists are the best judges of what is "good" for the people. In a democratic society, demands for public programs are supposed to originate in the political process from the felt needs of the people. But social accounting implies that social scientists will become "philosopher-kings" deciding what "problems" confront society and what are the "best" solutions for them.

---

[10]For an excellent discussion of the political implications of social measurement, see Peter J. Henriot's "Political Questions About Social Indicators," *Western Political Quarterly,* 23 (June 1970), 235–55.

[11]Irving Kristol, "Social Indicators, Reports and Accounts," *The Annals* (March 1970), 11.

EXPERIMENTAL POLICY RESEARCH:
THE GUARANTEED INCOME EXPERIMENT

Many policy analysts argue that "policy experimentation" offers the best opportunity to determine the impact of public policies. This opportunity rests upon the main characteristcs of experimental research: the systematic selection of experimental and control groups, the application of the policy under study to the experimental group only, and the careful comparison of differences between the experimental and the control groups after the application of the policy.

An interesting example of an attempt by the federal government to experiment with public policy was the New Jersey Graduated Work Incentive Experiment. The experiment was designed to resolve some serious questions about the impact of welfare payments on the incentives for poor people to work.[12] In order to learn more about the effects of the present welfare system on human behavior, and more importantly, to learn more about the possible effects of proposed programs for guaranteed family incomes, the federal Office of Economic Opportunity funded a three-year social experiment involving 1,350 families in New Jersey and Pennsylvania. The research was conducted by the Institute for Research on Poverty of the University of Wisconsin.

Debates over welfare reform had generated certain questions which social science presumably could answer with careful, controlled experimentation. Would a guaranteed family income reduce the incentive to work? If payments were made to poor families with employable male heads, would the men drop out of the labor force? Would the level of the income guarantee or the steepness of the reductions of payments with increases in earnings make any difference in working behavior? Because welfare programs did not provide a guaranteed minimum family income, or make payments to families with employable males, or graduate payments in relation to earnings, these questions could only be answered through *policy experimentation*. But policy experimentation raised some serious initial problems for OEO. First of all, any experiment involving substantial payments to a fair sampling of families would be expensive. For example, if payments averaged $1,000 per year per family, and if each family had to be observed for three years, and if 1,000 families were to be involved, a minimum of $3 million would be spent even *before* any consideration of the costs of administration, data collection, analysis and study, and reporting. Ideally a *national* sample should have been used, but it would have been more

---

[12]See Harold M. Watts, "Graduated Work Incentives: An Experiment in Negative Taxation," *American Economic Review*, 59 (May 1969), 463–72.

expensive to monitor than a local sample, and differing employment conditions in different parts of the country would have made it difficult to sort out the effects of income payments from variations in local job availability. By concentrating the sample in one region, it was hoped that local conditions would be held constant. Ideally *all* types of low-income families should have been tested, but that would have necessitated a larger sample and greater expense. So only poor families with an able-bodied man age 18 to 58 were selected; the work behavior of these men in the face of a guaranteed income was of special interest.

To ascertain the effects of different levels of guaranteed income, four guarantee levels were established. Some families were chosen to receive 50 percent of the Social Security Administration's poverty level income, others 75 percent, others 100 percent, and still others 125 percent. In order to ascertain the effects of graduated payments in relation to earnings, some families had their payments reduced by 30 percent of their outside earnings, others 50 percent, and still others 70 percent. Finally, a control sample was observed—low-income families who received no payments at all.

The experiment was begun in August 1968 and continued until September 1972. But political events moved swiftly and soon engulfed the study. In 1969 President Nixon proposed the Family Assistance Plan (FAP) to Congress, which promised all families a minimum income of 50 percent of the poverty level and a payment reduction of 50 percent of outside earnings. The Nixon administration had not waited to learn the results of the OEO experiment before introducing FAP. Nixon wanted welfare reform to be his priority domestic legislation and the bill was symbolically numbered HR 1 (House of Representatives Bill 1).

After the FAP bill had been introduced, the Nixon administration pressured OEO to produce favorable supporting evidence on behalf of the guaranteed income—specifically, evidence that a guaranteed income at the levels proposed in FAP would *not* reduce incentives to work among the poor. The OEO obliged by hastily publishing a short report, "Preliminary Results of the New Jersey Graduated Work Incentive Experiment," which purported to show that there were no differences in the outside earnings of families receiving guaranteed incomes (experimental group) and those who were not (control group).[13]

The director of the research, economics professor Harold Watts of the University of Wisconsin, warned that "the evidence from this preliminary and crude analysis of the earliest results is less than ideal." But he concluded that "no evidence has been found in the urban experiment to support the belief that negative-tax type income maintenance programs

---

[13]U.S. Office of Economic Opportunity, "Preliminary Results of the New Jersey Graduated Work Incentive Experiment," February 18, 1970. Also cited in Alice M. Rivlin, *Systematic Thinking for Social Action* (Washington, D.C.: Brookings Institution, 1971).

will produce large disincentives and consequent reductions in earnings." Moreover, the early results indicated that families in all the separate experimental groups, with different guaranteed minimums and different graduated payment schedules, behaved in a fashion similar to each other and to the control group receiving no payments at all. Predictably, later results confirmed the preliminary results, which were produced to assist the FAP bill in Congress.[14]

However, when the results of the Graduated Work Incentive Experiment later were *reanalyzed* by the Rand Corporation (which was not responsible for the design of the original study), markedly different results were produced.[15] The Rand Corporation reports that the Wisconsin researchers working for OEO originally chose New Jersey because it had no state welfare programs for "intact" families—families headed by an able-bodied, working-age male. The guaranteed incomes were offered to these families to compare their work behavior with control group families. *But* six months after the experiment began, New Jersey changed its state law and offered *all* families (experimental *and* control group families) very generous welfare benefits—benefits equal to those offered participants in the experiment. This meant that for most of the period of the experiment, the "control" group was being given benefits which were equivalent to the "experimental" groups—an obvious violation of the experimental research design. The OEO-funded University of Wisconsin researchers failed to consider this factor in their research. Thus, they concluded that there were no significant differences between the work behaviors of experimental and control groups, and they implied that a national guaranteed income would not be a disincentive to work. The Rand Corporation researchers, on the other hand, considered the New Jersey state welfare program in their estimates of work behavior. Rand concluded that recipients of a guaranteed annual income will work 6.5 fewer hours per week than they otherwise would work in the absence of such a program. In short, the Rand study suggests that a guaranteed annual income will produce a very substantial disincentive to work.

The Rand study was published in 1978 after enthusiasm in Washington for a guaranteed annual income program had already cooled. The Rand study conflicted with the earlier OEO study and confirmed the intuition of many members of Congress that guaranteed annual income would reduce willingness to work. The Rand study also suggested that a *national* program might be very costly and involve some payments to nearly half the nation's families. Finally, the Rand study noted that its own estimates

[14]*Final Report of the New Jersey Graduated Work Incentive Experiment*, David Kershaw and Jerelyn Fair, eds. (University of Wisconsin, Institute for Research on Poverty, 1974).

[15]John F. Cogan, *Negative Income Taxation and Labor Supply: New Evidence from the New Jersey-Pennsylvania Experiment* (Santa Monica, Calif.: Rand Corporation, 1978).

of high costs and work disincentives may "seriously understate the expected cost of an economywide . . . program."

PROBLEMS IN POLICY EXPERIMENTATION

The whole excursion into government-sponsored policy experimention raises a series of important questions.[16] First of all, are government-sponsored research projects predisposed to produce results supportive of popular reform proposals? Are social scientists, whose personal political values are generally liberal and reformist, inclined to produce findings in support of liberal reform measures? Would the OEO have rushed to produce "preliminary findings" in the New Jersey experiment *if* they had shown that the guarantees did in fact reduce the incentive to work? Or would such early results be set aside as "too preliminary" to publish? Because the participants in the experiment knew that they were singled out for experimentation, did they behave differently than they would have if the program had been applied universally? Would the work ethic be impaired if *all* American families were guaranteed a minimum income for life rather than a few selected families for a temporary period of time? Thus, the questions raised by this experiment affect not only the issues of welfare policy but also the validity of policy experimentation itself.

Experimental strategies in policy impact research raise still other problems. Do government researchers have the right to withhold public services from individuals simply to provide a control group for experimentation? In the medical area, where the giving or withholding of treatment can result in death or injury, the problem is obvious and many attempts have been made to formulate a code of ethics. But in the area of social experimentation, what are we to say to control groups who are chosen to be similar to experimental groups but denied benefits in order to serve as a base for comparison? Setting aside the legal and moral issues, it will be politically difficult to provide services for some people and not others. Perhaps only the fact that relatively few Americans knew about the New Jersey experiment kept it from becoming a controversial topic.

Another reservation about policy impact research centers on the bias of social scientists and their government sponsors. "Successful" experiments—where the proposed policy achieves positive results—will receive more acclaim and produce greater opportunities for advancement for social scientists and administrators than will "unsuccessful" experiments. Liberal, reform-oriented social scientists *expect* liberal reforms to produce positive

---

[16]For an excellent discussion of the problems and prospects of experimental policy research, see Frank P. Scioli and Thomas J. Cook, "Experimental Design in Policy Impact Analysis," *Social Science Quarterly*, 54 (September 1973), 271–91.

results. When reforms apear to do so, the research results are immediately accepted and published; but when results are unsupportive or negative, social scientists may be inclined to go back and recode their data, or redesign their research, or reevaluate their results because they believe a "mistake" must have been made. The temptation to "fudge the data," "reinterpret" the results, coach participants on what to say or do, and so forth, will be very great. In the physical and biological sciences the temptation to "cheat" in research is reduced by the fact that research can be replicated and the danger of being caught and disgraced is very great. But social experiments can seldom be replicated perfectly, and replication seldom brings the same distinction to a social scientist as does the original research.

People behave differently when they know they are being watched. Students, for example, generally perform at a higher level when something—anything—new and different is introduced into the classroom routine. This "Hawthorne effect"[17] may cause a new program or reform to appear more successful than the old, but it is the newness itself that produces improvement rather than the program or reform.

Another problem in policy impact research is that results obtained with small-scale experiments may differ substantially from what would occur if a large-scale nationwide program were adopted. For example, a guaranteed annual income for a small number of families in New Jersey and Pennsylvania—a guarantee that lasted only three years—may not trigger as much change in attitudes toward work as a *nationwide* program guaranteed to last *indefinitely*. In the New Jersey experiment, participants may have continued to behave as their neighbors did. But if everyone had been guaranteed a minimum income, community standards might have changed and affected the behavior of all recipient families.

Finally, we must acknowledge that the political milieu shapes policy research. Politics helps decide what policies and policy alternatives will be studied. Certainly the decision to study the effects of a guaranteed annual income arose from the interest of reformers in proving that such a program would not reduce incentives to work, as charged by some opponents. Politics can also affect findings themselves, and certainly the interpretations and uses of policy research are politically motivated. Can it be merely coincidental that the guaranteed annual income was found to have no adverse effects when it was widely supported in the early 1970s, but it was later found to have major adverse effects on working behavior in the late 1970s after support for the program had declined?

Despite these problems, the advantages of policy experimentation are

---

[17]The term is taken from early experiments at the Hawthorne plant of Western Electric Company in Chicago in 1927. It was found that worker output increased with any change in routine, even decreasing the lighting in the plant. See David L. Sills, ed., *International Encyclopedia of the Social Sciences*, 7 (New York: Free Press, 1968), 241.

substantial. It is exceedingly costly for society to commit itself to large-scale programs and policies in education, welfare, housing, health, and so on, without any real idea about what works. Increasingly, we can expect the federal government to strive to test newly proposed policies and reforms before committing the nation to massive new programs.

THE LIMITS OF PUBLIC POLICY

Never have Americans expected so much of their government. Our confidence in what governments can do seems boundless. We have come to believe that governments can eliminate poverty, end racism, ensure peace, prevent crime, restore cities, provide energy, clean the air and water, and so on, if only they will adopt the right policies.

Perhaps confidence in the potential effectiveness of public policy is desirable, particularly if it inspires us to continue to search for ways to resolve societal problems. But any serious study of public policy must also recognize the limitations of policy in affecting societal conditions. Let us summarize these limitations:

1. Some societal problems are incapable of solution because of the way in which they are defined. If problems are defined in *relative* rather than *absolute* terms, they may never be resolved by public policy. For example, if the poverty line is defined as the line which places one-fifth of the population below it, then poverty will always be with us regardless of how well off the "poor" may become. Relative disparities in society may never be eliminated. Even if income differences among classes were tiny, then tiny differences may come to have great symbolic importance, and the problem or inequality may remain.

2. Expectations may always outrace the capabilities of governments. Progress in any policy area may simply result in an upward movement in expectations about what policy should accomplish. Public education never faced a "dropout" problem until the 1960s when, for the first time, a majority of boys and girls were graduating from high school. At the turn of the century, when high school graduation was rare, there was no mention of a dropout problem. Graduate rates have been increasing every year, as has concern for the dropout problem.

3. Policies that solve the problems of one group in society may create problems for other groups. In a plural society one person's solution may be another person's problem. For example, solving the problem of inequality in society may mean redistributive tax and spending policies which take from persons of above-average wealth to give to persons with below-average wealth. The latter may view this as a solution, but the former may view this as creating serious problems. There are *no* policies which can simultaneously attain mutually exclusive ends.

4. It is quite possible that some societal forces cannot be harnessed by governments, even if it is desirable to do so. It may turn out that government cannot stop urban migration patterns of whites and blacks, even if it tries to do so. Whites and blacks may separate themselves regardless of government policies in support of integration. Some children may not be able to learn much in public schools no matter what is done. Governments may be unable to forcibly remove children from disadvantaged environments because of family objections even if this proves to be the only way to ensure equality of opportunity, and so on. Governments may not be *able* to bring about some societal changes.

5. Frequently people adapt themselves to public policies in ways that render the policies useless. For example, we may solve the problem of poverty by government guarantees of a high annual income, but by so doing we may reduce incentives to work and thus swell the number of dependent families beyond the fiscal capacities of government to provide guarantees. Of course, we do not really *know* the impact of income guarantees on the work behavior of the poor, but the possibility exists that adaptive behavior may frustrate policy.

6. Societal problems may have multiple causes, and a specific policy may not be able to eradicate the problem. For example, job training may not affect the hardcore unemployed if their employability is also affected by chronic poor health.

7. The solution to some problems may require policies that are more costly than the problem. For example, it may turn out that certain levels of public disorder—including riots, civil disturbances, and occasional violence—cannot be eradicated without the adoption of very repressive policies—the forceable break-up of revolutionary parties, restrictions on the public, appearances of demagogues, the suppression of hate literature, the addition of large numbers of security forces, and so on. But these repressive policies would prove too costly in terms of democratic values—freedom of speech and press, rights of assembly, freedom to form opposition parties. Thus, a certain level of disorder may be the price we pay for democracy. Doubtless there are other examples of societal problems that are simply too costly to solve.

8. The political system is not structured for completely rational decision making. The solution of societal problems generally implies a rational model, but government may not be capable of formulating policy in a rational fashion. Instead the political system may reflect group interests, elite preferences, environmental forces, or incremental change, more than rationalism. Presumably, a democratic system is structured to reflect mass influences, whether these are rational or not. Elected officials respond to the demands of their constituents, and this may inhibit completely rational approaches to public policy. Social science information does not exist to find policy solutions even if there are solutions. Moreover even where such information exists, it may not find its way into the political arena.

BIBLIOGRAPHY

HATRY, HARRY P., RICHARD E. WINNIE, and DONALD M. FISK, *Practical Program Evaluation.* Washington, D.C.: Urban Institute, 1973.

NACHMIAS, DAVID, *Public Policy Evaluation.* New York: St. Martin's, 1979.

PRESSMAN, JEFFREY L., and AARON WILDAVSKY, *Implementation.* Berkeley: University of California Press, 1974.

RIVLIN, ALICE M., *Systematic Thinking for Social Action.* Washington, D.C.: Brookings Institution, 1971.

SUCHMAN, EDWARD A., *Evaluative Research.* New York: Russell Sage Foundation, 1967.

WHOLEY, JOSEPH S., et al., *Federal Evaluation Policy.* Washington, D.C.: Urban Institute, 1970.

WILDAVSKY, AARON, *Speaking Truth to Power.* New York: John Wiley, 1979.

INDEX

INDEX